Theory Construction and Testing

Theory Construction and Testing

Edited By
Margaret T. Beard
    Professor
    College of Nursing
    Texas Woman's University

Information about the editor:
Margaret T. Beard is a professor, College of Nursing, Texas Woman's University. Her teaching-research interests focus on theory construction, research methodology and primary health care. Her research has appeared in *Advances in Nursing Science, The ABNF Journal, Nursing Research, Journal of Psychosocial and Mental Health Nursing, Issues in Mental Health Nursing* and *The Nurse Practitioner: The American Journal of Primary Health Care.*

TUCKER PUBLICATIONS, INC.
LISLE, ILLINOIS

Tucker Publications, Inc.
P.O. Box 580
Lisle, Illinois 60532-3164

Serving Minority Publishing Needs Since 1988

Library of Congress Catalog Card Number .... LC 95-060045

Beard, Margaret T,
Theory Construction and Testing

ISBN 0-923950-12-5

Typeset by Distinctive Designs • Batavia, Illinois
Printed and bound by BookMasters, Inc. • Mansfield, Ohio
Cover design by Distinctive Designs

CONTENTS

PART ONE: FOUNDATIONS OF THEORY CONSTRUCTION

PART TWO: METHODS AND APPLICATIONS OF THEORY CONSTRUCTION

CONTRIBUTORS

Betty N. Adams, PhD, RN
Associate Professor & Assistant Dean
College of Nursing
Texas Woman's University
Curriculum and Instruction
Higher Education

Donna Bachand, PhD, RN
Nurse Consultant
Dallas, Texas

Margaret T. Beard, PhD, RN
Professor
College of Nursing
Texas Woman's University

Helen A. Bush, PhD, RN
Professor Emeritus
College of Nursing
Texas Woman's University

Anita L. Comley, MSN, RN, OCN
Graduate Teaching Assistant
College of Nursing
Texas Woman's University
Denton, Texas
Oncology Nurse
Baylor University Medical Center
Dallas, Texas

Evelyn L. Curry, PhD
Assistant Professor
School of Information
and Library Studies
Texas Woman's University

Jennifer Gray, MSN, RN
Doctoral Candidate
Texas Woman's University
Specialist, The University of Texas
at Arlington
School of Nursing
Arlington, Texas

Patti Hamilton, PhD, RN
Professor and Director of Research
College of Nursing
Texas Woman's University

Carol Hodgson, MSN, RNCS
Doctoral Student
College of Nursing
Texas Woman's University
Professor and ADN Coordinator
Texarkana College
Texarkana, Texas

Patsy K. Keyser, PhD, RN
Professor
College of Nursing
Texas Woman's University

Verdell Marsh, MS, RN, CCRN
Doctoral Candidate
College of Nursing
Texas Woman's University
Staff Development Specialist
Department of Veteran's Affairs
Medical Center, Dallas Texas

David Marshall, PhD
Associate Professor
Mathematics & Computer Science
Texas Woman's University

Jan M. Nick, MS, RNC
Doctoral Student
College of Nursing
Texas Woman's University

Sally Northam, PhD, RN
Assistant Professor
College of Nursing
Texas Woman's University

Heidi Taylor, MS, RN
Doctoral Student
College of Nursing
Texas Woman's University
Instructor, West Texas A&M University
Canyon, Texas

Charles A. Walker, MSN, RN
Doctoral Student
College of Nursing
Texas Woman's University
Assistant Professor
Tarleton State University
Stephenville, Texas

PREFACE

A s indicated by the title of the book, the authors have attempted to present an integrated approach to theory construction and testing. An overview of the content, organization, and orientation of the book is given in Chapter 1. Here, there is a brief explanation of what was intended to be accomplished in writing the book. This project was undertaken to stimulate theory development and research in a specific area. Theory development should benefit researchers and is likely to serve the needs of practitioners. Theorists have the capability to develop frameworks that both incorporate accumulated knowledge and better guide implementation as prescriptive theory is sought.

Three methods of theory construction from a social science perspective, two rigorous methods for testing, and information on the analysis of categorical data are offered for reader purview. Bringing together models of theory in the process of construction is useful in learning the skills required to construct theory. The models will help students learn what is required in constructing theory and understand that theory is an ongoing process, cumulatively built on current knowledge, is continually being tested, refined, articulated, extended and reformulated.

This book is also meant to fill a major gap in the literature of most disciplines by presenting a detailed discussion of theory construction and testing. The emphasis is on methods of theory construction with examples and current methods of testing. The examples are beginning constructions and the testing focuses on structural equation modeling with Jöreskog and Sörbom's LISREL and Bentler's EQS computer software programs. These programs also offer assistance with categorical data. An illustration of LISREL 8 is included with example. Logit, probit, and loglinear for categorical and ordinal variables are presented. Information of interest to the novice and the accomplished scholar for constructing and testing theoretical formulations in building a scientific knowledge base is presented. The topic that I believe holds the greatest promise for furthering the development of scientific disciplines is structural equation models.

The linkage of theory construction and methods of testing from a systems perspective with the inputs and outputs delineated is also addressed in this book. Theory construction links the researcher and knowledge production. That is, theory construction and testing connects the theorist to the discipline's body of knowledge and is dependent on the philosophical view one holds and one's values. The philosophical or world view and values are the elements that eventually influence social policy.

An appreciation of the testing of theoretical constructions is enhanced if the reader has a background in statistics at the level of an introductory course. Some advanced topics are presented that until recently were accessible only to persons versed in mathematical language in which the topics were necessarily couched. However, with the widespread availability of computers and software, it is possible for persons lacking in mathematical skills to apply the most sophisticated of analytic approaches. The ease with which this can be done unfortunately can contribute to misapplications of analytic techniques and to misinterpretation of results. The techniques presented, LISREL and EQS, should be theory driven rather that data driven. Commentaries on inputs and outputs of computer programs in the context of the topics being presented are offered. The organization and mode of presentation afford a great deal of flexibility in the choice and sequencing of topics. It is hoped that this book will become a companion to which persons will keep returning as they broaden and deepen their understanding of theory and testing.

It is hoped that a service will be provided that supplements textbooks and also provide a vehicle to upgrade statistical methodology in the social sciences, as well as bionursing. The models, "optimal granulocyte colony stimulating factor administration," and "viral dormancy" are biologically encroached. It is hoped that by presenting some topics in theory construction and testing, a bridge will be provided between theoretical and statistical concepts. This book is a move in this direction.

Summary

The goal of this endeavor is to (a) introduce the reader to an understanding and appreciation of the advantages of "doing" theory construction and testing; (b) explicate the fundamental statistical theory that underlies structural equation modeling (SEM) as a powerful tool in testing theoretical constructions for knowledge development; (c) illustrate the use of recent LISREL and EQS software packages in the analysis of SEM; (d) bridge the gap between theory and research and (e) stimulate interest and curiosity in consulting advanced treatments of theory construction and testing the constructions.

It is hoped that an appreciation of the interrelations and interdependence among the various aspects of the research endeavor (theory and research) will be obtained. It is desirous that the reader will learn to appreciate the paramount role of theory in guiding the research enterprise. May the efforts here contribute to both the relevance and theoretical rigor of research as well as to the effectiveness of practice.

ACKNOWLEDGEMENTS

I would like to extend a very special thanks to the following people for their support and assistance in bringing this book to fruition.

Doctoral students for their inspiration to me to undertake this endeavor.

Secretaries, Sherry Darby, Vicki Daniloff and Elaine Cudd for typing, and Benita Eberhart for taking care of the little details always with a smile. Sue Thompson for providing assistance for secretarial support.

Dean Carolyn S. Gunning for the encouragement, support and being a good listener to me and all the faculty and students involved.

Publishers, Sallie Tucker-Allen, Monique Allen and her editorial staff, for giving this book their exceptional level of publishing vision and professionalism.

Most of all, my terrific family, Canarie Tillman, Valerie, Jonathan, Michael, Marcus and Allyson Beard, whose support and encouragement nurtured me and gave me the confidence to move forward. Also, friends Margie N. Johnson and Wilma Faye Edwards who incredibly put up with my not having the time for some of the other finer things in life.

Part One
Foundations of Theory Construction

Theory Construction and Testing: An Introduction and Overview

Margaret T. Beard

This chapter will present an introduction and overview of topics covered in this book. Theory will be defined; a metaphor of theories as maps will be given; the structure of theory indicated, formal theory defined; philosophy of science, creativity; theory and research linkage, testing and using structural equation modeling, categorical variables in testing, time in theory construction and social policy influence as an outcome of theoretical and empirical research will be presented.

T heory has been variously defined as an explanation between phenomena which are not as yet established as a law, as more than a hypothesis, as a hypothesis that has undergone verification and is applicable to a large number of related phenomena and as a statement of relations among concepts within a set of boundary assumptions. Kerlinger (1986) has defined theory as a set of interrelated concepts, definitions and propositions of phenomena put together with a systematic view of interrelations with the purpose of describing, explaining or predicting the phenomenon.

Selye (1964) indicated that theory is a bond between facts with fact assimilation and that a good theory unites the greatest number of facts. In the construction of theories, Selye suggested dissecting the complex phenomena of nature into units and then comparing the subunits of one unit with those of another. He further suggested that all biological theories can be fitted into the following three categories: (a) theories of unit formation; (b) theories of classification and (c) theories of causality. In theories of unit of formation, a biological unit designates any aspect of life that can be treated as one thing. The unit permits one to handle cognate objects as single packages. Theories of classification presuppose the recognition of smaller units common to a larger unit. The process of classification is fundamental and is usually the first step in the development of any science. Theories of causality allow one to infer lawful connections between physical antecedents and consequences. Symbolism can help in understanding the procedures of causal theory construction and testing. Selye suggested that one should always remember that symbols, like words, have only statistical validity. He further suggested that whatever one thinks of causality, scientific research would be impossible without the assumption of causal connections between antecedents and consequences and that orderly simplification is the first aim of science.

Theories as Maps

A theory is comparable to a map of a territory as opposed to its photograph (Barnum, 1994). The full terrain is not visible, but instead the parts that are important for its comprehension are highlighted. If the aim is to guide travelers, the map highlights roads; if the purpose is to describe the physical terrain, it illustrates mountains, plains and rivers.

Just as a map represents the relationship of significant objects or features within a geographic territory, a scientific theory represents an abstract set of ideas about particular phenomena. Attempts to describe phenomena through theory construction are similar in many respects to geographical mapmaking. Many facts that are true of maps are also true of scientific theories. Just as a map can never be the actual territory it represents, a theory about a phenomena can never be equivalent to the phenomena it describes.

Formal and informal tests of theories (like maps) can be tested for accuracy. Official agencies formally test the accuracy of maps. Maps are informally tested when put to practical use. Theories are formally tested in scientific research. They are informally tested each time an individual uses theory to understand a phenomena. Archaic theories, just as old maps, may still be useful. They may be improved upon or adapted for special application but are essentially correct. Old theories, as maps, may continue to serve as the basis on which newer theories or maps are built.

Whether referring to theory construction, theory development or theory building, the basic elements of theory are *concepts,* which are labels, categories or properties of objects to be studied. These are the bricks from which theories are constructed. Concepts are representative of the dimensions, aspects or attributes of reality in which the scientist is interested. When the scientist has a set of interrelated statements concerning the relationships between concepts, the scientist has a theory. The scientist constructs theories in the domain of interest by linking concepts of one class of attributes to concepts of other classes of attributes (Hardy, 1974). Concepts develop as a part of a theory and may be altered and refined as the body of knowledge grows. Hardy (1974) referred to the refinement of concepts as a continuous process involving sharpening theoretical and operational definitions in addition to modifying existing theory.

Theory Construction Defined

A dictionary definition of *con* is "to bring together;" *structure* is "a complex entity," "the configuration of elements, parts, of constituents in such an entity" (Morris, 1976). Construction then is the organization or arrangement of the interrelation of parts to give form to the entity or phenomenon. Theory construction is steering the configuration of a complex entity that is representative of the phenomena. Theory construction and testing steer the course of knowledge development.

In 1966, Berger, Zelditch and Anderson, began a series of theories in progress—systems of interrelated concepts and propositions that were abstract, general and had empirical import. All were theoretical beginnings, initial formulations, early stages in the ongoing process of testing, refinement, articulation, extension and reformulation of a theory. The works were published with the idea that training in theory is facilitated by having models of how to construct abstract, general, logically systematic, empirically-oriented theory and is further facilitated by contemporary models. The cumulative growth of knowledge does not begin with the master theorists. The foundation for the cumulative growth of theory is built upon the contemporary state of the art. In the process of testing and reformulating the hypothesized theoretical constructions, a substantive knowledge base will ensue.

Many disciplines feel that more middle-range theory is needed, that is, theory oriented to empirical knowledge of specific domains rather than overarching frameworks for the discipline. Middle-range theory is characteristically unfinished or "in progress."

Formal Theory

Formal theory is the use of symbols to represent theoretical terms and relations among them (Wells, 1986). The methodology of theory construction suggests that the development is facilitated by formally extracting theoretical principles from general discourse and formalizing them within supposed requirements of effective theories (Freese, 1980). Careful analysis of the requirements and applications of formal methods and techniques to the construction of substantive theories enable more effective consolidation of theories and data. A scientific theory may be considered a deductive system, but the relationships between variables may be expressed in a model. Like theories, models are isomorphic systems; they are selective representations of the empirical world.

How Should Theories be Constructed?

Cumulative theorizing builds a substantive body of knowledge. For the development of knowledge, there must be a natural transition from theoretical elaboration to empirical explanation.

Turner (1989 a & b) described theory building for scientific advancement as seeking answers to the following question: What are the critical and invariant properties of the universe and what are their operative dynamics? Turner described the development and expansion of knowledge along several paths including testing the plausibility of theoretical ideas with research findings. This path is usually associated with theoretical cumulation and is at the core of any science. Although the "logic" (or calculus) of deductive theory will not match that of the most advanced physical science, definitive tests of theories with data are possible. Knowledge develops through the assessment of a theoretical idea with data. The data may be historical, experimental, ethnographical, biographical or even impressionistic; but for knowledge development, theories should be examined with data that confirm their plausibility, provide a base for intellectual processes and produce cumulative knowledge. Cumulation extends beyond theory testing to creativity or creative arts where new ideas about the operative dynamics of the universe are incorporated into knowledge.

Theory development will usher in new advancements. Competing paradigms of theoretical constructions based on positivists view have served well in the past and will herald in new methodologies based on scientific advancement. What is needed is a position to open the way for greater methodological diversity.

STRUCTURE OF A THEORY

The structure of a theory can be conceptualized in systems terms. Systems thinking is a way of communicating across disciplines. Systems and theories are both considered to have boundaries. Systems can be considered as both a theoretical viewpoint and a methodological technique. In theory building, Dubin (1978) considers systems analysis as a vital component.

Theory can be viewed as a language consisting of elements, formulations and a set of definitions. Testing a theory's structure is facilitated if the concepts and the relationships between them are formalized (Hardy, 1974). In studying a scientific theory, one is interested in the logical structure of relationships between the concepts and the meaning given to the concepts. One then attends to the occurrence of concepts in the axioms, postulates or hypothesis of a theory.

Figure 1.1 Systems Perspective of Theory Construction

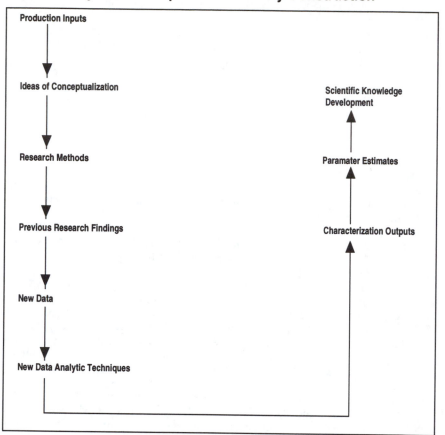

Research is often considered in terms of production (inputs) and character-izations (outputs). Inputs are conceptualizations, research methods, previous findings, new data and new analytic techniques. The outputs of these endeav-ors are advances in scientific knowledge (see Figure 1.1).

Theory construction links the researcher and knowledge production. That is, theory construction and testing connect the theorist to the discipline's body of knowledge. Knowledge is dependent upon the philosophical views of the researcher. Knowledge development is formally dependent on theory con-struction.

Theory construction has been considered as both a process and as a struc-ture (Bagozzi, 1984). The process involves logic, procedures, standards of conduct, evaluation and creativity (see Table 1.1). Theory construction has been described as disciplined imagination (Weick, 1990). As such, the quality of any theory is a function of the accuracy and detail present in the problem, independence among the conjectures that attempt to solve the problem and the diversity of the selection criteria used to test the conjectures. There are also standards of conduct for the theorists and for the researcher.

Table 1.1 The Theory Construction Endeavor

The Process of Theory Construction
Ideas
Creativity
Discipline of Imagination
Logic
Methods and Procedures
Standards of Conduct

Bagozzi (1984) characterizes theory construction by its structure (see Table 1.2). Structure includes the concepts, hypothesis of the theory, observations and measurements and the formal organizations of these elements.

Table 1.2 The Structure of Theory Construction

Formal Organization
Concepts/Constructs
Statements
Hypothesis (es)
Observations and Measurements

The Structure of Scientific Theory

Suppe (1977) indicates that correspondence rules are sometimes referred to as coordinating definitions, dictionaries, interpretative systems, epistemic correlations and rules of interpretation. In the Received View, three functions of correspondence rules are: (a) to define theoretical terms; (b) to guarantee the cognitive significance of theoretical terms; (c) and to specify the admissible experimental procedures for applying a theory to phenomena. The concept is synonymous with the corresponding set of operations.

A theory is a hypothesis of a correspondence between a definitional system for a universe of observations and an aspect of the empirical structure of those observations, together with a rationale for such a hypothesis. This is in contrast to uses of theory which connote a speculation or an unsubstantiated hypothesis or which do not refer directly to observations.

Scientifically, the effort can be described as the search for those combinations of formalized conceptualizations for data collections on one hand and structural aspects of the data that reveal regularities on the other hand. A theory is valuable if it has been convincingly verified by empirical evidence, that is, it asserts that data are observed in accordance with definitional systems that behave in a certain way and that these data are subsequently found to behave as specified by that theory. If such a theory is of sufficient generality, it may be called a law.

Innovation and Creativity

Innovation and creativity are often used interchangeably in theory construction. The distinction may be one of emphasis rather than substance (West & Farr, 1990). Innovation is the production and adoption of useful ideas and idea implementation (Kanter, 1988). Creativity is the production of novel and useful ideas (Mumford & Gustafson, 1988). Organizational creativity is defined by Woodman, Sawyer and Griffin (1993) as the creation of a valuable, useful new product, service, idea, procedure or process by individuals working together in a complex social system. This definition is commonly accepted for creative behavior or its products within an organizational context (Arleti, 1976; Barron, 1969; Golann, 1963).

The central issue in theory building is to recognize the materials out of which key components are inter-articulated. One must have a descriptive knowledge of the theoretical model and the theory should accurately mirror the empirical domain it describes. A proposition is a truth statement about a theoretical model. A hypothesis is the operational analog of such a truth statement (Dubin, 1978). Concepts must have empirical indicators, operations employed by the researcher to secure measurements or values for a unit concept (Dubin, 1978).

Theory building is the search for pervasive and determining elements and the making of laws pertaining to these elements. In building theory, Dubin (1978), names the concept or units put together in models of the perceived world as theories. The basic idea of models provides a method for developing theories of systems. Theories are built on properties and focus on characteristics. An attribute is a property present while a variable is an effect. The kind of unit used in building a theory makes a difference in the structure of a theory. Units of a theory can be placed into real and nominal classes as philosophers of science distinguish between realist and instrumentalists. Theory is, in structure, a complete holistic picture of the sensory or imaginative world as viewed by humans.

Theory Development

Proponents of theory development (Newman, 1979; Parkhe, 1993), argue that it be preceded by a deeper understanding and systematic incorporation of core concepts in research. Newman further presents theory building approaches that emphasize deductive theory testing and nomothetic research. A variety of theory building approaches and case studies are suggested. Theory development has been influenced by philosophy of science.

Philosophy of Science

The goals of science are to predict and understand observable phenomena. The hallmarks of good science are generalizability, predictability and objectivity. The philosophy of science influences the direction of scientific investigation. Some terms from philosophy of science are useful in theory development such as ontology, the fundamental assumptions about the elements of reality, that is, specifying what exists. Epistemology refers to study of the nature and grounding of knowledge about phenomena, that is, how one comes to know what is known. Axiology refers to study of the nature of values. Methodology is the nature of ways of studying phenomena.

Philosophy, philosophy of science and methods of inquiry have necessary linkages. In philosophy of science, questions are from metatheoretical presuppositions. Any knowledge obtained depends on the scientist's philosophical views. In considering knowledge as true beliefs, one validates a concept or construct. In considering doubts, one conducts pilot studies or similar methodologies to remove specific doubts. In other words, evidence is marshalled in favor of a single interpretation.

Philosophy of Science and Theory Testing

Various manifestations of positivism have been the predominant orientation of theory testing until recently. The basic tenets concerning the use of objective evidence for the purpose of theory confirmation was a generally accepted principle. The post-positivist view leads to newer thinking with complex formulations and choosing from among rival theories the same phenomenon. Theory connects the results of tested hypotheses toward the aim of becoming law. Tentative reasoning (theory) is viewed as giving way to accepted fact (law).

Laws

The ultimate aim of testing theories is to form empirical generalizations that become laws. Replications are important to this end as they justify a definitional system for observation and technical manipulation of data. The strengthening and improvement of laws require continued testing through experimental replications so the definitional and technical parts may be refined, modified or replaced. The crudest law is preferable to elaborate conceptual schemes and to sophisticated techniques which do not indicate promise of becoming partners in the formation of laws. A robust and well tested theory is usually known as a law, especially in the physical sciences (i.e., Newton's law, Ohm's Law) (Neelamkavil, 1987).

An objective of a generalizing theoretical strategy is to explain and generalize about the lawful phenomena of open systems (Freese, 1980). Laws are nomothetic universal or statistical generalizing of nonlimited spatio-temporal scope, having high information content and describing some regularity that observations of the world should confirm.

Theory and Research Linkage

In building knowledge with a theoretical base, one needs deductive types of arguments and empirical evaluations. Blalock (1969) identified the gap between language of theory and research as:

1. One thinks in terms of theoretical language with notions such as causes, forces, systems and properties.

2. One's tests are made in terms of covariations, operations and pointer readings. Theory and the testing of theory is most important in scientific research as explanations are formulated and implications submitted to empirical test.

Testing Theoretical Constructions

Ideally, research is cumulative, progressing forward through processes of theory generation, development, refinement, integration, and at times, disconfirmation or falsification. Kuhn's idea of a paradigm shift in thinking was a challenge to Darwin's evolution as Kuhn advocated revolution as a view of scientific progression.

Among contributors to current thinking about theory and testing are Feyerbend (1978), Kuhn (1970), Lakatos (1978) and Popper (1959, 1968, 1972). Popper did not believe that theories could be confirmed regardless of supporting evidence, but they could be falsified. In satisfying a theory, Lakatos (1978) distinguished among three models which he called dogmatic, methodological and sophisticated. Lakatos further distinguished between a theory's protective belt and its hard core. The hard core of a theory consists of a set of central principles impervious to challenge. The protective belt surrounds the hard core. Any progressive adjustments to the theory are made in the protective belt.

Categorical Variables in Testing

In recent years, progress has been made in developing a methodology for analyzing ordered categorical data. Advancements have been made in contingency table analysis. Distinctions are being made between nominal and ordinal data. No longer does one need to rely on Pearson's chi-square test designed for variables that have unordered categories. Advantages of the newer methods are that one can get a more complete description of the nature of the associations and there is greater power for detecting population associations (Agresti, 1989).

Regression

The most commonly employed tool of statistical model building is regression analysis. There are four basic characteristics of the regression model:

1. The regression model comprises an equation.
2. The equation specifies a directional relationship between the dependent variable and a set of independent variables.
3. The independent variables are assumed to be measured without error.
4. Each independent variable is assumed to be linearly related to the dependent variable.

The regression model has been used in testing hypothesized models in stages. Model testing works with both simple and highly complex models. Models that are poorly thought out in terms of the substantive theory rarely yield interpretable findings. Maximal likelihood estimates are robust in estimating model parameters and are robust against modest departures from the skewness and kurtosis of the nominal distribution for parameter estimates, but the standard errors, confidence intervals and likelihood ratio test of fit are more sensitive to such departures from characteristics of the normal distribution.

Multivariate Analysis of Variance

Multivariate analysis of variance is one of the traditional methods used to test whether a set of independent variables are significantly related to dependent variables. In theory testing, one can integrate a number of streams of research on the antecedents of a phenomena to develop and test an aspect of that phenomenon. Structural equation analysis can be utilized to test the parameter of the proposed model simultaneously and can also illustrate the mediating effects of the characteristics.

Causal Modeling

Causal modeling is a technique or method used to enhance the ability to draw causal inferences from empirical research. Causal modeling is useful in determining in as valid a manner as possible if certain "cause and effect" relationships among variables of interest exist in the real world. A variety of opinions exist regarding the usefulness and acceptability of causal models. Causal modeling is a useful heuristic tool to organize and express thoughts about the expected relationships among variables. This heuristic tool is helpful for producing empirical estimates of theoretically based hypothesized relationships among constructs. This is, at least, better than "armchair" theorizing.

Recursive and Nonrecursive Models

In causal modeling, the distinction between recursive and nonrecursive models is that recursive models are ones in which the causal flow is unidirectional. This indicates that there is no reciprocal causation between variables. A nonrecursive model has reciprocal causation.

From Theory to Statistical Model

To test a theory about relationships between theoretical constructs, structural equation models are frequently used. In the social and behavioral sciences, most theories are formulated in terms of hypothetical constructs that are latent variables. These latent variables have empirical indicators. The hypothetical construct is measured indirectly through these indicators.

In theory, the hypothetical constructs are defined by specifying their dimensions. The theory further specifies how the constructs are postulated to be interrelated. First, constructs are classified as dependent (caused, criterion, endogenous) or independent (causal, exploratory, exogenous). Second, for each dependent construct, the theory specifies any other constructs upon which it is dependent. The theory may include a statement about the sign and relative size of the direction of a construct on another construct. Because the constructs are not observed, the theory is tested indirectly. But, before the theory can be tested empirically, the researcher must define a set of observable indicators for each dimension. For example, an A/B behavior pattern would have two dimensions, the dimension of A and the dimension of B. The researcher would need indicators to represent the pattern of A behavior and B behavior. These could be urgency, hostility and hurriedness for A, with B behavior being just the opposite, quiet, serene and unhurried.

The structural equation part of the model is the theoretical relationships between the constructs. The measurement part of the model is the relationships between the observable indicators and the theoretical constructs. In order to test the model, each part must be formulated as a statistical model. This statistical model requires specifications of the form of the relationship as either linear or nonlinear. If the observed variables (indicators) are continuous (i.e., measured on an interval or ratio scale), the measurement equations are also

assumed to be linear, possibly after logarithmic, exponential or other nonlinear type of transformations of observable indicators. If the observed indicators are ordinal, the researcher usually assumes that there is a continuous variable underlying each ordinal variable and formulates the measurement model
in terms of these underlying variables.

Structural Equation Models

Structural equation models are generally applied to covariance matrices.
This procedure does not analyze the means of the indicators. The means for
the latent variables may be estimated by a method advocated by Sorbom (1974,
1978, 1982) known as an analysis with structured means.

In covariance matrices, the means of the latent variables may not be estimated since the means are set equal to zero. This is similar to regression
analysis applied to a covariance matrix whose matrix has been transformed
from correlations and standard deviations. In this case the intercept is zero.

Some highly sophisticated conceptual and analytical techniques are available to model and test scientific theories among which LISREL and EQS (X)
are popular in the analysis of structural equation models. Structural equation
models (SEM) bring together path analysis and factor analysis. SEM models
use statistical tools that are based upon and go well beyond conventional regression and analysis of variance. SEM, sometimes called latent variable
modeling, allow a joint analysis of theory and measurement. SEM can be
viewed as a product of the merging of two approaches of model fitting, multiple regression and factor analysis. Multiple regression expresses the relationship of a dependent variable to regressor or independent variables. The
partial relationship with each variable is expressed by the regression coefficient corresponding to the particular variable (Cuttance & Ecob, 1987). With
the factor analytic method one finds a number of latent variables that account
for the common relationship among a number of observed (or manifest) variables.

There are at present many varieties of structural equation modeling software programs available. These programs originated to meet specific needs of
researchers. As needs changed, commercially distributed programs have responded to market forces by gradually adding features which the larger body
of users desired. These programs required a great deal of time to learn a particular software program. In the beginning, not only were the computers programs costly, but they were only available on mainframes. Personal computer
programming for structural equation modeling has developed rapidly in recent
years from adapted versions of mainframe programs to newer graphical and
object oriented development environments.

Structural equation modeling (SEM) in theory testing is used by many academic disciplines. The term has come to mean not only the solving of a set of
simultaneous linear equations but also covariance structure analysis, latent
variables, multiple indicators and measurement errors in variables (Bollen &
Long, 1993). Most SEM applications are characterized by five sequential steps:
model specifications, identification, estimation, testing fit and respecification
(Bollen & Long, 1993). Future theory testing research using SEM will elaborate these areas and further expand current thinking regarding other approaches.
Expansions are already occurring in many areas of SEM.

In addition to testing for equal factor structures, one can also test for equal
regression coefficients and mean latent variable differences between groups.
Future trends will elaborate on latent variable interactions in hypothesized

models with more emphasis on models with nominal, ordinal and categorical variables (Bentler & Wu, 1993). Marsh (1994) demonstrated and expanded the typical confirmatory factor analysis approach. He indicated the substantive importance of tests for the invariance of factor loading and factor correlations. Factor loading reflects the relation between a particular indicator and the underlying latent constructs that it represents, that is, the validity of the indicator. One can test for factorial invariance across groups reflecting different levels.

TIME

There are models that allow relationships to vary through time, rather than requiring them to be fixed or forcing the analyst to specify and analyze the causes for the time-varying relationships. A researcher may want to understand methods dealing with relationships that vary slowly over time but in which the exact causes of variation cannot be identified.

Time in Research

Frequently researchers want to know the consequences of events such as, what are the health effects on workers at nuclear waste sites? Time is an important element in event history analysis as a researcher searches for events and their causes. Time in research occurs in many forms among which are time series, discrete and continuous time methods, time–independent and time–dependent covariates, event history analysis and panel analysis.

Events

The term events refer to a discontinuity in the history of an individual person, organization, nation, other institution (Allison, 1994), or entity. Events occur in time. With events, there are sharp changes from a distinct state to another state, or to put it another ways, from one level of a variable to a substantially higher or lower level. These changes represent a movement from one equilibrium state to another quite different equilibrium state. This is similar to the state and movement advocated by Stinchecombe (1968) in the demographic and in the functional form of theory construction.

Naturally occurring events are complex with shifts along different dimensions. Because of the complexity, any classification scheme will have a lot of residual heterogeneity. The complexity and heterogenity of events increases the difficulty of causal inference. The fact that events can be precisely situated in time, with a clear before and after is a distinguishing characteristic of the analysis of events. Reliable conclusions can be drawn about the existence of an effect. The problem, then is to determine which event features produced the outcome, or if the effect occurred for all events or a subset of the events. Time is an important consideration in event history analysis.

Time Series

Time series refer to observations taken chronologically on a given variable. The two main purposes of time–series data are: (a) to develop models to explain patterns that occur over time (i.e., cycles, trends, seasonal variations), and (b) to use the models for forecasting (Pedhazur & Schmelkin, 1991). Time series are observations over time on a given unit while cross–sectional refers to observations on a number of individuals over time (Hsiao, 1995). Panel data describe each of a number of individuals and, like time–series data, describe changes through time. Panel data (blending characteristics of cross–sectional and time–series) can be used to:

1. Obtain more accurate estimates.
2. Lessen the multicollinearity problems.
3. Reduce estimation bias.
4. Allow specification of more complex and realistic models.
5. Obtain more accurate prediction of individual outcomes (Hsaiao, 1995).

There are three types of variables in panel data analysis: individual time invariant, period individual-invariant, and individual time-varying variables. Variables that are the same for a given cross-sectional unit through time but vary across cross-sectional units are called individual time-invariant variables. Variables that are the same for all cross-sectional units at a given point in time, but vary through time are called period individual-invariant variables. Variables that vary across cross-sectional units at a given point in time and also exhibit variations through time are called individual time-varying variables.

The literature on time-series design and analysis is extensive. The purpose here is to introduce the existence of this promising methodological approach. This approach can vary from the very simple to the very complex. For general information and an introduction to time-series design, analysis, and illustration of application the reader is referred to Cryer (1986). For a book on the topic, see Cook and Campbell (1986) Chapter 5.

Interrupted Time Series Designs

Interrupted time-series, as the name implies, consist of a series interrupted by some discrete event or intervention. The purpose of this design is to assess the effect of the event or intervention, by attempting to infer if and in what way it has changed the time series data (Pedhazur & Schmelkin, 1991). In an interrupted time series design, observations are taken over under treatment one, then after a point previously selected, treatment two is implemented, and similar observations made (Mclaughlin & Marascuilo, 1990). Sometimes treatment one is a controlled condition without any treatment. When single subjects are used, the observations taken at time one are referred to as baseline, while observations taken under treatment two are referred to as intervention. The treatment effect is determined by the value of the mean for treatment two which is expected to exceed the mean of treatment one. In single subject designs (n=1), it is expected that the mean of treatment one will be larger than the mean of treatment two. .

There is long-term follow up of one group of subjects over a period of time in an interrupted time series design. In the first part of the study, subjects are observed repeatedly over the baseline period, then an intervention is imposed and observations are continued

Repeated Measurements Over Time

There are situations where repeated measurements are made at equally spaced intervals over time on each of a number of individuals or on experimental data. In these types of situations, measurements are taken repeatedly at long time intervals as in panel studies, or in learning experiments where measurements are made repeatedly at short intervals during a specified learning process. One type of model for these situations is the latent curve model. The latent curve model is used for situations where the repeated measurements appear to fol-low smooth and fairly similar trends over time for each individual, but there are variations in initial performance, final performance, and rate of change between individuals. Latent curve models originated with adaptations of prin-cipal component methods (Rao, 1958; Tucker, 1958) and have developed to models that yield testable structures for the mean vector and covariance matrix (Browne & Arminger, 1995).

An alternate model to repeated measurements design is fixed mean curves with time series deviations The assumptions of the model is a common fixed curve and that individual deviations from this curve follow a common autoregressive time series with moving average residuals. The deviation vec-tor variable is assumed to have elements generated by an ARMA process with homogenous autoregressive weights and homogeneous moving average weights but possibly nonhomogeneous white noise variance (Brown & Arminger, 1995).

Discrete-Time Hazard Rate

Risk set is a central concept in event history analysis, which is the set of individuals at risk for event occurrence at a given point in time (Allison, 1989). An example of risk is the development of heart disease which includes a pe-riod of time and a point in time at which symptoms appear. Another example is the probability of cancer as a result of exposure to waste products.

Another key concept is hazard rate, which may be referred to as hazard or rate. The hazard rate in discrete time is the probability that an event will occur at a particular time, in a particular individual, given the individual is at risk at that time (Allison, 1989). In the example, the hazard is the probability of hav-ing a heart attack or of developing cancer within a given year. The hazard is an unobserved variable, yet it controls the occurrence and timing of events. The hazard is the fundamental dependent variable in event history models.

Discrete-Time and Continuous-Time Formulations

What Gibbs (1972) in theory construction refers to as a temporal quantifier in terms of a point in time and a period of time is the same conceptualization as discrete-time and continuous time. In discrete-time formulations, one would proceed by specifying the probability for a given value if the state was left in the duration interval. One would specify the probability using a model for binary outcomes, that is, a logit or probit model. There is a drawback in apply-ing the discrete–time formulation to continuous-time (Peterson, 1995). The estimated coefficients will depend on the length of the time interval, which means that the results will not be comparable across studies that vary in the lengths of the time intervals for which the probabilities are specified. In mod-els such as the logit, only the constant term would be severely affected while the coefficients of explanatory variables would be less affected by the length of the time interval.

Time-Independent and Time-Dependent Covariates

The situation or entity considered in an investigation may be dependent not only on time, but other explanatory variables (covariates). Generally speak-ing, explanatory variables (covariates) may be considered of two broad types. There are those that stay constant over time and those that change or may change over time. Examples of variables that remain constant over time such as income, socioeconomic status, number of siblings, and marital status. Time-constant covariate problems may be solved using a formula advocated by Petersen (1995, p.465), and solving for x (the set of time-constant covariates), the hazard rate at duration t, given the covariates x; given the rate at which a transition occurs at duration t, given no transition before t, and given the covariates x.

Time-dependent covariates may be classified into three groups (Kafbfeisen and Prentice, 1980). The first is the deterministic time-dependent covariates such as the day of the week, or dock time, calendar time or any function of time that is prespecified. The second classified group are the stochastic covariates that are generated by a stochastic mechanism external to the process that is studied. An example would be changes of fluctuations in student fees which may change the behavior of a person but which themselves are not influenced by the behavior. These types of covariates are called exogenous. The last type consist of stochastic covariates that are generated by a stochastic mechanism internal to the process being studied. These types of covariates are called endogenous. There are no specific conceptual problems with the first type of covariates. To overcome conceptual problems following the selection of a problem for conceptualization in the second and third types see Petersen (1995). Structural equation modeling may be considered as one method of data analysis, especially with large sample sizes.

Social Policy

Scientific endeavors can help in the identification of substantive problems, suggest methods of control and assist in the measurement of decisions. As findings are translated into policy, that which is scientific blends with that which is political. Policy must be supported by science for TRUTH to be convincingly conveyed. Although scientists do not make policy, successful use of empirical validation by policymakers is dependent on a well defined delineation of the problem, the credibility of researchers, the nature of the researcher's arguments, the quality and availability of the research evidence, the ability of researchers to communicate ideas and research findings clearly, and the timeliness of the policymaker's interest in the issue.

Future Trends

Theory and research, that is theory and testing have influenced the past, the present and will impact the future of nursing as health care reform slowly evolves. The main impetus of health care reform is access to care, while health seems to be secondary. Economics, costs and humanitarian concerns will be guiding forces of the future. The development of scientific knowledge will be influenced by such terms as prevention, promotion, therapeutic interventions, effectiveness and outcomes. Better use can be made of philosophies and ideas by bridging the gap between theory and testing.

Overview of Book Layout

In this book, six examples of theoretical constructions are described—toward a theory of optimal granulocyte colony-stimulating factor administration, viral dormancy, fetal heart rate variability, adolescent risk taking, transformative change and experiential mastery. These are designed to serve as training in theory construction.

Figure 1.2 Diagramatic Indication of an Overview of Theory Construction and Testing

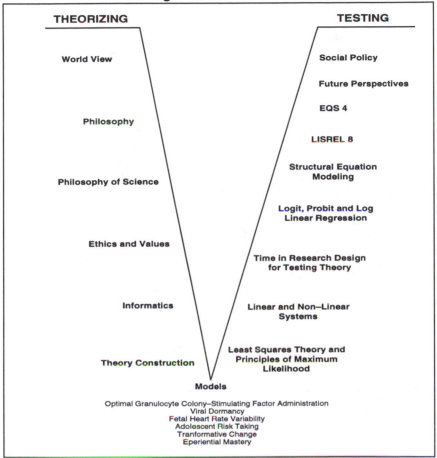

Testing will focus on structural equation modeling (SEM), with confirmatory factor analysis, a submodel of SEM using LISREL8 and EQS 4.02. Although there are many other computer software packages available for SEM, this discussion will be limited to LISREL and EQS. EQS does not resort to Greek notation nor matrix terminology for model specification. Both the LISREL and EQS programs have options for several estimation procedures. This presentation will be limited to the maximal likelihood procedure.

Figure 1.2 is a diagrammatic indication of an overview of this book. As noted in Figure 1.2, theorizing evolves from the world view and philosophy, philosophy of science and ethics and values of the theorist.

Informatics enables gathering background information in the construction of theory. Building models aids in theorizing and imaging phenomena. In testing the theoretical conceptualizations, least squares theory and the principles of maximum likelihood are frequently used as statistical foundations in linear and non-linear systems. Multivariate analysis can be used with categorical (nominal and ordinal) as well as interval and ratio level data. Structural equation modeling has become a well-respected multivariate data analysis method. Software packages such as LISREL and EQS handle a variety of ordinary least squares regression designs as well as structural equation models involving variables with arbitrary distributions. Computer software availability will influence knowledge development.

The choice of topics in this book were determined primarily on the basis of theory construction and testing endeavors and in light of their generality or pervasiveness. The book consists of three parts: foundations of theory construction, methods and application of theory construction and foundations and methods of theory testing.

Part One presents the theoretical arguments upon which Part Two is based. Chapter 1 outlines these arguments briefly. Chapter 2 presents the intellectual and moral virtues of theory construction and testing. Chapter 3 is a presentation of informatics with an illustration. Chapter 4 discusses conceptual models of phenomena.

Part Two contains the highlights of the book. An introduction and overview to the three selected methods of theory construction, Blalock, Gibbs and Stinchecombe, are provided in Chapter 5. Chapters 6 through 11 provide applications of the methods presented. Examples are abstract to concrete and include transformative change, adolescent risk-taking, viral dormancy, fetal heart rate variability, optimal granulocyte colony-stimulating administration and experimental mastery. Both recursive and nonrecursive models are included. Chapter 12 considers time in theory construction and testing.

Part Three includes Chapters 13 and 14 which are multivariate analyses of data at various levels including nominal and ordinal. Chapter 15 discusses structural equation modeling and is followed by Chapters 16 and 17 on specific computer software programs for analysis, LISREL and EQS. Chapter 18 is on social policy. Chapter 19, the final chapter, is future trends.

CONCLUSIONS

Through testing hypothesized relationships, empirical generalizations become laws. A robust and well tested theory is a law. Computer software programs for structural equation modeling and new developments in the analysis of categorical data will assist in facilitating a strong empirical base for social and public policy as outcomes of theory construction and testing.

REFERENCES

Agresti, A. (1989). Tutorial on modeling ordered categorical response data. *Psychological Bulletin, 105*(2), 290-301.

Allison, P.D. (1989). *Event history analysis.* Newbury Park: Sage Publications.

Allison, P.D. (1994). Using panel data to estimate the effects of events. *Sociological Methods and Research, 23 (2),* 174-199.

Arleti, G. (1976). *Creativity: The magic synthesis.* NY: Basic Books.

Bagozzi, R.P. (1984). A prospective for theory construction in marketing. *Journal of Marketing, 48,* 11-29.

Barnum, B.J. (1994). *Nursing theory: Analysis, application, evaluation. 4th ed.*

Barron, F. (1969). *Creative person and creative process.* NY: Holt, Rinehart & Winston.

Bentler, P., & Wu, E.J.C. (1993). *EQS/Windows user's guide.* Los Angeles, CA: BMDP Statistical Software.

Berger, J., Zelditch, M., & Anderson, B. (1966). *Sociological theories in progress Volume 1.* Boston, MA: Houghton Mifflin.

Blalock, H.M. (1969). *Theory construction: From verbal to mathematical formulations.* Englewood Cliffs, NJ: Prentice-Hall.

Bollen, K.A., & Long, J.S. (1993). *Testing structural equation models.* Newbury Park, CA: Sage Publications.

Browne, M.W. & Arminger, G. (1995). Specification and estimation of mean and covariance structure models. In G. Arminger, C.C. Clogg & M.E. Sobel (Eds.), *Handbook for statistical modeling for the social and behavioral sciences.* Plenum Press.

Cook, T.D. & Campbell, D.T. (1979). *Quasi–Experimentation: Design and analsysis issues for field settings.* Chicago: Rand McNally.

Cryer, J.D. (1986). *Time series analysis.* Boston. Duxbury.

Cuttance, P., & Ecob, R. (1987). *Structural modeling by example. Application in educational behavioral and social research.* Cambridge, UK: Cambridge University Press.

Dublin, R. (1978). *Theory building.* NY: The Free Press MacMillan Publishing Co.

Feyerbend, P. (1978). *Against method: Outline of anarchinistic theory of knowledge.* London: Verso.

Freese, L. (1980). Formal theorizing. *Annual Review of Sociology, 6,* 187-212.

Gibbs, J. (1972). *Sociological theory construction.* Hinsdale, IL: The Dryden Press, Inc.

Golann, S.E. (1963). Psychological study of creativity. *Psychological Bulletin, 60,* 548-565.

Hardy, M. (1974). Theories: Components, development, evaluation. *Nursing Research, 23*(2), 100-106.

Hsiao, C. (1995). Panel analysis for metric data. In G. Arminger, C.C. Clogg & M.E. Sobel (Eds.), *Handbook for statistical modeling for the social and behavioral sciences.* Plenum Press.

Kalbfleisch, J.D., & Prentice, R.L.. (1980). *The Statistical analysis of future time data.* Wiley.

Kanter, R.M. (1988). When a thousand flowers bloom: Structural collective, and social conditions for innovation in organization. In B.M. Shaw & L.L. Cummings (Eds.), *Research in Organizational Behavior, 10* (pp. 169-211). Greenwick, CT: IAI Press.

Kerlinger, F.N. (1986). *Foundations of behavioral research. 3rd ed.* NY: Holt.

Kuhn, T.S. (1970). *The structure of scientific revolutions 2nd ed.* Chicago, IL: Chicago University Press.

Lakatos, I. (1978). The methodology of scientific research programmes. In J. Worall & G. Currie (Eds.), *Philosophical Papers Vol. 1.* NY: Cambridge University Press.

Marsh, H.W. (1994). Confirmatory factor analysis models of factorial invariance: A multifaceted approach. *Structural Equation Modeling, 1,* 5-34.

McLaughlin, F.E., & Marascuilo, L.A.. (1990). *Advanced nursing and health care research.* Philadelphia, PA: W.B. Saunders Co.

Morris, W. (1976). *The American heritage dictionary of the English language.* Boston, MA: Houghton Mifflin Company.

Mumford, M.S., & Gustafson, S.B., Jr. (1988). Creativity syndrome: Integration, application and innovation. *Psychological Bulletin, 103,* 27-43.

Neeleamkavil, F. (1987). *Computer simulation and modeling.* NY: John Wiley and Son.

Newman, M. (1979). *Theory development in nursing.* Philadelphia, PA: F.A. Davis.

Parkhe, A. (1993). Messy research, methodological predispositions, and theory development in international joint ventures. *Academy of Academic Review, 18*(2), 227-268.

Pedhazur, E.J. & Schmelkin, L.P. (1991). *Measurement design and analysis: An integrated approach.* Hillsdale, NJ: Lawrence Erlbaum Assocation.

Peterson, T. (1995). Analysis of event histories. In G. Arminger, C.C. Clogg & M.E. Sobel (Eds.), *Handbook for statistical modeling for the social and behavioral sciences.* Plenum Press.

Popper, K.R. (1972). *Objective knowledge: An evolutionary approach.* Oxford: Clarendon Press.

Popper, K.R. (1959). *The logic of scientific discovery.* NY: Basic Books.

Popper, K.R. (1968) *Conjectures and refutations: The growth of scientific knowledge.* NY: Harper Torch Books.

Rao.C.R. (1958) Some Statistical Methods for Comparison of Growth Curves, *Biometrika, 14,* 1-17.

Selye, H. (1964). *From dream to discovery: On being a scientist.* NY: McGraw Hill.

Sorbom, D. (1974). A general method for studying differences in factor means and factor structures between groups. *British Journal of Mathematical and Statistical Psychology, 27,* 229-239.

Sorbom, D. (1978). An alternate to the methodology for analysis of covariance. *Psychometrika, 43,* 381-391.

Sorbom, D. (1982). Structural equation models with structured means. In K.G. Jordan & H. Wold (Eds.), *Systems under indirect observation: Causality, structure, prediction. 1* (pp. 183-185). Amsterdam: North Holland.

Stinchecombe, A.L. (1968). *Constructing Social Theories.* New York Harcourt, Brace & World.

Suppe, F. (1977). *The structure of scientific theories, 2nd ed.* Urbana, IL: University of Illinois Press.

Tucker, L.R. (1958). Determinants of parameters of a functional relation by factor analysis. *Psychometrika.* 23, 19-23.

Turner, J.H. (1989a). *Theory building in sociology.* Newbury Park, NJ: Sage Publications.

Turner, J.H. (1989b). General theory of macrostructural dynamica. In J. Berger, M. Zeldith, & B. Anderson (Eds.), *Sociological theories in progress.* Newbury Park, NJ: Sage Publications.

Weick, K.E. (1989). Theory construction as disciplined imagination. *Academy of Management Review, 14*(4), 516-531.

Wells, N. (1986). Strategies for theory development in nursing III. *Proceedings of Third Annual Nursing Science Colloquium.* Boston, MA: Boston University.

West, M.A., & Farr, J.L. (1990). *Innovation and creativity at work: Psychological and organizational strategies.* NY: John Wiley.

Woodman, R.W., Sawyer, J.E, & Griffin, R.W. (1993). Toward a theory of organizational creativity. *Academy of Management Review, 18*(2), 293-321.

Intellectual and Moral Virtues in Theory Construction and Testing

Patsy K. Keyser

The general ethical implications of the conceptual perspectives of an individual's research are enormous, not only because scientific conceptualizations are closely linked to the promotion of social good but because ethics and values are intrinsic to theory building. Values are interwoven with complex concepts, customs, attitudes, qualities or ideas by which we judge ourselves, others and our world. Such ideas involve culture, religion, beliefs, social norms and many other structural issues underlying communities in society.

Volumes of works discuss the value systems most common to Western civilization. The betrayal of a system's values for whatever reason is troubling. When there is a disintegration of values in communities, confidence is undermined, standards and guiding ideas are shaken, confusion occurs and standards are further threatened. Theorists contribute to this confusion when they build any theory in isolation from the greater society.

The aim of this chapter is to consider theorizing as an ethical activity and to base that activity on virtues. Virtues are the values that guide theoretical inquiry in a given discipline viewed as a community of practice. Virtues also help theorists to assess their standards and evaluative guidelines. Virtues focus on the development of character or what the theorist should **be** in a normative sense when seeking knowledge.

SCIENTIFIC ACCOUNTABILITY

Scientific theories that embrace the postpositivist tradition recognize the historical evolution of knowledge. Knowledge changes as it interacts with the culture as a whole and with those who contribute to perceptions of truth. History has shown that there is no *one* way to come to "the truth" and that what constitutes the truth is a vexing epistemological problem. Theorists are not allowed, once their body of knowledge has been discovered and described, to rest on those laurels without accountability for the consequences of their theories as explanations that contribute to perceptions of truth about the world.

Scientists create theories and test hypotheses. Some scientists emphasize theorizing, others emphasize testing, but neither creating nor testing theory singularly advances without the other. Theorizing is the reasoning process which frames scientific inquiry and its testing. Choices made in this process have ethical consequences, thus theory construction and testing are an ethical enterprise. Purposeful ethical inquiry needs to be an integral part of these activities (Reed, 1992).

Dewey (1948) saw theorizing as a "moral situation" which entailed reflective choice and deliberate consideration. Whether it occurs at the onset of inquiry or emerges during the process, theorizing is inherently linked to the theorist's value judgments and world view (Reed, 1992). To a certain extent, all research judgments are value judgments, and the principle activity of science is to make well-supported value judgments based on empirical observation.

Such observation is not free from conceptual adulteration, as observation is already cognition, valuation and belief (Laudan, 1981). Scientific inquiry in the social sciences is embedded in "normative commitments" (Bellah, 1981). Therefore, judgments of moral value occur in theorizing. For example, the theorist speculates about what may be good for the well-being of individuals or groups, why it may be good and what can be done to promote that good. Regardless of the methodology by which theories are advanced or tested, theorizing entails value choices made by the theorist/researcher that influence the good of society.

THE GOODS OF A PRACTICE

The "good of society" can be understood within the framework of the contemporary philosopher Alasdair MacIntyre (MacIntyre, 1981). Good is presented as *telos*, ends or goals that are sought by practices. The scientific discipline within which the theorist works can be viewed as a practice, a coherent, socially established, cooperative endeavor.

Practices are socially established human activities for the mutual advantage of those who establish them. The social sciences are established to seek knowledge in a given field and to build that knowledge through theory, research, teaching and application. As a cooperative activity in pursuit of "goods," expertise is developed and maintained. This expertise is beneficial to society and encourages education, accumulated expertise and amassed knowledge. Advantages are realized in the course of trying to achieve the standards appropriate to that activity. In the social sciences, the building of theories are a part of the activities of these disciplines. A discipline/practice generates satisfaction for those who are involved in its activities and who live up to the standards of the practice. One of the advantages of theory building is a sense of using one's knowledge and skills in increasing knowledge and understanding of the world. Such satisfaction is an *internal* good. To enjoy these goods, one submits to the standards of excellence for building theory in one's discipline. In addition to these internal goods, there are certain *external* goods related to building and testing theory in one's discipline. Some examples of external goods are a salary, job security and public rewards/recognition. Such goods are not internal to the discipline for they can be achieved in a variety of other ways. Moreover, if one is interested only in the external goods, he or she will be tempted to violate personal standards for the sake of such goods. Thus, virtues can be lost and scientific practices corrupted by the sacrifice of internal to external goods.

The manner in which new approaches to inquiry and scholarship are judged by the community of scholars depends in part on the principles by which the scholarship of the discipline is founded. By the same token, new approaches to the method serve to stretch the limits around which the principles and theories of a discipline are formed and reformed. Examples of practices are numerous and include such disciplines as anthropology, sociology, nursing and psychology. Each practice has a history, a tradition and standards, and each requires that participants in the practice cultivate certain virtues that are both intellectual and moral.

Virtue

Having sketched the notion of a practice, we can better understand MacIntyre's definition of virtue as "an acquired human quality the possession or exercise of which enables us to achieve those goods which are internal to practices and the lack of which effectively prevents us from achieving any such goods" (MacIntyre, 1981, p. 178). Using this approach, virtues are viewed as the dispositions or acquired qualities necessary to attain the goods internal to various practices such as the social sciences. Virtues both sustain the ongoing work of such practices and give them historical context. Although different disciplines may require different intellectual skills and standards of excellence, all theorists in the activity of theorizing and discovering draw from roughly the same virtues which are both intellectual and moral.

Intellectual virtues are frequently considered when discussing theory building, but both intellectual and moral virtues are necessary for theory building and testing. Moral virtues accompany intellectual virtues because they "are those goods by reference to which, whether we like it or not, we define our relationships to those other people with whom we share the kind of purposes and standards which inform practices" (MacIntyre, 1981, p. 178). Virtues, whether moral or intellectual, are a sort of readiness, a sort of being in the social world with a set of means to think and to act.

These related virtues by which the researcher pursues truth through theory construction and testing are honesty, courage, fairness and love. Victor Worsfold gives a useful framework for regarding these virtues' relationship to the process of scholarship and research (Worsfold, 1986).

INTELLECTUAL VIRTUES
Honesty

Honesty comes first because it is the first virtue of the pursuit of truth. While this may seem too obvious, it is also obvious that honesty is a hard virtue to exercise in the intellectual context. The exercise of honesty demands that all theorists face up to what they know and don't know about the subject matter in the field of their expressed and professed expertise. Honesty requires us to ask questions such as: Do I understand and pursue the standards of my subject matter? What kind of inquiry meets these standards? What do I need to explain or discover? Am I theorizing or simply reproducing and rearranging the views and opinions of others? Do I understand the intellectual purpose of theorizing or am I looking for personal acclaim? Do I understand and honestly reflect the analysis of my data? Am I prepared to defend my views about my field of expertise and at the same time be open to new ideas?

Honesty also requires that we ask additional questions about personal stresses of theory building and testing. Personal stresses are often related to external goods, one's needs for reward, acclaim or recognition. They can threaten one's intellectual honesty. These stresses may also relate to real or potential inadequacies of personal commitment or scholarship. Such inadequacies may threaten one's integrity in ways that destroy honesty, such as using the work of others as one's own or selling one's work to another for monetary gain. Falsifying data or inventing data are other examples.

Honesty is a hard task master because it is without equal in the pursuit of truth. As a result it must be at the heart of the theorist intellectual being. Honesty requires courage. What does it mean to be intellectually courageous?

Courage

Theorists as scholars demonstrate courage in the assertion of their convictions about the subject matter on which they are theorizing and about what they discover during the activity of constructing and testing theory. They exercise courage in their willingness to risk these convictions both in presentations and in writing for publication. What makes this intellectual virtue of courage risky and difficult to exercise is the realization that in risking the expression of one's convictions one may well be risking one's identity as a theorist and scholar. But the discovery of knowledge and the pursuit of truth demands that we risk the expression of our convictions. It is in developing these convictions that we need the virtue of fairness.

Fairness

Two approaches to fairness need consideration; fairness as fairmindedness and fairness as just treatment. Fairness as fairmindedness demands that theorists face the concepts of their subject matter from an open and reasonable point of view. Fairness requires that the theorist does not stretch or twist the approach to the concepts of the theory to serve a personal point of view that is self serving. Nor can the theorist claim that concepts make a contribution they do not make. One cannot, in fairness, have expectations or lead others to have expectations of a theory's ability to address issues when these expectations are false.

In fairness as just treatment, the theorist also considers the influence that the theory may have if applied in practice to society. Such fairness would ask, "How just are the concepts of the theory to various groups?" Certain theories applied in Nazi Germany in the 30s, for example, were unjust to several ethnic groups. This is not to say that theorists must or can anticipate how a given theory will be used. Rather they must consider their theory's general fairness. That is, theories must not advantage the elite at the expense of the disadvantaged of the world.

Intellectual fairness then requires that the limitations of the concepts be faced so that the theory of the subject matter proclaimed is honestly and courageously presented. Intellectual fairness also requires that we do not hold out concepts in a way that further disadvantage any one group. That such an intellectual pursuit must be upheld brings us to the last intellectual virtue, that of love.

Love

Worsfold (1986) in his discussion of excellence gives importance to the intellectual virtue of love which applies to the theorist. Intellectual love amounts to a deep commitment to the phenomenon explored by the theorist in the process of theorizing. Such commitment is evidenced by the theorist scholar in understanding what it is to give an account of oneself as a theorist. Love of the subject matter under study leads the theorist who has this love of subject to identify closely with the need for discovery. And to give an account of that area of discovery. Love of subject then requires stewardship of the subject area and it requires stewardship of the area of exploration. This stewardship implies willingness to keep up-dated so that one can give an account of the theoretical area not as it was when last investigated, perhaps as a graduate student, but as it is today and may be in the future. Love of subject area requires that the theorist understand and can explain what is happening on the leading edge of the phenomenon under study. It is this last intellectual virtue of love that requires the theorist to make contributions in the subject matter to the application of that subject in practice and thus to society.

Not to exercise this last virtue is to condemn oneself to little growth and lack of ability to achieve the internal goods of the practice. To pursue the virtues of honesty, courage, fairness and love is to continue the tradition of the discipline (practice) and to uphold its excellence. Pursuing truth by exercising the intellectual virtues of honesty, courage, fairness and love allow theorists a genuine sense of authority in the chosen subject and field. For theorists will be able to give an account of themselves to others, not in terms that are self serving but in terms that are more objectively justifiable. Thus, theorists who aspire to excellence are accountable to themselves and others, accountable for their conception of the field of exploration and expertise. Ultimately, the pursuit of excellence in theory building and testing rewards the theorist with the ability to be clearly authoritative about the theory. There are differences between authoritative and authoritarian theorist. Authoritarian theorist often occupy a defensive position based on the attitude, "This is the way it is, take it or leave it." They do not strive to objectively justify their position or to be open to change. Their relationship with others may be self serving and disconnected. But we are interested here in the authoritative theorist.

MORAL VIRTUES

If authoritative scholarship, as opposed to authoritarian scholarship, is to be practiced by theorists, it should be done with a careful consideration of the virtues: honesty, courage, fairness and love. At the same time that we consider these as intellectual virtues, we must also consider them as moral virtues. If the process of theory by which truth is discovered is to be acceptable, then it must be morally acceptable.

Theorists must be accessible to others to develop an understanding of the process of theorizing and theory building. To be honest in this way is to understand personal motivations for behavior. Honesty, defined as accessibility, requires the moral virtue of courage. This may at times require admitting that one may not have investigated every aspect of a subject. To be accessible requires courage to be open to others' criticism and evaluation.

Fairness is useful in this regard. As a moral virtue, it characterizes the treatment that the virtuous theorists offer others. They evaluate others with justice and without discriminating in favor of those they like. The Aristotelian conception of justice seems appropriate to the life of the theorist — fairness in terms of equality. The fair-minded scientist puts aside any preoccupations, biases and dislikes and evaluates a theory in a manner that gives others what they merit. Fairness also makes demands of theorists in self-evaluation. Fairness to self requires monitoring one's expectations of oneself. To demonstrate fairness to self is to demonstrate a concern for self or self-interest. To pursue self-interest, then, is to pursue a sense of self, in this case the professional self, within the community of one's discipline. Fairness to self and others is the moral center of justice when practicing theory construction and testing.

Finally, love in the context of theory building and testing amounts to compassion in the professional treatment of others and self. Compassion should be a part of all our dealing with others to whom we relate in the process of theory building and testing. This may apply to colleagues working with the theory construction process, students learning the process of theory testing or the public attending the presentation of the theoretical findings. In a community of theorists, ignorance induced by self-love betrays the integrity of the theorist and the community itself. To paraphrase Shklar, theorists who hate themselves are likely to spread their misery (Shklar, p.130).

Theory building and testing are done within a moral community for a moral enterprise binds a common moral purpose (Pellegrino, 1993). Theorists, researchers and scholars must be guided by a shared sense of morality, rules, principles or character traits to define a moral life in service to a given discipline.

SUMMARY

To theorize in a given discipline involves intellectual and moral modes of judgment. The intellectual theorist has an honest, courageous, fair and loving commitment to the subject matter in which the theorist is theorizing. The subject matter is pursued in terms of integrity and standards. Likewise, the moral theorist employs honesty, courage, fairness and love, not so much in commitment to the subject or its standards, but rather in the performance of intellectual virtues.

The excellent theorist is one who honestly pursues a life of theorizing and participates in ongoing debate. Such a theorist is able to risk criticism and pursues the standards of theory building and testing with courage, recognizing that all theories are limited. An even-minded fairness allows this theorizing to be measured against comprehensive truths about the world. This even-minded fairness allows the theorist to say "I do not know" and "I may be mistaken." With these qualities, the theorist has an intellectual love of "the truth," and the subject of the theory clearly before the mind's eye while living the vocation of theorizing. Essentially, the loving theorist is the person who knows risk and justly pursues the subject of life. With compassion for self and for others, the theorizing done by theorists will not be done in isolation. Theorists' speculations and conceptualizations will consider the well-being of individuals and groups in society, and address these as an ethical enterprise within the purposeful ethical standards of their discipline. In short, the best theorist is the virtuous person.

REFERENCES

Aristotle. (1967). Nicomachean ethics. In A.I. Melden (Ed.), *Ethical theories* (p. 88). Englewood Cliffs, NJ: Prentice-Hall.

Bellah, R.N. (1981). The ethical aims of social inquiry. *Teachers College Record, 83*(1), 1-18.

Carstens, R.W. (1986). Faculty excellence: Another dimension. *Perspectives, (16)*2, 1-11.

Dewey, J. (1948). *Reconstruction in philosophy.* Boston, MA: Beacon Press.

Laudan, L. (1981). A problem-solving approach to scientific progress. In Ian Hacking (Ed.), *Scientific revolutions* (pp. 144-155). NY: Oxford University Press.

MacIntyre, A. (1981). *After virtue.* Notre Dame, IN: University of Notre Dame Press.

Pellegrino, E., & Thomasma, D. (1993). *The Virtues in practice.* NY: Oxford Press.

Reed P.G. (1992). Nursing theorizing as an ethical endeavor. *In Perspectives on nursing theory.* Philadelphia, PA: J.B. Lippincott Co.

Shklar, J.N. (1984). *Ordinary voices.* Cambridge: Harvard University Press.

Worsfold, V.L. (1986). Faculty excellence. *Perspectives, (16)*2, 1-11.

The Role of Medical Informatics in Theory Construction

Evelyn L. Curry

Since the introduction of computer techniques to information processing in the 1940s, emerging technologies have provided increased access to a large body of data. This body of data allows researchers the opportunity to study in greater detail current professional practice, thus broadening the base for the formulation of theory.

Medical informatics (MI), a subset of information science, is generally defined as the organization and management of print and nonprint resources to support medical decisionmaking. This chapter will set forth the argument that medical informatics should be included in the paradigm for examining relationships in theory construction.

Three questions are addressed: What role does MI play in theory construction? Which patterns have been observed in this role? What is the future likely to be for the melding of MI and its relationship to practice and theory? First, information science (IS) will be defined within the context of social science theory. Second, MI will be considered and including a discussion of the three questions.

The purpose of this chapter is to set forth the argument that medical informatics should be included in the paradigm for examining relationships in theory construction.

INFORMATION SCIENCE DEFINED

Borko defines "information science" as an interdisciplinary investigation of the properties and behavior of information, the forces that govern the flow of information, and the techniques of processing it for optimum accessibility and usability (Samuelson, Borko, & Amey, 1977). Harmon (1990) continues the dialogue by proposing a different definition: "information science centers on the development of principles, laws, models, and theories that predict or explain information phenomena associated with natural and artificial systems. Such systems include, e.g., cells, molecules, organs, organisms, computers, organizations, communities, and atmospheric systems" (p. 32). Figures 3.1, 3.2, and 3.3, based on Harmon's definition, illustrate links between information science (IS) and the natural sciences; information science and various applications in *The Annual Review of Information Science and Technology* and information science concepts in Science/AI (artificial intelligence) departments.

In these figures, various attempts of selected disciplines to solve information problems are shown. For example, Figure 3.1 notes the underpinnings of IS (i.e., artificial intelligence, medicine, cybernetics, etc.); Figure 3.2 shows applications of artificial intelligence to selected subject areas (i.e., toxicology, energy, life sciences); Figure 3.3 presents subspecialties which have contributed to the current dialogue (i.e., instrumentation, citation mapping, modelling, metrics, etc.).

Figure 3.1 Some Scientific Roots of Information Science

Natural Science Research
Mathematics and Statistics
Information Theory
Cybernetics
Artificial Intelligence
Medicine
Science Information and Documentation
Biology

Figure 3.2 Links to Science and AI Departments

Annual Review of Information Science and Technology

Volumes	Chapter Topics
20	Information needs and uses
19	Expert systems
18	Energy information systems
18	Toxicological information
17	Biomedical communications
16	Information systems in the life sciences
15	Artificial intelligence applications
14	Empirical foundations of information science
13	Handling chemical structure information
13	Information systems in engineering

**Figure 3.3 Information Science Concepts in Science/AI
            Departments**

Systems theory
Cybernetics
Entropy
Models
Metrics
Scientific method
Systems analysis and design
Knowledge-based systems
Instrumentation
Citation mappings

THEORY CONSTRUCTION

Social science theory, of which information science is a part, is a "systematic explanation of the observed facts and laws that relate to a specific aspect of life" (Babbie, 1989, p. 46) and a powerful generalization about recurrent human behavior (Mohr, 1982). A theory is powerful if it is "accurate with respect to a large and well-defined scope of important human behavior" (Mohr, 1982, p. 5). Van House (1991) places IS research within the context of social science research by using Whetten's (1989) "litmus test" for a theoretical contribution. All theoretical research, she contends, does not consist of new theory; if it did, research would be fragmented and noncumulative. Theory advances through incremental refinements (Van House, 1991). Further, Whetten (1989) describes what actually constitutes theoretical breakthroughs:

- Important changes in a theory's "what" and "how"—frequently stimulated by surprising research results;
- Changes in "why" are probably the most fruitful, but also the most difficult avenues of theory development and
- Changes in "who," "when" and "where" (e.g., testing the applicability of a model in a new setting). New applications are of greatest value when they contribute to a refinement of the theory, that is, when tests of new "who," "when" and "where" refine the "what" and "why."

IS theory, based on the work of Shannon and Weaver (1963), models entropy as the amount of information required in a given situation in order to remove uncertainty. After reviewing several IS theories, Boyce and Kraft (1985) question their overall practical impact on the field. Citing the role of automata, formal languages and computability theory within the discipline of computer science, Hopcroft and Ullman (1979) note that mathematical modeling of the computing process has had an influence on many subareas of computer science, including applications (e.g., data structures, algorithms, compilers and programming languages) (Boyce & Kraft, 1985).

The so-called "mature professions have developed academic disciplines which provide a broad theoretical base for professional practice" (Larson, 1977, p. 55). Because of the central role of information transfer in the affairs of humankind and the ubiquitous nature of information, library and information science research (and similarly information theory) should take a holistic approach to problems and cross-disciplinary boundaries in the search for understanding of what goes on in the information transfer process (Grover & Greer, 1991).

THE ROLE OF MEDICAL INFORMATICS IN THEORY CONSTRUCTION

If the goal of IS theory is to improve information science practice, the role of MI in theory construction is to perform a similar function in the practices of medicine and health care delivery. In other words, the measure of a theoretical contribution should not be viewed apart from its practical application.

MI had its beginnings in the 1960s in research-oriented biomedical computing (instrumentation and biostatistics). In the 1970s, emphasis was on information systems (financial, statistical, and clinical). In the 1980s, a shift was observed toward the development of systems that support clinical decisionmaking. In the 1990s, the emphasis appears to be on the integration of systems based on a uniform medical language, standardized formats of records, gateway systems to access the plethora of resources available and effective communication between networks of medical personnel and organizations with patients and the public—both with and apart from the computer. These developments can lead to what Blum (Lunin, 1986) sees as a trend in medical informatics—a movement from learning about the tool to an understanding of how that tool enriches our understanding of the domain. Hence, the role of MI (or health informatics) is to improve medicine and health care delivery—indeed an overarching task which includes a wide range of subspecialties.

Expert Systems Research as a Metaphor for Theory Construction

Expert systems research profiles the role of MI in theory construction, particularly the interconnectedness between nodes to construct theoretical foundations. The role of the expert system is to simulate the thought patterns of an expert in the solving of designated problems. The work of theorists parallels this process. They both analyze sets of input conditions and construct paradigms by examining regularities and patterns in empirically-observed phenomena. The more temporal and contextual the observations (the wider the range of observations), the more powerful the resulting theory (Whetten, 1989).

Artificial Intelligence in Medicine

Shortliffe (1991) and Engle (1992) outline attempts to use computers as diagnostic aids in decisionmaking over the last 30 years—from decision support systems to automatic hospital recordkeeping systems, patient files, etc. This section highlights several expert systems (ESs) projects.

MYCIN, one of the first and most famous of the rule-based medical ESs, was developed at Stanford to aid in selecting the proper therapy for inpatients with certain systemic infections. MYCIN has the capability of dealing with uncertainty that is a part of medical practice and can also explain how it arrived at its decision, just like the best client resident (Madsen, 1991).

Perhaps the most comprehensive of the expert consultant type ESs is CADUCEUS/INTERNIST, a rule-based system designed to simulate the expert decision making of an experienced, board-certified internist. The outcome of more than 50 person years of work by a knowledge engineer and a physician domain expert (and several million dollars), INTERNIST is capable of making extremely complicated diagnostic decisions. The program can consider more than 3,500 patient manifestations and select diagnoses from more than 500 disease possibilities. The future standard of practice in diagnostic medicine may well include such systems (Madsen, 1991). Table 3.1 lists recently developed ESs in designated subspecialties.

Knowledge domains of the medical ESs developed so far also includes emergency medicine, rheumatology and many others. ESs have been designed to function as decision-making aids at the primary care level and to act as expert consultants at secondary and tertiary levels.

It is not clear presently what place, if any, computer-based decision support should have in medical practice. Engle (1992) finally concludes that researchers should concentrate on ways of making computer-generated relevant information available to physicians as they make decisions instead of on ways to make computers act as diagnosticians.

Table 3.1

Selected Knowledge Domains of Expert Systems	
Knowledge domains	**Research Investigators/Dates**
1) Cancer	Marchevsky and Coons, 1991 Leaning, Ng and Cramp, 1992 Marchevsky, 1991 Bibbo et al., 1991
2) Radiology	Lim, Walkup and Vannier, 1993
3) Diabetes	Lehmann et al., 1992
4) Cardiology	Greenwald, Patiland and Mark, 1992
5) Lymph node diseases	Heckerman, Horwitz and Nathwani, 1992 Heckerman and Nathwani, 1992
6) Obstetrics	Maresh, 1992
7) Psychiatry	Powsner and Miller, 1992
8) Pharmacology	Dasta, Greer and Speedie, 1992 Dasta, 1992
9) Hematology	Sorace et al., 1992
10) AIDS	Li and Xu, 1991
11) Optometry	Kastner et al., 1984

There is, however, increasing pressure on doctors to make correct diagnoses and to administer the correct therapies. This pressure comes from the public, the media, health service management and from the medical profession itself. Clinical audit is now an established part of medical practice; consequently, decision support tools and scoring systems are increasingly being used as a means of standardizing and improving practice (Kennedy, Harrison, & Marshall, 1993).

Another example which encourages the use of decision-support devices is that in which the diagnosis of acute chest pain could be improved by use of the data which is routinely gathered at presentation. Studies with statistical algorithms have demonstrated increased diagnostic performance as well as the potential for better use of resources and financial savings. The use of thrombolytic agents for acute myocardial infarction (MI), for example, is one of the most significant recent advances in medical therapy. However, they are used imperfectly because of the difficulty in making an accurate diagnosis. The effect of using decision-support systems on guiding therapy for acute chest pain has not been studied. Since the benefit of thrombolytic agents is greater the earlier they are administered, patients are increasingly presenting earlier and often before the full complex of symptoms has developed and ECG changes have evolved. It is important to make better use of clinical information, particularly since there seems little prospect of a diagnostic test to help in the emergency situation (Kennedy et al., 1993).

Myriad medical events handily support the argument. Situations frequently arise in practice where the opinion of a senior clinician is not immediately available. Casualty departments, for example, are largely staffed by relatively junior or inexperienced doctors. Sometimes nurses or ancillary staff, such as ambulance crew, are forced to make priority decisions, such as whether or not to summon urgent medical help. Again, computer-based decision support may be useful in these circumstances and may be seen as a means of disseminating expert information. The use of computer expert systems and other forms of artificial intelligence in education and training is only beginning to be explored.

Nursing Information Systems

Bobis (1993) discusses the expert system as an implement in the nurse's toolbox. Such tools can be implemented on small, inexpensive computing platforms, many having been written for the IBM/PC and the Apple Macintosh. They could assist the nurse in such specialized areas as drug-interaction, care plan preparation, acuity training and special techniques. Whenever a temporary staffing shortage develops, personnel could be rotated to different units with expert systems available to them as sources of patient care knowledge.

The nursing computer system is meant to be a tool for the bedside nurse. A craftsman would not consider accepting a job without access to the proper tools. He knows that, without the right tools, a task may take several times longer to accomplish—if it can even be accomplished at all. Although one does not necessarily look upon a computer system in the same vein as an artisan's chisel, a properly designed one could be a major component in the nurse's toolbox (Bobis, 1993).

Lange and Jacox (1993) describe empirical investigations based on large data bases. Clinical data bases, they note, have been used in epidemiologic studies and risk assessment and to study variation in physician practice. Administrative databases, they continue, have been used for technological assessment, geographic variation research, appropriateness research and effectiveness or outcomes research.

To date, nursing care issues have been noticeably absent from database-supported health policy research, partly because of the absence of the nursing care element in large administrative and clinical databases. One approach to this problem, Lange and Jacox (1993) contend is to include nursing data in various "minimum data sets." Standard or minimum data sets are comprised of sets of data elements that are necessary and sufficient to describe episodes of illness (Donovan & Saba, 1990) or the care given by particular providers (Werley & Lang, 1988). To date, much of the minimum data set research has focused exclusively on medical practice, partly because physician decisions drive much of the rest of the health care system. If nursing is to be able to analyze its practice in relationship to that of others and to determine how nursing care influences patient outcomes, nursing care elements must be included in the various minimum data sets (Lange & Jacox, 1993).

According to Lange and Jacox (1993), policy-related issues that could be addressed by nurse researchers using large clinical or administrative data bases are:

1. What is standard nursing practice in various settings?
2. What is the relationship between variations in nursing practice and patient outcomes?
3. What are the effects of different nursing staff mixes on patient outcomes and costs?
4. What are the total costs for episodes of treatment of specific conditions and what part of those are attributable to nursing care?
5. Who is being reimbursed for nursing care delivery?

Large health care databases are especially useful resources for addressing health policy questions.

Which role patterns are observable in the MI literature? Two clear strands appear to surface. First, the nature of the problem to be solved influences the type of information required. Secondly, a blend of data types more accurately reflects a definition of the problem. Additionally, the lines appear to be blurring between medical, nursing and health informatics in an attempt to pool a critical mass of up-to-the-minute data required for the efficient organization and management of health services delivery.

FUTURE DIRECTIONS OF MEDICAL INFORMATICS IN THEORY CONSTRUCTION

Elaine Larson, dean of the School of Nursing, Georgetown University, Washington, D.C., reports member responses of the Health Sciences Policy Board, Institute of Medicine (IOM), when asked to discuss the most pressing problems facing the U.S. biomedical and science communities today. Five responses are germane to the present discussion (Larson, 1993):

- Unless we are able to frame our interests in terms of public benefit, we will continue to be on the losing end of a highly competitive situation. The truth is that we are competing for other societal goods. The values that we present are poorly justified (physician employed in industry).

- The question of how do we nurture and protect the scientific infrastructure. The material infrastructure is deteriorating because nobody, especially the academic medical centers, planned for depreciation (industry physician).

- Scientists have to understand that we are entering a new era in which we must not only understand science as a method of inquiry and the values of science. You have to understand that in relation to others ideas (lawyer).

- The scientific community has got to demonstrate some cohesion and have a greater impact on the policy science research structure of this nation (academic physician).

- Serious mismatch between the scientific community's mindset and the government's decision making procedures. Tensions between strongly held moral positions in the society versus the rights of the public to draw benefits and value from biomedical research (government physician).

As Congressman George E. Brown, Jr. states in his plenary address at the annual meeting of the American Association for the Advancement of Science in February 1990, "the isolation of scientists from the federal decision-making process and their complacence about their roles in society. . . . has resulted in reduced funding for basic research—only one variable in a very complex equation which must be solved if we are to insure the strength of our economy in an increasingly competitive global marketplace. Science is, at best, only the first step in the innovation process" (Larson, 1993, p. 74).

Medicine, nursing and related health sciences do not exist in a vacuum. Their research must be tied to the larger national agenda. In the same vein, the political climate for nursing science is positive at present and nursing has managed to escape the critical scrutiny of the public with regard to research, perhaps primarily because nursing science accounts for such a small proportion of the biomedical research budget. However, as nursing science grows, the need to remain attuned to the public's health concerns is vital. The first wave of priorities selected for emphasis by the National Center for Nursing Research, low birthweight infants and human immunodeficiency virus infection are clearly responsive to the needs of society. As these priorities are reexamined and modified every 5 years or so, societal needs must be continuously highlighted (Larson, 1993).

More and more, the onus is on researchers to identify the societal relevance of their work (Larson, 1993). Kathleen McCormick (1993), from the Office of the Forum for Quality and Effectiveness in Health Care, offers the following solution:

> *A whole new world is on the horizon for the nursing profession and for nursing research to support nursing practice as we move toward health reform and broader nursing participation in health care. Moving into the role of participants in rather than deliverers of health care presents new challenges in describing what nursing does and evaluating its impact. The current focus on health reform in America requires the nursing profession to broaden its research skills to include scientific and research training in economics, health services, epidemiology, information science, anthropology, and evaluation research. (p. 191)*

Health services research is needed to address the shifts in delivery models of care which require an analysis of the impact of selected factors (environment, resources, settings, skills and education of providers, and types of coverage) on recipients of health care, including special population types. As the interest in outcomes research intensifies, nurses will need to learn the measurement techniques that can be used to assess the effectiveness of treatment plans on individual patients, pooled groups of patients, entire organizational data and even pooled societal data (McCormick, 1993).

Information science addresses information flow patterns in the matrix of health care delivery. As more population-based science unravels health care effectiveness and identifies the optimal community-level allocation of health interventions, automated patient record systems will become central to the processing of large data bases. The efficiency of collecting quality data in a reasonable time will necessitate the development of widespread systems for monitoring hospital and, more importantly, ambulatory practice patterns and patient outcomes (McCormick, 1993).

Why evaluation research? Comparisons of the validity and reliability of outcomes and products of one health reform methodology over another will become paramount in the decade ahead. Which users, what impact and what outcomes can be achieved will be critical to monitor. The overall health policy impact resulting from clinical and organizational research will be important to consider (McCormick, 1993).

The road ahead for medical information handling is unclear, but as research funds become more difficult to obtain, attention increasingly will be focused on health care reform and the societal relevance of research projects. The outcry to researchers and theorists will be to embrace inter- and intra-disciplinary perspectives to better understand the range of problems facing medical personnel.

SUMMARY AND CONCLUSION

The objectives of this chapter were threefold: to examine the role of MI in theory construction; to identify role patterns in the MI literature and to note future directions of MI in theory construction.

Medical informatics, as a tool, is needed to construct valid and reliable hypotheses with which to observe medical and health-related phenomena. The set of print and nonprint resources which comprises MI, assembles diverse data combinations, including bibliographic databases (MEDLINE, AIDSLINE, etc.); nonbibliographic databases (census reports, profile analyses); administrative databases (insurance files, quality assurance records, disease-specific registries, etc.) and clinical databases (patient files) in a host of innovative and existing data formats (e.g., minimum data sets).

Regarding role patterns in the MI literature, two threads were observed: (a) that careful problem definition influences information requirements and (b) that a mix of types of data sets enhances the investigator's understanding of designated information problems. Future directions point to the need for more socially relevant research which require multidisciplinary approaches to problem solving. The decade ahead promises a blurring of the lines between medical, nursing and health informatics.

This chapter suggests that the highest quality (grade A) information package is assembled heuristically, one layer at a time. The base layer (or mediocre, C-quality) includes primarily books and journals (print sources); the second layer (or B-quality) adds bibliographic databases (e.g., MEDLINE, AIDSLINE, etc.). A third layer (or A-quality) embraces the "virtual library"— an electronic array of information systems—which incorporates a variety of eclectic, cross-disciplinary approaches with which to test new hypotheses and reinterpret old ones. Researchers and practitioners will benefit most from an integrated, networked environment at their fingertips. More critically, however, the quality of the emerging health care system will depend on it.

REFERENCES

Babbie, E. (1989). *The practice of social research (5th Ed.)*. Belmont, CA: Wadsworth.

Bibbo, M., Kim, D.H., Pfeifer, T., Dytch, H.E., Galera-Davidson, H., & Bartels, P.H. (1991, February). Histometric features for the grading of prostatic carcinoma. *Analytic and Qualitative Cytology and Histology, 13,* 61-68.

Bobis, K. (1993, July). The expert system: The nurses' toolbox. *Nursing Management, 24,* 103-105.

Boyce B.R., & Kraft, D.H. (1985). Principles and theories of information science. *Annual Review of Information Science and Technology, 20,* 153-178.

Dasta, J.F. (1992, January). Enhancing the pharmacist-computer interface. *The Annals of Pharmacotherapy, 26,* 99-102.

Dasta, J.F., Greer, M.L., & Speedie, S.M. (1992, January). Computers in healthcare: Overview and bibliography. *The Annals of Pharmacotherapy, 26,* 109-111.

Donovan, U.R., & Saba, V. (1990). Initiatives regarding the effectiveness of health care and national uniform nursing data sets. In *Action report for the 1990 ANA house of delegates.* Kansas City, KS: American Nurses' Association.

Engle, R.L. Jr. (1992, Winter). Attempts to use computers as diagnostic aids in medical decision making a thirty-year experience. *Perspectives in Biology and Medicine, 35,* 207-219.

Greenwald, S.D., Patil, R.S., & Mark, R.G. (1992, March/April). Improved detection and classification of arrhythmias in noise-corrupted electrocardiograms using contextual information within an expert system. *Biomedical Instrumentation and Technology, 26,* 124-132.

Grover, R., & Greer, R.C. (1991). The cross-disciplinary imperative of LIS research. In C.R. McClure & P. Hernon, *Library and information science research: Perspectives and strategies for improvement* (pp. 101-113). Norwood, NJ: Ablex.

Harmon, G. (1990). Relationships with the natural sciences and knowledge engineering. In J. M. Pemberton & A. E. Prentice, *Information science: The interdisciplinary context.* NY: Neal-Schuman.

Heckerman, D.E., Horvitz, E.J., & Nathwani, B.N. (1992). Toward normative expert systems: Part I. The pathfinder project. *Methods of Information in Medicine, 3,* 90-105.

Heckerman, D.E., & Nathwani, B.N. (1992). Toward normative expert systems. Part II. Probability-based representations for efficient knowledge acquisition and inference. *Methods of Information in Medicine, 31,* 106-116.

Hopcroft, J.E., & Ullman, J.D. (1979). *Introduction to automata, theory, languages and computation.* Reading, MA: Addison-Wesley.

Kastner, J.K., Dawson, C.R., Weiss, S.M., Kern, K.B., & Kulikowski, C.A. (1984). An expert consultation system for frontline health workers in primary eye care. *Journal of Medical Information Systems, 8*(5), 389-397.

Kennedy, R. L., Harrison, R. F., & Marshall, S. J. (1993). Do we need computer-based decision support for the diagnosis of acute chest pain: Discussion paper. *Journal of the Royal Society of Medicine, 86,* 31-34.

Lange, L. L., & Jacox, A. (1993). Using large data bases in nursing and health policy research. *Journal of Professional Nursing, 9*(4), 204-211.

Larson, M. S. (1977). *The rise of professionalism: A sociological analysis.* Berkeley, CA: University of California Press.

Larson, E. (1993). Nursing research and societal needs: Political, corporate, and international perspectives. *Journal of Professional Nursing, 9*(2), 73-78.

Leaning, M.S., Ng, K.E.H., & Camp, D.G. (1992). Decision support for patient management in oncology. *Medical Informatics, 17,* 35-46.

Lehmann, E.D., Deutsch, T., Roudsari, A.V., Carson, E.R., Benn, J.J., & Sonksen, P.H. (1992). An integrated approach for the computer-assisted treatment of diabetic patients on insulin, *Medical Informatics, 17(2),* 105-123.

Li, L.X., & Xu, L.D. (1991, December). An integrated information system for the intervention and prevention of AIDS. *International Journal of Biomedical Computing, 29*(3-4), 191-206.

Lim, I., Walkup, R.K., & Vannier, M.W. (1993). Rule-based artificial intelligence expert system for determination of upper extremity impairment rating. *Computer Methods and Programs in Biomedicine, 39,* 203-211.

Lunin, L. F. (1986). What information science can contribute to medical informatics. *Proceedings of the Fifth Conference on Medical Informatics,* 285-288.

Madsen, E. M., Reinke, A.R., Fehrs, M.H., Yolton, R.L. (1991, February). Applications of expert computer systems. *Journal of the Optometric Association, 62,* 116-122.

Marchevsky, A.M. (1991, April). Expert systems for efficient handling of medical information I: Lung cancer. *Analytical and Quantitative Cytology and Histology, 13(2),* 89-92.

Marchevsky, A.M., & Coons, G. (1993). Expert systems as an aid for the pathologist's role of clinical consultant: CANCER-STAGE. *Modern Pathology, 6(3),* 265-269.

Maresh, M. (1992, March). Computers in obstetrics. *British Journal of Hospital Medicine, 47,* 336-339.

McCormick, K. (1993, July-August). Nursing research challenges within health care reform. *Journal of Professional Nursing, 9(4),* 191.

Mohr, L. B. (1982). *Explaining organizational behavior: The limits and possibilities of theory and research.* San Francisco, CA: Jossey-Bass.

Powsner, S.M., & Miller, P.L. (1992). Automated online transition from the medical record to the psychiatric literature. *Methods of Information in Medicine, 31,* 169-174.

Samuelson, K. H., Borko, H., & Amey, G. X. (1977). *Information systems and networks.* NY: North Holland.

Shannon, C.E., & Weaver, W. (1963). *The Mathematical theory of communication.* Urbana, IL: University of Illinois.

Shortliffe, E. H. (1991, October-December). Medical informatics and clinical decision making: The science and the pragmatics. *Medical decisionmaking: An International Journal of the Society of Medical Decision Making, 11,* S2-S14.

Sorace, J.M., Carnaham, G.E., Moore, G.W., & Berman, J.J. (1992, September). Automated review of blood donor screening test patterns at a regional blood center. *American Journal of Clinical Pathology, 98,* 334-344.

Van House, N. (1991). Assessing the quantity, quality and impact of LIS research. In C.R. McClure and P. Hernon, *Library and Information Science Research: Perspectives and Strategies for Improvement* (pp. 85-100). Norwood, NJ: Ablex.

Werley, H., & Lang, N. (1988). *Identification of the nursing minimum data set.* NY: Springer.

Whetten, D. A. (1989). What constitutes a theoretical contribution? *Academy of Management Review, 14(4),* 490-495.

BIBLIOGRAPHY

Aegerter, P., Auvert, B., Bertand, W.E., Emmanuelli, X., Benillouche, E., Landre, M.F., & Bos, D. (1992). An intelligent computer-assisted instruction system designed for rural health workers in developing countries. *Methods of Information in Medicine, 31,* 193-203.

Aronow, D. B., & Coltin, K. L. (1993, September). Information technology applications in quality assurance and quality improvement, Part I. *Journal of Qualitative Improvement, 19,* 403-415.

Aronow, D. B., & Coltin, K. L. (1993, October). Information technology applications in quality assurance and quality improvement, Part II. *Journal of Quality Improvement, 19,* 465-478.

Bakker, A. R., Nieman, H. B. J., & Pluyter-Wenting, E. S. P. (1986). Computers in nursing practice: Constraints and opportunities. *Proceedings of the Fifth Conference on Medical Informatics,* 602-606.

Beck, K. H., & Reldman, R. H. L. (1983). Information seeking among safety and health managers. *The Journal of Psychology, 115,* 23-31.

Broering, N. C. (1991, July). The MAClinical workstation project at Georgetown University. *Bulletin of the Medical Library Association, 79,* 276-281.

Chytil, M. K. (1986). Metadata and its role in medical informatics. *Proceedings of the Fifth Conference on Medical Informatics,* 149-154.

Coiera, E. (1991). Incorporating user and dialogue models into the interface design of an intelligent patient monitor. *Medical Informatics, 16*, 331-346.

Crawford, S. (1983, October). The origin and development of a concept: The information society. *Bulletin of the Medical Library Association, 71*, 380-385.

Dabke, K. P., & Thomas, K. M. (1992). Expert system guidance for library users. *Library Hi Tech, 10*, 53-60.

Dan, Q., & Dudeck, J. (1992). Certainty factor theory and its implementation in a medical expert system shell. *Medical Informatics, 17*, 87-103.

Demas, J. M., & Ludwig, L. T. (1991, January). Clinical medical librarian: The last unicorn? *Bulletin of the Medical Library Association, 79*, 17-27.

Dow, J. (1992). Using expert systems to elucidate library and information theory. *Library Hi Tech, 10*, 119-125.

Durbin, R. (1978). *Theory building.* NY: The Free Press.

Fairey, M. J. (1989). Management information: Its role in health care delivery. *Proceedings of the Sixth Conference on Medical Informatics*, xliii-xlix.

Forsythe, D. E., & Buchanan, B. G. (1991). Broadening our approach to evaluating medical information systems. *Symposium on Computer Applications in Medical Care*, 8-12.

Furfine, C. S. (1992). The FDA's policy on the regulation of computerized medical devices. *M.D. Computing: Computers in Medical Practice, 9*, 97-110.

Gage, J. S. (1992). Notes from StonyBrook. *M.D. Computing, 9*, 355-357.

Guo, D., Lincoln, M.J., Haug, P.J., Turner, C.W., Warner, H.R. (1991). Exploring a new best information algorithm for Iliad. *AMIA, 10*, 624-628.

Harris, D. L., Peay, W. J., & Lutz, L. J. (1989, January/February). Using microcomputers in rural preceptorships. *Family Medicine, 21*, 35-37.

Hayes-Roth, F. (1992). Knowledge systems: An introduction. *Library Hi Tech, 10*, 15-30+.

Huang, C. K. (1983, July). A leap forward in medical librarianship: A glimpse of the biomedical information center and network. *People's Republic of China, 71*, 299-303.

Johnson, N. R., Wu, E., Asu, G.V., Youngkin, M., & Strube, K. (1990, Winter). The best reference books in a medical school library. *Medical Reference Services*, 43-79.

Kelly, J. A., & Hillson, S. D. (1992, October). Searching for answers: Using computers to find the literature you need for patient care. *Minnesota Medicine, 75*, 39-41.

Kennedy, O. G., Davis, G. M., & Heda, S. (1992). Clinical information systems: 25-year history and the future. *Journal of the Society for Health Systems, 3*, 49-60.

Kingsland III, L. C. et al. (1993, April). Coach: Applying UMLS knowledge sources in an expert searcher environment. *Bulletin of the Medical Library Association, 81*, 178-183.

Kleinmuntz, B. (1992). Computers as clinicians: An update. *Computers in Biomedical Medicine, 22*, 227-237.

Lehmann, E. D., Deutsch, T., Roudsari, A.V., Carson, E.R., & Sonksen, P.H. (1993). Validation of a metabolic prototype to assist in the treatment of insulin-dependent diabetes mellitus. *Medical Informatics, 18(2)*, 83-101.

Levy, A. H. (1983). Teaching medical information. In J. C. Pages et al. (Eds), *Meeting the challenge: Informatics and medical education.* North Holland: Elsevier Science.

Massaro, D. W., & Friedman, D. (1990). Models of integration given multiple sources of information. *Psychological Review, 97*, 225-252.

McClure, C. R., & Hernon, P. (1991). *Library and information science research: Perspectives and strategies for improvement.* Norwood, NJ: Ablex.

Miaoulis, G., Skourlas, C., Christopoulou, A., & Xanthakis, S. (1992). New role of a medical documentation system. *Medical Informatics, 17(2)*, 165-178.

Miller, D. C. (1991). *Handbook of research design and social measurement (5th ed).* Newbury Park, CA: Sage.

Morris, A. (1991). Expert systems for library and information services: A review. *Information Processing and Management, 27*, 713-724.

Morris, A. (1992). Expert systems teaching: The needs of information professionals. *Library Hi Tech, 10*, 127-132.

News, news, news. (1989, December 6). *Journal of the National Cancer Institute, 81,* 1773-1776.

Nieman, H. B. J., Bakker, A. R., & Pluyter-Wenting, E. S. P. (1986). Computers in nursing practice: How? *Proceedings of the Fifth Conference on Medical Informatics,* 607-610.

Ozbolt, J. G. (1986). Developing decision support systems for nursing: Issues of knowledge representation. *Proceedings of the Fifth Conference on Medical Informatics,* 149-154.

Pemberton, J. M., & Prentice, A. E. (Eds.). (1990). *Information science: The interdisciplinary context.* NY: Neal-Schuman.

Peterson, H. E., & Gerdin-Jelger, U. (1986). A method on how to improve effective use of informatics in health care. *Proceedings of the Fifth Conference on Medical Informatics,* 335-337.

Pluyter-Wenting, E. S. P., Bakker, A. R., & Nieman, H. B. J. (1986). Computers in nursing practice: Why? *Proceedings of the Fifth Conference on Medical Informatics,* 597-601.

Powell, T. E. (1992, December). Laptop computer use in the health sciences library. *Computers in Libraries, 12,* 43-45.

Saba, V. K. (1986). Nursing information systems. *Proceedings of the Fifth Conference on Medical Informatics,* 579-584.

Schmandt, J., Bach, V., & Radin, B. A. (1979). Information and referral services for elderly welfare recipients. *The Gerontologist, 19,* 21-27.

Scott, R. (1993, March). Artificial intelligence: Its use in medical diagnosis. *The Journal of Nuclear Medicine, 34,* 50-514.

Shwe, M.A., Middleton, B., Heckerman, D.E., Henrion, M., Horvitz, E.J., Lehman, H.P., & Cooper, G.F. (1991). Probabilistic diagnosis using a reformulation of the INTERNIST-IQMR knowledge BASE I. The probabilistic model and inference algorithms. *Methods of Information in Medicine, 30(4),* 241-255.

Silverstein, N.M. (1984). (1984). Informing the elderly about public services: The relationship between sources of knowledge and service utilization. *The Gerontologist, 24,* 37-40.

Skywell B., & Stone, E.M. (1986). Using hospital mix data bases to manage nursing services. *Proceedings of the fifth conference on medical informatics,* 587-591.

Stead, Jr., E. A. (1988, July). The National Library of Medicine: The great equalizer between small hospitals and major medical centers. *North Carolina Medical Journal, 49,* 360.

Strozier, S. L. (1987, September). Microsearching online catalogs. *Small Computers in Libraries, 20,* 40-42.

Sullivan, M. G., & Brennen, P. W. (1984). Medical library services in Kuwait: History and future prospects. *Bulletin of the Medical Library Association, 72,* 12-17.

Sumner, W., & Shultz, E. K. (1992, October). Expert systems and expert behavior. *Journal of Medical Systems, 16 ,* 183-193.

Szecsebyi, J., Buschhorn, A., & Kochen, M. M. (1992). General practitioners' attitudes towards future developments in practice computing—A representative survey in the north of Germany. *Family Practice, 9,* 357-361.

Tiefel, V. (1993). The gateway to information: The future of information access today. *Library Hi Tech, 11,* 57-65, 74.

Veenstra, R. J., & Gluck, J. C. (1991, February 15). Access to information about AIDS. *Annals of Internal Medicine, 114,* 320-324.

Conceptual Models of Phenomena

Helen A. Bush

T he growth of scholarly thinking in nursing is reflected in a vital way in its models and theories and their application. Whereas in earlier years the focus was on learning about models and what constitutes a model or theory, more recently, uses of models and theories in practice, research, education and administration have become important.

This chapter opens with a brief review of contributions to the literature and continues with a discussion of nursing's worldviews. Values and their importance in building nursing science and the recent changes proposed for the substance of nursing constitute the latter part of the chapter.

A BRIEF REVIEW

In 1969, McKay's basic definitions for theory, model and system were derived from the classic definitions by Brodbeck, Meadows, Miller and von Bertalanffy. McKay stated that "...we should not remain content with mere factual data, averages, or correlations on which the researcher has imposed little rationale..." (p. 393). McKay recognized that theories, models and systems are essential to improved nursing practice since they aid the communication and extension of knowledge.

Jacox's 1974 article entitled, "Theory Construction in Nursing: An Overview" refers to conceptual frameworks and theoretical frameworks: "Such frameworks are more than isolated concepts and propositions, but do not yet meet the requirements of a theory" (p. 7). A review of the literature of the last two years revealed that these and other terms are used interchangeably: nursing conceptual model, nursing conceptual system, nursing model, nursing framework, nursing science framework, nursing science conceptual system, nursing conceptual framework, nursing systems and nursing theory.

Three years after the Jacox article, Phillips (1977) wrote "Nursing Systems and Nursing Models." This article emphasized to nurses that the medical, psychological, ecological and social models would not address the need for nursing models. Phillips indicated that when nursing models were constructed from concepts, nursing theory could then be generated. He did not elaborate on the probable origin of such concepts. When reprinted in Nicoll (1986), Phillips commented, "Even today... some nursing schools are still developing theory and doing research primarily from the perspective of another discipline" (p. 390). Phillips also made mention of colleagues who used the terms system and model synonymously. A review of the literature shows that this practice is continuing into the present time.

Four years after the Jacox article, Chinn and Jacobs (1978) offered their model for theory development in nursing. The operations within their model have been applied to defining nursing as a science. In clarifying the term theory, they explained: "Using our definition, it is only when events can be predicted, based on testing and application of the theoretical statements, that theory has been developed" (p. 2). Their presentation of the term conceptual framework supported Jacox (1974) and acknowledged the purposes of such frameworks "as categorizing data and investigating simple relationships between isolated phenomena, or may serve as a foundation for proposing and testing more complex interrelationships in research and practice" (p. 2).

In 1979, Bush stated, "The use of 'models' has been adopted (by nurses) as a system for observing, ordering, clarifying and analyzing events" (p. 13). In providing structure without a full discussion of concepts and their relationships, economy is a major benefit of a model. However, the danger of oversimplification and/or omission of critical components needs to be recognized.

Bush explained the relationship between models and theories and described the use of models in nursing research, education and practice.

Lancaster and Lancaster (1981) described, explained and classified various types of models. They defined a model as an entity which "may be used to define or describe something, to assist with analysis of a system, to specify relationships and processes, or to present a situation in symbolic terms that may be manipulated to derive predictions" (p. 32). Lancaster & Lancaster (1981) wrote that all theories are models since theories explain reality. However, all models are not theories if they lack the required components of theory.

Three advantages of models are: (a) to use trial and error techniques without the attending penalties; (b) to describe and predict events and (c) to assist in the better interpretation of events. A lack of evaluation instruments and use of a preordained set of concepts are designated as disadvantages (Lancaster & Lancaster, 1981).

MOVING AHEAD
Nursing's Worldview

In more recent years, the emphasis on explaining models and theories has shifted to the use of models to generate and develop the knowledge needed in nursing. The discovery, generation and testing of the knowledge which is important to nursing practice has rightfully taken precedence.

Fawcett (1993) asserted that four sets of paradigms or worldviews serve as the basis for the development of knowledge in nursing. In chronological order, they are the organismic and mechanistic worldviews (Reese & Overton, 1970), the change and persistence worldviews (Hall, 1981), the simultaneity and totality worldviews (Parse, 1987) and the particulate-deterministic, interactive-integrative and unitary-transformative worldviews (Newman, 1992). The characteristics of each worldview follow.

In the organismic worldview, the metaphor is the living organism. The organism is the source of acts and is "inherently and spontaneously active" (Reese & Overton, 1970, p. 133). The person is viewed as a whole organism whose behavior cannot be accurately predicted. The nature of change is qualitative as well as quantitative (Reese & Overton, 1970).

The metaphor for the mechanistic model is the machine. Since the focus is on parts and their interrelationships, the prediction of behavior is emphasized. This approach is also characterized by a tendency to quantification (Reese & Overton, 1970).

Hall (1981) challenged change as a major construct for nursing and offered persistence as a worldview. In the change paradigm, transition is continuous and natural progress is considered to be good. In the persistence view, however, stability is normal and solidarity is a major concept. Hall asserted "conservation and retrenchment are becoming necessary values" and reminded that as early as 1959, Dorothy Johnson emphasized the persistence view (p. 5).

Parse (1987) declared the totality paradigm as different from the simultaneity paradigm in "the assumptions about man and health, in the goals of nursing, and in the implications for research and practice" (pp. 31, 136). In the totality paradigm, the person is described as a bio-psycho-socio-spiritual being, while in the simultaneity view, persons are recognized by their behavioral patterns. Regarding nursing in the totality perspective, the central goals are health promotion, prevention of illness, care and cure. Causal and associative relationships are tested in the totality paradigm; and nursing care plans are used in determining person care. Quality of life and meaning in life rather than attention to a particular disease are important in the simultaneity paradigm. Qualitative research methods are appropriate in the simultaneity view. Meaning, rhythms and health patterns are significant to nursing care of the person.

In Newman's (1992) particulate-deterministic view, phenomena can be observed, isolated, reduced and measured. There is order and prediction. Antecedent conditions determine change; relationships are linear and causal. The interactive-integrative paradigm preserves control and predictability while acknowledging "reality as multidimensional and contextual" (p. 11). Antecedents and relationships are the basis of change. Objective and subjective events may interact. In the unitary-transformative paradigm, the human is a unitary being within a self-organizing field. Human fields are identified by pattern. Change is unidirectional and unpredictable. The unitary being moves through organization and disorganization to more complex organization. Personal knowledge is important.

In striving for parsimony, Fawcett analyzed the four sets of worldviews and reduced them to three sets which she named: the reaction worldview, the reciprocal interaction worldview and the simultaneous action worldview. For the reaction worldview, Fawcett brought together aspects of the mechanism, persistence, totality and particulate-deterministic worldviews.

In the reaction worldview, the person is a bio-psycho-social-spiritual being who reacts to the environment in a linear way. Survival is the only reason for change. Research depends on observed and measured events.

Organicism, totality, change and persistence were reformulated to become the reciprocal interaction paradigm. Persons are viewed holistically as they interact with their environment. What is real depends on the context. "Change is probabilistic and may be continuous or may be only for survival" (Fawcett, 1993, p. 58). Quantitative and qualitative research methods and techniques are used.

The simultaneous action worldview contains ideas from organicism, simultaneity and change. The major concepts in this worldview are pattern, mutual rhythmical interchange and the person as a self-organized field. Change takes place only in one direction and cannot be predicted. Persons become more complex as change occurs. Personal becoming is important.

Fawcett believed that nursing's knowledge fits well with reciprocal interaction and simultaneous action worldviews. While retaining the scope of the contents of the first four sets of worldviews, the three new paradigms provide simplicity and efficiency as well as clarifying our paths to theory construction. A simpler worldview is more useful for at least two reasons: it is easier to remember and should be easier to use to predict probable outcomes. Thus, the continuing development and refinement of nursing's worldview is basic since the worldview serves as a tool for decision-making.

PRESCRIPTIVE CONCEPTS — VALUES

Cody (1993) stated that scholars who consider quality of life issues realize the importance of values in building nursing science. Although that realization is present, according to Cody (1993), scientific knowledge has been used by those who manage human lives without a necessary basis in values. He insisted that personal patterns of living based on personal values are the focus for nursing science. Similarly, self-respect, self-determination and self-caring behaviors were noted by Donaldson and Crowley (1978) as values of the person which influence the value orientation of nursing as a discipline. They believed that nursing is "defined by social relevance and value orientations rather than by empirical truths" (p. 118).

Nurse leaders acknowledge that nursing is at a crossroads. A reevaluation of basic value priorities is necessary and beneficial to unifying nursing, fostering cohesiveness and interpreting world events. The need for reevaluation is essential for nursing in making better decisions in a changing world and to better understand which values are important to nursing.

Among the primary values for nursing is meaning — "values, beliefs and ideals all point to the centrality of meaning in human existence" (Cody, 1993, p. 110). In his article entitled, "Meaning and Mystery in Nursing Science and Art," Cody (1994) considered the contributions of Leininger, Newman, Parse and Watson to the study of meaning as an aim of nursing science. Leininger submitted, "Knowledge of meanings and practices derived from worldviews... cultural values, environmental context and language uses are essential to guide nursing decisions and actions... "(Cody, 1994, p. 48). Cody noted that Leininger did not speak to personal meanings but was more interested in meaning for a group or community. Regarding Newman (1986), Cody asserted her theory of health is "about meaning: the meaning of life and health ..." (Cody, 1994, p. 48). He described Parse's (1981, 1992) theory as revolving around meaning which, to Parse, is reality through valuing and imaging. For Watson (1985), fulfillment of the self can only be accomplished through the meaning of human existence.

The relationship of meaning to health, caring and living have been initiated by these four theorists. Further explanations will support the primacy of meaning as a value in the development of nursing as a science and an art.

DESCRIPTIVE CONCEPTS — SUBSTANCE

Donaldson and Crowley (1978) declared that nurse scholars need to focus on the substance of nursing. In 1993, Chinn submitted, "Most vexing of all, we ourselves still at times decry our not having a clear definition of what nursing is" (p. vi). She approached the issue in a positive manner by charging nurses to consider "our diversities and ambiguities as a real strength" (p. vi). Chinn believed that diversity and ambiguity can be advantageous in changing nursing in this era of redefining health care. Bower (1994) and Chinn (1993) are in agreement regarding our focus on technology, efficiency and cost-containment. While we must concern ourselves with these issues, our emphasis is misplaced unless we reaffirm our need for knowledge development through research, research-based practice especially of phenomena new to nurses but not new to the field of healing and therapeutics. Allopathic and alternative treatments were given by Bower and Chinn as examples of this point.

A different but important example of a concept new to nurses is chaos theory (Vicenzi, 1994). "Instead of equilibrium and homeostatic balance, the worldview of chaos elevates variation, change, surprise and unpredictability to the center of the knowledge process" (p. 37). Using chaos theory, disease or illness aligns with stability. Nurses would encourage chaotic motion and discard linear relationships. These notions also fit into Newman's (1992) unitary-transformative paradigm and the simultaneous action worldview (Fawcett, 1993). Also complementary to chaos theory is Newman's (1986) theory of health wherein disease is an inherent part of health.

Regarding the substance of nursing, Newman, Sime and Corcoran-Perry (1991) assert that although the concepts person, environment, health and nursing were significant, nursing's focus required further narrowing. They recommend health and caring as key concepts, pointing out that health has been central to nursing ever since Nightingale and continues so. Caring is described as the essence of nursing. Leininger (1984), Watson (1985) and Benner and Wrubel (1989) have related caring to health, healing and well-being. Newman and others (1991) stated, "Considerable evidence exists that caring, health and health experience are concepts central to the discipline of nursing" (p. 3). Also cited were Pender (1990), Newman (1990), Phillips (1990) and Parse (1981). "Nursing is the study of caring in the human health experience" (Newman et al., 1991). The identity of a discipline can be formulated to stipulate the area of study. The above definition of nursing implies a social commitment, the nature of service and the area for knowledge development.

Although specific theories of health and caring were not suggested, the compatibility of Newman's theory of health with chaos theory is clear. Further exploration of extant caring theories is necessary. Ultimately, a personal preference of the nurse may be in order as to the use of a theory of caring.

The above statements are in agreement with Smith (1994) when she writes of nursing practice in the next millennium. She envisions nursing practice as nursing theory based. The choice of that theory will derive from the nurse's value system. Inquiry as well as practice methods will continue to be centered on human health experiences, healing practices and quality of life issues.

SUMMARY

Nurse scholars have moved on from defining and describing models and their workings to determining a nursing worldview and its values (see Table 1). In the years since McKay (1969) exhorted us to improve nursing practice via the use of models, theories and systems, our worldview has developed from the reaction worldview and the reciprocal interaction worldview to the simultaneous action worldview (Fawcett, 1993).

While in the earlier years, our values provided support for nursing's philosophical and theoretical formulations, those values were not as manifest in nursing care. With the human health experience as a pre-eminent concept, meaning as a value for nurses has emerged as fundamental.

Our descriptive knowledge for facts to predict probable consequences of a proposed action has been narrowed from four broad concepts — person, health, environment and nursing — to health, caring and chaos. Thus, nursing practice in the

Table 4.1 From Definition of Models to Definition of Substance

1969 McKay	Definition and description of models models for nursing are presented.	Medical, ecologic, psychologic and social models are in use for nursing.
1978 Chinn & Jacobs	A model for theory development is introduced	1. Concept analysis. 2. Formulation and testing of relational statements. 3. Theory construction. 4. Practical application of theory.
1978, Leininger 1979, Watson 1981, Parse 1983, Newman	Theories for nursing which explicate the meaning of meaning are generated.	Meaning emerges as a core value for nursing.
1991, Newman, Sime and Corcoran-Perry	Concepts person, environment, health and nursing are narrowed.	Major concepts health and caring are determined.
1993, Fawcett	Four worldviews are reduced to three	Reciprocal interaction worldview and simultaneous action worldview guide nursing knowledge.
1994, Vicenzi	Chaos theory redefines health and nursing.	

future will have the support of an elegant worldview that is a combination of simplicity and scope. Core values will provide nurses' reasons for caregiving. The focus for the discipline of nursing will be clearly stated.

REFERENCES

Benner, P., & Wrubel, J. (1989). *The primacy of caring*. Menlo Park, CA: Addison-Wesley.

Bower, F. L. (1994, Summer). Research utilization: Attitude and value. *Reflections*, 4-5.

Bush, H.A. (1979). Models for nursing. *Advances in Nursing Science, 1*(2), 13-21.

Chinn, P. L. (1993). Advantages of ambiguity. *Advances in Nursing Science, 15*(4), vi.

Chinn, P. L. (1994). A window of opportunity. *Advances in Nursing Science, 16*(4), viii.

Chinn, P. L., & Jacobs, M. K. (1978). A model for theory development in nursing. *Advances in Nursing Science, 1*(1), 1-11.

Cody, W. K. (1993). Norms and nursing science: A question of values. *Nursing Science Quarterly, 6*(3), 110-112.

Cody, W. K. (1994). Meaning and mystery in nursing science and art. *Nursing Science Quarterly, 7*(2), 48-51.

Donaldson, S. K., & Crowley, D. M. (1978, February). The discipline of nursing. *Nursing Outlook*, 113-120.

Fawcett, J. (1993). From a plethora of paradigms to parsimony in worldviews. *Nursing Science Quarterly, 6*(2), 56-58.

Hall, B. A. (1981). The change paradigm in nursing: Growth vs. persistence. *Advances in Nursing Science, 3*(4), 1-6.

Jacox, A. K. (1974). Theory construction in nursing: An overview. *Nursing Research, 23*(1), 4-13.

Lancaster, W., & Lancaster, J. (1981). Models and model building in nursing. *Advances in Nursing Science, 3*(3), 31-42.

Leininger, M. (Ed.). (1984). *Care: The essence of nursing and health.* Thorofare, NJ: Slack.

McKay, R. (1969). Theories, models, and systems for nursing. *Nursing Research, 18*(5), 393-399.

Newman, M. A. (1986). *Health as expanding consciousness.* St. Louis, MO: Mosby.

Newman, M. A. (1990). Newman's theory of health as praxis. *Nursing Science Quarterly, 3,* 37-41.

Newman, M. A. (1992). Prevailing paradigms in nursing. *Nursing Outlook, 40,* 10-13, 32.

Newman, M. A., Sime, A. M., & Corcoran-Perry, S. A. (1991). The focus of the discipline of nursing. *Advances in Nursing Science, 14*(1), 1-6.

Nicoll, L. H. (1992). *Perspectives on nursing theory.* Philadelphia, PA: J. B. Lippincott.

Parse, R. R. (1981). *Man-living-health: A theory of nursing.* NY: Wiley.

Parse, R. R. (1987). *Nursing science: Major paradigms, theories, and critiques.* Philadelphia, PA: Saunders.

Pender, N. J. (1990). Expressing health through lifestyle patterns. *Nursing Science Quarterly, 3*(3), 115-122.

Phillips, J. R. (1977). Nursing systems and nursing models. *Image, 9*(1), 4-7.

Phillips, J. R. (1990). The different views of health. *Nursing Science Quarterly, 3*(3), 103-104.

Reese, H. W., & Overton, W. F. (1970). Models of development and theories of development. In L. R. Goulet & P. B. Baltes (Eds.), *Life span developmental psychology. Research and theory (pp.* 115-145). NY: Academic Press.

Smith, M. C. (1994). Beyond the threshold: Nursing practice in the next millennium. *Nursing Science Quarterly, 7*(1), 6-7.

Vicenzi, A. E. (1994). Chaos theory and some nursing considerations. *Nursing Science Quarterly, 7*(1), 36-42.

Watson, M. J. (1985). *Nursing: Human science and human care, a theory of nursing.* Norwalk, CT: Appleton-Century-Crofts.

Part Two
Methods and Applications of Theory Construction

Overview of Three Methods of Theory Construction

Charles A. Walker, Anita L. Comley, Carol Hodgson, Jan M. Nick and Heidi Taylor

I n its development as a scholarly discipline, nursing has benefitted from a variety of traditional and nontraditional approaches. Some nurse theorists encourage the use of alternative methods of investigation such as philosophic discourse, phenomenology and naturalistic inquiry (Carper, 1978; Munhall, 1989; Parse, Coyne, & Smith, 1985; Simmons, 1992; Younger, 1991; Watson, 1987). These alternative ways of knowing have enriched scientific knowledge and have become moderately accepted within the scientific community. Even so, the valuable theory construction strategies considered in this chapter fit neatly within the *traditional* mold of scholarship.

Theory construction, an architectural metaphor for knowledge development, conjures images of dazzlingly theoretical edifices built upon a foundation of *a priori* knowledge and assumptions. But acquired doctrines are not always reliable. In fact, they may present an impediment to novel and innovative thought. Sometimes the only legitimate way to proceed in developing new knowledge is to deconstruct what is known, to strip away any facade of myth and misconception and to level extant beliefs and dogmas (Rodgers, 1991).

The purpose of this chapter is to provide an overview of three theory construction strategies borrowed from sociology and applied toward nursing. Of the original works in which these methods were first introduced, two (Stinchcombe, 1968; Blalock, 1969) are no longer in print and the third (Gibbs, 1972) is difficult to find. Despite the relative inaccessibility of these resources, however, attention to the methods and ideas that they present has merit for theory development in nursing and related disciplines. Thus, what follows are summaries of the rudimentary characteristics of each theory construction strategy. Demonstrations of theory construction using these strategies shall be provided in subsequent chapters.

STINCHCOMBE'S METHODS OF THEORY CONSTRUCTION

Concerned with explaining social phenomena, Stinchcombe (1968) developed three complex causal explanations. These include demographic, functional and historicist models. The purpose of each is to provide a framework for constructing new theories. The demographic explanation defines the population under study and the differences between sub-populations. The functional explanation focuses on how homeostasis is accomplished in a system where a singular phenomenon may have many causes. The historicist explanation, a variant of the functional model, demonstrates the effect of historical influences on the structure of a phenomenon. Each of Stinchcombe's three causal explanations is described below.

Demographic Causal Explanation

The demographic model enables the researcher to examine population trends and to answer questions based on probabilities so that, despite individual differences, group behavior can be accurately predicted. This model is particularly helpful to the researcher in the case of large differences within the studied population. Demographic models are used to demonstrate causality in rates, proportions and quantities (Stinchcombe, 1968).

Stinchcombe (1968) defines a demographic causal model as one in which a causal force is assumed to be "proportional to the number of people of a certain kind" (p. 60). The purpose of the demographic model is to assist the researcher in describing the population while assigning subjects to categories. Two assumptions drive this model: (a) subjects more between mutually exclusive categories and (b) proportions of subjects moving from one category to another remains constant. Individuals move in and out of categories until proportions reach equilibrium, as occurs when the causal forces driving the population stabilize.

Stinchcombe's demographic model explains overall individual movement between categories. This explanation refines a theory in its developmental stages. Figure 5.1 demonstrates the movement of characteristics C and D from

Figure 5.1 Demographic Causal Model

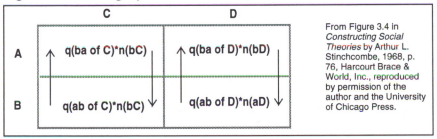

From Figure 3.4 in *Constructing Social Theories* by Arthur L. Stinchcombe, 1968, p. 76, Harcourt Brace & World, Inc., reproduced by permission of the author and the University of Chicago Press.

cell A to cell B and vice versa. According to Stinchcombe (1968), the arrows represent a certain number of people moving from one population to another at any given time. Even though movement into and out of a category is fairly constant, wide fluctuations in individual change may occur. A *proportionality factor* (q) is specified for each cell to indicate the net movement and the *number of people affected* (n).

According to Stinchcombe, the most conceptually satisfactory way to deal with different proportions in different subcategories of a population is to repeat the transition rate analysis in each subgroup. Within these guidelines, the researcher analyzes the various demographic variables in a theory. This causal model aids the theorist in making inferences about a group of people in relation to a given phenomenon.

Functional Causal Explanation

The functional causal model is defined as "a structure or an activity that is caused indirectly by its consequences" (p. 70). Stinchcombe (1968) states that the functional representations of causal structures give rise to a pattern in which the *consequences* (or outcomes) of a phenomenon tend to be constant while the *structures themselves* have great variability. This causal explanation would be the most appropriate model to implement if the phenomenon being studied remains constant while exhibiting multiple causes. A basic assumption underlying this model is that desired goals can serve as the drivers of future behaviors aimed at achieving those same goals. Hence, in the functional explanation, *consequences can act as causes*.

As Stinchcombe's own functional analysis of Marxist ideology reveals, many important social phenomena cannot be fully understood as a simple chronology of causes and effects occurring in neat linear progression. Thus, Stinchcombe introduces a "feedback loop" between the desired goal and sys-

Figure 5.2 Functional Causal Model

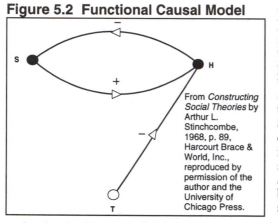

From *Constructing Social Theories* by Arthur L. Stinchcombe, 1968, p. 89, Harcourt Brace & World, Inc., reproduced by permission of the author and the University of Chicago Press.

tem-maintaining structures. Functional explanations consist of causal links among three variables: (a) the supporting maintenance structure, (b) a homeostatic variable (the outcome) and (c) tensions. A diagram of Stinchcombe's functional causal explanation is shown in Figure 5.2. The homeostatic variable (H) functions *indirectly* via a negative feedback loop to influence the structure. The structure (S)

maintains the homeostasis of the system. The tensions (T) threaten to destabilize the homeostatic variable. Tensions are viewed as the factors which disturb homeostasis and that may be controlled by the system's maintenance structure. Due to the supporting structure, the system is able to adapt, evolve or change to accommodate the tensions.

The purpose of the functional model is to assist the researcher in elucidating how system stability is achieved and maintained. According to Stinchcombe (1968), the employment of the functional explanation is appropriate if:

1. Many behaviors (or structures) are found with the same consequences.
2. A behavior varies with the amount of tensions in the system.
3. Outcomes are constant though causes vary.
4. Phenomena are erratic but nevertheless continue.
5. Behaviors (or structures) in a system are selected by certain consequences or outcomes.

Historicist Causal Explanation

Historicist explanations are special cases of functional explanations. In the historicist explanation, the original cause is not as important an influence on a phenomenon as is the loop generated by historical variables. Stinchcombe (1968) identified two ways to explain how historical variables develop and perpetuate themselves. First, similar causes, occurring year after year, produce the same effect (phenomenon) and second, certain social patterns are

Figure 5.3 Historicist Causal Model

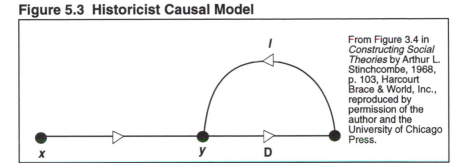

From Figure 3.4 in *Constructing Social Theories* by Arthur L. Stinchcombe, 1968, p. 103, Harcourt Brace & World, Inc., reproduced by permission of the author and the University of Chicago Press.

repetitive. The historicist causal explanation is, therefore, infinitely self-replicating. As Stinchcombe (1968) observes, the functional alternatives found in a particular society are generally determined by historical events. But once a functional alternative becomes established, it tends to eliminate the causes of other alternatives and regenerate itself.

The key components of the historicist model are the historical variables, functional alternatives and selective maintenance structures. The basic structure of Stinchcombe's historicist explanation is shown in Figure 5.3, in which X is an historical cause of Y. The variable D stands for a *delayer* which represents the passage of time during which Y operates as a cause. The return loop (1) indicates that Y will eventually repeat itself as an effect in succeeding periods. It is the infinite loop created by the delayer (D) and periodic measurement at "1" that makes the historicist explanation distinctive. In this form of explanation, empirical propositions can be derived about the conditions under which traditions tend to be preserved.

The logical structure of the historicist explanation of a phenomenon depicts how the effect of a cause at a previous point in time becomes the cause of the same effect at succeeding points in time (Stinchcombe, 1968). With this causal model, predictions can be fairly accurate since a theorist can predict future outcomes based on a knowledge of past behavior. This model serves as a predictor of contemporary social structures.

Prediction is both reliable and simple when viewing phenomena through a linear looking glass. However, when nonlinear processes are evident, prediction from an historical sequence of events becomes more challenging. Chaos theory informs the view of history as a series of repeatable events by insisting that where order and disorder mingle, a fringe of regenerative fractal patterns emerges (Gleick, 1987; Briggs, 1992). This delicate demarcation between predictability and unpredictability is consistent with the maxim of chaoticians that consequences are sensitive to initial conditions. Even the most minute error in measurement can yield grossly distorted results. Therefore, long term predictions of volatile and rapidly changing systems, like the weather and much of human behavior, is severely limited if not utterly impossible. For short term predictions, Stinchcombe's historicist model holds up to scrutiny; however, it fails to account for unexpected occurrences over time.

The causal models presented by Stinchcombe (1968) can assist the theorist in understanding any phenomenon of interest. Despite their complexity, all three models can prove useful in the initial phase of theory construction.

BLALOCK'S METHOD OF THEORY CONSTRUCTION

The goal of theory construction, according to Blalock (1969), is to state a theory in ways that can be tested. The strategies for theory construction suggested by Blalock are general enough to be used in diverse fields of study. He recommends moving from purely verbal theoretical formulations to simultaneous algebraic equations and, in the case of dynamic theories, to simultaneous differential equations. The verbal formulations of a theory are the simple, first approximations of a phenomenon which must ultimately be replaced or supplemented by testable mathematical formulations. In the chapters that follow, Blalock's block recursive method of theory construction will be used to develop the first approximations of verbal theories about various phenomena. These will identify relationships between and among testable variables.

According to Blalock (1979), "...a 'good' theory should be parsimonious or relatively simple, logically consistent, capable of making precise predictions, as complete or self-contained as possible in the sense of including virtually all of the important explanatory variables, and capable of being falsified" (p. 121). A theory which meets all of these criteria is not only difficult to construct, it is also more difficult to adequately test. Blalock suggests that theories may satisfy one or more criteria, therefore the importance of each criteria becomes a matter of preference. Theory construction is a process that lacks a specified beginning and ending, it is hoped that any unmet criteria will eventually be met as the process continues. For these reasons, the issue of criteria prioritization is left to judgment of the theorist (Blalock, 1979).

The important aspects of theory construction discussed by Blalock (1969) pertain to variables and their relationships. Exogenous variables are predetermined variables which are the givens or starting points of the theory. These variables are not considered to be dependent on other variables in the system. Conversely, endogenous variables are dependent on one or more variables in the system (Blalock, 1969).

Relationships among variables may be stated in the form of propositions (Blalock, 1969). Propositions assumed to be direct, causal links between variables are called axioms. Axioms are untestable because it is not possible to control for all the relevant variables. Propositions deduced by reasoning from axioms are called theorems. Theorems are testable if there are sufficient measures for the identified variables. They denote covariance and temporal sequences among the variables.

Blalock (1969) suggests the block-recursive system as a strategy for theory construction. A recursive system is one in which there is no feedback between variables. For instance, if variable X_1 (age) is considered to be a direct or indirect cause of variable X_2 (education), then X_2 cannot be a direct or indirect cause of X_1. Exogenous variables influence endogenous variables, but Blalock assumes no feedback from endogenous variables to exogenous variables in a block recursive system. Many phenomena of interest to nursing, involve complex feedback systems. A block-recursive system can be appropriate for constructing theories about such phenomena because it allows for feedback within but not between the system components.

Figure 5.4 illustrates a block-recursive system in which feedback is present within but not between blocks of variables. Blalock (1969) argues that as a theorist begins to delimit the number of variables to be considered in a theory, the theorist assumes "...that a block-recursive model can give a reasonably

Figure 5.4 A Block–Recursive System*

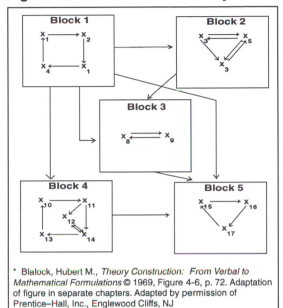

* Blalock, Hubert M., *Theory Construction: From Verbal to Mathematical Formulations* © 1969, Figure 4-6, p. 72. Adaptation of figure in separate chapters. Adapted by permission of Prentice–Hall, Inc., Englewood Cliffs, NJ

accurate representation of reality" (p. 73). As the theory is developed, the theorist may find that the model does not fit the data. If this occurs, the theory is modified often by adding more complexity and is compared again with the data. Through this process, the theory becomes increasingly representative of reality (Blalock, 1979).

The process for constructing a theory using Blalock's block-recursive system is described below:

1. *Review the Literature.* Carefully read the literature and clarify concepts. Translate existing verbal theories into common language. Search the literature for propositions and implicit assumptions regarding the relationships between concepts.

2. *Identify the Concepts and Variables.* Systematically list all the important concepts and variables. Eliminate and consolidate variables. Place related variables into categories. Categorization of theoretically related variables may result in the identification of typologies, which are forced dichotomies that tend to oversimplify a phenomenon. Blalock (1969) suggests that, while typologies are useful in identifying related variables, they are not sufficient for implying causal relationships.

3. *Analyze the Relationships Between Variables.* Analysis of propositions about theoretically related variables may lead to an inventory of causes and effects for selected dependent variables. As factors affecting the variables in causal sequences are identified, simple causal chains may be developed. If feedback is present, causal loops are indicated. Blalock (1969) argues that these methods, while more sophisticated than typologies, are limited by their failure to address covariance between dependent or independent variables.

4. *Create Blocks of Grouped Variables.* Place grouped variables in theoretical blocks. The relationship among the variables within a given block may be simple or complex. The nature of the relationships is depicted with arrows and positive or negative signs. *Within* the block, reciprocal causation or feedback among the variables may be present. If the variables within a block are so highly correlated that their individual effects cannot be separated, a researcher may treated them as a syndrome and give a general label to the block. By treating the block as a syndrome, a

researcher may use one or two measures to summarize the effect of the entire set of variables in this block.

5. *Depict the Nature of the Relationships Between Blocks.* The nature of the relationships between the blocks are also depicted with arrows and signs. Straight arrows indicate an explained association; curved or broken lines represent unexplained associations. The blocks are hierarchically arranged, with exogenous blocks depicted first followed by the endogenous blocks. Blalock assumes negligible feedback from the endogenous blocks (variables) to the exogenous blocks (variables). This creates the block recursive system; one in which there is a unidirectional flow of causality without feedback *between* the blocks.

6. *Generate Testable Hypotheses.* Each of the relationships depicted within and between the blocks are fertile ground for the generation of testable hypotheses. As these hypotheses are tested, the theory is modified to more accurately represent the reality of a phenomenon.

Blalock's block-recursive system is one strategy for identifying a first approximation or verbal formulation of a phenomenon. Over time, this verbal formulation must be replaced by mathematical formulas through which the identified relationships between variables can be tested. Blalock's block-recursive method may not be the appropriate model for all phenomena of interest to nursing. It is, however, a valuable strategy for identifying concepts and variables pertinent to a phenomenon and exploring the nature of their relationships.

GIBBS' METHOD OF THEORY CONSTRUCTION

Gibbs (1972a) believes that formal theory construction is essential for the progress of a discipline. His mode of theory construction, which can be characterized as positivistic, has three underlying assumptions: (a) theories should be stated formally, (b) theories should be testable and (c) predictive power should be the primary criterion for assessing theories.

Gibbs' idea that theory must move beyond a narrative of highly abstract concepts toward detailed specification of the underlying referents is not new. In *An Enquiry Concerning Human Understanding* published nearly two centuries ago, Hume (1798) argued that each complex idea (construct) must be made up of simpler ideas (concepts), every one of which must be a copy or mental replica of some sense experience (referent). Further, he maintained that for a word to be meaningful, it must stand for an idea, which in turn represents an antecedent impression, and the derivation from impression to idea must be clearly demonstrated. If this cannot be done, the word is meaningless.

In Gibbs' view, the primary purpose in formalizing a theory is to make it empirically testable. A formal theory is conveyed in accordance with some mode of theory construction. Elements of the mode selected stipulate the major components, the basic unit terms and the overall structure of a theory (Gibbs, 1972a). Like Blalock, Gibbs believes that because methods of theory development differ, the preference of one method over another is simply a matter of opinion.

Principle of Causality
 A discussion of the method of theory construction proposed by Gibbs cannot proceed without due consideration of the notion of causality. Causation, says Gibbs (1972b) can create problems in theory construction. Attempts to explain or predict phenomena based upon some causal mechanism are often problematic because theorists "infer causation; they do not observe it" (p. 816).
 Gibbs draws upon the work of Hume (1978) who posited two types of human knowledge: (a) knowledge derived from logical reasoning which Hume calls "relations of ideas" and (b) knowledge arrived at by observation which Hume calls "matters of fact." For example, one might see a brick being thrown at a window and then see the window shatter (matters of fact) and reason that one event is the cause of the other (relation of ideas). Here, causation implies not merely that one event preceded the other in time or was adjacent in space but that there exists some *necessary* connection between the two. Causation is

Figure 5.5 A 1-2-0-2 Theoretical Structure

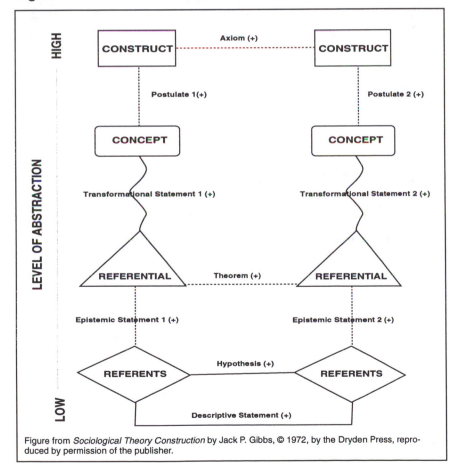

Figure from *Sociological Theory Construction* by Jack P. Gibbs, © 1972, by the Dryden Press, reproduced by permission of the publisher.

distinguished from coincidence by the notion of necessity — the cause is said to necessitate or compel the effect. And once a connection is discovered between two events, say A and B, confidence in prediction increases such that the next time A happens, other things being equal, B will follow.

But Hume and Gibbs maintain that all anyone can ever observe is the temporal and spatial conjunction between two events, one of which precedes the other. The inference of a causal connection arises from isolated and particular instances of observation. A large part of scientific investigation depends upon such a causal relation. The upshot of this intellectual skepticism is that the foundation of most scientific knowledge, namely the law of cause and effect, must be accepted as both limited and uncertain.

Consequently, Gibbs proposes a mode of theory construction which excludes causal language. He points out that his arguments should not be construed as a denial of causal thinking. Essentially, Gibbs permits the theorist to think causally in the development of theory but advocates excluding "causes" or other similar terms from theory construction. Causal language in social theories does not improve their testability, it only leads to confusion. He recommends, instead, using mathematical formulas to make relational statements within a theory.

Components of a Theory

According to Gibbs (1972a), a formally constructed theory has distinct intrinsic and extrinsic elements. Intrinsics are comprised of assertions about the properties of classes or events stated relationally. These relational statements hold the theory together. Each intrinsic statement is identified by a number or letter, and the statements are distinguished as to type such as axiom, postulate or theorem (see Figure 5.5).

The other part of Gibbs' paradigm is the extrinsic component of theory, which is comprised of the definitions of terms, along with formulas, procedural instructions and specifications of the kinds of data required. Gibbs (1972a) affirms the need to clarify a theory's structure to facilitate its testing. Therefore, theoretical assertions must include certain clearly defined terms.

Definitions of Terms

In Gibbs' model, three categories of terms are included, i.e., unit, substantive and relational terms. Other general terms, used to describe the model, must be understood if the reader is to comprehend the paradigm that Gibbs proposes. Some key definitions follow:

Unit terms are the designations given to classes of events or things. The theorist can increase the predictive accuracy of the assertions by limiting the theory to a single unit term and defining it explicitly in the theory. Examples from sociological theory include age, group and occupation.

Substantive terms designate properties of the class identified in the unit term. In Gibbs' model, they include constructs, concepts and referentials.

Constructs are not clearly defined by Gibbs, but his use of the term implies that they are a theory's most vague ideas and are not empirically testable. According to Gibbs, a construct may be used to denote an undefined idea (Gibbs, 1972a).

Concepts are substantive terms that are defined completely in a theory but are not empirically applicable.

Referentials are intrinsic terms that designate formulas in the extrinsic part of a theory and are represented as capitalized acronyms. Referential formulas are relevant only to the theory in which they are employed and should not be judged for predictive accuracy apart from that theory.

Temporal quantifiers of substantive terms are references to time. A substantive term designates a property but the designation is incomplete without temporal quantifiers. The reference to time may pertain to a particular point in time or to change over time.

Relational terms are words in intrinsic statements that denote a particular kind of association. They stipulate a relation either between the class and the property or between the properties of the class (Gibbs, 1972a).

Axioms are the intrinsic statements specifying a relation between two constructs.

Postulates are assertions of the empirical relation between a construct and a concept.

Propositions are assertions of the empirical relation between two concepts.

Transformational statements are assertions of the empirical relation between a concept and a referential. A theory is not testable without these statements.

Theorems are formally derived intrinsic statements linking referentials to other referentials. They constitute the final step of the intrinsic part of the theory.

Epistemic statements link referentials in a theorem with sets of referents.

Referents are unit terms or values that result from the measurement and computation of referential formulas.

Hypotheses are formally derived predictions about referents.

Descriptive statements stipulate values (perhaps correlation coefficients) which represent the association between two sets of referents.

Structure of a Theory

Gibbs (1972a) posits that a theory is not merely a collection of assertions. The intrinsic statements are interrelated syntactically and the resultant structure can be represented as in Figure 5.5. In Gibbs' method of theory construction, theories differ in structure depending on the number of each type of direct intrinsic statement present (axioms, postulates, propositions, and transformational statements). In denoting the structure of a theory, the number of each type of intrinsic statements is specified. For example, the hypothetical theory depicted in Figure 5.5 is a 1-2-0-2 structure, meaning that the theory has one axiom, two postulates, no propositions and two transformational statements. In the examples of theory construction using Gibbs' paradigm that appear in subsequent chapters, a variety of theoretical structures are used.

SUMMARY

In this chapter, the key ideas from the theory construction strategies promulgated by the sociologists Stinchcombe (1968), Blalock (1969) and Gibbs (1972) have been highlighted. Stinchcombe (1968) provides three heuristics useful for broadly conceptualizing a phenomenon of interest. His demographic model explains probabilities of occurrence within specified populations; his functionalist model examines the counterbalance between system-maintaining feedback and the tensions that shift a system toward disequilibrium; and his historicist model explores the power of the past in predicting present and future events.

Blalock (1969) advocates clustering (organizing) concepts into blocks and demonstrating relationships (covariations) within and among those blocks. The resultant schematic structure conveys some of the complexity demanded by the phenomenon being investigated.

Gibbs (1972) prompts the aspiring theorist to operationalize (or formalize) any putative theory by specifying empirical indicators. These indicators or methods of measurement, in turn, yield actual scores or values whereby the theory can be statistically tested.

The remaining chapters in this section will demonstrate how six emergent theories of relevance to nursing were developed. The phenomena which these theories represent differ greatly in their content, their level of abstraction and the immediacy of their practice applications. Each of the chapters (six through eleven) will begin with a general review of the literature relevant to the phenomenon under study. Next, the phenomenon will be addressed using the unique perspectives of the theory construction strategists whose works have been summarized here. Last, a path diagram, representing the culmination of theorizing about the particular phenomenon, will be presented and discussed briefly. The logic of causal modeling and methods for theory testing will receive due attention in Part III of this book.

REFERENCES

Blalock, H.M. (1969). *Theory construction: From verbal to mathematical formulations.* Englewood Cliffs, NJ: Prentice-Hall.

Blalock, H.M. (1979). Dilemmas and strategies of theory construction. In W. Snizek, E. Fuhrman & M. Miller (Eds.), *Contemporary issues in theory and research: A metasociological perspective.* Westport, CT: Greenwood Press.

Briggs, J. (1992). *Fractal patterns of chaos.* NY: Simon & Schuster.

Carper, B.A. (1978). Fundamental patterns of knowing in nursing. *Advances in Nursing Science, 1*(1), 13-23.

Gibbs, J. (1972a). *Social theory construction.* Hinsdale, IL: The Dryden Press, Inc.

Gibbs, J. (1972b). Causation and theory construction. *Social Science Quarterly, 52,* 815-826.

Gleick, J. (1987). *Chaos: Making of a new science.* NY: Penguin Books, USA, Inc.

Hume, D. (1978). *An enquiry concerning human understanding.* London: Oxford University Press. (Original work published in 1798).

Munhall, P.L. (1989). Philosophical ponderings on qualitative research methods in nursing. *Nursing Science Quarterly, 2*(1), 20-28.

Parse, R.R., Coyne, A., & Smith, M. (1985). *Nursing research: Qualitative methods.* Bowie, MD: Brady Communication Co.

Rodgers, B. (1991). Deconstructing the dogma of nursing knowledge and practice. *Image: Journal of Nursing Scholarship, 23*(3), 177-181.

Simmons, H. (1992). Philosophic and scientific inquiry: The interface. In J. K. Kikuchi & H. Simmons (Eds.), *Philosophic inquiry in nursing.* Newbury Park, CA: Sage.

Stinchcombe, A. (1968). *Constructing social theories.* NY: Harcourt, Brace & World, Inc.

Watson, J. (1987). Nursing on the caring edge: Metaphorical vignettes. *Advances in Nursing Sciences, 10*(1), 10-18.

Younger, J. B. (1990). Literary works as a mode of knowing. *Image: Journal of Nursing Scholarship, 22*(1), 39-42.

Toward a Theory of Optimal Granulocyte Colony-Stimulating Factor Administration

Anita L. Comley

Myelosuppression can occur among cancer patients when malignant tumors infiltrate bone mass. Traditional cancer treatments aim to destroy the rapidly replicating cancer cells but often yield, as a side effect, the suppression of the rapidly dividing myeloid tissue. Chemotherapy and total body irradiation prepare for bone marrow transplantation by destroying the patient's bone marrow to allow for growth of the donor's marrow in the host. As a result, cancer patients frequently experience anemia, thrombocytopenia and neutropenia (Rostad, 1991).

Complications due to anemia and thrombocytopenia are minimized by replacing red blood cells and platelets via blood transfusion (Rostad, 1991). However, neutropenia, a decrease in the number of circulating neutrophils, is not successfully treated in this manner. This condition severely compromises the client's ability to resist bacterial and viral infection and is thus associated with significant morbidity and mortality (Wujcik, 1992a).

Over the years, as the number of clients who have received and survived increasingly aggressive myelosuppressive therapy have grown, it has been a challenge to develop methods of appropriate supportive care for clients experiencing neutropenia. Standards of practice have evolved over time as empirical evidence to support or reject certain practices has grown. It also has been modified as technological, biological and pharmacological advances have provided new, more effective weapons in the fight against infection.

In February 1991, major advances in biotechnological research conducted in the 1980s resulted in the approval by the Food and Drug Administration (FDA) of a new colony-stimulating factor with profound implications for the care of cancer patients (Johnson, 1992). Recombinant granulocyte colony-stimulating factor is a naturally occurring hormone called a cytokine. It is produced through recombinant DNA technology from a strain of *E. coli* bacteria. Granulocyte colony-stimulating factor (G-CSF) regulates the proliferation and differentiation of neutrophil precursor cells in the bone marrow and enhances the infection-fighting functions of mature neutrophils (Wujcik, 1992a).

Recombinant G-CSF, given daily, subcutaneously, beginning 24 hours after the administration of the chemotherapy, has been shown to:

1. decrease the incidence, severity and duration of chemotherapy induced neutropenia
2. decrease the incidence of febrile neutropenia
3. decrease the incidence of documented infection
4. increase the number of patients whose bone marrow recovery allows them to maintain their chemotherapy dosing schedule
5. decrease the need for antibiotics

6. decrease the number of hospitalized days
7. decrease the incidence and severity of chemotherapy-related mucositis (Gabrilove et al., 1988; Wujcik, 1992a).

CONCEPTUALIZATION OF THE PHENOMENON: STINCHCOMBE'S STRATEGY

Stinchcombe's (1968) methodology for constructing social theories can be applied toward the phenomenon of caring for patients experiencing neutropenia due to cancer or its treatment. In a demographic explanation of the incidence of febrile neutropenia and documented infection in the cancer population, the people whose numbers must be specified are all individuals who experience neutropenia associated with their cancer or myelosuppressive therapy. The "proportionality factor" could realistically be the percent of the people who receive effective G-CSF therapy. The number of people with febrile neutropenia and documented infection form a sub-population of those with neutropenia as a result of cancer therapy (see Figure 6.1).

Figure 6.1 Stinchcombe's Demographic Causal Model

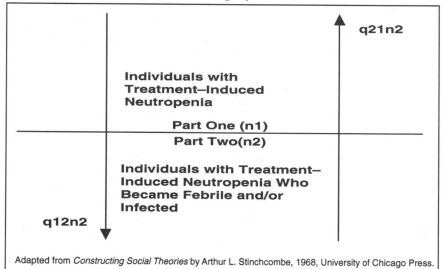

Adapted from *Constructing Social Theories* by Arthur L. Stinchcombe, 1968, University of Chicago Press.

At some future time, per Figure 6.1, Part One will be the number of people in that population to start minus the number who have moved to Part Two (downward arrow) plus the people who have come from Part Two (upward arrow). The proportionality rate, or rate at which people move from one part to the other, considered to be the percent of people who receive G-CSF therapy, is designated as "q". Theoretically, the number of people moving can be depicted mathematically as follows:

$q_{12}n_1$, Part One to Part Two
$q_{21}n_2$, Part Two to Part One

Stinchcombe (1968) posits that this movement will stop when $q_{12}n_1 = q_{21}n_2$ if the causal process is allowed to operate long enough.

In social phenomena, the important implication of this causal model is the ability to make predictions about groups of people and their reaction to the phenomenon in question, given that:

1. the population is classified into exhaustive categories which are recruited from each other;
2. the proportions of people in one category moving into another category per unit of time are approximately constant (Stinchcombe, 1968, pp. 66-67).

With respect to the care of neutropenic clients, this potential to predict the incidence of individuals who will suffer fever and infection, as it is influenced by G-CSF, could have important implications for health care providers. For example, this information would be useful in estimating the costs of myelosuppressive cancer therapy and in justifying the expense of this new, costly colony-stimulating therapy (Rafferty & Henry, 1993). It may also help clinicians in choosing appropriate precautions against infection in this population and provide additional information to clients involved in the process of informed consent for treatment.

Given the phenomenon of care of the neutropenic client, a historicist explanatory model can be transposed onto Stinchcombe's basic structure (see Figure 6.2). The original cause of y, x, can be theorized as the advent of myelosuppressive therapy for cancer, i.e., cytotoxic chemotherapy and radiation therapy. "y" stands for all those actions developed to protect this group of immunosuppressed clients from infection and to sustain them supportively through infections until their bone marrows had sufficiently recovered to resume this function. These include, but may not be limited to, protective isolation, low-microbial diet, immunoprophylaxis, antibacterial, antiviral and antifungal prophylaxis, antibiotic therapy and the management of septic shock (Rostad, 1991).

Figure 6.2 Care of Neutropenic Clients - Historicist Explanation

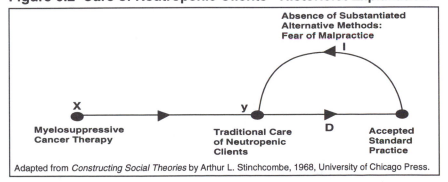

Adapted from *Constructing Social Theories* by Arthur L. Stinchcombe, 1968, University of Chicago Press.

As time progressed, these actions became an accepted standard of care for health care professionals. This caused the phenomenon to replicate itself, altered only when new methods of care were instituted. If insufficient evidence is available to contradict the efficacy of a standard practice, that practice will be retained. The "standard of practice" is viewed as a safe ground from malpractice or negligence for health care professionals and, indeed, it is this standard by which the judicial system measures the care provided.

A functional structure can be added to explain the effect of the advent of G-CSF therapy on the phenomenon of care of the neutropenic client. Figure 6.3 shows the application of this logical form to the phenomenon.

Figure 6.3 Care of Neutropenic Clients - Historic Functional Explanation

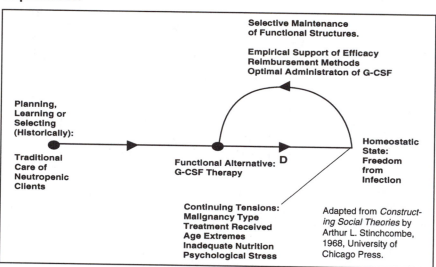

The traditional methods of care of the immunosuppressed client to prevent and treat infection leads to a "functional alternative" spawned from necessity. Despite the precautions of the standard of care, infection remains the leading cause of death in patients with cancer (Carter, 1993).

As a functional alternative to protecting the individual from sources of infection (an activity known to be less than ideal due to the high incidence of infection from endogenous sources) and treating the client with antibiotics prophylactically or once infected, G-CSF helps the client's immune system return to a state of competence more quickly. It also decreases the severity of the neutropenia and helps the neutrophils that are produced to be more functional defenders (Wujcik, 1992a). This functional alternative works to maintain the homeostatic state of freedom from infection. With the patients' increased ability to fight infection, they are made less susceptible to the tensions of infection during the neutropenic phase following treatment. The extent and severity of these tensions are influenced by the malignancy type, treatment received, age extremes of the client, inadequate nutrition and psychological stress (Carter, 1993).

According to Stinchcombe's logical structure, health care professionals have now undertaken the selective maintenance of the functional alternative. Research has continued to be conducted to add empirical support for the efficacy of G-CSF therapy in the treatment of neutropenia due to a wider spectrum of etiologies (Mann & Vance-Bryan, 1993). When this colony-stimulating factor was initially approved by the FDA, the indications for its use were clearly specified. The drug was quickly found to be useful in the treatment of neutropenia of similar etiologies that were not initially listed by the FDA. However, some insurers utilize the FDA-approved indications as strict criteria for reimbursement. In an effort to selectively maintain the alternative functional structure, the product manufacturer instituted a reimbursement hotline and began educating the health care providers about how to best file claims to obtain reimbursement for the client (Wujcik, 1992b).

ORGANIZATION OF THEORY ELEMENTS: BLALOCK'S METHOD

As the use of G-CSF and other colony-stimulating factors becomes increasingly prevalent, nurses will develop guidelines for the administration of these drugs (Johnson, 1992). Amgen, Inc., the manufacturer of filgrastim (Neupogen), indicates that the drug may be given intravenously or subcutaneously with equal effectiveness (Wujcik, 1992b). The subcutaneous route is most frequently utilized (Cunningham, 1992) and may be preferred for reasons of cost control and greater ease of self-administration in the outpatient setting.

Currently, there are no specific guidelines for or research supporting how to optimally administer filgrastim via the subcutaneous route. For example, discussion has ensued among oncology nurses in clinical practice regarding the appropriate maximum amount of the drug to administer in any given injection site, i.e., at what point the dose must be divided into two or more separate injections, whether there is the potential for bruising or abscess at the site if the amount of injectate is too large, whether the patient may receive a large injectate volume in one site without compromising the effect of the drug and whether one larger injection or multiple small injections are less painful to the patient.

A careful review of the literature produced an extensive list of variables pertinent to the administration of G-CSF. Major variables of the phenomenon as selected by the author are listed in Table 6.1. The variables are grouped into categories which each comprise a theoretical block in the causal diagram (see Figure 6.4). Each theoretical block of this recursive system is described, the variables are identified and the relationships are specified below.

Table 6.1 Variables Grouped by Theoretical Block

Patient Characteristics	Treatment Factors	Injection Factors	Outcome Parameters
Age Nutritional Status Emotional State Cardiovascular Status Propensity for Site Complications	Type of Malignancy Duration of Myelosuppresive Treatment Intensity of Treatment	Injectate Volume Site Selection Equipment Selection Injection Techniques	Drug Efficacy Site Complications Physical Discomfort

PATIENT CHARACTERISTICS BLOCK

G-CSF is known to have dose-dependent effects (Sheridan, 1992) but little literature addresses any variability in individual responses to similar doses. The efficacy of G-CSF in increasing the absolute granulocyte count, the occurrence of complications at the injection site and the perception of physical discomfort in individuals experiencing chemotherapy-induced neutropenia may be influenced by the physiologic and psychological characteristics of the client receiving therapy. These characteristics constitute a block of exogenous variables.

Figure 6.4 Optimal Subcutaneous Injection of C-CSF*

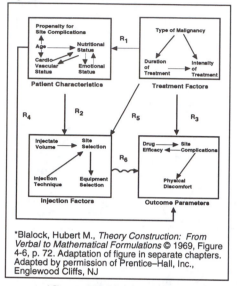

*Blalock, Hubert M., *Theory Construction: From Verbal to Mathematical Formulations* © 1969, Figure 4-6, p. 72. Adaptation of figure in separate chapters. Adapted by permission of Prentice–Hall, Inc., Englewood Cliffs, NJ

Age

It is known that very young or elderly patients are more susceptible to chemotherapy-induced neutropenia because of their immature or diminished immune response (Carter, 1993). Elderly or debilitated clients who have thinner skin and less subcutaneous tissue may have fewer injection sites of effective absorption (Newton, Newton, & Fudin, 1992).

Nutritional Status

Malnutrition, or inadequate intake of protein and calories, may increase the risk of neutropenic infection (Chandra, 1983). Malignancy increases the individual's need for protein and caloric intake to maintain neutrophil production, maturation and phagocytosis. Cachexia reduces both the inflammatory immune response and cellular immunity (Block, 1990; Chandra, 1983).

Emotional State

The prolonged effects of stress inhibit the protective function of the immune system including neutrophil chemotaxis, neutrophil oxidative killing and neutrophil phagocytosis. The adrenal glands respond to stress by producing increased amounts of glucocorticoids and catecholamines which compromise neutrophil production and the inflammatory response (Carter, 1993).

Cardiovascular Status

The cardiovascular and fluid status of the client may effect absorption of subcutaneous medications (Newton, Newton, & Fudin, 1992). For example, shock states may slow absorption. Absorption is facilitated by choosing sites for injection with large quantities of subcutaneous tissue that are well supplied with blood and lymphatic vessels (Wallace & Wardell, 1992). Areas that are edematous, contain stretch marks (Drass, 1992) or scar tissue, such as lipodystrophy (Hahn, 1990), may have poor absorption.

Propensity for Site Complications

Individual propensities for site complications have been observed. Local erythema at the injection site of G-CSF has been a noted adverse effect, however, swelling, unusual redness or itching may be indicative of allergic reaction (Shoemaker, 1992). In their study of three different subcutaneous injection sites for low-dose heparin, Fahs and Kinney (1991) found a large standard deviation in the surface area of bruises within all three treatment groups. They suspected that this was an indication of individual differences in bruisability and recommended that future research studies allow subjects to serve as their own control.

Relationships within the Patient Characteristics Block

Among neutropenic patients receiving subcutaneous G-CSF:

1. The greater the age, the greater the propensity for site complications (Woolridge & Jackson, 1988; Van Bree, Hollerbach, & Brooks, 1984).
2. The greater the age, the poorer the nutritional status (Eliopoulos, 1990).

3. The greater the age, the more impaired the cardiovascular status (Eliopoulos, 1990).
4. The poorer the nutritional status, the more impaired the cardiovascular status (LaQuatra and Gerlach, 1990).
5. The more impaired the cardiovascular status, the poorer the nutritional status (LaQuatra and Gerlach, 1990).
6. The poorer the nutritional status, the greater the emotional stress (Otto, 1991).
7. The greater the emotional stress, the poorer the nutritional status (LaQuatra and Gerlach, 1990).

TREATMENT FACTORS BLOCK

Three variables within this second exogenous block may affect the efficacy of the drug, the occurrence of complications and the client's perception of physical discomfort from the therapy. They are the type of malignancy being treated and the duration and intensity of the myelosuppressive treatment.

Type of Malignancy

Malignancies that cause neutropenia include leukemia, multiple myeloma and bony metastatic lesions from cancers with primary sites outside of the bone. The neutropenia results from healthy bone marrow displacement by malignant cells which destroy normal hematopoietic tissue (Carter, 1993).

Duration of Myelosuppressive Treatment

The rapidly replicating cells of the bone marrow are susceptible to chemotherapeutic agents and radiation therapy which destroy rapidly dividing malignant cells (Rostad, 1991). Chemotherapy and radiation given in smaller, intermittent doses over longer periods of time allow for the recovery of bone marrow and less severe neutropenia (Rubin, 1983).

Intensity of Treatment

Myelosuppression due to cancer chemotherapy is clearly dose-dependent. Larger doses of myelosuppressive drugs will cause greater neutropenia (Clark and McGee, 1992). The maximal tolerance dose of radiation of the bone marrow is the lowest of all the tissues in the body (Rubin, 1983). The greater the area of bone in the irradiated fields, especially the ilia, vertebrae, ribs, skull, sternum and metaphyses of the long bones, the greater the degree of myelosuppression (Rostad, 1991). Those patients who receive both radiation and chemotherapy — for example, preparation for bone marrow transplantation — will have the myelosuppressive effects of both modalities intensified (Otto, 1991).

Relationships within the Treatment Factors Block

Among neutropenic patients receiving subcutaneous G-CSF:

1. The type of malignancy treated will influence the duration of the treatment.
2. The type of malignancy treated will influence the intensity of the treatment.
3. The duration of the treatment will influence the intensity of the treatment.

INJECTION FACTORS BLOCK

Several variables of optimal subcutaneous injection of G-CSF are amenable to nursing management and intervention. These endogenous variables are aspects of how the drug is administered. They are the volume of injectate, the site selected for the injection, the technique used to inject the drug and the equipment selected for injection.

Injectate Volume

As is the case with many of the variables related to subcutaneous injection of medication, research has not determined the optimum amount of fluid to be given in a single subcutaneous site. Some guidelines are proposed but they seem to stem more from tradition than empirical generalization based on experimental studies.

The recommended dose of filgrastim is 5 mcgm/kg/day as a single daily injection (McKerrow, 1993). The drug concentration is 300 mcgm/ml. For example, this indicates a dose of 1.0 ml or 300 mcgm for a 60 kg individual (132 lbs), 1.6 ml or 480 mcgm for a 96 kg (211 lbs) person. This dose may be increased by 5 mcgms/kg increments with each chemotherapy cycle. In clinical trials, as much as 69 mcgm/kg/day has been administered via intravenous administration (Sheridan, 1992), but no information is available as to when the dose is considered too large for subcutaneous injection. Deglin and Vallerand (1993) state that "if the dose requires greater than 1.0 ml of solution it may be divided into two injection sites" (p. 493). No scientific rationale or empirical research evidence is cited for this recommendation.

Some sources limit the volume of injectate for a subcutaneous injection of any medication to 1.0 ml (Hahn, 1990; Newton, Newton & Fudin, 1992), while Wallace and Wardell (1992), Swonger and Matejski (1988), and Miller and Keane (1992) posit that the maximum amount that can be comfortably absorbed from one site is 2.0 ml. Absorption may be slowed by over-distension of the tissue with injectate by collapsing the adjacent blood and lymph vessels (Wallace & Wardell, 1992). Other discussions of subcutaneous drug administration fail to address the issue at all (Kosier, Erb, & Olivieri, 1991; Reiss & Evans, 1990; Schlafer & Marieb, 1989; Shannon, Wilson, & Stang, 1992, Shoemaker, D., 1992).

Site Selection

The information booklet for patients supplied by Amgen, Inc. (1992) illustrates sites on the posterior aspects of the upper arms, the lateral thighs and the abdomen on either side of the umbilicus. Fahs and Kinney (1991) studied these three anatomic regions for injection sites for low-dose heparin therapy. Group A subjects received injections in the abdomen, Group B, in the thigh, and Group C in the arm. They found no significant difference in activated partial thromboplastin time or bruising at 60 and 72 hours postinjection among the groups.

Variability of insulin effect by anatomic region used for injection has been demonstrated, resulting in the recommendation that only the abdomen be used, rotating sites of approximately 3 cm in dimension (Zehrer, Hansen, & Bantle, 1990). A variation of this recommendation is to use the same anatomical area at the same time every day. This is thought to reduce variability of blood glucose, while still utilizing all three of the traditional subcutaneous injection areas.

Equipment Selection

The size of syringe most frequently recommended for subcutaneous injections is a 1.0 ml tuberculin syringe for greater accuracy of small injectate doses. Woolridge and Jackson (1988) speculated that as the area of the syringe increases the force of the fluid exiting the needle decreases. Therefore, a 3.0 ml syringe might be preferable to decrease tissue trauma and bruising in patients receiving low dose heparin. They found a technique which included the larger syringe to be significantly more effective in reducing injection trauma than a technique that utilized a 1.0 ml syringe, however, there were three other variables investigated at the same time within the two techniques so it is impossible to tell which variable made the difference.

A range of needle sizes from 25 to 29 gauge and 3/8 to 5/8 inches is recommended in the literature for subcutaneous injection (Drass, 1992; Hahn, 1990; McConnell, 1990; Newton, Newton, & Fudin, 1992; Schumann & Bruya, 1988; VanBree, Hollerbach, & Brooks, 1984; Woolridge & Jackson, 1988). No research studies were found about the effect of needle size on site complications or patient perceptions of physical discomfort. Broadway (1991) warns that injections that are given too shallowly or that are intradermal may leak. The appropriate size needle for the site chosen is a factor in the depth of injection.

Injection Technique

Due to the myelosuppression that has resulted in neutropenia, clients receiving G-CSF are also generally thrombocytopenic. McKerrow (1993), Shoemaker (1992) and Wujcik (1992b) agree that "proper" or "appropriate" subcutaneous injection technique of G-CSF must be utilized by nurses to decrease the potential for tissue trauma, bleeding and bruising.

Bunching, pinching, rolling or folding the tissue one half to two inches is frequently recommended at the site of injection (Drass, 1992; Hahn, 1990; McConnell, 1990; Schumann, Bruya, & Henke, 1988). Spreading the skin is recommended less often (Kozier, Erb, & Olivieri, 1991). Amgen (1992) instructs clients to stabilize the skin either by pinching up a large area or by spreading the skin. Grasping the tissue in any way is sometimes cautioned against in the administration of heparin to prevent bruising (Schumann, Bruya, & Henke, 1988). Broadway (1991) suggests that the tissue grasped should be released prior to depressing the syringe plunger to prevent the medication from being squeezed out.

The angle of insertion of the needle to the skin most often recommended is 45 to 90 degrees, depending on the thickness of the subcutaneous tissue at the site (Kozier, Erb, & Olivieri, 1991; McConnell, 1990; Schumann, Bruya, & Henke, 1988). Amgen (1992) instructs clients in the narrative to insert the needle at a 90 degree angle.

Aspiration prior to injection of G-CSF is instructed by the manufacturer (Amgen, 1992). This is traditionally done in subcutaneous injection to prevent accidental intravenous injection of the medication. However, most sources caution against aspirating heparin and insulin because the subcutaneous tissue contains only small blood vessels making intravenous injection unlikely. Additionally, aspirating is thought to cause tissue damage and increase bruising (Drass, 1992; Hahn, 1990; McConnell, 1990; Schumann, Bruya, & Henke, 1988; VanBree, Hollerbach, & Brooks, 1984; Woolridge & Jackson, 1988).

Slow injection of the solution is suggested by Broadway (1991) to allow the tissue to expand and to decrease leakage. She also recommends allowing the needle to remain in the tissue for 30 to 60 seconds after the injection and then rapidly withdrawing it to prevent the drug from tracking back to the skin. This is thought to decrease the leaking of insulin and bruising associated with heparin. Many subjects in Woolridge and Jackson's (1988) study of bruising and induration resulting from subcutaneous heparin injection perceived rapid injection to be more painful than slow injection — the researchers recommend this as an area for further study.

Relationships within the Injection Factors Block

Among neutropenic patients receiving subcutaneous G-CSF:

1. The larger the injectate volume, the greater the amount of subcutaneous tissue and circulation required at the injection site (Wallace & Wardell, 1992).
2. The injection site chosen influences the injection technique utilized (Kozier, Erb, & Olivieri, 1991).
3. The injection site selected influences the equipment selected (Broadway, 1991).

OUTCOME PARAMETERS BLOCK

The second endogenous block is comprised of factors which may be thought of as the dependent variables of the phenomenon. All the other variables within the model have a direct or indirect causal relationship with the efficacy of the drug, the occurrence of complications at the injection sites and the degree of physical discomfort.

Drug Efficacy

The effectiveness of the G-CSF is evidenced by the degree of absorption of the drug and the resultant effect on stimulation and maturation of neutrophil precursors in the bone marrow and by the enhancement in function of the mature neutrophils. Absolute neutrophil counts are used to measure the incidence, severity and duration of neutropenia. The number of days of febrile neutropenia (temperature greater than 100.5, ANC less than 1500 cells/mm^3), the number of documented infections (positive microbial cultures or other positive diagnostic findings, such as pulmonary infiltrates on chest x-ray) and the number of days of antibiotic therapy and hospitalization are indicators of the treatment's efficacy (Haeuber, 1991; Wujcik, 1992a).

Site Complications

Tissue trauma, as evidenced by bruising, bleeding, inflammation, abscess formation or induration, may result from injections of G-CSF. The frequency and size of these areas of tissue damage have not been noted in the research literature.

Physical Discomfort

The clients' experience of noxious sensations such as pain, burning, tenderness or itching at the site during the injection of G-CSF or as a result of it is the third outcome variable of the phenomenon. These perceptions of the sensory dimension of pain or physical discomfort have also not been noted in the literature.

Relationships within the Outcome Parameters Block

1. The greater the drug efficacy, the fewer and less severe the site complications (theorem).
2. The more numerous and severe the site complications, the less efficacious the drug (Drass, 1992; Hahn, 1990).
3. The more numerous and severe the site complications, the greater the client perception of physical discomfort (Woolridge & Jackson, 1988).

Impact of Treatment Factors on Patient Characteristics (R$_1$)

The type of malignancy for which the client is undergoing treatment and the duration and intensity of that treatment will all affect the nutritional status and emotional state of the individual. The hypermetabolic process of malignancy requires increased caloric intake. Anorexia, nausea, vomiting, diarrhea, stomatitis and esophagitis, frequent side effects of antineoplastic therapies, contribute to malnutrition (Carter, 1993). The client's emotional state may be strongly influenced by the prognosis of the type of malignancy experienced. The effects of treatments of long duration and high intensity may deplete the coping mechanisms of the individual and the support system (Otto, 1991). The intensity of the treatment may also have a direct or indirect effect on the client's cardiovascular system. For example, the greater the dose of Adriamycin, the greater the potential for cardiotoxicity resulting in congestive heart failure (Clark & McGee, 1992). The greater the intensity of myelosuppressive therapy, the more susceptible the client will be to infection and bleeding at injection sites (Wujcik, 1992a).

Impact of Patient Characteristics on Injection Factors (R_2)

The nutritional status and age of the client will determine the availability of injections sites with adequate amounts of subcutaneous fat for effective absorption of the drug (Wallace & Wardell, 1992). This will influence site selection, injection technique and equipment selection. Cardiovascular status may be an important variable for the nurse to consider in deciding on the amount of injectate that will be effectively absorbed from one injection site. The emotional state of the client may also influence site selection; some clients fear injections in the abdomen and prefer to use sites on the extremities (Chamberlain, 1980).

Impact of Treatment Factors on Outcome Parameters (R_3)

The type of malignancy, the duration of treatment and the intensity of treatment all influence the severity of the neutropenia that the client experiences. They will strongly affect the measures of drug efficacy such as absolute neutrophil counts, documented infections, antibiotics administered and days of hospitalization required. As previously noted, the more severe the myelosuppression, the greater the potential for complications at the sites of injections of G-CSF. The overall distress and anxiety resulting from the cancer experience and its treatment will affect the person's ability to tolerate and cope with pain and, thus, will influence the perception of any physically uncomfortable procedure (Otto, 1991).

Impact of Patient Characteristics on Outcome Parameters (R_4)

Clients with a propensity for site complications will most likely experience an increased incidence as a result of G-CSF therapy (Fahs & Kinney, 1991). The influence of age on the competency of the immune system may also influence the efficacy of G-CSF in increasing absolute granulocyte counts and decreasing the incidence of infection in very young or elderly clients. Malnutrition will also compromise the immune system (Carter, 1993). Degree of absorption, a function of the cardiovascular status (Newton, Newton, & Fudin, 1992), will affect the efficacy of the drug. Again, the emotional state of the client influences their perception of physical discomfort (Otto, 1991).

Figure 6.5 Model of Subcutaneous Medication Administration*

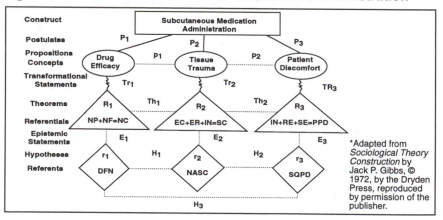

*Adapted from *Sociological Theory Construction* by Jack P. Gibbs, © 1972, by the Dryden Press, reproduced by permission of the publisher.

Impact of Treatment Factors on Injection Factors (R_5)

The intensity of the myelosuppressive therapy and the resultant degree of neutropenia will determine the dose of G-CSF required and, thus, influence the injectate volume (McKerrow, 1993).

Impact of Injection Factors on Outcome Parameters (R_6)

Large volumes of injectate potentially decrease absorption at the site by compressing the surrounding blood and lymph vessels (Wallace & Wardell, 1992). The drug may also leak from the site (Broadway, 1991). The tissue of the site selected may have poor absorption due to scar tissue, edema or lipodystrophy (Drass, 1992; Hahn, 1990). Problems of absorption will affect the efficacy of the drug. Injection technique and equipment selection, especially the rate of injection and gauge of needle, influence the client perception of physical discomfort (Woolridge & Jackson, 1988).

FORMALIZATION: GIBBS' PARADIGM

Figure 6.5 schematically represents the phenomenon of optimal subcutaneous injection of G-CSF constructed using Gibbs' paradigm.

Extrinsic Theory

For the phenomenon of interest here, the unit term is all individuals experiencing chemotherapy-induced neutropenia who are receiving daily subcutaneous injections of filgrastim (G-CSF).

Construct. Theoretically, the construct of "subcutaneous medication administration" is the combination of decisions made and actions taken by the individual administering the drug, equipment factors, drug factors and patient characteristics that maximize drug efficacy and minimize site complications and client perception of physical discomfort.

Concepts. The concepts of the theory include drug efficacy, tissue trauma and patient discomfort.

Drug efficacy - the degree of absorption of the drug and the resultant effect on stimulation and maturation of neutrophil precursors in the bone marrow and enhancement in function of the mature neutrophils.

Tissue trauma - bruising, bleeding, inflammation, abscess formation or induration, resulting from the injection of medication into the subcutaneous adipose layer.

Patient discomfort - patient report of the sensation (feeling), its intensity (strength) and their reaction (unpleasantness) experienced during a subcutaneous injection of a medication.

Referentials. Referentials are intrinsic terms that represent a formula in the extrinsic portion of the theory. Referential formulas are relative only to the theory in which they are employed and should not be judged for predictive accuracy apart from it.

$$R1: NP + NF = NC$$
Neutrophil Production + Neutrophil Function =
Neutrophil Competency
$$R2: EC + ER + IN = SC$$
Ecchymosis + Erythema + Induration = Site Complications

R3: IN + RE + SE = PPD
Intensity + Reaction + Sensation =
Patient Perception of Discomfort

Referents. Referents are unit terms that result from referential statements or formulas.

r1: DFN
Days of Febrile Neutropenia
r2: NASC
Number and Surface Area of Site Complications
r3: SQPD
Score on Tursky's Quantified Pain Descriptors

Intrinsic Theory

The following postulates, propositions, transformational statements and theorems comprise the intrinsic component of the theory.

Postulates. Postulates are assertions of the empirical relation between a construct and a concept. Among individuals experiencing chemotherapy-induced neutropenia who are receiving daily subcutaneous injections of G-CSF:

P1: The more optimal the subcutaneous administration of G-CSF, the > the drug efficacy.

P2: The more optimal the subcutaneous administration of the G-CSF, the < tissue trauma.

P3: The more optimal the subcutaneous administration of the G-CSF, the < patient discomfort.

Propositions. Propositions are assertions of the empirical relation between two concepts. Among individuals experiencing chemotherapy-induced neutropenia and receiving daily subcutaneous injections of G-CSF:

p1: The > the drug efficacy, the < the tissue trauma.

p2: The > the tissue trauma, the > the patient discomfort.

Transformational Statements. Transformational statements are assertions of the empirical relation between a concept and a referential. A temporal quantifier is added with t_0 representing the first day of G-CSF therapy, t_1 representing the last day of G-CSF therapy for a given cycle of chemotherapy administration and t_{0-1} representing the entire duration of the G-CSF therapy for that cycle. Among individuals experiencing chemotherapy-induced neutropenia who are receiving daily subcutaneous injections of G-CSF:

Tr1: The > the drug efficacy t_{0-1}, the > the NC at t_1.
Tr2: The > the tissue trauma t_{0-1}, the > the SC at t_1.
Tr3: The > the patient discomfort t_{0-1}, the > the PPD at t_1.

Theorems. Theorems are formally derived intrinsic statements in which the substantive terms are referentials. They constitute the final step of the intrinsic part of the theory. Among individuals experiencing chemotherapy-induced neutropenia who are receiving daily subcutaneous injections of G-CSF:

Th1: The > the NC at t_{0-1}, the < SC at t_1.
Th2: The > the SC at t_{0-1}, the > PPD t_{0-1}.

Epistemic Statements. Epistemic statements link referentials in a theorem with sets of referents. Among individuals experiencing chemotherapy-induced neutropenia who are receiving daily subcutaneous injections of G-CSF:

E1: The > the NC at t_{0-1}, the < the DFN at t_1.
E2: The > the SC at t_{0-1}, the > the NASC at t_1.
E3: The > the PPD at t_{0-1}, the > the SQPD at t_1.

Hypotheses. Hypotheses are statements that predict referents in the form of derived assertions. Among individuals experiencing chemotherapy-induced neutropenia who are receiving daily subcutaneous injections of G-CSF:

H1: The < DFN, the < NASC.
H2: The > NASC, the > SQPD.
H3: The < SQPD, the > DFN.

Figure 6.6 Path Diagram: Optimal Subcutaneous Administration of G-CSF

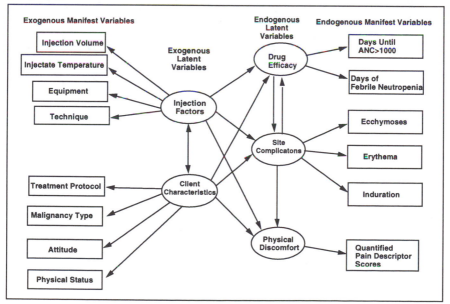

SUMMARY

In this chapter, the theory construction methods of the three sociologists, Stinchcombe (1968), Blalock (1969) and Gibbs (1972), have been utilized to initiate theory pertaining to the emergence of G-CSF therapy in the care of neutropenic clients and optimal subcutaneous administration of the drug. The demographic, historicist and historicist functional explanations proved useful in conceptualizing the role of this new therapy within the traditional standard of care and identifying the populations most likely to be impacted by its availability. Organization of the variables of the subcutaneous administration of G-CSF into a block recursive system necessitated identifying all potential variables and analysis of all possible relationships among those variables. Measurable empirical indicators of and testable relationships between these variables were delineated in the formal model based on Gibbs' (1972) paradigm. Ultimately, all three methods contributed to the formulation of organized thought about the phenomenon and the generation of testable relationships for future study.

REFERENCES

Amgen, Incorporated (1992). *Neupogen (Filgrastim): Information for patients.* (Serial No. P40047-1), 17-22.

Block, A.S. (1990). *Nutrition Management of the Cancer Patient.* Rockville, MD: Aspen.

Broadway, C. (1991) Prevention of insulin leakage after subcutaneous injection. *The Diabetes Educator, 17*(2), 90.

Carter, L. (1993). Influences of nutrition and stress on people at risk for neutropenia: Nursing implications. *Oncology Nursing Forum, 20,* 1242-1250.

Chamberlain, S. L., (1980) Low dose heparin therapy. *American Journal of Nursing, 80,* 1115-1117.

Chandra, R. (1983). Nutrition, immunity and infection. *Lancet, 1,* 688-691.

Clark, J.F., & McGee, R. (Eds.). (1992). *Oncology Nursing Society: Core curriculum for oncology nursing* (2nd ed.). Philadelphia: Saunders.

Cunningham, R. (1992). *Management of myelosuppression.* Prevention of Infection in Patients Receiving Myelosuppressive Chemotherapy, (Serial No. P40165-1), 5-11.

Deglin, J., & Valleran, A. (1993). *Davis's drug guide for nurses* (3rd Ed.) Philadelphia: Davis.

Drass, J. (1992). What you need to know about insulin injections. *Nursing92, 22*(11), 40-43.

Eliopoulos, C. (1990). *Health assessment of the older adult (2nd ed.).* Redwood City, CA: Addison-Wesley.

Fahs, P.S.S., & Kinney, M.R. (1991). The abdomen, thigh and arm as sites for subcutaneous sodium heparin injections. *Nursing Research, 40,* 204-207.

Gabrilove, J.L., Jakubowski, A., Scher, H., Sternberg, C., Wong, G., Grous, J., Yagoda, A., Fain, K., Moore, M., Clarkson, B., Oettgen, H., Alton, K., Welte, K., & Souza, L. (1988). Effect of granulocyte colony-stimulating factor on neutropenia and associated morbidity due to chemotherapy for transtional-cell carcinoma of the urothelium. *New England Journal of Medicine, 318,* 1414-1422.

Haeuber, D. (1991). Future strategies in the control of myelosuppression: the use of colony-stimulating factors. *Oncology Nursing Forum, 18*(2), 16-21.

Hahn, K. (1990). Brush up on your injection technique. *Nursing90, 20*(9), 54-58.

Johnson, J. (1992). Introduction. In R.M. Carroll-Johnson (Ed.), *A Case Management Approach to Patients Receiving G-CSF, Proceedings of the Sixteenth Annual Congress of the Oncology Nursing Society* (p. 7). San Antonio: Oncology Nursing Press.

Kozier, B., Erb, G., & Olivieri, R. (1991). *Fundamentals of nursing: Concepts, process and practice.* Redwood City, CA: Addison-Wesley.

LaQuatra, I., & Gerlach, M.J. (1990). *Nutrition in clinical nursing.* Albany: Delmar.

Mann, H., & Vance-Bryan, K. (1993). Immunotherapy targets in critical care. *Critical Care Nursing Clinics of North America, 5*(2), 333-343.

McConnell, E. (1990). Administering S.C. Heparin. *Nursing90, 20*(12), 24.

McKerrow, J. (1993). Management strategies in infection prevention. *Oncology Nursing Role in the Management of Patients Receiving CSFs, (Serial No. P40165-3),* 2-15.

Miller, B., & Keane, C. (1992). *Encyclopedia and dictionary of medicine, nursing and allied health (5th Ed.).* Philadelphia: Saunders.

Newton, M., Newton, D., & Fudin, J. (1992). Reviewing the "big three" injection sites. *Nursing92, 22*(2) 34-42.

Otto, S. (1991). *Oncology nursing.* St. Louis: Mosby.

Rafferty, K.M., & Henry, J.S. (1993). Ethical considerations in drug administration for critically ill patients. *Critical Care Nursing Clinics of North America, 5,* 377-382.

Reiss, B., & Evans, M. (1990). *Pharmacological aspects of nursing care.* Albany: Delmar.

Rostad, M.E. (1991). Current strategies for managing myelosuppression in patients with cancer. *Oncology Nursing Forum, 18*(2), Supp., 7-14.

Rubin, P. (Ed.). (1983). *Clinical oncology: A multidisciplinary approach. (6th ed.).* American Cancer Society.

Schlafer, M., & Marieb, E. (1989). *The nurse, pharmacology, and drug therapy.* Redwood City, CA: Addison-Wesley.

Schumann, L.L., & Bruya, M.A., & Henke, L. (1988). Administration techniques for low-dose sodium heparin. *Dimensions of Critical Care Nursing, 7*(6), 333-339.

Shannon, M., Wilson, B., & Stang, C. (1992). *Giovani and Hayes: Drugs and nursing implications (7th Ed.).* Norwalk, CT: Appleton and Lange.

Sheridan, C. (1992). Recombinant granulocyte colony-stimulating factor in patients receiving chemotherapy for bladder cancer. *A Case Management Approach to Patients Receiving G-CSF, Proceedings from the Sixteenth Annual Congress of the Oncology Nursing Society,* (pp. 20-24). San Antonio: Oncology Nursing Press.

Shoemaker, D. (1992). Recombinant granulocyte-stimulating factor in patients receiving chemotherapy for small cell lung cancer: clinical findings and case management. *A Case Management Approach to Patients Receiving G-CSF, Proceedings from the Sixteenth Annual Congress of the oncology Nursing Society,* (pp. 14-19). San Antonio: Oncology Nursing Press.

Stinchcombe, A.L. (1968). *Constructing social theories.* NY: Harcourt, Brace & World.

Swonger, A., & Matejski, M. (1988). *Nursing pharmacology: An integrated approach to drug therapy and nursing practice.* Glenview, IL: Scott, Foresman and Company.

VanBree, N.S., Hollerbach, A.D., & Brooks, G.P. (1984). Clinical evaluation of three techniques for administering low-dose heparin. *Nursing Research, 33,* 15-19.

Wallace, C., & Wardell (1992). *Nursing pharmacology: A comprehensive approach to drug therapy.* Boston: Jones and Bartlett.

Woolridge, J.B., & Jackson, J.G. (1988). Evaluation of bruises and areas of induration after two techniques of subcutaneous heparin injection. *Heart and Lung, 17,* 476-482.

Wujcik, D. (1992a). Overview of colony-stimulating factors: Focus on the neutrophil. In R.M. Carroll-Johnson (Ed.), *A Case Management Approach to Patients Receiving G-CSF, Proceedings of the Sixteenth Annual Congress of the Oncology Nursing Society* (pp. 8-13). San Antonio: Oncology Nursing Press.

Wujcik, D. (1992b). *Practical questions and answers for oncology nurses: Focus on G-CSF.* [Amgen Monograph]. NY: Triclinica Communications.

Zehrer, C., Hansen, R., & Bantle, J. (1990). Reducing blood glucose variability by use of abdominal insulin injection sites. *The Diabetes Educator, 16*(6), 474-477.

Toward a Theory of Viral Dormancy

Heidi Taylor

Viral dormancy in persons with Human Immunodeficiency Virus (HIV) is defined by Kaiser (1993) as "...a negative P-24 antigen (indicating an absence of viral activity), no loss of T-cells (the cells most often destroyed by HIV), and an absence of symptoms" (p. 6). Viral dormancy occurs when the genes that instruct the HIV to replicate are inactive (Kaiser, 1993)[1]. Biomedically modelled therapies are directed toward the use of agents to eradicate the invading organism. The progression of HIV to the development of Acquired Immune Deficiency Syndrome (AIDS) is a process which varies greatly among individual cases. Because the biomedical model explains only part of the development of AIDS, new approaches to well-being for the HIV positive individual are suggested.

Gallo and Montagnier (1988), the discoverers of HIV, state that any work in finding effective treatments has two facets. "In addition to combating a complex and evasive pathogen, it must pioneer entirely new areas of medicine" (Gallo & Montagnier, 1988, p. 47). These new areas of medicine may, in fact, be a synthesis of ancient, traditional, contemporary and as yet undiscovered approaches. AIDS is beginning to be approached as a chronic illness and as an opportunity for self-actualization (Berridge, 1993; Gloerson, Kendall, Gray, McConnell, Turner, & Lewkowicz, 1993). This calls for a shift from the biomedical paradigm which considers "cure" to be the treatment imperative.

Holistic practices in combination with standard medical therapy have promising outcomes for prolonging viral dormancy (Kaiser, 1993). This chapter will utilize three theory construction methods to explore viral dormancy and Kaiser's therapeutic approaches (1993). Each method suggests various theoretical relationships. While all three methodologies move the theorist from verbal to formal mathematical formulations, the focus of this chapter will be the refinement of the verbal formulations which suggest a path analysis for exploring viral dormancy.

STINCHCOMBE'S METHODS
Demographic Explanation

According to Stinchcombe (1968), a demographic causal theory is one in which "...a causal force is assumed to be proportional to the number of people of a certain kind" (p. 60). He identifies two problems of causal explanation: explaining how many people of a certain kind there are and explaining the proportion between the numbers of different kinds of people and the causal force which produces the differences (Stinchcombe, 1968, p.60).

To help explain the phenomenon of viral dormancy in HIV positive individuals using the demographic approach, the number of HIV positive individuals must be specified. The symptomology (presence or absence of symp-

---

[1] Our understanding of the period of time between infection with HIV and the development of AIDS is changing as research in this area rapidly unfolds. The activity of HIV during this period is not well understood. This work represents the use of various theory construction methods that formalize the work of Kaiser (1993).

Table 7.1 Demographic Explanation of Viral Dormancy

To Explain	Kinds of People Whose Number Must Be Specified	Proportionality Factors
Viral Dormancy	HIV Positive Individuals	Symptomology

toms) is used as the proportionality factor between the number of people with HIV and those experiencing viral dormancy. These elements are demonstrated in Table 7.1.

Table 7.1 describes a closed demographic explanation where the number of a certain kind of people results from previous demographic processes (Stinchcombe, 1968). At any given time, all of the symptomatic HIV persons come from either the symptomatic group in the past or from the asymptomatic group. Likewise, the asymptomatic group of HIV positive individuals come from either the asymptomatic group in the past or the symptomatic group.

It may be useful to identify which health care practices, standard or holistic, keep asymptomatic persons in the asymptomatic group or move symptomatic persons to the asymptomatic group. Standard health care practices include those derived from the biomedical model — antiviral and antibiotic treatment guided by laboratory values. Holistic health care includes the biomedical model of care but also incorporates nutrition, exercise, psychological and spiritual dimensions of care and other approaches. This complex demographic explanation in which there are two groups of people with a different balance of forces is depicted in Figure 7.1.

Figure 7.1 Demographic Explanation*

	Standard Healthcare Practices	Holistic Healthcare Practices
Symptomatic	↑ q sa s N a s ↓	↑ q sa h N a h ↓
Asymptomatic	q as s N s s ↓	q as h N a h ↓

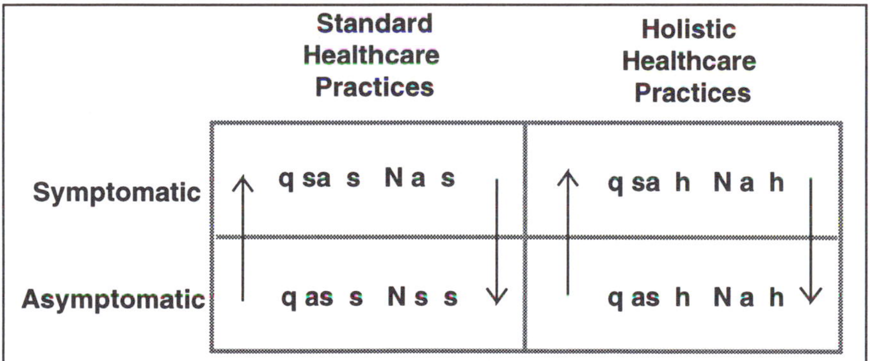

*Adapted from *Constructing Social Theories* by Arthur L. Stinchcombe, 1968, p. 76, figure 3.4. Harcourt, Brace & World, Inc., reproduced by permission of the author and the University of Chicago Press.

The arrows in this figure demonstrate the movement of different groups from one characteristic to another. The q stands for the proportion of the group; the subscripts define the direction of the movement. For instance, in the first cell, q_{sa} stands for the proportion of the group moving from symptomatic to asymptomatic. The second subscript s indicates the transition rate for those receiving standard medical therapy. The n, subscript a s, stands for the number of asymptomatic individuals receiving standard medical therapy. This cell demonstrates that the number of asymptomatic individuals who receive standard medical therapy is a combination of the number of symptomatic individuals moving from symptomatic to asymptomatic and the number who remained asymptomatic. The logic of this explanation follows for the other cells.

If the movement from cell to cell operates long enough, the net number in all groups will be the same. In this case, one could not suggest stronger causal processes in any group. When the proportions in one group are larger than those in another, it follows that the causal forces in that group are stronger. In this example, if there were a larger proportion of asymptomatic individuals in the holistic health care practices group, one would deduce that the causal processes involved are stronger for patients receiving holistic health care than for other patients.

A proposition can be derived from the demographic explanatory process, that the larger the proportion of HIV positive individuals moving from symptomatic to asymptomatic, the greater the efficacy of the treatment modality.

Functional Explanation

Stinchcombe (1968) suggests that a functional explanation of a phenomenon is "...one in which the consequences of some behavior or social arrangement are essential elements of the causes of that behavior" (p. 80). Stinchcombe elaborates that it is, in fact, the desire for the consequences that causes the behavior (p. 80). In situations where the consequences of actions are the same but the actions that achieve the consequences are different, a functional explanation is suggested. He borrows from Heider the notion of equifinality, that is, when various means are perceived to lead to the same end (p. 80).

Equifinal patterns are suggested when:

1. *There is an increase in activity because the end is difficult to achieve.* When a person is diagnosed as HIV positive, there is an increase in the activity of the individual in learning about the disease and treatment modalities which will offer the best possible future. Many patients change lifestyle patterns in an effort to control their future (Kaiser, 1993).
2. *The end is achieved even though there are reasons for it not to be achieved.* In some patients, viral dormancy, or remaining asymptomatic, is achieved despite low T-cell counts (Kaiser, 1993).
3. *People offer a variety of explanations, including inadequate or inconsistent ones, to explain their behavior.* Asymptomatic HIV positive individuals offer a variety of explanations for choosing particular treatment options and achieving a symptom-free state. The choices for treatment may include standard, experimental and holistic methods (Kaiser,1993).

4. *Patterns of behavior are selected because of known and proven conse-*
    quences. The HIV positive individual who seeks health care, whether
    standard or holistic, does so because of a desire for optimizing health and
    prolonging life. If there is no desire to prolong life or improve the quality
    of remaining life, the individual may choose to forego any treatment meth-
    odology so that the natural process of the disease and earlier death may
    result. In both examples, the behavior can be explained by the desired
    consequences.

The essential elements of a functional explanation are (Stinchcombe, 1968):

1. The homeostatic variable (H) is the consequence which is maintained. It
    tends to stay stable despite forces that try to change it.
2. The structure (S) or behavior that has a causal impact on the homeostatic
    variable (H).
3. The other causal forces or tensions (T) which tend to upset the homeo-
    static variable (H).
4. The causal processes which maintain the structure (S).

The causal structure in this phenomenon is demonstrated in Figure 7.2. In
this structure, the homeostatic variable (H) is a prolonged, asymptomatic life
for the HIV positive individual. This is the desirable state and also the consequence which causes the person with HIV to select health care practices that
promote viral dormancy.

Figure 7.2 Functional Explanation*

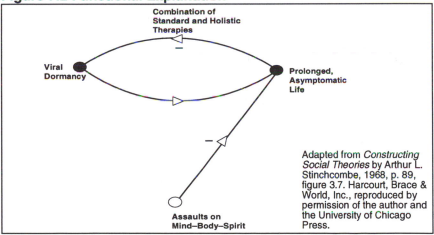

Adapted from *Constructing Social Theories* by Arthur L. Stinchcombe, 1968, p. 89, figure 3.7. Harcourt, Brace & World, Inc., reproduced by permission of the author and the University of Chicago Press.

The structure (S) which has a causal impact on H is viral dormancy. Viral
dormancy exists when the virus is at rest, the person remains asymptomatic
and T-cell counts remain stable or improve. As long as this is the case, the
person remains asymptomatic. Prolongation of an asymptomatic life is both a
consequence of viral dormancy and a cause of viral dormancy.

The tensions (T) which upset the homeostatic variable (H) are any assault on the mind-body-spirit which disrupt the asymptomatic life of the HIV individual. The HIV virus is the major tension. It is impossible to extricate HIV from the genetic code of the individual's own cells once it is incorporated. Standard medical treatment, including antiviral therapy, can be a tension because in order to control the HIV, antivirals may damage the individual's own cells.

Opportunistic infections are a major tension because they cause the morbidity and mortality due to HIV (Kaiser, 1993). These include pneumocystis carynii pneumonia (PCP), toxoplasmosis, mycobacterium avium complex, fungal infections, cryptococcal meningitis, histoplasmosis and cytomegalovirus (Kaiser, 1993). Poor nutrition is a tension which negatively affects the prolonged asymptomatic life (Law & Baldwin, 1993; Corman, 1985). Stress (physical and psychological) also alters the immune system's ability to effectively protect the individual (Kaiser, 1993; Ornish, 1990; Borysenko, 1987; Palmblad, 1981; Plaut & Friedman, 1981).

The causal processes that support the functional structure (S) as it maintains the homeostatic variable (consequence or H) become stronger when H is not maintained. Since this force is stronger when H is not naturally maintained (when the tensions are higher) and decreases when H is maintained, it has a negative direction from H to S (Stinchcombe, 1968). In the case of the HIV positive individual, the combined use of standard medical therapies (antiviral and antibiotic treatment) and holistic health care practices (nutrition, exercise, yoga, emotional and spiritual healing activities) serve as the support systems (causal processes) that maintain the functional structure of viral dormancy.

Propositions which can be derived from this functional explanation are:

1. The greater the viral dormancy, the more the individual's life is asymptomatic and prolonged.
2. The greater the assault on the mind-body-spirit (invasiveness of HIV, the use of antiviral therapies, opportunistic infections, poor nutrition, stress and inactivity), the greater the symptoms which shorten the individual's life span.
3. The greater the assault on the mind-body-spirit, the greater the use of a variety of health care practices to maintain viral dormancy.

HISTORICIST EXPLANATION

Stinchcombe (1968) describes a historicist explanation as one in which an effect created by causes at some previous period becomes a cause of that same effect in succeeding periods. In this form of explanation, empirical propositions can be derived about the conditions under which traditions tend to be preserved or decayed.

As a form of explaining tradition in the phenomenon of viral dormancy in the HIV positive individual, the historicist model may seem inappropriate. While the disease's history has been profound, it is difficult to identify traditions in the therapeutic modalities used to treat the disease. However, a great deal of history has affected public health policy regarding AIDS and HIV.

Berridge (1993) suggests that lessons from history have long been a significant theme in public health policy. Policy makers believed that mandates for dealing with AIDS could be derived from past experiences with epidemics; that the way society reacted to past epidemics provided clues for approaching the AIDS epidemic. Historical input has focused on three areas: the associations between disease and stigma and disease and moral panic; the historical record of sexually transmitted diseases and the history of the public health response to disease, particularly the tensions between individual rights and the public good (Berridge, 1993, p. S244). Brandt (1988) suggests that the fear of disease has a powerful influence on medical approaches and public health policy.

The AIDS epidemic has been approached in the same way public health concerns in the past have been approached. Other epidemics have, over time, become less threatening because of the development of effective treatments for the diseases. The success of the biomedical approach in the past established a historical cause for the approach to AIDS management.

Following Stinchcombe's (1968) model, the functional structure in this schema is the "cure" ethic, that is, the focus on the elimination of the disease through biomedical methods. This focus has led to the maintenance of the homeostatic variable (H), standard medical therapy. Fear, homophobia, inadequate research funding and a lack of support for non-standard, holistic therapies has maintained the cure ethic as a functional structure. The tensions (T) which tend to disrupt the homeostatic variable of standard medical therapy include the inability to find a cure for the disease, the lack of adequate funding for research, the development of the science of psychoneuroimmunology (which is demonstrating the immune system's link to psychological and neurological factors) and the growing body of literature suggesting positive health outcomes using non-standard, holistic therapies. The tradition of standard medical therapy has continued in the approach to HIV infection and AIDS as a result of the causal forces in the historical development of medicine. Figure 7.3 illustrates the historicist explanation for this phenomenon.

Figure 7.3 Functional Historicist Explanation*

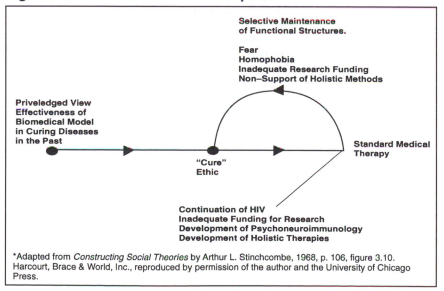

*Adapted from *Constructing Social Theories* by Arthur L. Stinchcombe, 1968, p. 106, figure 3.10. Harcourt, Brace & World, Inc., reproduced by permission of the author and the University of Chicago Press.

Propositions which can be derived from this historicist approach are:

1. The greater the effectiveness of the biomedical model in managing diseases in the past, the greater the adherence to the "cure" ethic.
2. The greater the power of the privileged view of the medical community, the greater the adherence to standard medical therapies in public health policy.
3. The greater the tensions on standard medical therapy (continuation of HIV, inadequate funding for research, development of psychoneuroimmunology, development of holistic therapies), the lesser the efficacy of standard medical therapy.
4. The lesser the efficacy of standard medical therapy, the greater the use and acceptance of alternative therapies.

ORGANIZATION OF THEORY ELEMENTS: BLALOCK'S METHODS

Blalock's (1969) methods of theory construction are helpful in organizing conceptual relationships from simple verbal statements to more formal mathematical models. One method recommended by Blalock is a block-recursive system. A block-recursive system serves as a first approximation of the phenomenon to reality. It is a verbal construction which identifies theoretical relationships and suggests testable hypotheses. These first, verbal approximations are ultimately replaced by mathematical formulas for testing.

The block-recursive system recognizes the complexity of some phenomena in which feedback occurs between certain variables in the phenomenon but not all variables. The variables which are theoretically linked and demonstrate feedback are grouped together into theoretical blocks. The theoretical blocks are then arranged to demonstrate how one group of variables relates to other groups of variables.

The variables in the phenomenon of viral dormancy can be categorized into theoretical blocks: demographics, therapeutic approaches, mind-body-spirit connections and viral dormancy (see Table 7.2). Once grouped into a block, the relationships among the variables *within* the block are identified by arrows, as are the relationships *between* the blocks of variables.

Table 7.2 Theoretical Blocks

Demographic Variables	Therapeutic Approaches	Mind-Body-Spirit	Viral Dormancy
Age	Immune System	Active Coping	Stable or Improving Immune Status
Education	Medication Regime	Positive Emotions	Viral Inactivity
Socioeconomic Status	Exercise	Spiritual Growth	Absence of Symptoms
Social Support	Hatha Yoga	Physiological Balance	Viral Dormancy
	Immune Enhancement Diet		

THEORETICAL BLOCK OF DEMOGRAPHIC VARIABLES
Identification of the Variables
The exogenous variables, age, education, socioeconomic status and social support, describe the conditions of the person which are relatively stable at any given time. These represent independent variables which influence viral dormancy indirectly. The availability of social and financial support impacts access to health care by the HIV patient (see Figure 7.4).

Figure 7.4 Block–Recursive Model of Viral Dormancy*

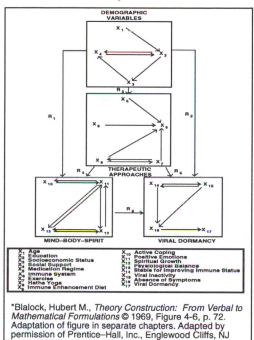

X₁ Age
X₂ Education
X₃ Socioeconomic Status
X₄ Social Support
X₅ Medication Regime
X₆ Immune System
X₇ Exercise
X₈ Hatha Yoga
X₉ Immune Enhancement Diet

X₁₀ Active Coping
X₁₁ Spiritual Growth
X₁₂ Physiological Balance
X₁₃ Stable for Improving Immune Status
X₁₄ Viral Inactivity
X₁₅ Absence of Symptoms
X₁₇ Viral Dormancy

*Blalock, Hubert M., *Theory Construction: From Verbal to Mathematical Formulations* © 1969, Figure 4-6, p. 72. Adaptation of figure in separate chapters. Adapted by permission of Prentice–Hall, Inc., Englewood Cliffs, NJ

Description of the Variables
The person's age describes chronological age and the physical and psychological development of the individual. Education is the amount of formal education completed by the individual. Socioeconomic status refers to the amount of personal financial resources available to the individual. Social support is the support received through social networks which may include family, friends and community organizations. Social support may also include financial support received from social agencies.

Relationships Within the Block
Age (X_1) has a direct relationship with opportunities for education. Education (X_2) is positively related to socioeconomic status and social support. As a person's education increases, so does the likelihood they will improve their socioeconomic status (X_3). As the person engages in educational activities, social support is enhanced. Social support (X_4) enhances accessibility to educational opportunities. The relationships among these variables is demonstrated in the Demographic Variables Block (see Figure 7.4).

THEORETICAL BLOCK OF THERAPEUTIC APPROACHES
Identification of the Variables
The variables included in the block of Therapeutic Approaches include medication regime, immune enhancement diet, exercise, hatha yoga and immune system. These variables are representative of the combined therapeutic approach of standard and holistic therapies proposed by Kaiser (1993). Through the use of these approaches, the HIV positive individual may prolong the period of viral dormancy.

Description of the Variables

Medication regime is defined as the use of antiviral, immunomodulating and antibiotic medications to contain viral replication, improve immunological status and prevent opportunistic infections. Antivirals and immunomodulators have demonstrated some effectiveness in extending the period of viral dormancy, but have not demonstrated efficacy in improving survival rates (Kaiser, 1993; Vanham et al., 1993; Hamilton et al., 1992; Collier, 1990; Hague et al., 1989; Clumeck & Hermans, 1988). These therapies do not necessarily improve the quality of life. They can cause severe side effects and, in some cases, resistance to the drug (Kaiser, 1993, Hamilton et al., 1992; Collier, 1990). Using medication alone as the only treatment to extend the period of viral dormancy is an expensive and incomplete therapy and one in which the risks of toxic side effects may outweigh the limited benefits of administration (Jennings, 1994; Kaiser, 1993).

The **immune enhancement diet** is considered by Kaiser (1993) to be the foundation for a holistic approach to healing for HIV patients. The diet consists of natural and minimally processed foods, vitamins, minerals, calories, protein and herbal supplements. Law and Baldwin (1993) recommend a diet adequate in protein, calories and nutrients to relieve symptoms and prevent weight loss in HIV positive individuals. Certain Chinese herbs have been demonstrated to improve the immune functions in animals and *in vitro* (Chu, Wong, & Mavligit, 1988). Patients who follow herbal recommendations in the comprehensive healing program for HIV require lower doses of antiviral medications in order to maintain stability (Kaiser, 1993). Compromising on the nutritional status of patients with HIV may have a negative effect on treatment outcomes and may lead to malnutrition-related immunosuppression (Thommessen & Runberget, 1993).

Exercise is defined by Kaiser (1993) as a regular activity performed three to five times a week which achieves the following goals: deep breathing (cleanses the lungs and acts as a pump for the lymph system), sweating (increases the body temperature which inhibits viral replication) and maintaining increased circulation for one-half hour (allows sufficient time for increased circulation to impact the deep tissues of the organs). These goals can be achieved by a combined exercise regime which includes aerobic activity and hatha yoga.

Hatha Yoga is a method of yoga which utilizes breathing and bodily mastery to attain relaxation and develop the mental discipline needed for work at the level of consciousness (Hewitt, 1977). Because it employs the mind, body and spirit, hatha yoga may be a particularly appropriate holistic approach to viral dormancy. Ornish (1990) has demonstrated that yoga along with dietary changes and emotional therapy can reverse the effects of heart disease. Kaiser (1993) and Borysenko (1987) discuss yoga as a relaxation technique. Although there is a paucity of published research on the use of yoga in health-related studies, there is evidence that the practice of yoga has positive health outcomes (Jain & Talukdar, 1993; Bulavin, Kliuzhev, Kliachkin, Lakshmankumar, Zuilkin, & Vlasova, 1993; Wood, 1993; Berger & Owen, 1992; Singh, Wisniewski, Britton, & Tattersfield, 1990; Stanescu, 1990). Hatha yoga may be a useful strategy for viral dormancy because the effect of relaxation and breathing are believed by Kaiser (1993) to influence the immune system.

The **immune system** is described as a widely dispersed network of organ, tissue and fluids which protect the body from invasive antigens and pathogens. The immune system is most affected by the presence of the HIV as it binds directly to the CD4 positive helper T lymphocytes and causes immuno-suppression (Zeller, 1991). The individual's immune system mounts a massive response. A brief, flu-like illness occurs and the immune system is able to contain the virus for a period of time, delaying the onset of further symptoms (Bollinger & Siliciano, 1992). This is the period of viral dormancy or latency.

Relationships Within the Block

Within the block of Therapeutic Approaches (see Figure 7.4), medication regime (X_5), immune enhancement diet (X_9), hatha yoga (X_8) and exercise (X_7) all have a positive relationship with the immune system (X_6). The immune system is improved or stabilized in the HIV positive individual as a result of these approaches (Kaiser, 1993). Additionally, the practice of hatha yoga may encourage the use of the Immune Enhancement Diet since it and yogic eating patterns are similar. Hatha yoga and exercise have a reciprocally positive relationship. As one exercises, the mastery of the body enhances the experience of hatha yoga.

THE THEORETICAL BLOCK OF THE MIND-BODY-SPIRIT

Identification of the Variables

The variables of the mind-body-spirit theoretical block are active coping, positive emotions, spiritual growth and physiologic balance (see Figure 7.4). These variables represent a holistic understanding of the individual's life experience.

Description of the Variables

Active coping is defined as the process by which the individual chooses and participates in strategies which enhance a positive adaptation to stress. Goodkin and others (1992a) found that an active coping style may deter the loss of natural killer cell function in asymptomatic HIV positive individuals. In a separate work, Goodkin and others (1992b) found that life stressors and coping styles may be predictors of the development of AIDS. Higher life stressor impacts and passive coping styles were related to lower T-cell counts.

Positive emotion is defined as an affective state of consciousness in which positive feelings such as joy and happiness are experienced. In the classic work by Solomon and Moos (1964), negative emotional responses have been demonstrated to have adverse effects on the immune system in patients with rheumatoid arthritis. More recent research has demonstrated that immunologic changes are related to depression and significant reductions in PHA, a stimulator of T lymphocytes among depressed, bereaved individuals (Schleifer, Keller, Bond, Cohen, & Stein, 1989; Linn, Linn, & Jensen, 1984). Positive emotional states have been found to enhance immune system responses (Kaiser, 1993; Antoni et al., 1991).

Spiritual growth is defined as the process of attaining meaning and purpose in life and the movement toward transcendence, "...the ability to reach or exceed the limits of usual experience; the capacity, willingness or experience of rising above or overcoming bodily or psychic conditions; or the capacity for achieving wellness and/or self-healing" (Howden, 1992, p.12). One achieves spiritual growth through a variety of avenues — illness may prompt a spiritual experience. Stuart, Deckro and Mandle (1989) view spiritual well-being as the cornerstone to health, enabling the holistic integration of one's inner resources (p.36). Presti (1990) suggests that in a spiritual search, people look for hope, meaning, purpose and a sense that their life matters. Persons with AIDS see their diagnosis as positively enhancing their spirituality because their spiritual perspectives alter as they face their own mortality (Belcher, Dettmore, & Holzemer, 1989). Lamendola and Newman (1994) describe a pattern of identifying a more meaningful connectedness to the self, others and spiritual values among HIV positive individuals and persons with AIDS.

Physiological balance is the state in which all physical systems are harmonious and complementary to one another. Physiological balance does not imply a disease-free state. It is a state in which the physical systems of the body form an integrated network that optimizes the physical experience even in the presence of illness. This variable is the "body" component of the mind-body-spirit connection and may be measured in many ways.

Relationships Within the Block

Active coping (X_{10}) and positive emotions (X_{11}) have a reciprocal relationship. If one utilizes active coping styles, positive emotional states can be achieved. A positive emotional state leads to the use of active coping styles. Positive emotions impact spiritual growth (X_{12}) positively. Spiritual growth leads to more positive emotional states. Physiological balance (X_{13}) has reciprocal relationships with positive emotions and spiritual growth. The relationships in this block demonstrate the reciprocal and inextricable nature of the elements of the mind-body-spirit (see Figure 7.4).

THEORETICAL BLOCK OF VIRAL DORMANCY
Identification of the Variables

The variables depicted in this theoretical block are a stable or improving immune status (T-cell panel), viral inactivity (p-24 antigen and beta 2 microglobulin), absence of symptoms and viral dormancy. These variables indicate the degree of viral activity and the status of viral dormancy. When the immune status remains stable and viral activity is limited, an absence of symptoms results and viral dormancy is prolonged.

Description of the Variables

Stable or Improving Immune Status is defined by stabilized or increasing T-cell counts. T-cell counts are measured by a T-cell panel which includes T4 (CD4) absolute count, T8 (CD8) absolute count, T4/T8 ratio and T4%. The T4 (CD4) absolute count indicates the number of T4 (CD4) cells present. The absolute CD4 level is not considered as predictive of the onset of AIDS as the rate in which the value drops (Alcabes, Schoenbaum, & Klein, 1993). The T8 (CD8) absolute count indicates the level of cytotoxic and suppressing activities against HIV. The antiviral effects of CD8 cells is strongest in asymptomatic HIV positive individuals (Levy, 1993). The T4/T8 ratio is an additional measure of T-cell status. It is preferred along with T4% as a measure of immune status because T4/T8 ratio and T4% are not as affected by stress and illness as the absolute counts. As a result, they provide a more stable picture of the immune status (Kaiser, 1993, Gallagher, 1991).

Viral Inactivity is measured by the p24 antigen, a protein which is part of HIV. A positive p24 antigen indicates that the virus is actively replicating

(Kaiser, 1993; Gallagher, 1991). Elevated beta-2-microglobulin indicates damage to the T-cells (Kaiser, 1993; Gallagher,1991) and is reflective of the level of viral activity.

The **absence of symptoms** is empirically identified as the absence of the conditions listed by the CDC (1992). These include opportunistic infections which decrease the length and the quality of the HIV positive individual's life.

Viral Dormancy is defined as the period of time when the virus is inactive, T cell counts are stable or improving and the person remains asymptomatic. A decline in the activity of the virus and stabilizing or increasing T-cells lead to an asymptomatic state. As long as the person is asymptomatic, there is significant stability (Kaiser, 1993). Numerous researchers have identified the latent period of the HIV infection which is difficult to predict (Slade, Turner, Abrams, Carlo, & Salk, 1992; Fauci, 1991; Haseltine & Wong-Staal, 1988). The mechanism of the latency period is not well-defined, but it is thought that the host immune response can control the virus spread through antiviral antibodies or cellular immune responses (Levy, 1993).

Relationships Within the Block

A stable or improving immune status (X_{14}) increases viral inactivity (X_{15}). Viral inactivity stabilizes or improves the immune system. A stable or improving immune system and viral inactivity have positive relationships with the absence of symptoms. The absence of symptoms (X_{16}) leads to viral dormancy (X_{17}) (Kaiser, 1993).

Model of Viral Dormancy in HIV Positive Individuals

Figure 7.4 demonstrates a block-recursive model of the phenomenon of viral dormancy in HIV positive individuals. The prior discussion focused on the relationships among the variables *within* the blocks. To understand how the blocks of variables relate to one another, the relationships *between* the blocks are discussed. These relationships are identified in the model (see Figure 7.4) by the notations R1 through R6.

Relationship Between the Demographic Variable Block and the Mind-Body-Spirit Block (R_1)

An individuals' age, education, socioeconomic status and social support can impact coping styles, emotional status, spirituality and physiological balance. As a person ages, coping styles and emotional states may mature and enhance spiritual growth. Educational level and socioeconomic status impact physiological balance by improving access to health care support. Social support may influence spiritual growth through establishing relationships in which spirituality is discussed and explored.

Relationship Between the Demographic Variable Block and Viral Dormancy Block (R_2)

Demographic characteristics have an influence on viral dormancy. Age has been demonstrated to have an inverse relationship with CD4 counts. As the individual ages, the rate of the decline of CD4 counts increases, causing a rapid progression to AIDS (Longini, Clark, Gardener, & Brundage, 1991; Blaxhult, Granath, Lidman, & Giesecke, 1990; Goedert et al., 1989). The extent of social support is believed to influence coping and life stressors (Goodkin et al., 1992b). Coping styles may have an impact on viral dormancy.

Relationship Between the Demographic Variable Block and Therapeutic Approaches (R_3)

As described in the previous relationship, age plays a role in immune system stability. Age may also be a factor in the selection of specific therapeutic approaches. A person's educational background may influence the choice of standard or holistic therapies. Because of the relationship between education and socioeconomic status, educated individuals with greater financial resources generally have increased access to all therapeutic approaches.

Relationship Between Therapeutic Approaches Block and Mind-Body-Spirit Connectivity (R_4)

The identified therapeutic approaches are designed to enhance physiological balance and psychological characteristics such as coping and emotions. Hatha yoga is a particularly appropriate therapeutic approach because it uses the body to improve mental discipline which prepares one for work in the area of consciousness and spirituality. The immune enhancement diet and exercise positively impact physiological balance.

Relationship Between the Therapeutic Approaches Block and the Viral Dormancy Block (R_5)

The therapeutic approaches block is representative of the comprehensive healing program for persons with HIV developed by Kaiser (1993). It is believed that the use of these approaches, in conjunction with positive emotional states, will stabilize or improve the immune system, decrease viral activity and provide for a longer asymptomatic period of viral dormancy (Kaiser, 1993). Persons who use this approach have demonstrated asymptomatic states even when CD4 counts have been below 200 (Kaiser, 1993).

Relationship Between the Mind-Body-Spirit Block and the Viral Dormancy Block (R_6)

Active coping, positive emotions, spiritual growth and physiological balance interact together to have a positive influence on the immune system. The mind-body connection has been demonstrated in research conducted in the area of psychoneuroimmunology (Kaplan, 1991; Houldin, Lev, Prystowski, Redei, & Lowery, 1991; Ader, 1981; Solomon & Moos, 1964). The role of spirituality in the area of immunology has not been so clearly demonstrated but is believed by this author to impact emotions, coping and feelings of physical well-being. Because of this, the relationship between spirituality and viral dormancy is believed to be a positive one.

FORMALIZATION OF GIBBS' PARADIGM

Gibbs (1972) defines theory as a "...set of logically interrelated statements in the form of empirical assertions about properties of infinite classes of events or things" (p.5). Gibbs (1972) identifies causation as a controversial idea in science and is critical of the trend in sociology to look to philosophers of science as arbitrators of the controversy. He argues that the debate in philosophy is inconclusive and should be limited to sociology since there is not just one conception of causality. He proposes that the conception of causality adopted by sociologists should depend upon the practical problems and conditions of work in the sociological field.

This argument is important for nurse theorists. The acceptance of the conception of causation by other disciplines (particularly medicine and the basic sciences) may limit the usefulness of nursing theory in nursing practice because it is not reflective of the unique practical problems of nursing. A major question proposed by Gibbs is "What kind of research findings is evidence that one phenomenon is the cause or a cause of another?" (p.20) He states that without answering this crucial question, the use of the word "cause" in formulating theory is not justified. It is a particularly important issue when one considers that a theorist may answer the question of causality but stipulate a research procedure that is alien to the conditions of work in a particular specialty. Specialists working in that area would gain nothing from adopting that conception of causation (Gibbs, p. 20).

Gibbs suggests that a definition of causation is useless unless it incorporates the issues of spatial and temporal relations between variables, but causation cannot rest solely on that issue (1972, p.22). Space-time relationships demonstrate nothing more than a correlation between variables unless the particular type of relationship which would be decisive in arguments of causation can be determined. Gibbs (1972) argues that there is not likely to be agreement in the discipline about decisive conditions for causation.

Because of these issues, Gibbs offers a proposed mode of theory construction which excludes causal language. The reasons for this exclusion are that "1) it is doubtful that a definition of causation can be formulated that will truly satisfy anyone, let alone everyone; 2) numerous conceptions of causation and related rules and procedures of inference are alien to some sociological specialties; and 3) theories can be constructed without employing a causal language" (1972, p.24). Gibbs emphasizes that his notions of causality do not imply that the theorist should deny causal thinking. He proposes that the use of the term "causes" and similar terms be excluded from theory construction because they can create confusion.

The position taken by Gibbs regarding causal language is particularly salient to nursing. Nursing work is similar to sociology in that many issues faced by nursing clients revolve around social issues. Beyond that scope, however, nursing is concerned with the elements of basic sciences as well. As nursing has attempted to develop a scientific base, research approaches have embraced the causal language and causal thinking of the basic sciences. In so doing, theories which do not attempt to explain phenomena through causal processes are given less attention. It would appear that Gibbs' recommendation to sociologists, that the conception of causation should depend on the practical problems and conditions of work in the field, is relevant to nursing as well. Nursing's field is ever changing and falls along the continuum from highly intuitive to highly technical. As such, multiple conceptions of causation seem most appropriate for nursing.

INTRINSIC AND EXTRINSIC COMPONENTS OF THE THEORY
Unit Terms

The **unit term** of a theory identifies the social unit to which the intrinsic statements of the theory will apply. For the purpose of constructing a theory about viral dormancy in persons with HIV infection, the unit term "asymptomatic, HIV positive adults" will be used.

Substantive Terms

The substantive terms of the proposed theory are identified and defined as follows (see figure 7.5):

Viral Dormancy. The time during which the HIV positive individual is symptom free, has a stable or improving T-cell count and the virus is inactive.

Figure 7.5 Model of Viral Dormancy in HIV Positive Adults: Gibbs' Paradigm*

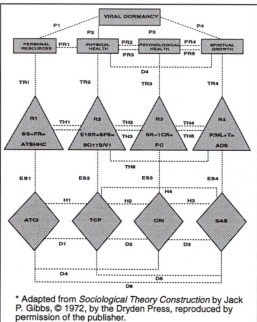

* Adapted from *Sociological Theory Construction* by Jack P. Gibbs, © 1972, by the Dryden Press, reproduced by permission of the publisher.

Personal Resources. The degree of social support, including family, friends and agencies, and financial resources available to the individual.

Physical Health. The immune status of the HIV positive individual, which determines the susceptibility to opportunistic infections.

Psychological Health. The ability to cognitively and behaviorally manage internal and external demands which may exceed the person's resources.

Spiritual Growth. The process of attaining meaning and purpose in life and the movement of the individual toward transcendence.

Acronyms of the Theory

SS -	social support
FR -	financial resources
ATSHHC-	access to standard and holistic health care
EISR -	enhanced immune system response
SFS -	symptom free state
SOIIS/VI-	stable or improving immune status/ viral inactivity
SR -	stress reduction
ICR -	increased coping resources
PC -	positive coping
P/ML -	purpose and meaning in life
T -	transcendence
AOS -	attributes of spirituality
ATCI -	access to care inventory
TCP -	T - cell panel
CRI -	Coping Resources Inventory
SAS -	Spirituality Assessment Scale

THEORETICAL STATEMENTS
Theoretically asserted and derived statements are identified and defined below. Temporal conditions are specified where appropriate. In this model, T_0 is used to demonstrate that the relationship described in the statement occurs at any point in time. The use of T_0 to describe the temporal condition for both variables in a statement suggests that the relationship is synchronous.

Postulates
Postulates are direct, intrinsic statements in which the substantive terms are constructs and concepts. *Constructs* are depicted by quotation marks and *concepts* are depicted by single quotation marks. In this model, the postulates are:
Among asymptomatic, HIV positive adults:

P1 The greater the 'viral dormancy at T_0', the greater the 'personal resources at T_0'.
P2 The greater the 'viral dormancy at T_0', the greater the 'physical health at T_0'.
P3 The greater the 'viral dormancy at T_0', the greater the 'psychological health at T_0'.
P4 The greater the 'viral dormancy at T_0', the greater the 'spiritual growth at T_0'.

Propositions
Propositions are direct, intrinsic statements in which the substantive terms are concepts. Propositions link concepts. Concepts are depicted by single quotation marks. In this model, the propositions are:
Among asymptomatic, HIV positive adults:

Pr1 The greater the 'personal resources at T_0', the greater the 'physical health at T_0'.
Pr2 The greater the 'physical health at T_0', the greater the 'psychological health at T_0'.
Pr3 The greater the 'psychological health at T_0', the greater the 'physical health at T_0'.
Pr4 The greater the 'psychological health at T_0', the greater the 'spiritual growth at T_0'.
Pr5 The greater the 'spiritual growth at T_0', the greater the 'psychological health at T_0'.
Pr6 The greater the 'spiritual growth at T_0', the greater the 'physical health at T_0'.

Referentials
The referentials are intrinsic terms that designate a formula in the extrinsic part of a theory. The referentials for this model are:

R1 SS + FR = ATSHHC
R2 EISR + SFS = SOIIS/VI
R3 SR + ICR = PC
R4 P/ML + T = AOS

Transformational Statements

Transformational statements are direct, intrinsic statements which link the substantive terms of concepts and referentials. They are:

Among asymptomatic, HIV positive adults:

Tr1   The greater the 'personal resources at T_0', the greater the access to standard and holistic health care (ATSHHC) at T_0.

Tr2   The greater the 'physical health at T_0', the greater the stable or improving immune status and viral inactivity (SOIIS/VI) at T_0.

Tr3   The greater the 'psychological health at T_0', the greater the positive coping (PC) at T_0.

Tr4   The greater the 'spiritual growth at T_0', the greater the attributes of spirituality (AOS) at T_0.

Theorems

Theorems are derived, intrinsic statements in which the referentials are the substantive terms. The theorems for this model are:

Among asymptomatic, HIV positive adults:

Th1   The greater the ATSHHC at T_0, the greater the SOIIS/VI at T_0.

Th2   The greater the SOIIS/VI at T_0, the greater the PC at T_0.

Th3   The greater the PC at T_0, the greater the SOIIS/VI at T_0.

Th4   The greater the PC at T_0, the greater the AOS at T_0.

Th5   The greater the AOS at T_0, the greater the PC at T_0.

Th6   The greater the AOS at T_0, the greater the SOIIS/VI at T_0.

Epistemic Statements

Referents become evidence for a theory only when a prediction about them can be derived from a theory (Gibbs, 1972, p.292). Epistemic statements link the referentials in a theorem with a set of referents. The epistemic statements in this model are:

Among asymptomatic, HIV positive adults:

ES1   The greater the ATSHHC at T_0, the greater the ATCIS (access to care inventory score)   at T_0.

ES2   The greater the SOIIS/VI at T_0, the greater the TCPV (T-cell panel values) at T_0.

ES3   The greater the PC at T_0, the greater the CRIS (Coping Resources Inventory score) at T_0.

ES4   The greater the AOS at T_0, the greater the SAS (Spirituality Assessment Score) at T_0.

Hypotheses

Hypotheses are formally derived assertions about predictions concerning referents. The formally derived hypotheses in this model are:

H1   The greater the ATCI score, the greater the TCP values.

H2   The greater the TCP values, the greater the CRI score.

H3   The greater the CRI score, the greater the SAS score.

H4   The greater the SAS score, the greater the TCP values.

Descriptive Statements

Descriptive statements refer to the actual relation between the two sets of referents determined from research. As such, it is not possible to provide descriptive statements about this model since the hypotheses have not been tested and actual values are not available which represent the demonstrated association between the referents.

The Model

A model depicting the substantive terms and statements of the theory appears in Figure 7.5. The path diagram which can be constructed from this theoretical work appears in Figure 7.6. A structural equation model based on the path diagram is depicted in Figure 7.7. The structural equations and matrices which are based on this model are included in the appendix.

Figure 7.6 Path Diagram of Viral Dormancy in HIV Positive Adults*

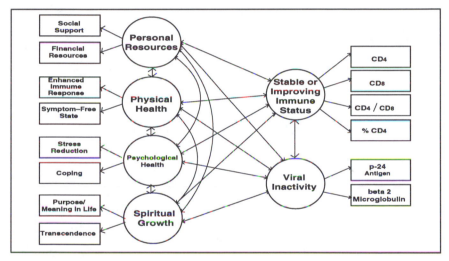

CONCLUSION

Combining holistic health care practices with standard medical therapy in prolonging viral dormancy in the HIV positive individual has implications for individual health, public health policy and nursing. The theory construction methods presented in this chapter have illumined the phenomenon as described by Kaiser (1993) and have suggested theoretical relationships which can be tested by nurses. The combined approach of holistic therapies with standard medical therapy provides rich research and practice opportunities for nurses. In fact, nursing may be the profession best prepared for researching holistic interventions. Holistic practices, including health promotion activities such as nutrition, exercise and emotional, social and spiritual support, are common to nursing practice but are usually less valued than the prescriptive biomedical approaches. Through the use of holistic methods, the nurse can facilitate the patient's self-healing. In this way, nursing decreases the dependency of the patient on health care providers and promotes the patient's autonomy.

Figure 7.7 Path Diagram with LISREL Notation for Viral Dormancy in HIV Positive Adults*

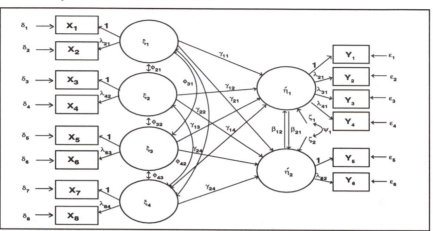

* See Appendix for corresponding equations.

Holistic health care practices encourage the inclusion of families and communities by expanding the domain of treatment beyond the physician's control. Once therapeutic decisions are transferred from the exclusive domain of the physician, patients and those around them have increased participation in the choice of therapeutic approaches. The participant role encourages a sense of ownership of health and the healing process. This sense of ownership may increase positive outcomes.

Promoting holistic approaches in which persons are able to make decisions about diet, exercise and emotional health, allows for greater participation of non-healthcare providers in the care of the individual, potentially decreasing cost and increasing the availability of health care. If viral dormancy can be extended as a result of combining holistic and standard therapies, the utilization of scarce resources in treating opportunistic infections will decrease. Families and communities whose resources are not drained are better able to provide for their members.

Perhaps the greatest influence on public health policy regarding HIV and AIDS is fear of the disease. Within the framework of the biomedical model, the only weapons against AIDS and HIV are antivirals and immunomodulators. These approaches have shown limited success in improving survival rates. Although fear perpetuates the sense of urgency in eradicating the disease, approaching HIV and AIDS as chronic conditions may demonstrate that simple and common practices can prolong the asymptomatic period.

REFERENCES

Ader, R. (1981). *Psychoneuroimmunology*. NY: Academic Press.

Antoni, M., Baggett, L., Ironson, G., LaPerriere, A., August, S., Klimas, N., Schneiderman, N., & Fletcher, M. (1991). Cognitive behavioral stress management intervention buffers distress responses and immunologic changes following notification of HIV-1 seropositivity. *Journal of Consulting and Clinical Psychology, 59*(6), 906-915.

Belcher, A., Dettmore, D., & Holzemer, D. (1989). Spirituality and sense of well-being in persons with AIDS. *Holistic Nursing Practice, 3*(4), 16-25.

Berger, B., & Owen, D. (1992). Mood alteration with yoga and swimming: Aerobic exercise may not be necessary. *Perceptual and Motor Skills, 75*(3), 1331-1343.

Berridge, V. (1993). The history of AIDS. *AIDS, 7*(suppl 1), S243-S248.

Blalock, H. (1969). *Theory construction: From verbal to mathematical foundations.* Englewood Cliffs, NJ: Prentice-Hall, Inc.

Blaxhult, A., Granath, F., Lidman, K., & Giesecke, J. (1990). The influence of age on the latency period to AIDS in people infected by HIV through blood transfusion. *AIDS, 4*(2), 125-129.

Bollinger, R., & Siliciano, R. (1992). Immunodeficiency in HIV-1 infection. In G. Wormser (Ed.), *AIDS and Other Manifestations of HIV Infection.* NY: Raven Press.

Borysenko, J. (1987). *Minding the body, mending the mind.* NY: Bantam Books.

Brandt, A. (1988). AIDS in historical perspective: Four lessons from the history of sexually transmitted diseases. *American Journal of Public Health, 78,* 367-371

Bulavin, V., Kliuzhev, V., Kliachkin, L., Lakshmankumar, V., Zuilkin, N., & Vlasova, T. (1993). Elements of yoga therapy in the combined rehabilitation of myocardial infarct patients in the functional recovery period. (Russian) *Voprosy Kurortologii, Fizioterapii i Lechebnoi Fizicheskoi Kultury, 4,* 7-9. (Abstract from Medline, No. 94055204).

CDC (1992). 1993 revised classification system for HIV infection and expanded surveillance case definition for AIDS among adolescents and adults. *Morbidity and Mortality Weekly Report, 41*(RR-17), 1-19.

Chu, D., Wong, W., & Mavligit, G. (1988). Immunotherapy with Chinese medicinal herbs. Reversal of cyclophosphamide-induced immune suppression by administration of fractionated Astralgus membranaceus in vivo. *Journal of Clinical Laboratory Immunology, 25,* 119-125.

Clumeck, N., & Hermans, P. (1988). Antiviral drugs other than Zidovudine and immunomodulating therapies in Human Immunodeficiency Virus infection. *The American Journal of Medicine, 85*(suppl 2A), 165-172.

Collier, A. (1990). Clinical research 1990: A summary. *AIDS, 4*(suppl 1), S15-S18.

Corman, L. (1985). Effects of specific nutrients on the immune response. *Medical Clinics of North America, 69,* 758-791.

Fauci, A. (1991). Immunopathogenic mechanisms in human immunodeficiency virus (HIV) infection. *Annals of Internal Medicine, 114*(8), 678-693.

Goedert. J., Kessler, C., Aledort, L., Biggar, W., White, G., Drummond, J., Vaidya, K., Mann, D., Eyster, M., Ragni, M., Lederman, M., Cohen, A., Bray, G., Rosenberg, P., Friedman, R., Hilgartner, M., Blattner, W., Kroner, B., & Gail, M. (1989). A prospective study of human immunodeficiency virus type 1 infection and the development of AIDS in subjects with hemophilia. *New England Journal of Medicine, 321*(17), 1141-1148.

Gallagher, D. (writer) & Kaiser Permanente (producer). (1991). *Now that you know: Living healthy with HIV* [Film]. CA: Concept Media.

Gallo, R., & Montagnier, L. (1988). AIDS in 1988. *Scientific American, 259*(4), 41-48.

Gibbs, J. (1972). *Sociological Theory Construction.* Hinsdale, IL: The Dryden Press, Inc.

Gloerson, B., Kendall, J., Gray, P., McConnell, S., Turner, J., & Lewkowicz, J. (1993). The phenomenon of doing well in people with AIDS. *Western Journal of Nursing Research, 15*(1), 44-58.

Goodkin, K., Blaney, N., Feaster, D., Fletcher, M., Baum, M., Mantero-Atienza, E., Klimas, N, Millon, C., Szapocznik, J., & Eisdorfer, C. (1992a). Active coping style is associated with natural killer cell cytotoxicity an asymptomatic HIV-1 seropositive homosexual males. *Journal of Psychosomatic Research, 35*(7), 635-650.

Goodkin, K., Fuchs, I., Feaster, D., Leeka, J., & Rishel, D. (1992b). Life stressors and coping style are associated with immune measures in HIV-1 infection. *International Journal of Psychiatry in Medicine, 22*(2), 155-72.

Hague, R., Yap, P., Mok, J., Eden, O., Coutts, N., Watson, J., Hargreaves, F., & Whitelaw, J. (1989). Intravenous immunoglobulin in HIV infection: Evidence for the efficacy of treatment. *Archives of Diseases in Childhood, 64,* 1146-1150.

Hamilton, J., Hartigan, P., Simberkoff, M., Day, P., Diamond, G., Dickinson, G., Drusano, G., Egorin, M., George, W., Gordin, F., Hawkes, C., Jensen, P., Klimas, N., Labriola, A., Lahart, C., O'Brien, W., Oster, C., Weinhold, K., Wray, N., & Zolla-Pazner, S. (1992). A controlled trial of early versus late treatment with Zidovudine in symptomatic human immunodeficiency virus infection. *The New England Journal of Medicine, 326*(7), 437-443.

Haseltine, W., & Wong-Staal, F. (1988). The molecular biology of the AIDS virus. *Scientific American, 259*(4), 52-62.

Hewitt, J. (1977). *The complete book of yoga.* NY: Schocken Books.

Houldin, A., Lev, E., Prystowski, M., Redei, E., & Lowery, B. (1991). Psychoneuroimmunology: A review of the literature. *Holistic Nursing Practice, 5*(4), 10-21.

Howden J. (1992). *Development and psychometric characteristics of the spirituality assessment scale.* Unpublished doctoral dissertation, Texas Woman's University, Denton.

Jain, S., & Talukdar, B. (1993). Evaluation of yoga therapy programme for patients of bronchial asthma. *Singapore Medical Journal, 34*(4), 306-308. (Abstract from Medline, No. 94090448).

Jennings, P. (Reporter). (1994, March 17). *ABC World News Tonight.* NY: American Broadcasting Company.

Kaiser, J. (1993). *Immune power.* NY: St. Martin's Press.

Kaplan, H. (1991). Social psychology of the immune system: A conceptual framework and review of the literature. *Social Science in Medicine, 33*(8), 909-923.

Lamendola, F., & Newman, M. (1994). The paradox of HIV/AIDS as expanding consciousness. *Advances in Nursing Science, 16*(3), 13-21.

Law, V., & Baldwin, C. (1993). Nutritional support in HIV disease. *Physiotherapy, 79*(6), 394-399.

Levy, J. (1993). Features of Human Immunodeficiency Virus infection and disease. *Pediatric Research, 33*(suppl,1), S63-S70.

Linn, M., Linn, B., & Jensen, J. (1984). Stressful events, dysphoric mood and immune responsiveness. *Psychological Review, 54*, 219-222.

Longini, I., Clark, W., Gardener, L., & Brundage, J. (1991). The dynamics of CD4+ T-Lymphocyte decline in HIV infected individuals: A Markov modeling approach. *Journal of Acquired Immune Deficiency Syndrome, 4*(11), 1141-1147.

Ornish, D. (1990). *Dr. Dean Ornish's program for reversing heart disease.* NY: Ballantine Books.

Palmblad, J. (1981). Stress and immunologic competence: Studies in man. In R. Ader (Ed.), *Psychoneuroimmunology (pp. 229-254).* NY: Academic Press.

Plaut, S., & Friedman, S. (1981). Psychosocial factors in infectious disease. In R. Ader (Ed.), *Psychoneuroimmunology (pp. 3-30).* NY: Academic Press.

Presti, H. (1990). AIDS: The spiritual challenge. *American Journal of Occupational Therapy, 44*(1), 87-102.

Schleifer, S., Keller, S., Bond, R., Cohen J., & Stein, M. (1989). Major depressive disorder and immunity: Role of age, sex, severity and hospitalization. *Archives of General Psychiatry, 46*, 81-87.

Singh, V., Wisniewski, A., Britton, J., & Tattersfield, A. (1990). Effect of yoga breathing exercises (pranayama) on airway reactivity in subjects with asthma. *The Lancet, 335*(8072), 1381-1383.

Slade, H., Turner, J., Abrams, C., Carlo, D., & Salk, J. (1992).Immunotherapy of HIV-seropositive patients: Preliminary report on a dose ranging study. *AIDS Research and Human Retroviruses, 8*(8), 1329-1331.

Solomon, G., & Moos, R. (1964). Emotions, immunity and disease. *Archives of General Psychiatry, 11*(6),657-674.

Stanescu, D. (1990). Yoga breathing exercises and bronchial asthma. *The Lancet, 335*(8072), 1192.

Stinchcombe, A. (1968). *Constructing social theories.* NY: Harcourt, Brace & World, Inc.

Stuart, E., Deckro, J., & Mandle, C. (1989). Spirituality in health and healing: A clinical program. *Holistic Nursing Practice, 3*(3), 35-46.

Thommessen, M., & Runberget, J. (1993). Nutritional counseling to patients with HIV infection. Can nutritional intervention prevent, expose or relieve symptoms in HIV-positive persons? *Tidsskrift for Den Norske Laegeforening, 113*(3), 324-326. (Abstract from Medline, No. 93181870).

Vanham, G., Kestens, L., Hoof, J., Penne, G., Colebunders, R., Goilav, C. Vandenbruaene, M., El Habib, R., & Gigase, P. (1993). Immunological parameters during treatment with ditiocarb (Imuthiol). *AIDS, 7,* 525-530.

Wood, C. (1993). Mood change and perceptions of vitality: a comparison of the effects of relaxation, visualization and yoga. *Journal of the Royal Society of Medicine, 86*(5), 254-258.

Zeller, J. (1991). Immune mechanisms in AIDS. In J. Durham & F. Cohen (Eds.), *The person with AIDS: Nursing perspectives (pp. 60-71).* NY: Springer.

Toward a Theory of Fetal Heart Rate Variability

Jan M. Nick

Healthy People 2000 clearly conveys a commitment to fetal well being: "improving the health of mothers and infants is a national challenge" (p. 366). Unfortunately, progress in the prevention of neonatal mortality has slowed (Healthy People 2000, 1990, p.366). Over the last decade, the percent of infant deaths resulting from intrauterine hypoxia and birth asphyxia has dropped only one percent (U.S. Bureau of the Census, 1993). New explanations of fetal heart rate behavior are necessary if the goals outlined in *Healthy People 2000* are to be achieved.

Current analysis of fetal heart rate patterns is based on the linear behavior of the fetal "system." The prediction of fetal outcomes are fairly good, however, as the above paragraph indicates; progress in predictive abilities has also slowed. Analysis using a nonlinear framework may provide new insights into fetal heart rate patterns and could increase the predictive outcomes of fetal well-being.

This chapter will present several models of analysis of fetal heart rate patterns using chaos theory as the theoretical framework. The theory construction methods used to develop the models were Stinchcombe's (1968), Blalock's (1969) and Gibbs' (1972).

The fetal unit depicted in this chapter is portrayed as a dynamic system. A dynamic system is one that changes, moves forward or adapts to external stimuli (Gleick, 1987). Dynamic systems can behave in two ways. One way is linearly; small tweaks only cause small changes thereby making long-term prediction possible. The system is "insensitive" to tweaks or perturbations. A dynamic system may also behave nonlinearly. Small tweaks cause great changes to the course of behavior and render long-term prediction impossible. However, current views held by chaoticians is that prediction is possible with nonlinear dynamics but not in the traditional sense of the word (Lampton, 1992).

The analysis of fetal heart rate patterns began in the 1960s and is currently used extensively to predict fetal outcomes (Daddario, 1992; Freeman, Garite, & Nageotte, 1991). Patterns such as long-term and short-term heart rate variability, and accelerations and decelerations all provide valuable information about the status of the fetus. Decisions about medical and nursing care are based on the patterns obtained with the electronic fetal monitor.

The electronic fetal monitor is applied to the mother to simultaneously monitor fetal heart rate and uterine contractions. Since the fetal heart rate is controlled by the parasympathetic and sympathetic nervous systems, any pattern produced by the fetal heart rate provides a window into the central nervous system which is affected by the oxygenation status of the maternal-fetal unit. Therefore, fetal heart rate patterns can help clinicians determine the oxygenation status of the fetus by the patterns produced by the fetal heart rate.

However, this linear model for prediction is not perfect. Fetal outcomes do not always match pattern predictors. Fetuses who demonstrate a reassuring fetal heart rate pattern (i.e., presence of accelerations, no late decelerations) often times have low apgars at delivery. Conversely, fetuses who demonstrate a non-reassuring fetal heart rate pattern (i.e., presence of late and/or variable decelerations, no short-term variability) may have adequate apgars at delivery. Cotton (1991) recommends that clinical patterns that do not fit a linear model may need to be examined nonlinearly. The addition of nonlinear dynamical analyses into the fetal heart rate variability may provide more understanding and lead to an increase in predictive outcomes.

Nonlinear dynamics

The science of nonlinear dynamics has recently allowed dynamic systems to be evaluated with the help of micro-computers. Using linear models, any error and unexplained outcomes were considered to be random behavior and outliers were excluded from data analysis. Nonlinear analysis includes outliers in the data. Outcomes that do not follow a predicted course may be due to a system that is also driven by nonlinear forces.

Below are several nonlinear behavioral characteristics that are now accepted characteristics of chaos theory. The usefulness of chaotic systems will be discussed in order to link human systems and nonlinear dynamics. For the purposes of this chapter, nonlinear dynamics is used interchangeably with chaos theory and is partially brought about by the systems theory approach.

Interactivity, interdependence. Any systems theory contains the basic assumption of interactivity and mutual interdependence. Due to the complexity and interaction of the "parts," the system is affected even by a seemingly insignificant change. Small changes in a dynamic system will create oscillations in the regulatory mechanism of the system. Nonlinear dynamics assumes a holistic approach in its behavior and is systems oriented — dynamic systems are more than the sum of their parts.

Sensitivity to initial conditions. Sensitivity to initial conditions is one of the most basic tenets of chaos theory. This sensitivity or "butterfly effect" was described in 1961 when a mathematical meteorologist named Edward Lorenz modelled the weather using three variables (Lorenz, 1963). Inadvertently, Lorenz discovered that minuscule changes in the equation caused great differences in outcomes. He then realized that even small changes in the initial conditions of a system could be amplified over time causing entirely different results. In science, this was coined the "butterfly effect" figuratively meaning that a butterfly flapping its wings in Asia could affect the weather in New York days later. Depending on a variable's origination, end results may drastically differ from predictions. As Lampton (1992) states, tiny errors in data can develop into large errors. Therefore, long term predictions are impossible in any system with a sensitive dependence on initial conditions (p. 69). This should not prove troublesome however because not many outcomes can be perfectly predicted using linear modelling.

Self-similarity. The concept of self-similarity or fractals has been around for centuries, but not until recently have fractal patterns been placed in a scientific theoretical framework. Self-similarity or fractals, are patterns that are reproduced at smaller and smaller scales in an extensive system. Examples of common fractals produced by mathematical equations include Mandelbrot sets and Julia sets. Fractals found in nature include the branching of tree limbs, lung tissue and heart muscle Purkinje fibers.

Fractals are caused by iterations from feedback loops in a system (see explanation of feedback loops below). The iterations allow the system to repeat a pattern using the same code while the scale changes. The ability to produce fractals is part of the adaptive process that is vital to the survival of any dynamic system. Once this ability is lost, the transfer of correctly coded information ceases and the system cannot survive.

Feedback loops. Another defining attribute of chaos theory/nonlinear dynamics is the existence of iteration and feedback loops (Briggs & Peat, 1989; Gleick, 1987). Feedback can be either positive or negative. The purpose of feedback loops is to regulate and control the system (Gleick, 1987, p. 292). Positive feedback *amplifies* the message. Negative feedback provides information to increase or decrease system output. A classic biologic example is the negative feedback loop that exists in regulating serum blood sugar in mammals. If blood sugar is elevated, the feedback loop tells the pancreas to secrete more insulin. If the blood sugar is low, the feedback loop tells the pancreas to secrete less insulin. Briggs and Peat (1989) state that it is now recognized that negative and positive feedback loops are commonly found in many complex systems.

Attractors. The characteristic of "attractors" in nonlinear dynamics is an important one. It is the influence of the attractors which constrain the behavior of a system, allowing for short-term predictions. Attractors can be thought of as a force causing the trajectory or path to stay in certain planes. This force is inherent in chaotic systems. Attractors can be detected by visually inspecting the plotted phase plane graph of data obtained from the chaotically behaved system.

Bifurcation. The reason chaotic systems have difficulty predicting long term behavior is because bifurcations occur rapidly and without warning. A bifurcation is the splitting of a pathway into two or more trajectories. Where the system moves from order to disorder is called the bifurcation. Bifurcation in dynamic systems is important because such a perturbation ultimately changes the course of a behavior. Even so, knowing when something has happened is sometimes as important as knowing what happened. The bifurcation point may provide a lot more information about a system and its environment.

Usefulness of Nonlinear Dynamics

Prediction from linear systems is fairly easy (barring outliers). Until recently, prediction with nonlinear systems was thought to be impossible. However, Garfinkle, Spano, Ditto and Weiss (1992) report that sensitivity to initial conditions makes these systems highly susceptible to control pending the appropriate analyzation of any developing chaos. In a personal conversation with Cotton (1991), William Schaeffer reported that prediction with nonlinear systems is possible but not in the way prediction was used previously. This supports the view taken by Lampton (1992) that if data can be shown to fit a nonlinear model, it is possible to write a set of deterministic equations that describe various events, whereas if the system behaves randomly, outcomes cannot be determined.

In summary, the history of the development of chaos theory has been rich with contributions from many of the basic sciences. New terminology such as fractals, attractors and sensitivity to initial conditions have developed because of that influence. It was determined that chaotic systems behaved in certain ways that could be detected using mathematical modeling. Viewing dynamic systems chaotically promises to provide new insights into the behavior of systems that were once thought to be randomly driven. In addition, short-term prediction is possible for systems that behave chaotically.

Using this information, a theory can be constructed about the relationships between fetal heart rate variability and nonlinear dynamics. To achieve this goal, several theory construction methods will be employed below as outlined by sociologists Stinchcombe (1968), Blalock (1969) and Gibbs (1972).

STINCHCOMBE'S THREE CAUSAL EXPLANATIONS
Demographic Causal Explanation

Using Stinchcombe's demographic model as a template, Figure 8.1 presents a tentative *a priori* model to show possible fetal outcomes using the theory of linear and nonlinear dynamics. This is probably the easiest of Stinchcombe's causal models and one of the most beneficial during the initial stages of theory development. In all four cells, the reader will notice that the proportions that

Figure 8.1 Fetal Outcomes Model Using the Demographic Causal Model*

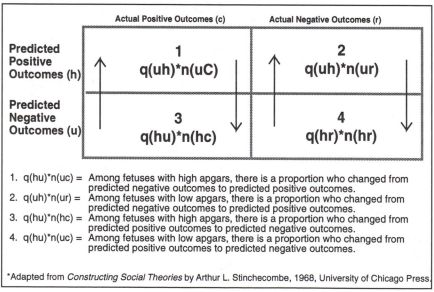

	Actual Positive Outcomes (c)	Actual Negative Outcomes (r)
Predicted Positive Outcomes (h)	1 q(uh)*n(uC)	2 q(uh)*n(ur)
Predicted Negative Outcomes (u)	3 q(hu)*n(hc)	4 q(hr)*n(hr)

1. q(hu)*n(uc) = Among fetuses with high apgars, there is a proportion who changed from predicted negative outcomes to predicted positive outcomes.
2. q(uh)*n(ur) = Among fetuses with low apgars, there is a proportion who changed from predicted negative outcomes to predicted positive outcomes.
3. q(hu)*n(hc) = Among fetuses with high apgars, there is a proportion who changed from predicted positive outcomes to predicted negative outcomes.
4. q(hu)*n(uc) = Among fetuses with low apgars, there is a proportion who changed from predicted positive outcomes to predicted negative outcomes.

*Adapted from *Constructing Social Theories* by Arthur L. Stinchecombe, 1968, University of Chicago Press.

move in and out of cells are well defined with all possible combinations included. The arrows indicate the movement of a proportion of the population from one cell to another.

The first cell (1) demonstrates that the number of full term fetuses with actual *positive* outcomes (high apgars) is a combination of the fetuses with reassuring heart rate tracings plus a portion of fetuses with non-reassuring heart rate tracings. The second cell (2) shows that the number of full term fetuses with *negative* outcomes (low apgars) is also a combination of fetuses whose heart rate tracing looked reassuring plus a portion of fetuses whose heart rate tracing looked non-reassuring. The third cell (3) identifies the proportion of full term fetuses that have non-reassuring EFM strips (indicating anticipated low apgars) plus fetuses who have predicted and positive outcomes the same. Finally, the fourth cell (4) indicates the number of fetuses who moved from predited positive outcomes (high apgars) and those whose heart rate tracing indicated negative outcomes (low apgars) and were born with low apgars.

In the demographic model, the primary concern is not the proportion or the end result of the populations that move, it is the movement itself that is so interesting (Stinchcombe, 1968, p. 79). Proportions can be manipulated upon the identification of the underlying causes. With Stinchcombe's demographic causal explanation, causality can be examined in detail.

Figure 8.2 Nonlinear Fetal Heart Rate Behavior Using the Functional Causal Model*

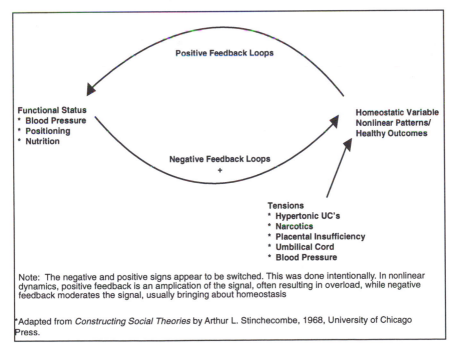

Note: The negative and positive signs appear to be switched. This was done intentionally. In nonlinear dynamics, positive feedback is an amplication of the signal, often resulting in overload, while negative feedback moderates the signal, usually bringing about homeostasis

*Adapted from *Constructing Social Theories* by Arthur L. Stinchcombe, 1968, University of Chicago Press.

FUNCTIONAL CAUSAL MODEL

Stinchcombe (1968) states that functional theories are useful for explaining phenomena (variables) by examining the consequences or outcomes. When the aim is to look for explanations, the functional causal model provides answers. The basic functional model by Stinchcombe was presented in Chapter 5. By taking this functional model and applying it to the possible chaotic influences on fetal heart rate variability, the reader notices in Figure 8.2 that the stability of the fetus (homeostasis) is brought about by several functional factors. These functional variables include maternal blood pressure, maternal and/or fetal positioning and prenatal nutrition. These are representative examples, not inclusive examples of the variables affecting fetal oxygenation system homeostasis.

If any of the functional variables are altered, the homeostatic balance of the fetus is affected. This is demonstrated as a "positive feedback loop" which produces a negative effect, on balance. In nonlinearity, positive feedback *amplifies* a signal or message resulting in further augmentation of the signal. Positive feedback produces increasingly larger effects and ultimately can produce havoc in the system. Therefore, the positive feedback is actually viewed negatively and assigned accordingly.

Negative feedback loops, on the other hand, regulate a system by encoding the signal as either too little or too much. The system is then able to increase or decrease the signal to maintain homeostasis. In this model, the homeostatic variable is the outcome. If it is receiving too much positive feedback (amplification rather than regulation), then the negative feedback loop responds by trying to maintain homeostasis. Negative feedback has a positive effect on a system. Therefore, it is viewed positively and is assigned accordingly. It is easy to see that if a system only has positive feedback, outcomes could be detrimental. Nonlinear systems have both negative and positive feedback built into the system.

Tensions in Stinchcombe's functional causal model are temporal, current, negative effects that tend to throw the fetus out of homeostasis during the labor process. These may include variables such as hypertonic uterine contractions, narcotics, umbilical cord compression, maternal blood pressure (similar to the functional variable) and placental insufficiency. These tensions have an effect on the fetal oxygenation which, in turn, affects the fetal heart rate pattern. Fetal heart rate patterns are the clue to the reassuring or non-reassuring status of the fetus. As mentioned above in the demographic model, reassuring patterns indicate that the fetus is well-oxygenated, and at birth, high apgar scores are usually obtained. Non-reassuring patterns indicate that the fetus is stressed or in distress, which would produce low apgar scores at birth.

This second model was not as helpful in revealing the nonlinear model's shortcomings as was the demographic causal model. It also seems that the functional causal model omits a very important factor — history. The third model provided by Stinchcombe, the Historicist Causal Model (1968), does add this factor. The historicist model is helpful in developing theories that explain stable and repeating phenomena.

HISTORICIST CAUSAL EXPLANATION

Applying the historicist causal method to the chaotic properties of fetal heart rate variability, the reader is instructed to view Figure 8.3. The homeostatic

Figure 8.3 Nonlinear Fetal Heart Rate Behavior Using the Historicist Causal Model*

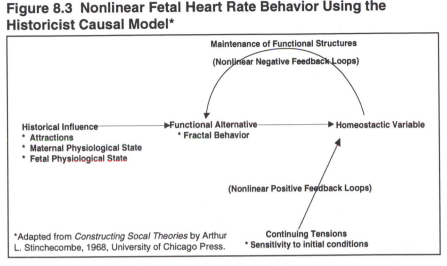

Maintenance of Functional Structures
(Nonlinear Negative Feedback Loops)

Historical Influence————▶Functional Alternative————————▶ Homeostactic Variable
* Attractions   * Fractal Behavior
* Maternal Physiological State
* Fetal Physiological State

(Nonlinear Positive Feedback Loops)

*Adapted from *Constructing Socal Theories* by Arthur   **Continuing Tensions**
L. Stinchecombe, 1968, University of Chicago Press.   * Sensitivity to initial conditions

variable is again identified as the well-oxygenated fetus producing high apgar scores at birth. However, using the nonlinear framework, various historical influences may include the influence of attractors, forces which constrain the system to act a certain way. Attractors pull a system into a certain pattern of behavior and may also influence the fetal heart rate to stay within certain boundaries. Additional historical influences include maternal physiologic state (pre-conception and postconception) and the fetal physiologic state (appropriate fetal growth and development).

The functional alternative portion in the historicist causal model can be viewed as the portion introducing fractal behavior. Encoded messages may receive similar signals which cause the system, from point to point in its totality, to appear similar. The function that affects the ability to adapt (homeostasis) are fractals developing over time.

Continuing tensions that negatively affect the homeostasis of the fetus may include the nonlinear characteristic of sensitivity to initial conditions. The sensitivity, small perturbations that produce large differences in outcomes, constantly impacts the homeostatic properties of the fetal heart rate variability.

Summary

Stinchcombe's three causal models (1968) were applied to the link between nonlinearity (chaos theory) and the fetal heart rate patterns produced during electronic fetal monitoring. The demographic causal model provided insights into the study's population domain; this will assist in refining the theory during development phases. The functional causal explanation was not as helpful, yet it did lay the groundwork for the third explanation, the historicist causal model, which provided the most significant insights into the proposed link. Many characteristics of nonlinearity became clearly apparent to the researcher. Attractors, sensitivity to initial conditions and feedback loops were logically placed.

It is important to note that Stinchcombe (1968) did not intend for all three models to be used concurrently in an investigation of one phenomenon. The theorist must decide which model would be appropriate to employ, then use the model as a template for theory construction. Reworking the model(s) is recommended to further the developing theory.

BLALOCK'S BLOCK METHOD OF THEORY CONSTRUCTION
Identification of Blocks

Blalock (1969) developed a block-design model for theory construction. For the phenomenon of fetal heart rate variability and nonlinear behavior, three blocks/categories of variables are identified using Blalock's model: the demographic block (containing five variables), the dynamic system block which contains four variables and the fetal outcome block (four variables). The demographic variables are exogenous influences on the dependent variable. These are variables which cannot be changed or manipulated.

Dynamic systems variables are endogenous influences inherent in the system. These include linear behavior and nonlinear behavior. This relationship is depicted inversely: as linear influences increase, nonlinear influences decrease. Linear behavior is predictable and insensitive to minute changes in the system. Nonlinear behavior is sensitive to minute changes and provides short-term prediction only.

The fetal outcomes block includes four categories of outcome (2 X 2 table). Stinchcombe's (1968) demographic model was helpful in the identification of this block. Both demonstrate that fetal outcomes can move from one state to another rapidly. Each block will be explained in detail. Table 8.1 below demonstrates the three blocks used to explain this phenomenon and the variables included under each block.

Table 8.1 Identification of Blocks and Variables within Blocks

Block	Variable Name
Demographic Block	x_1 Maternal Blood Pressure x_2 Maternal Position x_3 Maternal Antepartal Course x_4 Analgesia/Anesthesia During Labor x_5 Placental Functioning
Dynamic System Block	x_6 Insensitivity to initial conditions x_7 Sensitivity to initial conditions x_8 Presence of attractors x_9 Presence of fractals
Fetal Outcomes Block	x_{10} Predicted positive but actual negative outcome x_{11} Predicted negative and actual negative outcome x_{12} Predicted positive and actual positive outcome x_{13} Predicted positive but actual negative outcome

Identification of Demographic Variables

This demographic block is recursive in nature. There is no feedback from any of the variables within the block itself. The demographics placed in this block are not the traditional demographics, nevertheless they affect the dependent variable(s). As seen in Figure 8.4, the variables inside the demographic block include exogenous influences such as maternal blood pressure, maternal position, maternal antepartal course, analgesia during labor and placental functioning. All the variables except analgesia during labor directly influence the fifth variable, placental functioning. The fifth variable (x_5) is the most important as it provides all the oxygen, nutrients and blood supply to the fetus. In essence, it is the lifeline from the mother to the fetus. The five variables are discussed in detail below. Included are the interrelationships within the block.

Figure 8.4 Block Recursive Model of Analysis of Fetal Outcomes with Dynamic Systems*

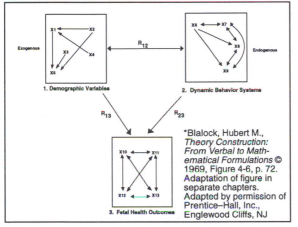

1. Demographic Variables
2. Dynamic Behavior Systems
3. Fetal Health Outcomes

*Blalock, Hubert M., *Theory Construction: From Verbal to Mathematical Formulations* © 1969, Figure 4-6, p. 72. Adaptation of figure in separate chapters. Adapted by permission of Prentice–Hall, Inc., Englewood Cliffs, NJ

Maternal blood pressure. Maternal blood pressure (x_1) can greatly affect the placental functioning (x_5) which directly affects the fetal oxygenation. A direct negative relationship exist. After a point, as blood pressure increases, placental functioning decreases.

Maternal position. Maternal position (x_2) also directly influences the blood pressure (x_1). However this relationship is indicated both negatively and positively. Many positions can raise blood pressure and others can lower blood pressure. The position depends on the desired effect.

Maternal antepartal course. Maternal antepartal course (x_3) can also directly influence how a fetus, and subsequently the fetal heart rate pattern, behaves. Therefore, this variable is negatively related to placental functioning (x_5). The antepartal history can also negatively or positively affect the maternal blood pressure. Diseases during pregnancy such as pregnancy-induced hypertension, pregnancy-induced diabetes, substance abuse and poor nutrition are some of the more common antepartal variables affecting maternal and fetal outcomes. Prenatal care does alter the course of pregnancy only in the early detection and intervention of problems. However, it does not directly influence other variables included in the block therefore it was not included in this exogeneous block.

Analgesia/Anesthesia during labor. Analgesia and anesthesia (particularly regional blocks) can also affect blood pressure negatively. A common side effect of analgesia is lowered maternal blood pressure which affects placental functioning. As the amount of anesthesia increases, blood pressure may decrease.

Placental functioning. Several other variables directly affect placental functioning. As depicted in the model, maternal blood pressure negatively affects placental functioning. Maternal antepartal course also affects placental functioning. Maternal position can directly affect placental functioning either negatively or positively depending on the maternal position and its relationship to the fetus. Placental functioning directly influences the fetal heart rate patterns depicted on the electronic fetal monitor tracing.

The exogenous variables have been identified and their relationships within the block are discussed. The endogenous block (dynamic system block) is discussed in the section below.

Identification of Dynamic system Variables

The "dynamic system" block is non-recursive in nature. Feedback loops exists between the single linear variable and the three nonlinear variables. This feedback loop is a negative loop in that if one subsystem is dominant, the other subsystem becomes non-dominant in its influence on the system. A dynamic system can take on linear and/or nonlinear behavior. The variable x_6 is a linear variable. Variables x_7, x_8 and x_9 are nonlinear variables.

Insensitivity to initial conditions. Insensitivity (x_6) is a descriptor of linearity — small perturbations do not disrupt the path or trajectory taken. Outcomes are predicted with fair accuracy. The hypothesized relationship between variables x_6 and x_7 is reciprocal and negative. As linear behavior dominates, nonlinear behavior decreases. It is also reciprocal because a feedback loop tells the system which influence is dominant at any one time.

Sensitivity to initial conditions. Variable (x_7), sensitivity to initial conditions, is a classic descriptor of nonlinear behavior. A positive relationship exists between this variable and variable x_8. As the amount of nonlinear behavior increases, the amount of influence of attractors also increases. In addition, a positive relationship exists between sensitivity to initial conditions and the presence of fractals. As variable x_7 increases, so does variable x_9.

Presence of Attractors. Attractors (x_8) are inversely proportional to variable x_6 (insensitivity to initial conditions). As the linear influence "insensitivity" dominates, the presence of attractors weakens. Conversely, the relationship between other nonlinear characteristics sensitivity, and presence of fractals are positively correlated. The more those influences are present, the more attractors are present.

Presence of Fractals. Fractals (self-similarity) of a pattern (x_9) are present in nonlinear systems. The relationships between fractals and sensitivity to initial conditions and fractals and attractors are portrayed positively. Conversely, the relationship between fractals and the linear insensitivity to initial conditions is depicted negatively. One dominates the other at any given time.

Identification of Fetal Outcomes Variables

The third and final block is the fetal outcomes block. This block can be non-recursive also. The variables in this block are the dependent variables for the other two blocks. The block was constructed using a 2 X 2 table with the categories of predicted positive/negative and actual positive/negative outcomes as the headings. The classes are mutually exclusive. Linear models are fairly good at predicting positive and negative outcomes. However, non-linear models may also prove helpful in predicting outcomes. Below is each of the possible fetal outcomes and the relationships within the block.

Predicted positive/negative outcome. The variable x_{10} is related negatively to all the other variables in the block (x_{11}, x_{12}, x_{13}). They are reciprocal in nature. As the fetus moves from one variable to another, all the others variables are excluded.

Predicted negative/negative outcome. The variable x_{11}, (predicted negative fetal outcome with actual negative outcome) is negatively related to variables x_{10}, x_{12}, x_{13}. Each variable is mutually exclusive with the others.

Predicted positive/positive outcome. Using linear methods for analysis, predicted identifications of reassuring fetal heart patterns with resultant high apgars are well documented (Freeman, Garite, and Nageotte, 1991). The variable x_{12} is reciprocal with the other three variables in this block.

Predicted negative/positive outcome. Unexpected positive outcomes may be produced when the monitor strip indicates fetal distress. This variable (x_{13}), even though unexpected, is not unsatisfactory — the end result is a healthy fetus. Due to fetal monitoring tracings, however, public policy has changed and the cesarean section rate has increased dramatically (Freeman, Garite, and Nageotte, 1991). Unnecessary cesarean deliveries and other medical interventions have caused health care costs to skyrocket.

Relationships between Blocks

During initial theory construction, Blalock recommends that variables be kept to a minimum (Blalock, 1969). He states that simplicity is preferable and that more variables can always be added later. Figure 8.4 demonstrates the block recursive model of the analysis of fetal outcomes with dynamic systems behavior. Blalock (1969) states that relationships within blocks can be non-recursive, but that between blocks, the relationship is recursive (p. 72). However, some phenomena may be better explained if non-recursive relationships between the blocks are used. The reader is encouraged to use these theory construction methods as guides only. Strict implementation would not justify the fit with varying phenomena.

Relationship between Demographic Block and Dynamic Behavior Block (R_{12})

Exogenous factors such as maternal blood pressure and position, the antepartal course, analgesia/anesthesia and placental functioning can impact the linear and nonlinear behavior of the fetal central nervous system (and thus the heart rate variability). If any of the exogenous factors negatively impact the system, the fetal system may be unable to respond and may bifurcate into another level of behavior. The relationship between the demographic block (B_1) and the dynamic behavior block (B_2) is portrayed as a unilateral direct relationship. For example, if the placental function is optimal, the dynamic system is able to maintain and respond to changes. However, if maternal blood pressure is too low/high, the fetal system may be unable to respond to the changes and bifurcate to an unhealthy pattern. The relationship is unilateral because the exogenous factors can positively/negatively impact how the fetus responds to the environment. However, the endogenous factors of the fetus do not impact the maternal blood pressure or placental functioning.

Relationship between Demographic Block and Fetal Outcomes Block (R_{13})

Exogenous variables directly affect the outcome of the fetus. Therefore, the relationship between blocks one and three are portrayed as unilateral with a positive or negative effect on block three. Demographic variables $x_{1,2,3,}$ affect the placental functioning which correlates very highly with fetal outcomes.

Relationship between Dynamic Behavior Block and Fetal Outcomes Block (R_{23})

The endogenous block (dynamic behavior) also directly affects the fetal outcome. However the relationship is not reciprocal. Fetal outcome does not positively/negatively affect the linear and nonlinear behavior of the fetus since the outcome is after the fact.

Summary

This section provides a theory construction method for analyzing fetal heart rate patterns using linear and nonlinear dynamics. The model was constructed using Blalock's (1969) method of theory construction. Relationships within and between each block were identified and the nature of the relationships was explained. This model's strength is its requirement that the researcher consider the relationships within and between the blocks and specify these relationships. Blalock's is a relatively simple theory construction method that promises to assist the theorist in defining important variables and relationships in the model.

GIBBS' MODEL

Gibbs' (1972) classic model for theory construction uses traditional terminology such as axioms, propositions, constructs and theorems into the building phase of model specification. In his book, *Sociological Theory Construction*, Gibbs divides the model into intrinsic and extrinsic components. Intrinsics includes statements and assertions that will be tested. The extrinsic portion includes definitions of terms. Using Gibbs' model as a template, the relationship between fetal heart rate variability and nonlinear behavior is depicted in Figure 8.5.

Figure 8.5 Model of Fetal Heart Rate Variability Using Gibbs' Paradigm*

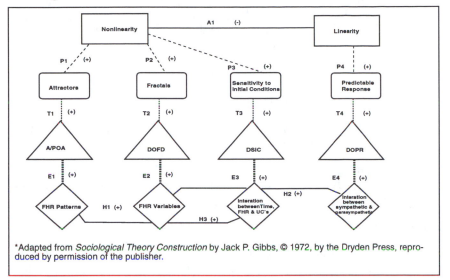

*Adapted from *Sociological Theory Construction* by Jack P. Gibbs, © 1972, by the Dryden Press, reproduced by permission of the publisher.

In the application of Gibbs' model with fetal heart rate monitoring, two constructs are identified: linearity and nonlinearity. A proposed inverse relationship exists between the two constructs. The presence of linearity does not exclude nonlinear behavior. However, they are inversely proportional. The more the system behaves linearly, the less the system behaves nonlinearly. The axiom that links these two constructs intrinsically is:

A_1: As linearity increases in a system, nonlinearity decreases, and vice versa.

Postulates
Attractors, fractal behavior and sensitivity to initial conditions are all aspects of nonlinearity. Predictable response is an aspect of linearity. Figure 8.5 demonstrates where the concepts and constructs are placed in the model. Postulates link concept with construct. The postulates articulated for the construct of nonlinearity include:

P_1: Among "dynamic systems", the greater the nonlinearity, the greater the presence of attractors.

P_2: Among "dynamic systems", the greater the nonlinearity, the greater the fractal dimension.

P_3: Among "dynamic systems", the greater the nonlinearity, the greater the sensitivity to initial conditions.

P_4: Among "dynamic systems", the greater the linearity, the greater the predictable response.

Referentials and Transformational Statements

The referentials are acronyms that assist in deriving testable formulas. Referentials are extrinsic substantive terms. There are three referentials in the construct of nonlinearity. They include: 1) A/POA, the absence or presence of attractors, 2) DOFD, the degree of fractal dimension and 3) DSIC, the degree of sensitivity to initial conditions. One referential parallels the construct of linearity, DOPR, the degree of predictable response. The transformational statements that operationalize the concepts into referentials include:

T_1: Among "dynamic systems," the greater the degree of attractors, the greater the A/POA.

T_2: Among "dynamic systems," the greater the presence of fractal behavior, the greater the DOFD.

T_3: Among "dynamic systems," the greater the sensitivity to initial conditions, the greater the DSIC.

T_4: Among "dynamic systems," the greater the predictable response, the greater the DOPR.

Epistemic statements

The link between referentials and empirical indicators are called epistemic statements. The empirical indicators are the measurements used to demonstrate a concept in some way. The epistemic statements that connect referentials to indicators are:

E_1: Among dynamic systems, the greater the A/POA, the greater the A/P of FHR patterns.

E_2: Among dynamic systems, the greater the DOFD, the greater the FHR variability.

E_3: Among dynamic systems, the greater the DSIC, the greater the interaction between the variables of time, FHR and UC's.

E_4: Among dynamic systems, the greater the DOPR, the greater the interaction between the sympathetic and parasympathetic systems.

Analysis of fetal heart rate patterns using a linear framework has been effective for many cases. However, the analysis of fetal heart rate patterns using nonlinear techniques promises to add a new dimension of understanding of the fetal system. New understanding may bring about new predictive abilities that, when coupled with linear prediction, can approach 100% accuracy.

Hypotheses

For this model, hypotheses are considered to be general assertions regarding links within the empirical referents in the model. The hypotheses derived for this model are:

H_1: The greater the FHR variability, the more reassuring the FHR patterns.

H_2: The greater the interaction between sympathetic and parasympathetic branches of the central nervous system, the greater the the FHR variability.

H_3: The greater the interaction between time, FHR, and US's, the greater the complexity of FHR patterns.

Figure 8.5 is the model of fetal heart rate behavior using Gibb's paradigm. Please note that this model is still in the developing stages of theory construction.

Changes in Public Policy

As stated in the above paragraph, public policy and standards for obstetrical care practice have changed due to technology and information gains in fetal monitoring. Although the technology is currently available for the surveillance of fetal development, the perimortality rate has not decreased proportional to the technology available today. Linear dynamics have been used for initial analysis and evaluation, however, refinements in fetal monitoring interpretation by the addition of nonlinear analysis and evaluation is necessary if the perimortality rates are impacted to any degree.

REFERENCES

Blalock, H. (1969). *Theory construction: From verbal to mathematical foundations.* Englewood Cliffs, NJ: Prentice-Hall, Inc.

Briggs, J., & Peat, F. (1989). *Turbulent mirror.* NY: Harper & Row, Publishers.

Cotton, P. (1991). Chaos, other nonlinear dynamics research may have answers, applications for clinical medicine. *JAMA, 266*(1), 12-18.

Daddario, J. (1992). Fetal surveillance in the intensive care unit: Understanding electronic fetal monitoring. *Critical Care Nursing Clinics of North America, 4*(4), 711-719.

Freeman, R., Garite, T., & Nageotte, M. (1991). *Fetal heart rate monitoring (2nd ed.).* Baltimore, MD: Williams & Wilkins.

Garfinkle, A., Spano, M., Ditto, W., & Weiss, J. (1992). Controlling cardiac chaos. *Science, 257,* 1230-1235.

Gibbs, J. (1972). *Social theory construction.* Hinsdale, IL: The Dryden Press, Inc.

Gleick, J. (1987). *Chaos: Making a new science.* NY: Penguin Books.

Lampton, C. (1992). *Science of chaos.* NY: A Venture Book.

Lorenz, E. (1963). Deterministic nonperiodic flow. *Journal of Atmospheric Sciences, 20,* 130-141.

Stinchcombe, A. (1968). *Constructing social theories.* NY: Harcourt, Brace & World, Inc.

U. S. Bureau of the Census. (1993). *Statistical abstracts of the United States: 1993 (113th ed.).* Washington, DC: U.S. Government Printing Office.

U.S. Department of Health and Human Services [DHHS]. (1990). *Healthy people 2000: National health promotion and disease prevention objectives.* (DHHS Publication. PHS No. 91-50213).

Toward a Theory of Adolescent Risk-Taking

Carol Hodgson

A dolescence is the period of development between childhood and adulthood during which individual decisions may enduringly affect character. According to Erikson (1950), during the adolescent years, the individual is faced with a particular crisis in self-perception. Erikson terms this dilemma "identity versus role confusion." One's identity is sought through new behaviors which due to immaturity and lack of life experience may include risk-taking activities. Any resolution of this adolescent crisis effectively persists into adulthood, and if maladaptive, may result in severe limits to the individual's personal freedom or health.

The negative consequences of adolescent risk-taking are well-documented. The current focus of the media on the problems of adolescence, including accidental injuries, death, substance abuse, smoking, suicide, HIV infection and unwanted pregnancy clearly indicate a societal interest in the adolescent's developmental dilemma. With the increasing incidence of high risk behaviors in the population of persons aged thirteen to twenty, there is an urgent need for health care professionals, including nurses, to understand adolescent risk-taking behavior. A thorough understanding of the phenomenon is essential so that strategies may be planned and implemented to reduce any resulting morbidity and mortality.

In this chapter, a beginning theory of adolescent risk-taking is described, using the three methods of theory and model construction proposed by Stinchcombe (1968), Blalock (1969) and Gibbs (1972).

BACKGROUND OF THE PHENOMENON: LITERATURE REVIEW

Several theories provide concepts useful to exploring adolescent risk-taking behavior. Erikson's developmental theory (1950) provides the basis for initial understanding. His theory does not mention risk-taking *per se*, but addresses the development of identity in adolescence and the role confusion, diffusion, experimentation and transition that occur in the growth toward maturity.

From Erikson's theory, Busen (1990), in developing a tool to measure adolescent risk-taking, developed the concepts of vulnerability, impulsivity and thrill-seeking to describe the possible negative outcomes of failure to establish a positive identity during the adolescent stage of development. From Selman (1971), Busen (1990) adopted the concepts of self-esteem, autonomy and social adaptation to represent role-taking, the positive outcome of adolescence. Age, socioeconomic status and education, which change with time, were depicted as antecedent to the independent variables (the positive and negative outcomes of adolescence) which affect the dependent variables of perceived and experienced risk-taking. Gender and race were depicted as variables which may influence risk-taking but are not affected by time and change.

Neo-cognitive learning theory described by Kelley (1993) provides additional background information for the understanding of adolescent risk-taking. One of the key concepts of the theory, learned insecurity, is defined as a frame of mind which may cause young people to move from healthy levels of functioning to dysfunctional levels. Learned insecurity is developed and reinforced by exposure to conflict, negative beliefs and other forms of unhealthy parenting. High-risk youths have higher levels of learned insecurity, but according to Kelley (1993), in a supportive, optimistic educational climate, even high-risk youths have been shown to recognize the distortions of their thought systems and begin to act in a more mature, objective manner.

Mead's (1934) theory of symbolic interaction helps in explaining the meaning and influence that symbols may have on behavior. The use of harmful substances such as tobacco and alcohol may have symbolic meaning for the young person. The possession and use of such substances may invoke feelings of control or belonging, especially if the peer group approves of the behavior.

The term role in symbolic interaction refers to a cluster of related meanings and values that guide an individuals's behavior (Rose, 1980). Role models are those individuals who pattern the behavior expected in certain social situations. Adolescents learn the role of the adult by trying the behaviors being patterned by the role model.

During childhood, parents are the primary role models for most children, but Erikson (1950) emphasized that during adolescence, parents are replaced by peers for support and values. According to Whatley (1991), association with risk-taking peers may increase risk-taking behaviors in adolescents.

RECONCEPTUALIZATION OF THE PHENOMENON: STINCHCOMBE'S STRATEGY

The construct of adolescent risk-taking was examined through the method of theory construction proposed by Stinchcombe (1968). Three types of explanations of the theory, demographic, functional and historicist, are given and propositions are derived.

Demographic Causal Explanation

According to Stinchcombe (1968), a demographic causal theory is one in which a causal force is assumed to be "proportional to the number of people of a certain kind" (p. 60). The explanation includes two steps: explaining how many people of a given kind there are and explaining the proportionality between numbers of different kinds of people and the causal forces producing a phenomenon. To explain the prevalence of adolescent risk-taking, the sample must specify individuals aged thirteen to twenty years from various social classes and ethnic groups. The proportionality factor is the proportion of groups engaging in various risk-taking behaviors.

In Stinchcombe's method of theory construction, there are two main variants of demographic explanations: closed and open. In a closed demographic

explanation, the number of people of certain kinds is the result of past demographic processes. The proportions of people of one category moving into
another category per unit of time are approximately constant even though there
may be a good deal of individual change.

Incomplete or open demographic explanations are ones in which the numbers of people in the groups are not determined by the same causal process
involved in the proportionality factors. Adolescent risk-taking is best explained
by the open demographic method.

The labels "calculated" and "non-calculated" were selected to represent two
types of adolescent risk-taking engaged in by both males and females. Figure

Figure 9.1 An Illustration of an Open Demographic Explanation of Adolescent Risk–Taking Using Stinchecome's (1968) Method*

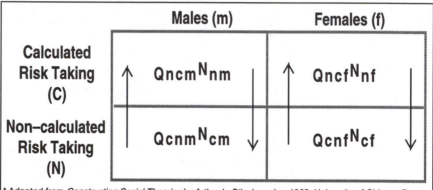

	Males (m)	Females (f)
Calculated Risk Taking (C)	$\uparrow$ $Q_{ncm}N_{nm}$	$\uparrow$ $Q_{ncf}N_{nf}$
Non–calculated Risk Taking (N)	$Q_{cnm}N_{cm}$ $\downarrow$	$Q_{cnf}N_{cf}$ $\downarrow$

* Adapted from *Constructing Social Theories* by Arthur L. Stinchcombe, 1968, University of Chicago Press.

9.1 illustrates the open demographic explanation of gender non-calculated risk-
takers. Calculated risk-taking (C) equates with the "mature adolescent decision-making pattern" (Strauss & Clarke, 1992, p. 71) evidenced by consideration and acceptance of the consequences of decisions. Non-calculated risk-
taking (N) parallels the "immature decision-making pattern" characterized by
lack of awareness of the consequences or the "transitional pattern" evidenced
by factual knowledge of consequences coupled with failure to use the knowledge to reduce personal risk (Strauss & Clarke, 1992).

From the preceding figure, among adolescent males in a given time, a proportion (qncm) change from calculated to non-calculated risk-taking and vice
versa. Among females, in the same given time, a proportion (qcnf) change
from non-calculated to calculated risk-taking and vice versa. If this process
continues long enough, it will appear to end when the same number of persons
change from calculated to non-calculated risk-taking as change in the opposite
direction. The proportions tend to be stable even with individual change.

According to Stinchcombe (1968), the most conceptually satisfactory way
to deal with different proportions in different subcategories of a population is
to repeat the transition rate analysis in each subgroup. Using these guidelines,

analyses could be done for the various demographic variables in the theory of adolescent risk-taking: age, gender, socioeconomic status, race and education. The dichotomous variables of calculated and non-calculated risk-taking could be specified as to the particular high risk behaviors such as smoking/nonsmoking, use of alcohol/abstinence from alcohol and use of condoms/non-use of condoms.

Functional Causal Explanation

Functional causal imagery is indicated whenever there is a pattern of equifinality — various means are perceived to lead to the same end. An equifinal structure is evident in circumstances when some causal process selects patterns of behavior according to consequences. Elements in the functional explanation of adolescent risk-taking are:

1. **Homeostatic variable (H):** the consequence or end which tends to be maintained and which in turn, functions as a cause of the behavior or structure. The homeostatic variable is a sense of identity, the developmental task of adolescence according to Erikson (1950) or adult role-taking (Busen, 1990).
2. **Structure (S),** which has a causal impact on H. The S represents peer group identification or conforming to the norms of the selected peer group, which, depending on the norms of the particular group may include both calculated and non-calculated risk-taking behaviors.

Figure 9.2 An Illustration of a Functional Causal Explanation of Adolescent Risk–Taking Using Stinchecombe's (1968) Method*

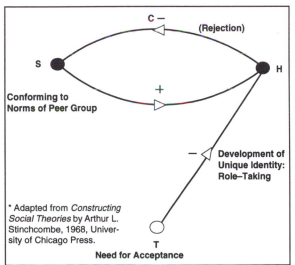

* Adapted from *Constructing Social Theories* by Arthur L. Stinchcombe, 1968, University of Chicago Press.

Conforming to the norms of the peer group tends to maintain H (development of a unique identity and adult role-taking). More elaborate functional causal explanations include tensions (T). They are other causal forces which tend to upset H (the homeostatic variable) to keep it from happening regularly unless the structure, S, causes it. In the explanation of adolescent risk-taking, T is need for acceptance.

Also included in the functional causal explanation may be a causal process (a system of rewards) which causes the structure, $\underline{S}$, maintaining the homeostatic variable, $\underline{H}$, to be selected or reinforced. In the explanation of adolescent risk-taking, the causal process, $\underline{C}$, is rejection or non-recognition. Figure 9.2 demonstrates the functional causal explanation of adolescent risk-taking with a causal loop.

An advantage in using Stinchcombe's (1968) method is that propositions may easily be derived from the pictorial representations. Those derived from the functional explanation of adolescent risk-taking include the following:

1. As $\underline{T}$ (need for acceptance) increases, $\underline{H}$ (development of unique identity and adult role-taking) decreases.
2. As $\underline{T}$ (need for acceptance) increases, $\underline{S}$ (conformity to the norms of the peer group) increases. Depending on the propensity of the peer group, the resulting behavior may be calculated or non-calculated risk-taking.
3. If $\underline{T}$ (need for acceptance) is high, but $\underline{H}$ (development of unique identity and adult role-taking) remains constant, the compensating causal loop $\underline{C}$ is operating.
4. If $\underline{T}$ is high, and $\underline{H}$ (development of unique identity and adult role-taking) decreases, $\underline{C}$ (rejection, non-recognition) will have a causal effect on $\underline{S}$ (conformity to the norms of the peer group) so that behaviors that indicate conformity will be disproportionately exhibited in an attempt to maintain $\underline{H}$.
5. If $\underline{S}$ (conformity to the norms of the peer group) is successful, $\underline{H}$ (unique identity and adult role-taking) is maintained.

Figure 9.3 An Illustration of the Functional Historicist Explanation of Adolescent Risk–Taking Using Stinchecombe's (1968) Method*

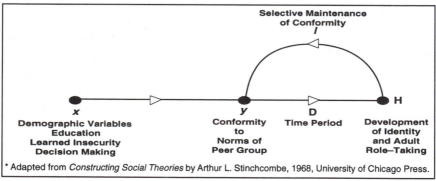

* Adapted from *Constructing Social Theories* by Arthur L. Stinchcombe, 1968, University of Chicago Press.

Historicist Explanation

According to Stinchcombe (1968), a functional historicist explanation is one in which "an effect created by causes at some previous period becomes a cause of that same effect in succeeding periods" (p. 103). Functional alternatives tend to exist in society because they fill a need in the society and are maintained for that reason.

A functional historicist explanation of adolescent risk-taking may be demonstrated by Figure 9.3 in which $\underline{X}$ represents the demographic variables age, gender, socioeconomic status, race and education (Busen, 1990); level of learned insecurity (Kelley, 1993); and level of maturity in decision-making (Strauss & Clarke, 1992) tending to produce $\underline{Y}$, the functional alternative (conformity to norms of the peer group). This conformity may take the form of either calculated or non-calculated risk-taking. $\underline{D}$ indicates the delayed or extended time period in which $\underline{Y}$ operates to cause $\underline{H}$ (the development of identity and adult role-taking). The selective maintenance loop indicates that $\underline{Y}$ (conformity to norms of the peer group) reproduces itself as an effect.

Propositions derived from the functional historicist explanation are similar to those derived from the functional structure because of the similarity in the explanations; however, because of the addition of $\underline{X}$ (historical cause of $\underline{Y}$), additional propositions may be derived including the following:

1. Change in demographic variables or antecedents ($\underline{X}$) of the adolescent population causes a change in conformity to norms of the peer group.
2. An increased level of learned insecurity leads to increased conformity to norms of the peer group.
3. An adolescent's level of maturity in decision-making correlates with conformity to the norms of the peer group.

Conclusion

Stinchcombe (1968) provides three basic methods for constructing theories: demographic, functional and functional historicist. Each of these has been used to construct an explanation of adolescent risk-taking. Of the three methods, the functional historicist method seems most appropriate for this phenomenon, as it provides the most comprehensive explanation. By studying the variables and their relationships, one may derive propositions which suggest empirical referents for testing.

ORGANIZATION OF THEORY ELEMENTS: BLALOCK'S METHOD

The construct of adolescent risk-taking was next examined using the method of theory construction proposed by Blalock (1969). His method proved to be useful in organizing the variables and identifying the interrelationships among them. To use his method, one must first complete an inventory of causes and effects of the phenomenon of interest. This is accomplished by reviewing relevant literature and listing axioms and propositions linking the variables.

A thorough review of descriptive reports and research studies was accomplished. Variables of the phenomenon were listed and relationships between the variables were noted. The variables were then grouped and consolidated into four blocks to be included in a beginning model of adolescent risk-taking. The individual blocks and the relationships within the blocks will first be described. The model depicting the phenomenon will then be presented and described in detail.

Theoretical Block of Demographic Variables

Description of Block. Demographic variables form an exogenous block that describes the characteristics of the population of adolescents. These are the "givens" of the system according to Blalock (1969) and are not variables that can be altered. These variables, age, socioeconomic status, education, ethnic background and gender, impact the way an individual views the self and the environment, resulting in an effect on risk-taking. The variables are numbered to distinguish them in the model which will be depicted later.

Age (X_1) refers to chronological age in years from thirteen to twenty, the generally accepted age of adolescence in North American society. Socioeconomic status (X_2) is the level of financial income of the household where the adolescent resides. Education (X_3) refers to formal education in years, performance in school and to informal education or life experience. Ethnic background (X_4) is the social group in which the individual is born and reared. Ethnicity includes the traits of religious preference, race, language, ancestry and physical traits which distinguish the social group. Gender (X_5) is the classification of male or female.

Relationships within the Demographic Block

Education (X_3) is the central demographic variable, with the other four variables having a direct relationship to it. Age (X_1) is related to education in that the longer the adolescent has lived, the more opportunities he or she has had to gain both formal education and life experience.

Socioeconomic status (X_2) is related to education (X_3) in that the risk of poverty is greater among low-education families (Nord, Moore, Morrison, Brown, & Myers, 1992). Higher socioeconomic status and higher educational goals are related. Parents with more formal education tend to have greater incomes; therefore, their children are less likely to live in poverty and more likely to be motivated toward educational goals (Santelli, & Beilenson, 1992).

Ethnic background (X_4) has a positive relationship with education and a reciprocal relationship with socioeconomic status. In fact, ethnicity and socioeconomic status are so closely linked, and socioeconomic status is so difficult to measure in adolescents, that it is often difficult to separate them (Santelli & Beilenson, 1992).

Gender (X_5) is related to education in that fewer females than males are high school drop-outs (Roper, 1991). Gender may be related to informal education or life experience, but no supporting evidence was found in the literature. Socioeconomic status and role expectations associated with ethnic background may impact informal education more than does gender.

In summary, the block of demographic variables shows the relationships between demographic variables. Age and gender influence education only, but there is a reciprocal relationship between other pairs of variables: socioeconomic status and education and socioeconomic status and ethnic background.

Theoretical Block of Intrapersonal Variables

Description of Block. Intrapersonal variables are the psychological traits of the adolescent which affect the propensity to take risks: ego identity, health locus of control and autonomy.

Identification of Intrapersonal Variables. According to Erikson (1950), the adolescent is concerned with acquiring a sense of identity while overcoming a sense of identity confusion. Since development occurs gradually over time, a sense of identity is not an either/or circumstance. Presumably, depending on the adolescent's level of maturation, differing levels of identity or sense of self are found in different individuals of the same age group. Identity is designated X_6 in the model of adolescent risk-taking.

Health locus of control (X_7) refers to perceptions of health and health responsibility and whether or not individuals believe they can make decisions and take actions that affect their health status. Internal or external control is the degree to which a person perceives that events are dependent on one's own behavior (internal) or are a result of chance (external) (Whatley, 1991).

Autonomy (X_8) is the use of independent reasoning in problem solving (Lewis, 1981). Adolescents who view themselves as having autonomy usually describe themselves as self-reliant (Steinberg & Silverberg, 1986).

Relationships within the Block. The block of intrapersonal variables, which include identity, health locus of control and autonomy, form a loop of relationships with one reciprocal. A person with a strong identity (X_6) will have an internal locus of control (X_7), as will a person with a high degree of autonomy (X_8). An individual with a less-developed sense of identity and less autonomy or self-reliance, will be more external.

A high level of personal identity (X_6) is positively related to autonomy (X_8). The reverse is also true. Steinberg and Silverberg (1986) state that genuine autonomous functioning develops in late adolescence and coincides with the development of a coherent sense of identity. Strauss and Clarke (1992) describe development of identity and self-reliance as dimensions of autonomy.

The theoretical block of intrapersonal variables displays the relationships between variables within the block. A sense of identity and autonomy are related to health locus of control, while autonomy and identity have a reciprocal relationship.

Theoretical Block of Environmental Variables
Description of Block. Four variables form the block of environmental factors that impact adolescent risk-taking. These are role models, social network, availability of resources and peer pressure.

Jessor and Jessor (1977) identified environmental factors that contribute to risk-taking. They include the existence of peers who model the behaviors, a low degree of support or control from adult significant others, friends exceeding parents as sources of influence and social pressure from peers who model problem behavior.

Role models (X_9) may be peers, as suggested by Jessor and Jessor (1977) or adults whose behaviors the young person imitates. People in the media, such as movie stars or rock music stars, may in themselves be role models, but young people also may be influenced by the particular life-style they portray in their film or stage presentations and seek to emulate the behavior suggested. Radio, television, printed media and images promoted on advertising billboards and promotions are also sources of role models (Boyd & Glover, 1989).

Social network (X_{10}) refers to the social ties one has, including family, friends, school and religious affiliations. According to Whatley (1991), social networks may provide a sense of psychological well-being or support, but they also may be destructive or at least, in some instances, not helpful.

Availability of resources or accessibility (X_{11}) defines the ease with which the individual obtains what is needed to engage in a certain behavior. For example, an adolescent who does not have access to an automobile will not be at risk for a fatal accident due to his or her careless driving. Many high-risk behaviors in which adolescents engage require considerable financial resources which may not be readily available to people with limited income.

Peer pressure (X_{12}) is the urging and supporting of behaviors by one's age group. Peer pressure manifested by dares or challenges can be viewed as stimuli for actions which affirm, strengthen or test a person's affiliation with certain groups (Lewis & Lewis, 1984).

Jessor and Jessor (1977) listed peer pressure as one of the environmental factors contributing to problem behavior in adolescents. A study by Jessor, Chase and Donovan (1980) demonstrated that the existence of role models and peer pressure accounted for the greatest part of the variance in studies of the use of marijuana and alcohol in adolescents. Lewis and Lewis (1984) stated that peer pressure is both a normal process of psychological development and a major contributor to the development of risk-taking behaviors.

Relationships within the Block. Role models (X_9) have a reciprocal relationship with social network (X_{10}) and a positive relationship with peer pressure (X_{12}). For adolescents, role models are likely to be peers, but social network includes all contacts in the environment. Therefore, the greater the social network, the more potential role models. Likewise, the more role models, the greater the social activity and social network. The more role models (especially if they are peers), the more peer pressure.

Social network (X10) also has a reciprocal relationship with availability of resources (X11). The more social contacts the adolescent has, the more likely the exposure to and availability of resources, either harmful or beneficial.

Availability of resources (X11) and peer pressure (X12) are reciprocally related. An adolescent who has the resources to participate in a variety of activities will likely be exposed to more peer pressure. An example is driving while drinking. As the adolescent and the peer group age, driving allows them access to situations where alcohol is available (Whatley, 1991).

The theoretical block of environmental variables demonstrates the relationships between variables within the block. Role models and social network have a reciprocal relationship, as do social network and availability of resources, availability of resources and peer pressure and peer pressure and social network. In addition, role models have a positive relationship with peer pressure.

Theoretical Block of Outcome Variables

Outcome variables form an endogenous block that includes an understanding of probability and chance, decision-making and consequences. All three variables affect not only the propensity toward, but also the behavioral manifestations of adolescent risk-taking.

Identification of Outcome Variables. The understanding of probability and chance (X_{13}) is a cognitive skill acquired as one lives and accumulates experiences in risk-taking. The level of understanding is an important dimension of risk-taking behavior (Strauss & Clarke, 1992).

Decision-making (X_{14}) as defined by Kaufman (1985), is the strategic process of making choices. It requires the ability to use logical thinking to solve problems. Three decision-making patterns were identified by Strauss and Clarke (1992). They are immature, transitional and mature. Although the patterns are described in relation to adolescent mothers, the same patterns likely exist in other adolescents.

Consequences (X_{15}) refer to the logical results of an action or decision and may be positive or negative. In the report of a study of peer pressure and risk-taking in children, Lewis and Lewis (1984) stated that children often are presented with challenges to place themselves at risk at an age before they are capable of understanding the causal relationship between an act and the non-reversibility of its consequences.

Relationships within the Block. Variables within the outcome block form a triad of reciprocal relationships. The relationship between understanding the notion of probability and chance (X_{13}) and decision-making (X_{14}) was described in relation to sexual decision-making in adolescence by Smith, Weinman and Mumford (1982). According to Strauss and Clarke (1992), a lack of understanding of probability and chance leads to immature decision-making. Presumably, more understanding results in more mature decision-making.

Decision-making (X_{14}) and consequences (X_{15}) appear to be closely related. In their review of the literature on decision-making in adolescent mothers, Strauss and Clarke (1992) state that the adolescent demonstrating an immature risk-taking pattern is unaware of the consequences of that behavior. In the transitional pattern, the adolescent girl has factual information but did not use it to reduce personal risk. For the adolescent demonstrating a more mature pattern of decision-making, evidence of acceptance of responsibility for the consequences of the decision is present. Should pregnancy occur, "I knew better" is likely to be expressed by the girl (Strauss & Clark, 1992).

Understanding the consequences of a behavior, either by experiential or observational knowledge, impacts decision-making. The mature pattern of decision-making takes into account alternatives to the risk-taking behavior based on the possible consequences (Strauss & Clarke, 1992).

Consequences (X_{15}) and understanding probability and chance (X_{13}) have a reciprocal relationship — the consequences of risk-taking impact understanding and understanding impacts the personal meaning of a behavior. According to Kirby (1992), Bandura's social learning theory provides an explanation of the impact of consequences on decision-making in that people learn to estimate important factors in a decision by observing the behavior and the rewards and punishments that result.

MODEL OF ADOLESCENT RISK-TAKING

Blalock (1969) proposed a block-recursive system of theory construction in which feedback is present within blocks of variables but not between blocks. As this model of adolescent risk-taking was developed, the relevant variables were blocked for better organization and to demonstrate relationships. However, the model has feedback loops between blocks. It does not adhere to Blalock's block-recursive method. This may indicate that the construct of

Figure 9.4 A Model of Adolescent Risk–Taking Using Blalock's (1969) Method*

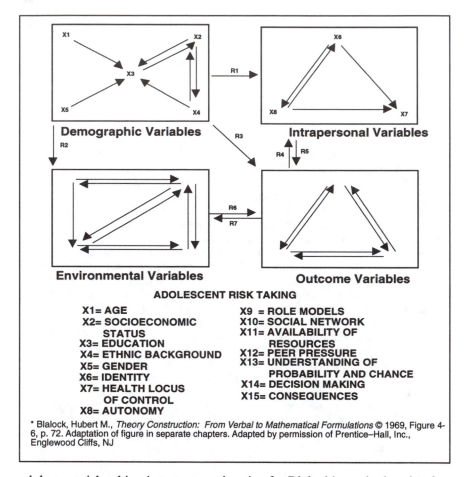

adolescent risk-taking is too comprehensive for Blalock's method or that further modification is needed to make the model fit the data. For the purposes of this chapter, the beginning model of adolescent risk-taking is presented in Figure 9.4 with inclusion of the feedback loops. The relationships between the blocks are described to explain the model.

Impact of Demographic Block on Intrapersonal Block (R1)

Age, because it is one indicator of the developmental stage, is related to the sense of identity, the developmental task of adolescence (Erikson, 1950). Many adolescents engage in risk-taking behaviors due to unrealistic optimism or a sense of invulnerability (Bueno, Redeker, & Norman, 1992).

Poverty and ethnicity are often cited in the literature as factors contributing to adolescent risk-taking. Santelli and Beilenson (1992) report that Black teens living in impoverished neighborhoods are more likely to initiate sexual behavior than other Black teens. Rates of teen childbearing remain higher in poor, minority communities. Black and Hispanic teens are disproportionately represented among the poor and poorer youth are more likely to begin sexual activity at a younger age than their more affluent peers (Newcomer & Baldwin, 1992).

In the national school-based Youth Risk Behavior Survey conducted by the Centers for Disease Control in 1990 (cited by Roth, 1993), 54.2 percent of all high school students reported having had sexual intercourse. Male students were more likely than females to have had intercourse, and Blacks were more likely than Whites or Hispanics.

Education impacts intrapersonal variables. The more education one has, the better the chance for establishing a positive identity and for learning internalizing values and beliefs.

Impact of Demographic Block on Environmental Block (R2)

Demographic variables determine in large measure the peer group for an adolescent. Demographic variables influence the availability of resources and the social network. Adolescents from affluent backgrounds have the financial resources to engage in high risk behaviors, especially if the behavior involves the use of expendable goods such as tobacco or alcohol. It is evident that the availability of automobiles supports adolescent risk-taking.

Figure 9.5 A Model of Adolescent Risk–Taking Using Gibb's (1972) Method*

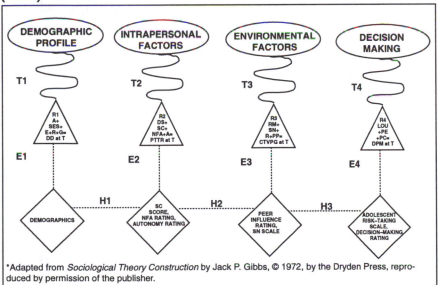

*Adapted from *Sociological Theory Construction* by Jack P. Gibbs, © 1972, by the Dryden Press, reproduced by permission of the publisher.

Impact of Demographic Block on Outcome Block (R3)

The literature abounds with studies on the relationship of demographics to outcomes. According to Lewis and Lewis (1984), children reported they were dared by peers to engage in problem behaviors and risk of personal injury. With increasing age, the dares occurred more often and more frequently in the school setting. The junior high school setting was almost twice as common a site for such challenges as the elementary school.

Older, better educated adolescents are more likely to have more mature decision-making skills (Strauss & Clarke, 1992). They also have the cognitive abilities to learn and profit from the consequences of their behavior and the behavior of others.

Relationship Between Outcome Block and Intrapersonal Block (R4 and R5)

As illustrated by Figure 9.4, outcome variables impact intrapersonal variables and vice versa. Adolescents who have a strong sense of identity, an internal health locus of control and autonomy have a greater understanding of probability and chance, more mature decision-making skills and a greater likelihood of learning from consequences. Conversely, the outcome variables increase the development of intrapersonal characteristics.

Relationship Between Environmental and Outcome Blocks (R6 and R7)

Environmental variables have a positive relationship to outcome variables. Religious practice, one example of social network, exerts a protective effect in preventing early sexual initiation, according to Santelli and Beilenson (1992). Family influence, a component of social network, may impact a teen's sexual behavior and is an area that warrants more investigation. In their review of the literature on adolescent sexual behavior, Santelli and Beilenson cite several studies that indicate that family influences do not equally influence adolescent sexual activity and they may have differing effects on initiation of sexual activity and the use of contraception.

Strauss and Clarke (1992) reported that decision-making skills are enhanced by supportive environments. Kirby (1992) advocates school-based programs to reduce sexual risk-taking behaviors. One component of the program would be training in decision-making.

FORMALIZATION OF THE THEORY: GIBBS' PARADIGM

The method of theory and model construction proposed by Gibbs (1969) is comprised of two main parts: the intrinsic and the extrinsic. In this discussion, the intrinsic and extrinsic components of adolescent risk-taking are described. Figure 9.5 illustrates the theoretical model of the phenomenon, a 0-0-3-4 design, which indicates that no constructs, axioms or postulates are given. Four concepts and three propositions give direction to the examination of adolescent risk-taking behavior.

Explanation of the Model

In Gibbs' model, three types of terms are included: unit, substantive and relational. The unit term refers to the designation of a class of events or things as units. In the model under discussion, the unit term is adolescents who are defined as young people in the United States ranging in age from twelve to twenty years.

Relational Terms

In Gibbs' method, relational terms describe a relationship between class and property or between properties of the class (Gibbs, 1972). In this model, the relational terms are "greater, greater" and "greater, less."

Temporal Quantifiers

Temporal quantifiers or time parameters are essential in Gibbs' paradigm. In the model under discussion, the temporal quantifier is represented by T to denote some point in time during the life of an individual, age twelve to twenty.

Substantive Terms

Substantive terms, which include constructs, concepts and referentials, designate properties of the class identified in the unit term (Gibbs, 1972). In Figure 9.5, there are no constructs. The concepts are demographic profile, intrapersonal factors, environmental factors and decision-making patterns.

Demographic Profile—characteristics of the population of adolescents including age, socioeconomic status, education, IQ, race and gender.

Intrapersonal Factors—factors within an individual that influence behavior. Included are developmental stage, ego identity, autonomy and propensity to take risks.

Environmental Factors—the components in an individual's surroundings, including relationships, that influence behavior. Factors included in the model are role models, social network, resources and peer pressure.

Decision-making Patterns—sequences of logical thought involving a series of choices. Three levels may be differentiated: immature, transitional and mature (Strauss and Clarke, 1992). Included in the model are level of understanding of probability and chance, prior experience and perceived consequences of behavior.

Referentials

R1: $A + SES + E + IQ + R + G = DP$
Age + Socioeconomic Status + Education + Intelligence Quotient + Race + Gender = Demographic Profile

R2: $DS + SC + NFA + A = PTTR$
Developmental Stage + Self Concept + Need for Acceptance + Autonomy = Propensity to Take Risks

R3: $RM + SN + R + PP = CTVPG$
Role Models + Social Network + Resources + Peer Pressure = Conformity to Values of the Peer Group

R4: $LOU + PE + PC = DMP$
Level of Understanding + Past Experiences + Perceived Consequences = Decision-making Pattern

Referents
Referents are unit terms or values that result from computation of the referential formulas.

Propositions
Per Gibbs (1972), a proposition is an intrinsic statement in which the substantive terms are concepts. The proposed model of adolescent risk-taking has three propositions.

P1: The greater the changes in the demographic profile, the greater the influence of intrapersonal factors.

P2: The greater the influence of intrapersonal factors on risk-taking behaviors, the less the influence of environmental factors.

P3: The greater the influence of environmental factors, the greater the change in decision-making.

Transformational Statements
A transformational statement is defined by Gibbs (1972) as a direct intrinsic statement in which the substantive terms are a concept and a referential. He further states that a theory is not testable without these statements because the stipulation of formulas and requisite data (in the referentials) are a distinct step in theory construction. There are four transformational statements in the proposed theory of adolescent risk-taking.

T1: Among adolescents, the greater the change in the demographic data, the greater the change in the demographic profile at T.

T2: Among adolescents, the greater the intrapersonal factors, the greater the propensity to take risks at T.

T3: Among adolescents, the greater the environmental factors, the greater one's conformity to values of the peer group at T.

Figure 9.6 A Path Diagram of Adolescent Risk–Taking

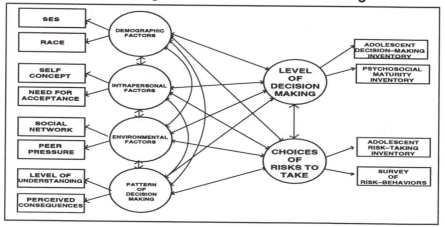

T4: Among adolescents, the greater maturity of decision-making, the greater the maturity of decision-making pattern at T.

Other Relational Statements

Other relational statements include epistemic statements, designated by E1 through E4 in the model. They link referentials in the theory with sets of referents or indicators. Hypotheses, designated H1 through H3, are formally derived predictions about referents. No epistemic statements or hypotheses have been formally stated, but the next step in the testing of model is their identification.

PREPARATION FOR THEORY TESTING: PATH DIAGRAM

A path diagram is often useful in discussing a theoretical model. It helps to communicate the basic conceptual ideas of the model in a clear and concise manner. The diagram may be tested by path analysis. Figure 9.6 depicts the path diagram of the model of adolescent risk-taking. To simplify the description, only two manifest (measurable) variables for each latent (theoretical) variable are included.

Several testable hypotheses are generated by the path diagram of adolescent risk-taking. The list is not exhaustive but is given for illustration.

Among adolescents:

1. Demographic factors influence the level of decision-making and choices of risks to take.
2. Demographic factors and intrapersonal factors have a reciprocal relationship.
3. Intrapersonal factors and environmental factors affect each other reciprocally.
4. The pattern of decision-making influences the level of decision-making and the choices of risks to take.
5. Intrapersonal factors influence both the level of decision-making and choices of risks to take.

CONCLUSION

This chapter has depicted an evolving theory of adolescent risk-taking using the theory construction methods proposed by Stinchcombe (1968), Blalock (1969) and Gibbs (1972). The use of three different techniques to examine the same phenomenon has made possible the conceptualization of highly theoretical to empirical constructs.

REFERENCES

Blalock, H.M., Jr. (1969). *Theory construction: From verbal to mathematical formulations.* Englewood Cliffs, N.J.: Prentice-Hall.

Boyd, G.M., & Glover, E.D. (1989). Smokeless tobacco use by youth in the U.S. *Journal of School Health, 59*(5), 189-194.

Bueno, M.M., Redeker, N., & Norman, E.M. (1992). Analysis of motor vehicle crash data in an urban trauma center: Implications for nursing practice and research. *Heart & Lung, 21*(6), 558-567.

Busen, H.H. (1990). *Development of an adolescent risk-taking instrument* (Doctoral dissertation, Texas Woman's University, 1990).

Erikson, E. (1950). *Childhood and society.* NY: W.W. Norton.

Gibbs, J.P. (1972). *Sociological theory construction.* Hinsdale, IL: The Dryden Press, Inc.

Jessor, R., Chase, J.A., & Donovan, J.E. (1980). Psychosocial correlates of marijuana use and problem drinking in a national sample of adolescents. *American Journal of Public Health, 70,* 604-613.

Jessor, R., & Jessor, S.L. (1977). *Problem behavior in psychological development: A longitudinal study of youth.* NY: Academic Press.

Kaufman, D.J. (1985). An interview guide for helping children make health-care decisions. *Pediatric Nursing, 11,* 365-367.

Kelley, R.M. (1993). Neo-cognitive learning theory: Implications for prevention and early intervention strategies with at-risk youth. *Adolescence, 28*(110), 439-460.

Kirby, D. (1992). School-based programs to reduce sexual risk-taking behaviors. *Journal of School Health, 62*(7), 280-287.

Lewis, C. (1981). How adolescents approach decisions: Changes over grades seven to twelve and policy implications. *Child Development, 52,* 538-544.

Lewis, C.E., & Lewis, M.A. (1984). Peer pressure and risk-taking behaviors in children. *American Journal of Public Health, 74*(6), 580-584.

Mead, G.H. (1934). *Mind, self, and society.* Chicago, IL: The University of Chicago Press.

Newcomer, S., & Baldwin, W. (1992). Demographics of adolescent sexual behavior, contraception, pregnancy, and STDs. *Journal of School Health, 62*(7), 265-270.

Nord, C., Moore, K.A., Morrison, D.R., Brown, B., & Myers, D. E.(1992). Consequences of teen-age parenting. *Journal of School Health, 62*(7), 310-317.

Roper, W.L. (1991). Current approaches to prevention of HIV infection. *Public Health Reports, 106,* 111-115.

Rose, A.M. (1980). A systematic summary of symbolic interaction theory. In J. Riehl & C. Roy (Eds.), *Conceptual models for nursing practice (Chap. 40).* NY: Appleton-Century-Crofts.

Roth, B. (1993). Fertility awareness as a component of sexuality education. *Nurse Practitioner, 18*(3), 40-48.

Santelli, J.S., & Beilenson, P. (1992). Risk factors for adolescent sexual behavior, fertility, and sexually transmitted diseases. *Journal of School Health, 62*(7), 271-279.

Selman, R. L. (1971). Taking another's perspective: Role-taking development in early childhood. *Child Development, 42,* 1721-1734.

Smith, P., Weinman, M., & Mumford, R. (1982). Social and affective factors associated with adolescent pregnancy. *The Journal of School Health, 52,* 90-93.

Steinberg, L., & Silverberg, S.B. (1986). The vicissitudes of autonomy in early adolescence. *Child Development, 57,* 841-851.

Stinchcombe, A.L. (1968). *Constructing social theories.* NY: Harcourt, Brace & World, Inc.

Strauss, S.S., & Clarke, B.A. (1992). Decision-making in adolescent mothers. *Image: Journal of Nursing Scholarship, 24*(1), 69-74.

Whatley, J.H. (1991). Effects of health locus of control and social network on adolescent risk taking. *Pediatric Nursing, 17*(2), 145-148.

Toward a Theory of Transformative Change

Charles A. Walker

N urses are familiar with change. The health care delivery system in which they work is in a constant state of flux, and their patients commonly confront challenging life transitions (Schumacher & Meleis, 1994). Yet Chinn (1992) concedes that nurses "think of change as something 'out there' noticeable only when they see dramatic shifts in edifice, or structure, or effect" (p. 102). Chinn goes on to assert that any significant change in nursing must begin with the willingness of each and every nurse to boldly experiment with transformative change.

The aim of this chapter is to demonstrate how a theory of transformative change was developed according to the strategies for theory construction described by Stinchcombe, Blalock and Gibbs. First, extant conceptions of change derived from the literature will be reviewed. Second, the phenomenon of change will be reconceptualized (Stinchcombe, 1968). Third, elements of the emergent theory will be organized (Blalock, 1969). And last, the theory will be formalized for testing (Gibbs, 1972).

REVIEW OF LITERATURE

Literature relevant to the phenomenon of change crosses many disciplines. Here, various perspectives on change from philosophy, the human sciences and nursing will be considered.

Philosophy of Change

The writer of Ecclesiastes observes that life is characterized by rhythmical cycles or seasons: "A time to weep/ And a time to laugh/ A time to mourn/ And a time to dance/ A time to keep/And a time to throw away/A time to be silent/And a time to speak" (New King James Version of the Holy Bible [NKJV], 1977, p. 722). People of faith have always recognized that life is a journey in which every step executes some divinely ordained plan, and they have found comfort in the belief that "there is a time for every purpose under heaven" (NKJV, 1985, p. 721). Despite the fact that their own lives are propelled by seemingly continuous change, the faithful are reassured by a divine order that remains invariable and unchanging. Through Plato's picture of an idealized world, this idea of ultimate truth as unchanging was formally introduced into Western philosophic thought (Durant, 1977).

Another early reference to change was in the philosophy of Heraclitus (530-470 B.C.), who maintained that there is nothing permanent except change. All things forever flow and change — even in the stillest matter there is seen flux and movement. "Through strife," says Heraclitus, "all things arise and pass away... where there is no strife there is decay: the mixture which is not shaken decomposes" (Durant, 1977, p. 64).

Some of the same ideas were developed by Hegel several centuries later. Hegel (1833/1985) posits that the end (achievement of the higher, more embracing truth) justifies the means (subordination and suppression of particular, limited truths). The evolution of thought thus entails contradictions, oppositions and negations. But in the end, everything of value is enhanced because of the conflict.

Hegel's philosophy of strife as dialectical growth was most popularly translated into human terms by Marx (1959) who offers mass movements and economic forces as the basic causes of every fundamental change. Struggle, suffering and death are justified because he views the ultimate in life as achievement, rather than contentment or happiness.

In the mid-nineteenth century, Darwin published the then controversial *Origin of Species* and presented a detailed and richly documented theory of the mode and process of evolution "by means of natural selection, or the preservation of favored (species) in the struggle for life" (Darwin, 1859/1979). Darwinian evolution has found tribute in such diverse writings as Nietzsche's (1876/1989) philosophy of pessimism and the optimistic theology of Teilhard de Chardin (1959).

During the last decade or so, the study of nonlinear dynamics has become influential in the physical and biological sciences. Popularly known as chaos theory, this new paradigm exposes the order hidden within disorder and the disorder that emerges through processes that appear to be orderly (Gleick, 1987). These ideas threaten to shatter the clockwork precision of Newtonian science. Scientists are beginning to accept that uncertainty and unpredictability may be the *modus operandi* of the universe. Chaos theory has significant implications for understanding the nature of change.

Transformation: Change of Change

Change, note Watzlawick, Weakland and Fisch (1974), often involves a move to the next higher level. Going from one level to another entails a shift, a discontinuity or a transformation; it provides a way out of a system. Watzlawick and others (1974) call this second-order change (first-order change being change within an existing framework). Second-order change is thus the change of change (Watzlawick et al., 1974).

Watzlawick, a psychotherapist and research associate with the renowned Palo Alto group, presents a pragmatic look at second-order change under the rubric "reframing." To reframe is to change the conceptual viewpoint or emotional setting of an experience — to place it in another context, another frame. Therapeutically, reframing "breaks the illusion inherent in any world image and thereby reveals that what appeared unchangeable can indeed be changed" (Watzlawick, 1978, p. 120).

Ferguson (1980) addresses the ways people change in *The Aquarian Conspiracy*. "Change itself changes," asserts Ferguson (1981, p. 72) with confidence. Ferguson challenges her reader to explore how the national health care delivery system might be transformed so that all Americans who need health care can receive it. In light of the escalating costs of medical treatment, she wisely observes that "the question automatically equates health with hospitals, doctors, prescription drugs and technology. Instead," reflects Ferguson, "we should be asking how people get sick in the first place and what is the nature of wellness." (Ferguson, 1980, p. 29)

Parse's View of Transforming

In her theory of human becoming (formerly Man-Living-Health), Parse (1992) views health as a way of living and of an ongoing participation with the universe: "disease is not something a person contracts but rather a pattern of interrelationships with the world" (Parse, 1981, p. 41). Parse believes in the integrality of personal evolution and change as manifestations of health. Human becoming is fostered and supported through illuminating meanings multidimensionally, synchronizing rhythmical patterns of relating and potentiating transcendence within an infinite array of possibilities. Parse's (1981) third principle is thus stated, "Cotranscending with the possibles is powering unique ways of originating in the process of transforming" (p. 41).

In transformation, a person increases in complexity through integrating new discoveries. Transforming is the struggle to integrate the unfamiliar with the familiar. The process of transforming is the incarnation of "chosen values in a coherent connectedness of the familiar-unfamiliar." (Parse, 1981, p. 63) According to Parse, transforming occurs through the language of connecting-separating as an individual parts from one place or person, dwells awhile with another and in turn seeks new unions.

Other Perspectives on Change

Nurses have employed a number of substantive theories borrowed from diverse disciplines like psychology and organizational science to explain personal and institutional change (Brown, 1990; Cashman, 1989; Conger, 1992; Davidhizar & Kuiper, 1989; Koerner, Bunkers & Nelson, 1991; Massey, 1991; Pearlman & Takacs, 1990; Robinson, 1991; Smith, 1991; Wagner, 1990). These additional perspectives on change include force field analysis (Lewin, 1951), grief and loss (Kuebler-Ross, 1969), dynamical systems (Porras, 1987), hardiness and health (Kobasa, 1979; Pollock, 1989), human development (Wilber, 1983) and conservationism (Marris, 1984).

Broadly speaking, though, the nursing literature construes change as something to be managed or controlled. Those who advocate "change management" view trends in health care as chaotic and argue that nurses must gain control over change and its potentially catastrophic consequences (Brown, 1990; Jones, Kopjo, Goodner-Laff, & Weber, 1990). In order for change to be truly transformative, however, the people involved need to change the way they think, not merely the ways they behave.

RECONCEPTUALIZING CHANGE

By applying Stinchcombe's (1968) method of theory construction to the phenomenon of change, new explanations emerge for the act of human becoming. From the resultant explanations, eleven propositions are derived to guide future research endeavors.

The Demographics of Change

Stinchcombe's demographic explanation invites the reader to consider the mechanism by which persons are transformed from perceiving and responding to change as a liability (or threat that they must somehow control) to envisioning change as an opportunity for exercising choice and experiencing growth. In Figure 10.1, the four cell matrix represents the intersection of an individual's view of change and the type of change that the individual encounters. In cell

Figure 10.1 The Demographics of Change*

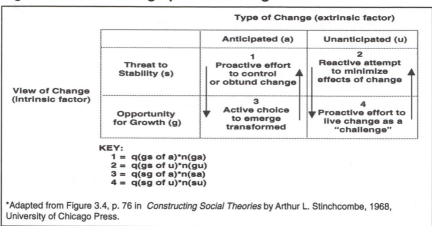

		Type of Change (extrinsic factor)	
		Anticipated (a)	Unanticipated (u)
View of Change (intrinsic factor)	Threat to Stability (s)	**1** Proactive effort to control or obtund change	**2** Reactive attempt to minimize effects of change
	Opportunity for Growth (g)	**3** Active choice to emerge transformed	**4** Proactive effort to live change as a "challenge"

KEY:
1 = q(gs of a)*n(ga)
2 = q(gs of u)*n(gu)
3 = q(sg of a)*n(sa)
4 = q(sg of u)*n(su)

*Adapted from Figure 3.4, p. 76 in *Constructing Social Theories* by Arthur L. Stinchcombe, 1968, University of Chicago Press.

one, when change is anticipated by one who views it as a threat to stability, efforts are made to control or obtund change. In cell two, when a change comes without anticipation, attempts are made to minimize the effects of the change. In cells three and four, an individual who values change as an opportunity for growth encounters change by choosing to emerge transformed or to live the change as a challenge.

Reaction represents a reflexive response to change elicited by circumstances beyond one's control. Proaction is the mobilization for change that serves as the bridge between managing change and choosing change. Efforts to predict change or to protect ourselves from its effects are often futile. Instead of reacting or proacting, the active participant in change recognizes its inevitability and responds by structuring new meanings and creating emergent realities (Parse, 1992; Defeo, 1990). To participate in the creative act of change, to be actively involved in the natural unfolding of events, involves risking personal choice.

The Historical Flow of Change

Stinchcombe's historicist model is useful for understanding the transitional nature of first-order change (see Figure 10.2). The historical variables that influence change are (1) past experiences with change, (2) perception of change and (3) susceptibility to change. The first of these variables is bound to influence the latter two. For example, if one's family life were subject to periodic and dramatic upheaval, one would expect that such an individual might adopt a fatalistic view, perceive change as a threat to self and assume a rigid approach to living marked by a fierce resistance to change.

While humans are an extremely adaptive species, they also desire a modicum of permanence and stability in their lives. This homeostatic centering process connects the unfamiliar events of the present with the familiar events of the past. The struggle for stability serves to delay our experience of change. Perhaps this explains why humans describe profound distortions of perception

Figure 10.2 First–Order Change*

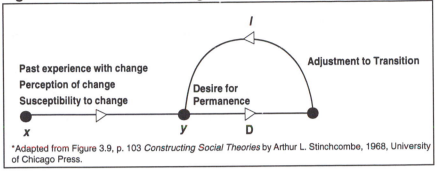

Past experience with change

Perception of change

Susceptibility to change

Desire for Permanence

Adjustment to Transition

*Adapted from Figure 3.9, p. 103 *Constructing Social Theories* by Arthur L. Stinchcombe, 1968, University of Chicago Press.

during times of drastic change. The sense that time is just creeping along supports the delayer function (D) in the model of first-order change shown in Figure 10.2.

After a within-system change, the individual's adjustment to a transition determines his or her continued desire for permanence. If the change is construed as chaotic and its effects represent a severe disruption to everyday existence, the person may cling more tenaciously to familiar, stabilizing structures and well established patterns of behavior (Hall, 1981 & 1983). If the change is viewed as a challenge that offers choice, then the individual may be willing to forsake equilibrium and engage the unfamiliar in innovative ways (Defeo, 1990).

The Functionality of Change

Stinchcombe's functionalist model aids in explaining the transformative nature of second-order change. To participate in the creative act of change involves a desire for growth. The use of the term "homeostatic variable" pre-

Figure 10.3 Second–Order Change*

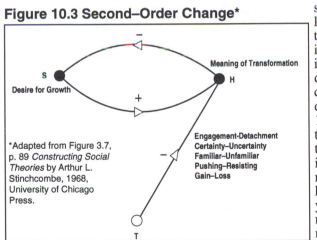

Meaning of Transformation

S

Desire for Growth

Engagement–Detachment
Certainty–Uncertainty
Familiar–Unfamiliar
Pushing–Resisting
Gain–Loss

*Adapted from Figure 3.7, p. 89 *Constructing Social Theories* by Arthur L. Stinchcombe, 1968, University of Chicago Press.

sents a distressing limitation of the functional model because it is philosophically inconsistent with the dynamic concept of change. The kind of dynamism (Porras, 1987) aimed at maintaining the status quo through minor shifts in equilibrium does not leave room for upheavals that move beyond system maintenance toward a totally new paradigm.

According to Stinchcombe, "tensions" are those causal factors which disturb homeostatic equilibrium. They, therefore, bear striking similarity to the driving and restraining forces featured in Lewin's (1951) field analysis theory of change. In the model of second-order change shown in Figure 10.3, the ten-

sions engagement-detachment, certainty-uncertainty, familiar-unfamiliar, pushing-resisting and gain-loss are identified in the manner of Hegel's dialectic.
However, the anti-Hegelian slant adopted by Parse (1981 & 1992) prompts us
to look beyond the arbitrary absolutes derived through dialectical synthesis to
discover the diverse realities that might be possible.

Derived Propositions
The following statements result from applying Stinchcombe's (1968) demographic, historicist and functional explanations to the phenomenon of change.
These eleven propositions can be used to develop testable hypotheses and guide
research about change and its relevance for nursing.

From the Demographic Model:
1. In circumstances where change is anticipated, as persons shift from
    viewing change as a threat to seeing change as a challenge, efforts to
    exert control over change will diminish.
2. In circumstances where change is not anticipated, as persons move
    from viewing change as a liability to seeing change as an
    opportunity, attempts to minimize the effects of change will decline.

From the Historicist Model:
3. Past experience with change, in which the change is perceived as be-
    yond the person's control, will decrease susceptibility to change in the
    future.
4. Past experience with change, in which the change is perceived as re-
    storing control or supporting the will to choose, tends to increase fu-
    ture susceptibility to change.
5. A decreased susceptibility to change tends to enhance the individual's
    desire for permanence or stability.
6. An increased susceptibility to change will inhibit the individual's de-
    sire for permanence.
7. Transitional maladjustment will create a greater desire for permanence
    or stability.
8. Transitional adjustment will lessen desire for permanence.

From the Functional Model:
9. A desire for growth accompanied by an active choice to emerge trans-
    formed will increase the likelihood of genuine transformation.
10. Sacrificing the familiar to the unfamiliar while pushing for and resist-
    ing change will enlarge the meanings derived through transformation.
11. Negotiating gain-loss in the face of certainty-uncertainty adds richness
    and depth to the transformative process.

ORGANIZING THEORY COMPONENTS
By using Blalock's (1969) prescription for theory construction, fifteen variables are organized into four blocks: (1) encountering the "not yet," (2) living
paradoxical rhythms, (3) adjusting to transition and (4) co-transcending with
the possibles (Parse, 1981). Relationships within and among the blocks are
also discussed (see Figure 10.4 and Table 10.1).

Block 1: Encountering the "Not Yet"

Encountering the "not yet" is to confront future contingencies in the "here and now," a momentary, transient time situated precariously on the convergence of two eternities. An historic past provides context for the fleeting present as it merges with future realities.

Figure 10.4 A Model of Transformative Change*

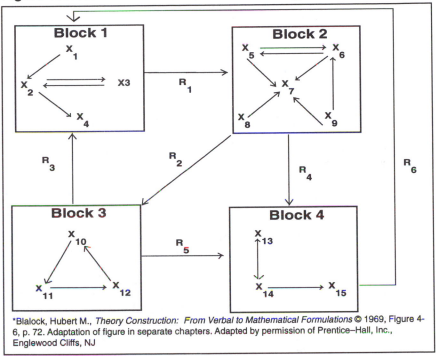

*Blalock, Hubert M., *Theory Construction: From Verbal to Mathematical Formulations* © 1969, Figure 4-6, p. 72. Adaptation of figure in separate chapters. Adapted by permission of Prentice–Hall, Inc., Englewood Cliffs, NJ

Description of the Variables

Past experience with change (X_1) includes all involvements in the change process that precede the present encounter. Perception of change (X_2) is the lens through which changes are viewed and interpreted. The change process is experienced uniquely when seen through different lenses or from various vantage points. Thus, no singular view of a change should be accepted as absolute.

Susceptibility to change (X_3) represents the likelihood that one will eagerly encounter the "not yet." This complex concept is demonstrated in Kobasa's (1979) construction of hardiness which has three components: control, commitment and challenge. A challenge represents the degree of enthusiasm with which persons invite change into their lives. Recent discussion of the conceptual and methodological issues associated with hardiness (Tartasky, 1993) questions whether the constellation of characteristics attributed to hardiness constitute a unified whole. For example, Pollock and Duffy (1990) demonstrate in their health-related modification of Kobasa's work that "commitment" and "challenge" can be collapsed into a single entity.

Table 10.1 Variables Identified in the Model*

Encountering the "Not Yet"	Living Paradoxical Rhythms	Adjusting to Transition	Co–transcending with the Possibles
x_1= Past experience with change	x_5= Gain-Loss	x_{10}= Coping	x_{13}= Will to power
x_2= Perception of Change	x_6= Certainty-Uncertainty	x_{11}= Mastery	x_{14}= Transcendence
x_3= Susceptibility to change	x_7= Engagement-Detachment	x_{12}= Adaptation	x_{15}= Meaning
x_4= Subjective response to change	x_8= Pushing-Resisting		
*see Figure 10.4	x_9= Familiar-Unfamiliar		

Subjective response to the change process (X_4) suggests that how one responds to change cannot be ascertained independent of the individual undergoing change. No completely detached, objectified instrument can be devised to decipher the immediate response to change and any subsequent desire for permanence versus growth.

Relationships Within the Block
The block identified as encountering the "not yet" displays unidirectional relationships connecting the variables: past experience (X_1), perception (X_2) and subjective response to change (X_4). Perception of change is powerfully influenced by past experience and, in turn, influences one's response to the change process. Perceived as a consummate threat to stability or as an opportunity for growth, change is responded to subjectively. Some persons view change as a liability or crisis with which they must contend so they respond by attempting to control change or to minimize its effects. Other persons who value change as an opportunity to exercise choice encounter the "not yet" by choosing to emerge transformed.

Susceptibility to change (X_3) is a measure of how amenable one is to the change process. To the extent that one cherishes involvement and courageously lives change as a challenge, the person's perception of change is subject to revision. Hardiness (Kobasa, 1979) is hypothesized to influence and be influenced by perception. "Hardy" individuals are identified, in part, because of the way in which they perceive change. On the other hand, the presence of "hardiness" as a stable personality trait can be used to predict one's inclination for perceiving and responding to particular changes in the future. Consequently, susceptibility to change (X_3) and perception of change (X_2) share a pairwise reciprocation that mediates the recursive relations among perception and the other two variables in block one (Blalock, 1969).

Block 2: Living Paradoxical Rhythms
"Rhythmical patterns of relating" are posited by Parse (1981, p. 50) as paradoxical unities requiring no neat synthesis. Dwelling with these dialectical rhythms, rather than attempting to achieve a synthetic resolution, maintains the essence of struggle (see Figure 10.4 and Table 10.1).

Description of the Variables

The rhythm gain-loss (X_5) emerges from the work of numerous grief theorists and transcendental psychologists involved with such diverse groups as the elderly, survivors of war, and bereaved caregivers of family members with Alzheimer's disease (Garrett, 1987; Lifton, 1967; Jones & Martinson, 1992). Far more than a material or emotional cost-benefit analysis, gain-loss (X_5) occurs as an individual is suddenly thrust from a position of spiritual synchrony and serenity into a situation fraught with sorrows, profound emptiness and a sense of disorientation. Efforts to deny the reality of change or to compromise it out of existence are intermediate steps experienced before the individual finally comes to terms with the struggle known as gain-loss (Kuebler-Ross, 1969).

Certainty-uncertainty (X_6) arises from the theoretical work of Mischel (1988 & 1990) who defines uncertainty as "the inability to determine the (outcome) of illness-related events... because sufficient cues are lacking" (1990, p. 256). Uncertainty indicates that a situation is, in at least some aspect, vague and unpredictable. In her reconceptualization of uncertainty, Mischel (1990) points out that uncertainty does not imply a situation which one must, necessarily, dread or desire. Its consequences are by definition indeterminate. Predictability, she asserts, is consistent with a Western cultural bias toward coherent order.

Engagement-detachment (X_7) is closely akin to Parse's (1981) notion of connecting and separating. Continuously moving back and forth between engagement and detachment occurs as persons separate from the stable structures of the past and tentatively connect with the unknown future. This variable constitutes the fundamental *action* involved in the process of change.

Pushing-resisting (X_8) is the rhythm that animates the change process. It is the struggle between search and resistance that Marris (1984) identifies as central to his "conservation" principle whereby persons survive major changes in their lives. He persuasively argues that the conservative impulse inherent in simultaneously pushing for and resisting change is not incompatible with growth as long as the "threads of continuity" tying past to present and future are preserved.

Participation in change assumes some encounter with conditions that are at once familiar-unfamiliar (X_9). The ostensible unfamiliarity of a situation often recedes to reveal much that is readily, though unexpectedly, recognizable. Familiarity merges with unfamiliarity until what was once exotic or strange becomes conventional and commonplace.

Relationships Within the Block

Pairwise causation is witnessed within two adjacent triads endogenous to the block identified as living paradoxical rhythms (Blalock, 1969). Only one variable, engagement-detachment (X_7), is influenced by all four others. Gain-loss (X_5) reciprocates with certainty-uncertainty (X_6) since, according to Mischel's (1988 & 1990) probabilistic theory of uncertainty, the desire for surety in a particular situation is due in large part to the probable risk of gain-loss. And, despite the Western bias that uncertainty is feared and certainty is valued (Mischel, 1990), an accurate expectation of certainty-uncertainty serves as a guide for calculating a gain-loss ratio and evaluating the consequent risk.

Gain-loss (X_5) demonstrates direct and indirect influences on engagement-detachment (X_7). Carmack (1992) states that balancing engagement and detachment comprises the basic process relating how gay persons respond to the multiple and cumulative losses associated with AIDS. Functionality is seen as a dynamic reverberation between the extremes of over-attachment and disengagement, either of which can occur in the face of profound loss.

Authentically living familiarity-unfamiliarity (X_9) happens as persons place the new and unfamiliar within the context of the old and familiar. This rhythm helps to restore balance (Marris, 1984) and to ease the tension of engagement-detachment (X_7). Recognizing the familiar embedded within the unfamiliar strengthens the sway of certainty-uncertainty (X_6) on engagement-detachment, since familiarity confirms what is already known (the certain) and discloses what remains to be known (the uncertain).

Pushing-resisting (X_8) is an exogenous variable that propels the rhythmical pattern of engagement-detachment (X_7), which was characterized earlier as the active component of change. From this perspective, resistance is not an impediment to change, but rather serves as a necessary precursor to real and lasting transformation (Parse, 1981; Marris, 1984).

Block 3: Adjusting to Transition

The third theoretical block, though inconsistent with Parse's (1981 & 1992) theory of human becoming and contrary to most eudaemonistic theories, gives due recognition to nursing's preoccupation with adaptation models. Implicit in this block is a philosophical concession that concepts like stress, coping (X_{10}), homeostasis, mastery (X_{11}) and adaptation (X_{12}) describe aspects of human behavior that coexist with or antecede transformative change (see Figure 10.4 and Table 10.1).

Description of the Variables

Researchers have noted that some people are less vulnerable to the deleterious effects of stress than others (Antonovky, 1979, Kobasa, 1979). Even Mischel's (1984) original theorizing about uncertainty reflected on the perceived stress associated with illness. All behaviors aimed at alleviating emotional distress or ameliorating stressful situations constitute coping (X_{10}).

Mastery (X_{11}) refers to achieving full command of some skill or knowledge that fosters emotional equilibrium. It is the ability to mitigate adversity for successful adaptation (X_{12}).

Relationships Within the Block

Adjustment to emotional distress was addressed by Mischel and others (1991) in a study of women receiving treatment for gynecological cancer which explored the mediating functions of coping and mastery on uncertainty in illness. Diverse forms of coping (X_{10}) coalesce into an emergent sense of mastery. Mastery (X_{11}) enables the individual to respond adaptively. Once accomplished, adaptation (X_{12}) in turn reinforces coping. The three variables in this block are joined via a nonrecursive, feedback loop (Blalock, 1969).

Block 4: Co-transcending with the Possibles

The epithet applied to the fourth theoretical block is lifted verbatim from Parse's (1981) third principle. Juxtaposing transcendence (X_{14}) with transition contrasts the major distinctions between these two modes of change. As conceptualized above, transition rests on theories of stress and adaptation, whereas transcendence relies on the tenets of existentialism and transpersonal psychology (see Figure 10.4 and Table 10.1).

Description of the Variables

Meaning (X_{15}) has a pervasive and enduring effect on all of life, and aesthetics is the act of experiencing meaning (Whitehead, 1925). Nietzsche (1886/ 1967) defines aesthetic experience as a reflection of the tragic composition that is human life. The elusive concept, transcendence (X_{14}), is clarified by Haase, Britt, Coward, Leidy and Penn (1992): "Reaching beyond self-concern, stepping back from and moving beyond what is, and extending self-boundaries inwardly, outwardly and temporally" (p. 144) are listed as the critical attributes of transcendence. Outcomes of transcendence include connectedness, personal growth and finding purpose. The will-to-power (X_{13}) establishes a strong link between aesthetic experience (Nietzsche, 1886/1967) and the quest for form and meaning.

Relationships Within the Block

Recursivity denotes the relations between variables in block four (Blalock, 1969). A coherent sense of meaning develops as one transcends tragedy (Frankl, 1966 & 1972). Much has been written about structuring meaning through suffering as if an awareness of one's mortality and the threat of extinction motivate humans to experiment with alternative ways of being and becoming (Frankl, 1972; Steeves & Kahn, 1987). Parse (1987) refers to this energizing force as powering, "the pushing-resisting of interhuman encounters that originates uniqueness in the process of transforming" (p. 165). The will-to-power (X_{13}) provides the impetus for transcendence (X_{14}). Transcendence, in turn, inspires meaning (X_{15}) in the change project called human becoming.

Model of Transformative Change

A complex phenomenon like change compels the aspiring theorist to map the multiple variables involved. Blocking variables (Blalock, 1969) organizes them into a conceptual schema which depicts relationships within and among the variable blocks. Block-recursive structures misrepresent as static realities those social phenomena of concern to nurses. The model of transformative change (shown in Figure 10.4) illustrates two non-recursive feedback loops intended to convey the dynamic nature of the change process.

Description of Relationships Between Blocks

Persons move from encountering the "not yet" to living paradoxical rhythms (R_1) once change has been appraised as an opportunity or a danger. Sacrificing the familiar to the unfamiliar while pushing for and resisting change occurs concurrently with negotiating gain-loss in the face of certainty-uncertainty. Engagement-detachment renders a bifurcation in the change process. Persons may proceed along one of two distinct but potentially overlapping paths. The path of greatest predictability (R_2) advances precipitously in the direction of transitional adjustment, while the path of greatest potentiality (R_4) launches transcendence with the possibles. Both of these destinations feed back to modify or enrich future encounters with the "not yet" (via R_3 and R_6, respectively). Additionally, persons may liberate themselves from the adaptive cycle in Block

3 and experience a jump, discontinuity or paradigmatic shift (R_5) toward transcendent meaning.

Description of the Non-recursive Loops

The R_1-R_2-R_3 loop represents first-order change. First-order change, note Watzlawick and others (1974), is the change that occurs within an existing system. Wilber (1983) calls this phenomenon "translation," the fleshing out of experience that, taken to its extreme, becomes an undulating preoccupation with sameness and stability. Alternately, the R_1-R_4-R_6 and R_1-(R_2-R_5)-R_6 loops represent second-order change. Second-order change is "the change of change" that pushes beyond the perimeters of an existing system (Watzlawick, Weakland, & Fisch, 1974). According to Wilber (1983), "transformation" is the upward spiral in human development that creates higher levels of complexity and diversity.

FORMALIZING THE THEORY

By employing Gibbs' (1972) rigorous method, the theory of transformative change is translated into a system of formal logic. According to Gibbs, theory consists of both intrinsic and extrinsic components. Empirical assertions and other relational statements unique to the theory comprise the intrinsic part; these are made explicit in Tables 10.2 and 10.3 with schematic representations in Figures 10.5 and 10.6. The extrinsic part of the theory includes those concepts and terms derived from other sources (see Table 10.4 for definitions of terms utilized in the proposed theory). Theory formalization and preparations for testing are tedious processes that convert a vivid verbal narrative into an amalgam of esoteric equations and mathematical notations. However, despite its apparent complexity, the proposed theory of transformative change, through exposure to Gibbs' method, is anchored solidly to the *terra firma* of the empirical world.

Path Diagram

Once formalized in the manner prescribed by Gibbs (1972), a theory can be subjected to statistical analysis. Path analysis and linear structural relation (LISREL) modeling (Jöreskog & Sörbom, 1989) are two means of theory testing used by theorists and researchers in nursing and the behavioral sciences (Mason- Hawkes, & Holm, 1989). Neither of these techniques can establish causation with certainty. But they do permit researchers to draw conclusions about a causal model based upon available data.

A path diagram of the proposed model of transformative change (shown in Figure 10.7) demonstrates hypothesized relations between the exogenous (predictor) variables and the endogenous (criterion) variables. The exogenous latent variables include: past experience with change, perception of change, susceptibility to change and response to change; the endogenous latent variables are: transitional adjustment and transcendental meaning. Correspondence between latent (theorized) variables and the manifest (measurable) variables are also depicted.

Derived Hypotheses

1. Past experience with change contributes directly to one's perception of change.
2. Perception of change reciprocates with susceptibility to change.

Table 10.2 Explication of Relational Statements*

Axiom:
A. The greater the degree of hardiness, the greater the degree of uncertainty that the individual can tolerate.

Postulates:
P_1 The greater the uncertainty, the greater the perception of change.
P_2 The greater the hardiness, the greater the susceptibility to change.

Propositions:
Pr_1 The greater the past experience with change, the greater the perception of change.
Pr_2 The greater the perceived change, the less the susceptibility to change.
Pr_3 The greater the susceptibility to change, the less the response.
Pr_4 The greater the response to change, the greater the influence of past experience on changes in the future.
Pr_5 The greater the perceived change, the greater the trend toward transitional adjustment.
Pr_6 The greater the transitional adjustment, the greater the likelihood of deriving transcendental meaning.
Pr_7 The greater the susceptibility to change, the greater the trend toward transitional adjustment.
Pr_8 The greater the perceived change, the greater the likelihood of deriving transcendental meaning.
Pr_9 The greater the susceptibility to change, the greater the likelihood of deriving transcendental meaning.

Transformational Statements:
Tr_1 The greater the sum of GL, CU, ED, PR and FU, the greater the EWC.
Tr_2 The greater the sum of TTS and OFG, the greater the AOC.
Tr_3 The greater the sum of DFS and BAC, the greater the STC.
Tr_4 The greater the sum of ED and SR, the greater the RTC.
Tr_5 The greater the sum of MAS and COP, the greater the A.
Tr_6 The greater the sum of SE, SW, WB, PG and CO, the greater the T.

Theorems:
Th_1 The greater the EWC, the greater the AOC as measured by DA/OA.
Th_2 The greater the AOC, the less the SOC as measured by SS/CSS.
Th_3 The greater the SOC, the greater the RTC as measured by POMS/SI
Th_4 The greater the RTC, the greater the EWC as measured by SI.
Th_5 The greater the AOC, the greater the A as measured by MMS/WOCS
Th_6 The greater the A, the less the T as measured by SI.
Th_7 The greater the T, the greater the SOC as measured by SS/CSS.
Th_8 The greater the AOC, the greater the T as measured by SI.
Th_9 The greater the SOC, the less the A as measured by MMS/WOCS.

Epistemic Statements: E_1 - E_6 are possible.
Hypotheses: H_1 - H_9 are deferred.

* Acronyms are fully identified in Table 10.3.

3. Susceptibility to change contributes directly to one's response to change.
4. Response to change feeds back to inform one's experience with change.
5. Perception of change may mediate either transitional adjustment or transcendence depending upon the appraisal of threat versus opportunity.

Figure 10.5 Relationships Among Exogenous Variables*

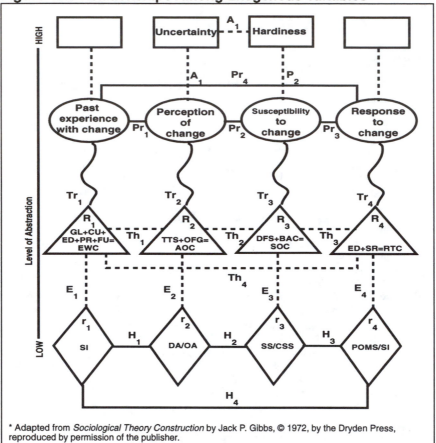

* Adapted from *Sociological Theory Construction* by Jack P. Gibbs, © 1972, by the Dryden Press, reproduced by permission of the publisher.

6. Susceptibility to change may yield transitional adjustment or transcendence depending upon the degree of challenge versus security desired.
7. Transitional adjustment may predispose the individual to derive new meanings that are transformative.

SUMMARY

Each of the strategies for theory construction recommended by Stinchcombe (1968), Blalock (1969) and Gibbs (1972) contributes uniquely to an understanding of transformative change. Using these strategies is, admittedly, antithetical to Parse's preference for a program of qualitative research and theorizing (Parse, Coyne, & Smith, 1985); however, the causal formulations presented in this chapter bridge the existential concepts and language of phenomenology found in Parse's theory of human becoming to recent products of nursing's quantitative tradition. The resultant models (see Figures 10.4 and 10.7) coax new insights and discoveries without supplanting other portraits of change in the nursing literature.

Table 10.3 Explication of Referential Formulas and Empirical Referents

R_1 GL + CU + ED +PR + FU = EWC
Gain-loss + certainty-uncertainty + engagement-detachment + pushing-resisting + familiarity-unfamiliarity = experience with change (Kuebler-Ross, 1969; Marris, 1984; Mischel, 1990; Parse, 1981).

r_1 Obtained by structured interview (SI)

R_2 TTS + OFG = AOC
Threat to stability + opportunity for growth = appraisal of change (Marris, 1984;Mischel, 1990).

r_2 Measured by Danger and Opportunity appraisal (DA/OA) subscales developed by Folkman and Lazarus (1982).

R_3 DFS + BAC = SOC
Desire for security + beliefs about change = sense of "challenge" (Kobasa, 1978).

r_3 Measured by the Security and Cognitive Structure Scales (SS/CCS) of the California Life Goals Evaluation Schedule (Hahn, 1966).

R_4 ED + SR = RTC
Emotional distress + subjective report = response to change

r_4 Measured via the Profile of Mood States (POMS) published by McNair, Lorr and Droppleman (1971) and by structured interview (SI).

R_5 MAS + COP = A
Mastery + Coping = Adaptation

r_5 Measured by MMS/WOCS, a modified five-item Mastery Scale (Pearlin & Schooler 1978; Mischel, 1991) and the Ways of Coping Scale (Mischel, 1988).

R_6 SE + SW+ WB + PG + CO = T
Serenity + self worth + well being + personal growth + connectedness = transcendence (Haase, Britt, Coward, Leidy & Penn, 1992).

r_6 Obtained through carefully designed and conducted structured interview (SI) or other sensitive measure(s), such as Reed's (1991) Self–Transcendence Scale.

The philosophers, psychologists, political theorists and nurses whose ideas have been considered in this chapter agree that change requires effort. Many people perceive change as a burden imposed by external forces (Van den Berg, 1961). But, transformative change is precisely the sort of change called for by health care reformers — radical change that rejects conventional wisdom, oppressive institutions and bureaucratic structures that don't work. Change can re-form our moral obligation to those persons who are underserved by the present system. At the macro level of change, nurses can be instrumental in interpreting social movements and influencing public policy. At the micro level, nurses represent role models for their clients who are often persons confronting progressive diseases or life-changing injuries.

Clinical nurses must be equipped to respond to the increasing morbidity and mortality rates associated with teenage pregnancy, domestic violence, tuberculosis, cancer, aging and AIDS. Likewise, nurse theorists and researchers must prepare themselves for a different sort of nursing scholarship in which the discourse of science gives way to emergent methodologies derived from

Figure 10.6 Relationships Between Exogenous and Endogenous Variables*

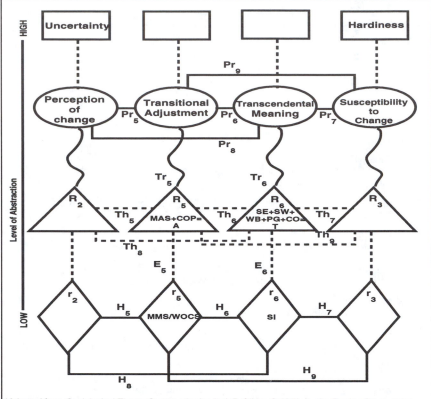

*Adapted from *Sociological Theory Construction* by Jack P. Gibbs, © 1972, by the Dryden Press, reproduced by permission of the publisher.

Figure 10.7 Path Diagram of Transformative Change Model

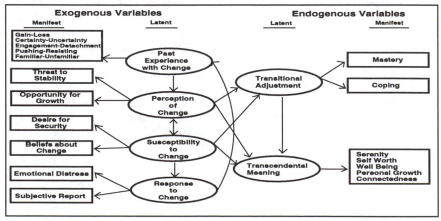

Table 10.4 Definitions of Terms

Uncertainty. Mischel (1990) defines uncertainty as "the inability to determine the (outcome) of illness-related events...because sufficient cues are lacking" (p. 256). Uncertainty implies that a situation is, in at least some aspect, vague and unpredictable; however, since consequences are by definition indeterminate, the situation need not arouse dread or desire.

Hardiness. Kobasa's (1979) construction is a complex motivating factor that moderates stress-illness events. Using an existential perspective, Kobasa views hardiness as a personality trait that enables persons to resolve conflict or to remain healthy in stressful situations. The hardiness construct includes three components: control, commitment and challenge.

Past experience with change. All individual and corporate involvements in the change process that precede a present encounter constitute experience with change.

Perception of change. The lens through which changes are viewed and interpreted describes the perception of change. The change process is experienced uniquely from various vantage points; thus, no singular view of a change should be accepted as absolute.

Susceptibility to change. Characterized as how amenable an individual is to change, susceptibility is roughly equivalent to Kobasa's (1979) concept of "challenge" or the conviction that the world is ever changing and that change, itself, offers exciting challenge for further development of the self.

Response to change. Change cannot be ascertained independent of the person(s) undergoing the change. No completely detached, objectified instrument can be devised to decipher the immediate and highly subjective response to change.

Transitional adjustment. A homeostatic resolve to maintain permanence and continuity during change based on theories of stress and adaptation (Antonovsky, 1979). This path of predictability includes the subconcepts of mastery and coping.

Transcendental meaning. This path of potentiality launches the will-to-power in transformative change which manifests as a jump, a discontinuity, or a paradigmatic shift. Transcendence inspires meaning and purpose in the change process known as human becoming.

the humanities. As nurses become more acutely aware of the incongruities inherent in quantifying the essence of human care and human becoming, they must be willing to tolerate the resistance of their peers while, at the same time, pushing for desired changes.

A growing cadre of nurses are persuaded that change can be a source of empowerment. In an editorial entitled "Inventing Ourselves Forward," Copp (1991) challenges nurses to take initiative for their own personal and professional lives. By deepening their commitment to change, acknowledging its universality and actively seeking transformation, nurses can create new possibilities for themselves and those entrusted to their care.

REFERENCES

Antonovsky, A. (1979). *Health stress and coping.* San Francisco, CA: Jossey-Bass.

Blalock, H.M. (1969). *Theory construction: From verbal to mathematical Formulations.* Englewood Cliffs, NJ: Prentice-Hall.

Brown, K. (1990). Managing change. *American Association of Occupational Health Nurses Journal, 38*(12), 586-587.

Carmack, B.J. (1992). Balancing engagement/detachment in AIDS-related multiple losses. *Image: Journal of Nursing Scholarship, 24*(1), 9-14.

Cashman, J. (1989). Effecting change through the stream analysis process. *Journal of Nursing Administration, 19*(5), 37-44.

Chinn, P.L. (1992). Where and when does change begin? *Nursing Outlook, 40*(3), 102-103.

Conger, M.M. (1992). Application of change theory to a clinical problem. *Nursing Management, 23*(10), 89-90.

Copp, L.A. (1991). Inventing ourselves forward. *Journal of Professional Nursing, 7*(1), 1.

Darwin, C. (1979). *The origin of species by mean of natural selection, or the preservation of favored races in the struggle for life.* NY: Avenel Books. (Original work published 1859).

Davidhizar, R., & Kuiper, J. (1989). How to plan and implement change. *Advancing Clinical Care, 4*(3), 38-39.

de Chardin, P.T. (1959). *The future of man* (N. Denny, Trans.). NY: Harper & Row.

DeFeo, D.J. (1990). Change: A central concern of nursing. *Nursing Science Quarterly, 3*(2), 88-94.

Durant, W. (1977). *The story of philosophy.* NY: Simon & Shuster.

Ferguson, M. (1980). *The aquarian conspiracy: Personal and social transformation in the 1980's.* Los Angeles, CA: J. P. Tarcher, Inc.

Folkman, S. (1982). An approach to the measurements of coping. *Journal of Occupational Behavior, 3,* 56-107.

Frankl, V. (1972). *Man's search for meaning.* NY: Simon and Schuster.

Frankl, V. (1966). Self-transcendence as a human phenomenon. *Journal of Humanistic Psychology, 6,* 97-106.

Garrett, J.E. (1987). Multiple losses in older adults. *Journal of Gerontological Nursing, 13*(8), 8-12.

Gibbs, J.P. (1972). *Sociological theory construction.* Hinsdale, IL: The Dryden Press, Inc.

Gleick, J. (1987). Chaos: Making of a new science. NY: Penquin Books, USA, Inc.

Haase, J.E., Britt, T., Coward, D.D., Leidy, N.K., & Penn, P.E. (1992). Simultaneous concept analysis of spiritual perspective, hope, acceptance and self-transcendence. *Image: Journal of Nursing Scholarship, 24*(2), 141-148.

Hahn, M. (1966). *California life goals evaluation schedule.* Palo Alto, CA: Western Psychological Services.

Hall, B.A. (1981). The change paradigm in nursing: Growth versus persistence. *Advances In Nursing Science, 3*(4), 1-6.

Hall, B.A. (1983). Toward an understanding of stability in nursing phenomena. *Advances in Nursing Science, 5*(1), 15-20.

Hegel, G.W.F. (1985). *Introduction to the lectures of the history of philosophy* (T.M. Knox & A.V. Miller, Trans.). Oxford: Clarendon Press. (Original work published 1833)

Jones, K., Kopjo, R., Goodner-Laff, L., & Weber, C. (1990). Gaining control in a changing environment. *Caring, 9*(7), 38-42.

Jones, P.S., & Martinson, I.M. (1992). The experience of bereavement in caregivers of family members with Alzheimer's disease. *Image: Journal of Nursing Scholarship, 24*(3), 172-176.

Jöreskog, K.G., & Sörbom, D. (1989). *LISREL 7: A guide to the program and applications (2nd ed.).* Chicago, IL: SPSS, Inc.

Kobasa, S.C. (1979). Stressful events, personality and health: An inquiry into hardiness. *Journal of Personality and Social Psychology, 37*(1), 1-11.

Koerner, J.G., Bunkers, S.S., & Nelson, Jr. (1991). Change: A professional challenge. *Nursing Administration Quarterly, 161*(1), 15-21.

Kuebler-Ross, E. (1969). *On death and dying.* NY: Macmillian Publishers.

Lewin, K. (1951). *Field theory in social science: Selected theoretical papers.* NY: Harper and Row.

Lifton, R. J. (1967). *Death in life: Survivors of Hiroshima.* NY: Random House.

Marris, P. (1984). *Loss and change.* London: Rutledge and Kegan Paul.

Marx, K. (1959). *Basic writings on politics and philosophy* (L.S. Fever, Trans. and Ed.). NY: Doubleday.

Mason-Hawkes, J., & Holm, K. (1989). Causal modeling: A comparison of path analysis and LISREL. *Nursing Research, 38*(5): 312-314.

Massey, P. (1991). Institutional loss: An examination of a bereavement reaction in 22 mental nurses losing their institution and moving into the community. *Journal of Advanced Nursing, 16,* 573-583.

McNair, D., Lorr, M., & Droppleman, L. (1971). *POMS manual for profile of mood states.* San Diego, CA: Educational and Industrial Testing Service.

Mischel, M.H. (1984). Perceived uncertainty and stress in illness. *Research in Nursing and Health, 7,* 163-171.

Mischel, M.H. (1988). Uncertainty in illness. *Image: Journal of Nursing Scholarship 20,* 225-232.

Mischel, M. (1990). Reconceptualization of the uncertainty in illness theory. *Image: Journal of Nursing Scholarship, 22*(4), 256-62.

Mischel, M.H., Padilla, G., Grant, M., & Sorenson, D.S. (1991). Uncertainty in illness theory: A replication of the mediating effects of mastery and coping. *Nursing Research, 40*(4), 236-240.

New King James Version of the Holy Bible. (1977). La Habra, CA: The Lockman Foundation.

Nietzsche, F. (1967). The will to power. (W. Kaufmann and R.J. Hollingsdale, Trans.). NY: Random House. (Original work published 1886).

Nietzsche, F.W. (1989). *Human, all too human* (M. Faber & S. Lehmann, Trans.). Lincoln: University of Nebraska Press. (Original work published in 1876)

Parse, R.R. (1981). *Man-living-health: A theory of nursing.* NY: Wiley & Sons.

Parse, R.R. (1987). Nursing science: Major paradigms, theories and critiques. Philadelphia, PA: W.B. Saunders.

Parse, R. R. (1992). Human becoming: Parse's theory of nursing. *Nursing Science Quarterly, 5*(1), 35-42.

Parse, R.R., Coyne, A., & Smith, M. (1985). *Nursing research: Qualitative methods.* Bowie, MD: Brady Communications.

Pearlin, L.I., & Schooler, C. (1978). The structure of coping. *Journal of Health and Social Behavior, 19,* 2-21.

Pearlman, D., & Takacs, G.J. (1990. The 10 stages of change. *Nursing Management, 21*(4), 33-38.

Pollock, S.E. (1989). The hardiness characteristic: A motivating factor in adaptation. *Advances in Nursing Science, 11*(2), 53-62.

Pollock, S.E., & Duffy, M.E. (1990). The health related hardiness scale: Development and psychometric analysis. *Nursing Research, 39,* 218-222.

Porras, J.I. (1987). *Stream analysis.* Reading, MA: Addison-Wesley.

Reed, P.G. (1991). Toward a nursing theory of self–transcendence: Deductive reformulation using developmental theories. *Advances in Nursing Science, 13* (4), 64-77.

Robinson J. (1991). Project 2000: The role of resistance in the process of professional growth. *Journal of Advanced Nursing, 16,* 820-824.

Schumacher, K.L., & Meleis, A.I. (1994). Transitions: A central concept in nursing. *Image: Journal of Nursing Scholarship, 26*(2), 119-127.

Smith, J. (1991). Changing traditional nursing home roles to nursing case management. *Journal of Gerontological Nursing, 17*(5), 32-39.

Steeves, R. H., & Kahn, D.L. (1987). Experience of meaning in suffering. *Image: Journal of Nursing Scholarship, 25*(3), 225-230.

Stinchcombe, A.L. (1968). *Constructing social theories.* NY: Harcourt, Brace & World.

Tartasky, D.S. (1993). Hardiness: Conceptual and methodological issues. *Image: Journal of Nursing Scholarship, 25*(3), 225-230.

Van den Berg, J. (1961). *The changing nature of man.* NY: W. W. Norton & Company.

Wagner, C. (1990). On the move. *Nursing Management, 23*(4), 76.

Watzlawick, P., Weakland, J., & Fisch, R. (1974). *Change: Principles of problem formation and problem resolution.* NY: W. W. Norton & Company.

Watzlawick, P. (1978). *The language of change: Elements of therapeutic communication.* NY: Basic Books.

Whitehead, A.N. (1925). *Science and the modern world.* London: Hogarth Press.

Wilber, K. (1983). *Eye to eye: The quest for the new paradigm.* NY: Anchor.

Toward a Theory of Experiential Mastery in Women with HIV Infection

Jennifer Gray

T he epidemic caused by the human immunodeficiency virus (HIV) radically alters the lives of those it touches, placing them at risk for maladaptive coping (Van Servellen, Nyamathi, & Mannion, 1989). Changes in the lives of AIDS (acquired immunodeficiency syndrome) patients intensify as the disease progresses. The life changes can potentiate a worsening physical condition and psychosocial difficulties (Derdiarian & Schobel, 1990) or the changes can challenge patients to "do well" despite the disease.

Persons who view themselves as doing well with AIDS have conceptualized the disease as a "manageable chronic illness or an opportunity for self-actualization" (Gloersen, Kendall, Gray, McConnell, Turner, & Lewkowicz, 1993, p. 47). Long-term survivors report that living with AIDS is a question of outlook (Gavzer, 1993), emphasizing the importance of psychosocial variables in "doing well" (Gloersen et al., 1993). They utilize health-promoting behaviors to fight the disease and transcend in the midst of illness.

What applications from the life experiences of long-term survivors can be made to persons with HIV infection? Can we as nurses promote an outlook in persons who are infected that will positively impact length and quality of life? Five theoretical explanations will be offered for the phenomenon of HIV-infected women experiencing lived well-being. The first three theoretical explanations will be the results of applying Stinchcombe's (1968) demographic, functional and historicist methods of theory construction. Blalock's (1969) and Gibb's (1972) methods of theory construction will be used for the fourth and fifth explanations. Each explanation will include a visual diagram and conclude with propositions.

CONCEPTUAL AND HISTORICAL CONTEXT

Contextual information is needed to understand theoretical explanations. To provide the conceptual context, definitions of three pertinent phenomena, i.e., spiritual perspective, well-being and mastery will be given. A description of the historical context places the discussion on a timeline within the phenomena.

Definitions of Spiritual Perspective, Well-Being and Mastery

Spiritual Perspective. Reality is primarily what we make it to be (Watzlawick, Beavin, & Jackson, 1967). A person develops a "generalized way of looking at the world, a way of perceiving stimuli" (Antonovsky, 1984, p.118). One's perspective creates possibilities and limitations of action (Omer, 1984).

Spiritual perspective is defined as an "integrating and creative energy based on belief in, and a feeling of interconnectedness with, a power greater than self" (Haase, Britt, Coward, Leidy, & Penn, 1992). The power greater than self may be God, a Higher Power, or other forces in nature. Connectedness, belief and creative energy are descriptive attributes of a spiritual perspective. The realization and development of these attributes results in purpose and meaning in life, guidance of values and self-transcendence (Haase et al., 1992).

Well-Being. The spiritual dimension is a unifying force that "plays a vital role in determining the state of well-being of the individual" (Banks, 1980, p. 210.) Well-being is the enduring, yet dynamic feeling that life is manageable. Antonovsky (1984) calls this feeling a sense of coherence. Roth (1988) describes well-being as a "way of being in the world" that is congruent with one's beliefs (p.153).

Mastery. Closely related to well-being is the concept of mastery. Younger (1991) defines mastery as a "human response to difficult or stressful circumstances in which competency, control, and dominion are gained over the experience of stress" (p. 81). Mastery implies a new level of functioning due to the development of new capabilities or reorganization of self that allows the person to transcend the difficulty of the experience. This new level of functioning facilitates an appraisal of the future as less-threatening.

HISTORICAL EVOLUTION OF THE PHENOMENON IN CONTEXT

The context for theorizing is the AIDS epidemic as it impacts women, spirituality in nursing and spirituality in the epidemic.

AIDS Epidemic. In 1981, medical attention was drawn to the incidence of specific strains of pneumonia and sarcoma in previously healthy homosexual men (Jones, Adinolfi, & Gallis, 1991). The HIV virus itself was identified in 1984. The occurrence of the disease in an already-networked group facilitated the eventual mobilization of social pressure for widespread testing and the development of new medications (Penney, 1991). Homosexual males were the primary risk group, but reports of the infection grew among IV drug users, minority women infected by bisexual partners or IV drug use and infants born to these women (Carson & Green, 1992). The link of HIV infection with homosexuality, then IV drug use and bisexual behaviors, led to the stigmatization of the disease (Smeltzer, 1992).

Women are the fastest growing segment of the AIDS population (Frick, 1992). In 1982, women comprised 6% of the AIDS population; by 1989, women comprised 11% of the AIDS population (Smeltzer, 1992). The number of HIV positive women in the world is expected to equal the number of HIV positive men by the end of the 1990s (Laurence, 1991). Women comprise 30 to 50% of the new patients in clinics in San Francisco and New York (Gorman, 1992).

Science and medicine have been slow to recognize that health care problems manifest themselves differently in men and women. This prevailing view of women's health delayed research and intervention efforts targeting women. Finally, in 1992, the National Institute for Health put out a major call for proposals addressing HIV infection in women (National Institutes of Health [NIH], 1992).

Spirituality in Nursing. Centuries ago nursing was a religious calling that emphasized the care of the sick. Social change exploded as industrialization, secularization and technological advances impacted history. The spirit was devalued in the scientific view of reality that was predominant. Nursing reflected the prevailing values of science and avoided mention of the spirit or spiritual care.

Spirituality has gradually become a popular topic of lay literature and open discussion. Nursing, following the movement of society, has begun to recognize the importance of meaning and spirituality in nursing the whole person (Dickinson, 1975). The spirit has been considered in nursing literature for twenty years (Sodestrom & Martinson, 1987) with spiritual distress being accepted as a nursing diagnosis in 1985. "Efforts to build empirical knowledge about the spiritual dimension in health have been gaining momentum during the last ten 10 years" (Reed, 1992, p. 349).

Spirituality in AIDS Epidemic. Confronting one's mortality forces the person with HIV infection to confront vital questions about the meaning of life (Belcher, Dettmore, & Holzemer, 1989). The existential issues may be complicated by "unresolved conflicts and concerns about life choices" (Carson, Soeken, Shanty, & Terry, 1990, p. 29). The spiritual nature of the disease is evident in the comments of long-term survivors who report participation in spiritual activities (Carson & Green, 1992).

Summary of Context. Historical trends have shaped the present and provide compelling evidence for an active role for nurses in the spiritual care of women with HIV infection. Whereas the HIV infection epidemic is increasing among women, whereas the disease has a spiritual component, and whereas nurses have a professional heritage grounded in spiritual care and advocacy, nurses are the logical and legitimate leaders to identify and implement interventions to promote well-being and mastery in women with HIV infection. What theoretical explanations can guide nursing interventions in this population? The first theoretical explanation was constructed using Stinchombe's demographic method and considers women who may achieve mastery, in the presence of HIV infection and substance abuse.

DEMOGRAPHIC EXPLANATION
Discussion

Analyzing the population proportion of HIV-infected women who achieve mastery is actually a problem of classifying the "population into categories that have different balances of causal forces operating to change individuals" (Stinchcombe, 1968, p. 78). In considering women with HIV infection and demographic variables, the writer noted that over half of the women with HIV infection were or are intravenous drug users (Butz et al., 1993). Women who have or are using IV drugs would be expected to have fewer coping mechanisms and be less likely to experience well-being after diagnosis. Thus, the causal forces toward mastery on women who had contacted the disease through IV drug use would be markedly different than the causal force on women who contacted the disease in other ways. The proportion achieving mastery in each group would be different. The difference in proportionality makes a closed demographic explanation of the phenomena a valuable tool (Stinchcombe, 1968) for implementing and evaluating specific interventions to change methods of transmission and coping. While the number of infected women is growing and suggests the open demographic method, the population can be conceptualized as closed with subgroups recruited from each other (Stinchcombe, 1968).

One way to deal with different proportions in different subgroups of the population is to conduct a transition rate analysis for each subgroup. Figure 11.1 gives a visual representation of the demographic explanation.

Figure 11.1 Mastery in Women with HIV Infection: IV Drug Users and Other–Infected Women Visual Diagram for Demographic Explanation*

	IV Drug Users ($_i$)	Other Infected ($_o$)
Mastery ($_m$)	↑ $q_m n_{si}$ ↓	↑ $q_{sm} n_{so}$ ↓
Struggle ($_s$)	$q_{ms} n_{mi}$ ↓	$q_{ms} n_{mo}$ ↓

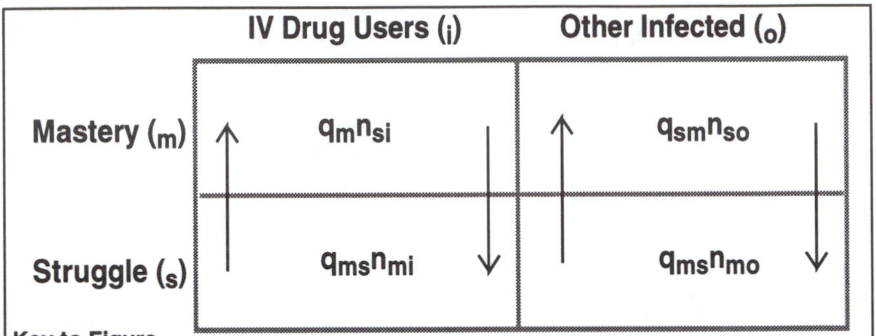

Key to Figure

N=women with HIV infection n_{mo}=mastery other-infected women
n_{mi}=mastery IV drug users q_{ms}=proportion of change from mastery to struggle
n_{si}=struggling IV drug users q_{sm}=proportion of change from struggle to mastery
n_{so}=struggling other-infected women

*Adapted from *Constructing Social Theories* by Arthur L. Stinchcombe, 1968, University of Chicago Press.

Description of Visual Diagram for Demographic Explanation

In a given time period, a proportion (q_{msi}) of women with HIV infection who are also IV drug abusers will move from mastery to struggle. A smaller proportion (q_{smi}) will achieve mastery. During the same time period, a proportion (q_{mso}) of women who were "other-infected" will move from mastery to struggle and a larger proportion (q_{smo}) will move from struggle to mastery.

The nurse researcher interested in this population could randomly sample women with HIV infection identifying the method of transmission and measuring the degree of mastery. Using the number of subjects in each group, the researcher could calculate the proportion of change for each group based on the following formula:

$$q_{ms}\, n_m = q_{sm}\, n_s$$

This formula is based on the principle of equifinality so that proportions of people in the groups tend to equilibrium even in the face of significant individual change (Stinchcombe, 1968).

Propositions from Demographic Explanation

One purpose of a "scientific model is to generate predictions about the empirical domain it represents" (Dubin, 1978, p. 159). Predictions take the form of propositions about the values of the units of the model. From the demographic explanation of women with HIV infection who are experiencing mastery, the following propositions can be stated:

1. A change in the causal force from struggling to mastery will have a greater impact on the number of masterful IV drug users than on the number of masterful other-infected women.

2. The number of women with HIV infection who are experiencing mastery is negatively related to the proportion of change from mastery to struggle.
3. The number of women with HIV infection who are struggling is negatively related to the proportion of change from struggle to mastery.

Stinchcombe also proposed a functional method for explaining phenomena such as women with HIV infection.

FUNCTIONAL EXPLANATION
Discussion

When the consequences of behavior are its principle cause, a functional explanation of cause is appropriate (Stinchcombe, 1968). Stinchcombe (1968) identifies the essential elements of a functional explanation to be a homeostatic variable, a structure with causal impact on the homeostatic variable, tensions that disturb the homeostatic variable and a causal process that causes the structure to be reinforced. The essential elements of a functional explanation among the population of interest are listed in Table 11.1.

Table 11.1 Essential Elements of Functional Explanations

Element	Application to Women with HIV Infection
Homeostatic Variable	Lived experience of well-being
Structure	Spiritual perspective
Tensions	Meaning/Personal investment
Causal Process	Uncertainty and Life events

The homeostatic variable is the lived experience of well-being. The structure causing this experience is the frame of reference by which the person determines meaning of life events, called one's spiritual perspective.

Meaning of life and meaning in life are produced by the spiritual perspective (Conrad, 1985; Dickinson, 1975; Forbis, 1988; Vastyn, 1986). Meaning in this functional explanation is viewed as an operator along with personal investment. The spiritual perspective with its resulting meaning and personal investment has been selected because of its consequence of modifying the value of the homeostatic variable, well-being, to compensate for variations induced by changes in uncertainty and life events (Stinchcombe, 1968).

The tensions that disturb the lived experience of well-being are uncertainty and life events. As the degree of lived well-being decreases, there is an increase in the causal process of focused personal investment. Personal investment is defined as a pattern of concentrated and consistent actions chosen by the person (Maehr & Braskamp, 1986). There is a negative correlation as personal investment attempts to return the life experience to a state of well-being via increasing the activity of the spiritual perspective.

Women with HIV infection have the additional tension of a life-threatening illness to increase their perception of uncertainty. Uncertainty is a common theme identified in qualitative studies of persons with HIV infection (Brown & Powell-Cope, 1991; Cowles & Rodgers, 1991; Hall, 1990; Nokes & Carver, 1991). Circumstances beyond one's control influence one's well-being (Ochs, 1983) and produce both fear and "aliveness."

The change in tension can be diagrammed as a source in order to study the effects of the changes on well-being. The H^1 can be conceptualized as mastery. Figure 11.2 illustrates the relationships between these essential elements.

Figure 11.2 Functional Explanation of Mastery in Women with HIV Infection*

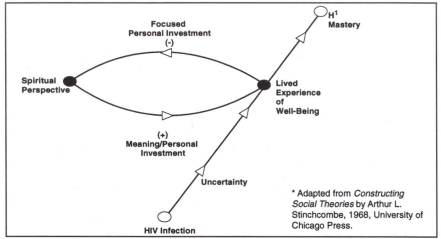

Stinchcombe's formula to express the effect of increased tension in the form of HIV infection on well-being can be used as an example. While recognizing the potential for measurement error obscuring the effects, the following formula was conceptualized:

$$\frac{R}{1-KC^2}$$

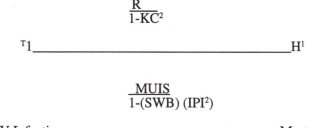

For this explanation, R would be a measurement of uncertainty, such as Mishel's Uncertainty in Illness Scale (MUIS) (Mishel, 1981). K is how effective the maintenance of the homeostatic variable, well-being, is as a selective cause. This could be measured by Ellison and Paloutzian's Spiritual Well-being Scale (Ellison, 1983; Ellison & Paloutzian, 1978). C^2 is the proportion of effect from spiritual perspective to well-being. This path was conceptualized to be meaning/personal investment. A modification of Maehr and Braskamp's instrument, Inventory of Personal Investment (IPI), could be used to measure C (Maehr & Braskamp, 1986). The product of the equation would be a measure of the impact that the change in tension had on the endpoint of mastery.

Propositions from Functional Explanation
Stinchcombe (1968) gives clear examples of propositions for functional explanations. Using his examples as a prototype, the following propositions are identified:

1. As the perception of uncertainty due to HIV infection increases, the experience of well-being decreases.
2. If uncertainty is high and mastery achieved, the value of focused personal investment has increased.
3. A high degree of spiritual perspective is related to mastery in the presence of high uncertainty.

HISTORICIST EXPLANATION
Discussion
The historicist explanation looks for a set of causes that at a given point in time established a pattern that continues to produce the same thing over time (Stinchcombe, 1968). In the case of spiritual perspective in women with HIV infection, the cause may be a conversion experience or a slower process of spiritual development.

Conversion experiences have been studied in relation to meaning and purpose in life (Paloutzian, 1991). The person is confronted with "perceiving themselves in relation to the whole of life" and have a need to complete the picture. The conversion experience is "adopting an encompassing world view" to complete the picture (Paloutzian, 1991, pp. 1153-1154). These religious and spiritual experiences play a formative role in the development of religious attitudes (Kass, Friedman, Leserman, Zuttermeister, & Benson, 1991).

Less dramatically, spiritual perspective can evolve from developmental processes. Intellect is a basic or inherent quality of human beings. Spirituality is also seen as a basic or inherent quality of human beings (Haase et al., 1992; Muldoon & King, 1991). Intellect is developed through the processes of mental stimulation. Spirituality is developed through spiritual stimulation. Processes that stimulate spiritual awareness, increase spiritual resources, and utilize spiritual skills foster spiritual development.

One of the outcomes of intellectual development is an increased awareness of one's intellectual capabilities. In the same way, one of the outcomes of spiritual development is an increased awareness of one's own spiritual perspective. How a person functions each day and rises to meet life's challenges is greatly influenced by the degree of intellectual development. Similarly, spiritual development will influence daily functioning and responses in times of crises.

Once present, the spiritual perspective tends to reproduce itself. "People become committed to what they are doing... in order to reduce cognitive dissonance" (Stinchcombe, 1968, p. 116). Investments are made in the structure that create self-generating resources (Stinchcombe, 1968) so that it is easier to maintain the spiritual perspective than it is to forsake it.

Description of Figure 11.3: Historicist Explanation
The conversion experience or the process of spiritual development estab-lishes a structure the writer calls spiritual perspective. This spiritual perspec-tive produces well-being. The meanings and personal investment that are the operators are reinforced by well-being to maintain the spiritual perspective.

Propositions from Historicist Explanation
From the discussion of the historicist explanation and the description of the diagram come these propositions.

Figure 11.3 Historicist Explanation for Well–Being in Women with HIV Infection*

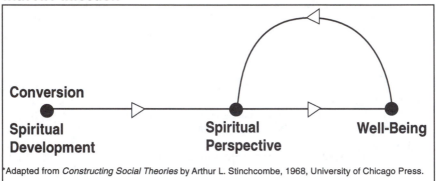

*Adapted from *Constructing Social Theories* by Arthur L. Stinchcombe, 1968, University of Chicago Press.

1. The history of a conversion is related to higher levels of well-being.
2. Commitment to a spiritual perspective over time is a sunk cost, in that the efforts to create the resource are no longer recoverable.
3. Spiritual perspective improves with use and tends to regenerate itself.
4. Personal investment activities improve with use and tend to regenerate them-selves.

BLALOCK'S METHOD OF THEORY CONSTRUCTION
The fourth theoretical explanation is based on Blalock's method of theory construction. A block non-recursive system of theory will be used to organize the variables and identify the interrelationships.

Since a very complex and intricate network of variable relationships is re-quired to explain experiential mastery, a preliminary analysis was needed to select the variables to be included in the model. One method for identifying variables is to consider theories-in-use (Zaltman, LeMasters, & Heffring, 1982). Persons who exemplify a desired outcome or characteristic are interviewed or observed to identify what "theory" they are using.   The writer analyzed qualitative studies, anecdotal reports, and research reports to identify clues as to why some persons do well and survive for long periods of time and others do not. These clues helped organize the abundance of stress and coping vari-ables into five blocks of variables to be included in the model. Table 11.2 displays the blocks and variables within each. The theoretical blocks and rela-tionships within the blocks will be described first. In the process of this description, each variable will be identified. The model of the system will then be presented followed by a detailed description of the phenomenon.

Theoretical Block of Demographic Variables

Description of Block. Demographic variables form an exogenous block that describes the life situation of the person with HIV infection. These variables impact the woman's ability to access internal and external resources to cope with the complexities of the disease. Age, education, socioeconomic status and social support are the identified variables.

Identification of Demographic Variables. Age refers to chronological age as an indicator of development. Education is the number of years completed in formal schooling, such as high school and college. The socio-economic

Table 11.2 Categories and Listing of Variables

Demographic Parameters	Disease in Mastery	Meaning	Personal Investment
Social Support	CD4 Counts	Health-Related Hardiness	Transformational Coping
Age	Opportunistic Infections	Spiritual Perspective	Problem-solving Coping
Education	HIV Counts		
Social-Economic Status		Sense of Mastery	Affect-Control Coping
		Uncertainty	
		Conflict	
		Situational Meaning	

status is an estimate of availability of financial resources to seek treatment and the treatment options available. Social support is the "perceived availability or enactment of helping behaviors by members of the social network" (Tilden, Nelson, & May, 1990, p. 338).

Relationships within the Block. Age (X_1), an exogenous variable, is related to education in that the longer one has been living the more opportunities one may have had to pursue an education. The relationship may actually be curvilinear with teens and those over 50 being the least likely to have completed formal schooling.

Education (X_2) has a positive relationship with socio-economic status (Pearlin & Schooler, 1978). In calculating socio-economic status for research purposes, the last completed year of education is included (Nam & Powers, 1983). Education also has a positive relationship with social support (Tilden et al., 1990). Socio-economic status (X_3) has a positive relationship with social

Figure 11.4 Demographic Variables*

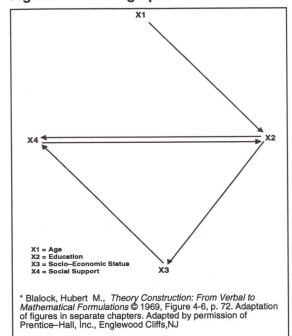

X1 = Age
X2 = Education
X3 = Socio-Economic Status
X4 = Social Support

* Blalock, Hubert M., *Theory Construction: From Verbal to Mathematical Formulations* © 1969, Figure 4-6, p. 72. Adaptation of figures in separate chapters. Adapted by permission of Prentice–Hall, Inc., Englewood Cliffs,NJ

support (Tilden et al., 1990). Social support (X_4) has a reciprocal relationship with education. A woman with social support is more likely to have remained in school or returned to school.

The Demographic Variable Block displays these relationships between variables. The loop formed by education, socio-economic status, and social support also has a pairwise reciprocation between social support and education (Blalock, 1969). Age is an exogenous variable impacting one variable (education) in the loop.

Theoretical Block of Disease Parameters

Description of Block. Disease parameters are the physiological and behavioral manifestations of the infectious process caused by the human immunodeficiency virus. The actual count of human immunodeficiency virus (HIV), the CD4 count and the number of opportunistic infections are the identified variables.

Identification of Disease Parameter Variables. The number of human immunodeficiency viruses present (X_5) is only indirectly measurable by the p24 antigen and reflects the virility of the infection. The more viruses present the more damage that has been done to the immune system.

The CD4 count (X_6) is the number of receptor sites available on the helper T-lymphocytes. The helper T-lymphocytes coordinate and stimulate the body's defense against infection. The HIV organisms actually take over the nucleus of the helper T-lymphocytes, severely compromising the immune system (McMillan, 1992).

As a result of this damage to the immune system, infections develop in the person with HIV infection. These secondary infections are called "opportunistic" infections (X_7) since they only develop when the immune system can no longer protect the body, giving them the opportunity to develop (Mikluscak-Cooper & Miller, 1991).

Relationships within the Block. The more HIV present, the lower the CD4 count will become. The lower the CD4 count, the more likely the person is to develop opportunistic infections. Opportunistic infections further inhibit and damage the immune system, causing additional decreases in the CD4 count.

More HIV can replicate since the immune system is even more compromised. The double pairwise reciprocal causation (Blalock, 1969) is shown in the Disease Parameter Block.

Theoretical Block of Meaning

Description of Meaning. Spiritual perspective is one of several variables that will determine situational meaning. Situational meaning is an outcome of one's perspective. Situational meaning is the individualized appraisal of the situation that will influence one's response. Other variables that have been identified include health-related hardiness, sense of mastery, uncertainty and conflict.

Figure 11.5 Disease Parameters*

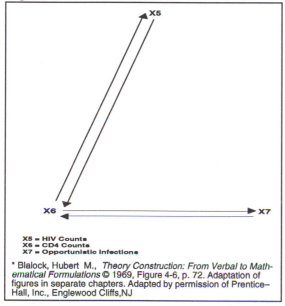

X5 = HIV Counts
X6 = CD4 Counts
X7 = Opportunistic Infections

* Blalock, Hubert M., *Theory Construction: From Verbal to Mathematical Formulations* © 1969, Figure 4-6, p. 72. Adaptation of figures in separate chapters. Adapted by permission of Prentice–Hall, Inc., Englewood Cliffs,NJ

Identification of Meaning Variables. Health-related hardiness (X_8) is described as a personality resource that buffers the negative effects of stress (Pollock & Duffy, 1990). The construct of health-related hardiness is composed of control, commitment, and challenge. Control is the "sense of mastery or self-confidence needed to appropriately appraise and interpret health stressors." Commitment is the "motivation and competence to effectively cope with the threat." The "reappraisal of the health stressor as stimulating and potentially beneficial" or as an opportunity for growth comprise the definition of challenge (Pollock & Duffy, 1990, p. 219).

Spiritual perspective (X_9) is the frame of reference consisting of beliefs and attitudes about connectedness and is an exogenous variable in this block. Spiritual well-being has been studied in persons with HIV infection (Carson, Soeken, Shanty, & Terry, 1990; Carson & Green, 1992) and found to be related to hope and hardiness. Spiritual perspective is a slightly differently construct strongly influenced by a new paradigm for studying spirituality (Haase et al., 1992). Connectedness is the substantive term of the new paradigm with spiritual perspective being a construct of transpersonal, interpersonal and intrapersonal connectedness (Gray, 1993).

Sense of mastery (X_{10}) is an affirmation of self as capable of overcoming a stressful situation. Uncertainty (X_{11}) is the "inability to determine the meaning of illness-related events" (Mishel, 1988, p. 225). Managing the uncertainty that accompanies a life-threatening, chronic illnesses is an essential task in adaptation (Mishel, 1988). Conflict (X_{12}) is defined as "perceived discord or stress in relationships caused by behaviors of others or the absence of behaviors of others" (Tilden et al., 1990, p. 338).

Situational meaning (X_{13}) is the appraisal made by the woman that will determine the type of personal investment that will be made in achieving mastery over the illness. The situational meaning is influenced by the interrelationships of the variables in the block.

Relationships within the Block. Within the block, there are two triads that have pairwise causation, with no loops and no reciprocation (Blalock, 1969). In the first triad, the variable acting on the other two is spiritual perspective. In the second triad, the variable acting on the other two is uncertainty. These two variables are exogenous to the others in the block. Uncertainty has a reciprocal causation relationship with conflict.

Figure 11.6 Meaning*

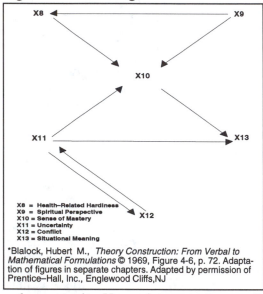

X8 = Health-Related Hardiness
X9 = Spiritual Perspective
X10 = Sense of Mastery
X11 = Uncertainty
X12 = Conflict
X13 = Situational Meaning

*Blalock, Hubert M., *Theory Construction: From Verbal to Mathematical Formulations* © 1969, Figure 4-6, p. 72. Adaptation of figures in separate chapters. Adapted by permission of Prentice-Hall, Inc., Englewood Cliffs,NJ

Spiritual perspective has a direct positive impact on health-related hardiness and sense of mastery. A woman with a high level of health-related hardiness will also have a high sense of mastery. Uncertainty and conflict will have a negative impact on the woman's perception of her ability to master the situation. Conflict in relationships has been shown to negatively impact mental health states (Pollock & Duffy, 1990).

The appraisal of situational meaning is heavily influenced by the presence of uncertainty. The presence of uncertainty has been linked to situational appraisals of danger and opportunity. Uncertainty as reconceptualized by Mishel (1990) can lead to personal growth as well as adaptation.

Theoretical Block of Personal Investment in Mastery

Description of Personal Investment in Mastery. Maehr and Braskamp (1986) state that meaning is the antecedent for personal investment. Personal investment in mastery is the energy and time given to coping with the infection and to growing through the resulting life changes. Three types of coping strategies impact experiential mastery.

Identification of Personal Investment Variables. Behaviors aimed at reducing or eliminating psychological distress or stressful situations are coping behaviors (Fleishman, 1984). The qualitative studies analyzed in the preliminary stages of theory construction yielded common themes describing three types of coping behaviors. Fighting to survive with HIV infection involved everyday and illness work (Gaskin & Brown, 1992). This type of coping was called problem solving (X_{15}). Problem-solving as a coping strategy in this block is taking action in response to a stressor that changes the stressor or the consequences of the stress. These behaviors include seeking social support, problem-solving, and accepting responsibility.

Figure 11.7 Personal Investment*

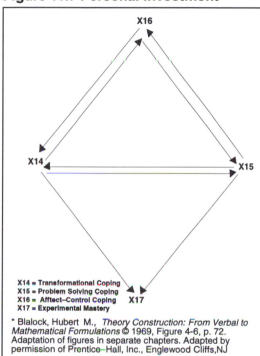

X16

X14

X15

X14 = Transformational Coping
X15 = Problem Solving Coping
X16 = Afftect–Control Coping   X17
X17 = Experimental Mastery

* Blalock, Hubert M., *Theory Construction: From Verbal to Mathematical Formulations* © 1969, Figure 4-6, p. 72. Adaptation of figures in separate chapters. Adapted by permission of Prentice–Hall, Inc., Englewood Cliffs,NJ

In qualitative studies with persons with HIV infection, changes in hopes and dreams led to setting new priorities and changing lifestyles (Gaskin & Brown, 1992; Hall, 1990; Nokes & Carter, 1991). Behaviors leading to these outcomes can be called transformational coping (X_{14}). Transformational coping is cognitively restructuring a stressor or attempting change through trying new behaviors in response to the stressor. These new behaviors include positive reappraisal, confrontive coping or growth-promoting.

Other behaviors are temporary solutions that decrease emotional distress but do not promote problem-solving or transformation. These behaviors can be called affect-control coping (X_{16}) and attempt to diminish emotional distress by avoidance or distancing.

Persons with HIV infection have demonstrated the ability to master their illness and experience well-being in the midst of illness. Personal accounts of transcendence and prolonged survival are well-documented. A person who is "beset with threatening circumstances and overcomes is tempered by the experience and emerges with greater strength and resilience" (Younger, 1991, p. 81). This experience of competency, control and dominion over stress is experiential mastery (X_{17}).

Relationships within the Block. Problem-solving coping, transformational coping and affect-control coping form a general three-variable model (Blalock, 1969). Positive relationships exist between each variable and the other two. To meet the condition of stability, the sum of the negative feedback must equal the sum of the positive relationships (Blalock, 1969). Problem-solving coping and transformative coping also have a relationship with experiential mastery. As either of these two types of coping increase, experiential mastery will also increase (Gloersen et al., 1993). Experiential mastery is described as acceptance, growth, change and certainty during and after stress (Younger, 1993).

Blalock Model of Experiential Mastery

When multiple relevant variables are involved in a complex phenomenon, blocking the variables organizes the variables and allows conceptual discrimination between different types of relationships (Schwirian, 1981). Recursive models display a process unique in space and time, without feedback. Experiential mastery has a feedback loop that clearly portrays the urgency of mastery research for this population. Experiential mastery has an impact on disease parameters (Mikluscak-Cooper & Miller, 1991). This feedback loop makes the model non-recursive. The relationships between the blocks will be described to complete the description of the phenomenon (see Figure 11.8).

Figure 11.8 Experimential Mastery in Women With HIV Infection*

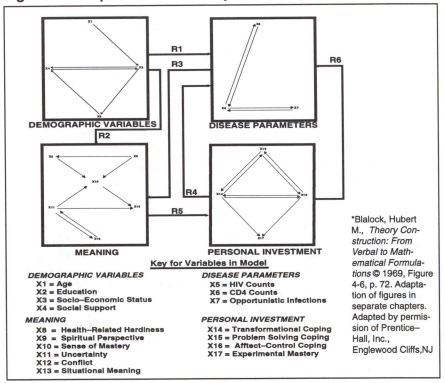

DEMOGRAPHIC VARIABLES
DISEASE PARAMETERS
MEANING
PERSONAL INVESTMENT

Key for Variables in Model

DEMOGRAPHIC VARIABLES
X1 = Age
X2 = Education
X3 = Socio–Economic Status
X4 = Social Support

MEANING
X8 = Health–Related Hardiness
X9 = Spiritual Perspective
X10 = Sense of Mastery
X11 = Uncertainty
X12 = Conflict
X13 = Situational Meaning

DISEASE PARAMETERS
X5 = HIV Counts
X6 = CD4 Counts
X7 = Opportunistic Infections

PERSONAL INVESTMENT
X14 = Transformational Coping
X15 = Problem Solving Coping
X16 = Afftect–Control Coping
X17 = Experimental Mastery

*Blalock, Hubert M., *Theory Construction: From Verbal to Mathematical Formulations* © 1969, Figure 4-6, p. 72. Adaptation of figures in separate chapters. Adapted by permission of Prentice–Hall, Inc., Englewood Cliffs, NJ

Impact of Demographic Block on Disease Block (R_1). Schwirian (1981) notes that variables within a block can have relationships with another block and the individual variables within the block. The age (X_1) of the woman has a relationship to the condition of the immune system. The age may also be an indirect indicator of how long a woman has been engaged in high-risk behaviors that may have led to the transmission of the virus. The more prolonged the exposure, the higher the HIV count (X_5) will be and the lower the CD4 count (X_6) may be. Education (X_2) as a demographic variable may influence how quickly a woman recognizes disease symptoms and seeks medical care, hopefully arresting the disease process.

Impact of Demographic Block on Meaning Block (R_2). Age (X_1) is believed to influence one's spiritual perspective (X_9) (Reed, 1992). Education (X_2) may influence the ability to use cognitive strategies in developing health-related hardiness.

Social support (X_4), another demographic variable, is considered to be an intervening variable in the appraisal of stress (Boyle, Grap, Younger, & Thornby, 1991). A lack of social support (X_3) would interfere with the interpersonal connectedness component of the spiritual perspective (X_9). Appropriate social support and education (X_2) have been linked to health-related hardiness (X_8)(Johnson-Saylor, 1991; Boyle et al., 1991). Socio-economic status (X_3) has been shown to influence one's sense of mastery (X_{10}). Age (X_1), education (X_2), social support (X_3) and socio-economic status (X_3) impact uncertainty (X_{11}), another meaning-block variable (Johnson-Saylor, 1991; Mishel, 1988; Nyamathi & Flaskerud, 1992). These relationships are a sampling of how the demographic-block variables impact the meaning block.

Impact of the Disease Block on the Meaning Block (R_3) Disease parameters influence meaning by providing the situational constraints and potentials with which the woman must deal. Maehr and Braskamp (1986) would theorize that the disease parameters shape meaning by impacting one's perceived options (health-related hardiness, X_8) and personal incentives (spiritual perspective, X_9). Uncertainty (X_{11}), one of the meaning variables is directly determined by the disease parameters (Mishel, 1990) since changes in the disease condition make it more difficult to predict outcomes, a component of uncertainty.

Impact of Disease Parameters on Personal Investment Block (R_4). The emotional response of the person dealing with physiological changes due to the HIV infection will impact the choice of coping strategies and the potential for mastery. The disease parameters are in effect the stressors to which the coping strategies are the response.

Impact of Meaning Block on Personal Investment Block(R_5). Maehr and Braskamp (1986) developed their theory on the proposition that meaning is the antecedent of personal investment. Several of the meaning variables have been linked to the coping strategies and to mastery, the variables in the personal investment block.

A spiritual perspective (X_9) impacts ones's ability to utilize transformational (X_{14}) and problem-oriented coping (X_{15}) (Dunkel-Schetter, Feinstein, Taylor, & Falke, 1992; Gavzer, 1993). High-level health-related hardiness (X_8) is related to problem-solving coping (Pollock, 1989) and low-level is related to affect-control coping (X_{16}) (Boyle et al., 1991). A sense of mastery (X_{10}) is related to problem-solving coping (Holahan & Moos, 1987). Uncertainty (X_{11}) and conflict (X_{12}) work against the defined components of mastery (X_{17}). A sense of mastery (X_{10}) and health-related hardiness (X_8) potentiate mastery (Gavzer, 1993).

Non-Recursive Relationship of Experiential Mastery on Disease Parameters (R_6). Gavzer (1993) advocates that mastery in the midst of HIV infection directly influences the disease parameters. Long-term survivors of HIV infection credit transformational coping and mastery to their victory over the disease. Mind states produced by problem solving and transformational coping help the immune system function better (Mikluscak-Cooper & Miller, 1991). Each statement about relationships within the blocks and between the blocks can be utilized as propositions for this theoretical explanation.

GIBBS' METHOD OF THEORY CONSTRUCTION

The last method of theory construction to be applied to the phenomenon of women doing well with HIV infection is Gibbs' method. Gibbs' paradigm of theory construction mandates that the theory include both extrinsic and intrinsic portions. Congruent with his views of causation, Gibbs proposes that relations between substantive terms be stated as either 'the greater X, the greater Y' or 'the greater X, the lesser Y'. To enhance a reader's understanding of the derivations of a theory, Gibbs (1972) proposes that a theorist use one type of relational term (p. 102). The relational term signifies the direction of the association between properties and predicts an ordinal difference (Gibbs, 1972). These principles will be used in constructing the last theoretical explanation.

Extrinsic Theory

Gibbs (1972) notes that the unit term, substantive terms, temporal quantifiers and formulas for referentials should be designated in the extrinsic part of the theory. The unit term is the class of events or things that is included in each intrinsic statement (p. 114). Substantive terms are words that designate properties of units (Gibbs, 1972, p. 122). Substantive terms may be as abstract as constructs and as empirically applicable as referentials. Temporal quantifiers refer to time and must be used with substantive terms to avoid ambiguity in theory construction. The formulas for the referentials are the last component of the extrinsic part of the theory. The formulas specify how values for each referential will be calculated (Gibbs, 1972, p. 132).

Unit Terms. The unit term in the theory of experiential mastery is the group of persons confronting life-threatening conditions. Younger (1991) notes that persons in difficult and stressful situations can find "a meaning and purpose in living that transcends the difficulty of the experience" (p. 81). The life-threatening condition of particular interest to the theorist is infection with the human immunodeficiency virus (HIV). The theory will be tested with a sample of women with HIV infection.

Substantive Terms. Constructs of experiential mastery. The theorist uses her own judgment to determine whether a phenomenon is a construct. Constructs may be defined but the definitions are not empirically applicable (Gibbs, 1972). Constructs are identified by double quotation marks. In reviewing mastery as an outcome of living with and coping with a life-threatening condition, the following constructs emerged : "personal resources," "network resources," "stressor," "appraisal" and "personal investment." These constructs are defined as follows:

1. "Personal resources": "personality characteristics that people draw upon to help them withstand the threats posed by events and objects in their environment" (Pearlin & Schooler, 1978. p. 5).
2. "Network resources": configuration of people available to the person undergoing stress.
3. "Stressor": life-strains or "structured social experiences that adversely penetrate people's emotional lives" (Pearlin & Schooler, 1978, p. 3).
4. "Appraisal": the individual's determination whether a "person-environment transaction is regarded as significant for well-being" and whether the transaction holds potential for loss, harm, mastery, or benefit (Folkman, Lazarus, Dunkel-Schetter, DeLongis, & Gruen, 1986, p. 993).

5. "Personal investment": the energy and time given to coping with the stressor and to growing through the resulting life changes. Maehr and Braskamp (1986) state that personal investment is impacted by situational factors.

Substantive Terms. Concepts of experiential mastery. Concepts are terms with "a designated property or relation between properties, with all other conceivable properties excluded" (Gibbs, 1972, p. 127). Concepts are identified by single quotation marks. The construct of "personal resources" has the two concepts of 'spiritual perspective' and 'health-related hardiness.' 'Social support' is the concept linked to the construct of "network resources." 'Pathology' is the concept limiting the construct of "stressor." The construct of "appraisal" is conceptualized as 'perceived opportunity'. "Personal investment" is linked to the concept of 'coping.' Definitions of the concepts are as follows:

1. 'Spiritual perspective': the frame of reference consisting of beliefs and attitudes about transpersonal, intrapersonal, and interpersonal connectedness (Haase et al., 1992).
2. 'Health-related hardiness': personality resource composed of control, commitment, and challenge that buffers the negative effects of stress (Pollock & Duffy, 1990).
3. 'Social support': "perceived availability or enactment of helping behaviors by members of the social network" (Tilden et al., 1990, p.338).
4. 'Pathology': physiological and behavioral manifestations of the infectious process caused by the human immunodeficiency virus.
5. 'Perceived opportunity': assignment of meaning to a situation that includes the possibility of positive outcomes (Mishel, 1988).

Table 11.3 Referential for Spiritual Perspective=TIIC: Transpersonal, Intrapersonal, and Interpersonal Connectedness

Referent	Subcomponents	Instrument to Measure
SWBSRS: Spiritual Well-Being Scale/Reciprocity Scale	Transpersonal Connectedness=Religious Well-Being Subscale of the SWBS. **Scores range from 1-60, with higher scores indicating higher religious well-being.**	Spiritual Well-Being Scale by Ellison and Paloutzian (1978).
	Intrapersonal Connectedness=Existential Well-Being Subscale of the SWBS. **Scores range from 1-60, with higher scores indicating higher existential well-being.**	Spiritual Well-Being Scale by Ellison and Paloutzian (1978).
	Reciprocity Subscale of the IPRI. **Scores range from 13-65, with higher scores indicating higher reciprocity.**	Interpersonal Relationship Index (IPRI) by Tildent, Nelson, and May (1990)

$$TIIC = 3X_1 + 2X_2 + X_3$$

where x_1 is religious well-being score (RWB), X_2 is existential well-being (EWB), and X_3 is the reciprocity subscale score. Of the three variables, RWB is seen as being the most important with EWB close behind. RS is important, but similar to social support that will be included in another equation. Consequently, it carries its normal weight in this equation.

Table 11.4 Referential for Health-Related Hardiness
HCCC: Health-Related Commitment, Challenge, and Control

Referent	Subcomponents	Instrument to Measure
HRHS Health-Related Hardiness Scale	HRHS: Commitment /Challenge (COCH) Subscale of the HRHS. **Scores range from 20 to 120 with higher scores indicating higher commitment and challenge in regards to health stressors.**	Health-Related Hardiness Scale by Pollock and Duffy (1990).
	HRHS: Control Subscale(CON) of the HRHS. **Scores range from 14 to 84 with higher scores indicating greater sense of locus of control in regards to health stressors.**	Health-Related Hardiness Scale by Pollock and Duffy (1990).

$$HCCC = X_4 + X_5$$

where X_3 is commitment/challenge score (COCH) and X_4 (CON) is control score on HRHS. COCH and CON are seen as equally contributing to HCCC.

Table 11.5 Referential for Social Support
PIPS: Referential of Interpersonal Support

Referent	Subcomponents	Instrument to Measure
IPRI Interpersonal Relationships Index	SSS: Perceived availability of help. **Score on the Social Support Scale of the Interpersonal Relationships Inventory (IPRI).**	Interpersonal Relationships Index by Tilden, Nelson, and May (1990)
	CF: Perceived discord in current relationships. **Score on the Conflict Scale of the Interpersonal Relationships Inventory (IPRI).**	Interpersonal Relationships Index by Tilden, Nelson, and May (1990)

$$RIPS = 2X_6 - X_7$$

where X_6 is social support scale score (SSS) and X_7 is conflict score (CF). Social support is seen as being crucial to experiencing mastery, but can be diminished by conflict.

6. 'Coping': "the person's constantly changing cognitive and behavioral effort to manage specific external and/or internal demands that are appraised as taxing or exceeding the person's resources" (Folkman et al., 1986, p. 993).

Referentials identified. Referentials are acronyms that identify formulas to be found in the extrinsic part of the theory (Gibbs, 1972). Tables 11.3-11.8 identify the referentials, referents and the instruments to measure the referents. Each table is followed by the formula for the referential.

Temporal Quantifiers. Designation of a substantive term is incomplete and ambiguous without reference to time (Gibbs, 1972). T_0 refers to any point in time when personal resources and network resources were developed. T_0, as a temporal quantifier, signifies a point in time that "need not and will not be the same for all units or all tests" (Gibbs, 1972, p. 157). $_0T_d$ is the time of diagno-

Table 11.6 Referential for Pathology
RHIVI: Referential of Human Immunodeficiency Virus Infection

Referent	Subcomponent	Instrument to Measure
CDMLO: Combined Scores on Physical Measures	CD4: Number of T-lymphocytes . **Values scored as follows: >1,000=1; 500-999=2; 200-499=3; 100-199=4;<100=5. Range 1-5.**	Laboratory measurement of lymphocytes in blood serum.
	MT: Mode of Transmission. **Data scored as follows: Partner of bisexual male=1; IV drug use=2; Blood products=3; Sex for pay=4; Combination of high-risks=5.**	Contact with HIV noted in patient's chart by physician and confirmed by woman.
	DI:Duration of Infection. **Actual number of months, range from 1 to 120.**	Months since the time the subject identifies as the likely beginning of exposure.
	LI: Length of Illness **Actual number of months from the date of first positive Western blot test documented on patient's chart, range from 1 to 120.**	Patient report of months since the first positive blood test for HIV, confirmed by chart review.
	OI:Opportunistic Infections. **Number of opportunistic infections documented in patient's chart since date of first positive Western blot test scored as the sums of different infections.**	Patient report of number of different opportunistic infections since diagnosis as being HIV positive, confirmed by chart review.

$$RHIVI= \frac{[X_9 X_{10} X_{11}] X_{12}}{X_8}$$

where X_8 is CD4 count, x_9 is mode of transmission (MT), X_{10} is duration of the infection (DI), X_{11} is length of illness (LI), and X_{12} is opportunistic infection (OI). Opportunistic infections are the strongest indicator of worsening pathology so that the product of three other indicators is raised by the power of the OI indicator. A low CD4 count indicates worsening pathology.

sis with the life-threatening condition. The placement of the T after the subscript 0 means that the diagnosis occurred after the development of the personal and network resources. T_{d+6} refers to the time six months after diagnosis, when personal investment will be measured. Figure 11.9 presents the schematic representation of the theory of experiential mastery.

In considering the theory of experiential mastery, the referentials have varying degrees of influence on mastery. The exogenous factors of spiritual perspective, health-related hardiness, and social support interact and together have a greater effect. Pathology (RHIVI) will diminish the energy available for coping and is found in the divisor of the equation. These internal and situational factors are weighted by multiplying by 3. The appraisal component is added as well as the coping strategies. Coping strategies are weighted more heavily than any other element, because of the belief that the person can always choose how to respond (Frankl, 1978).

Table 11.7 Referential for Perceived Opportunity
ODUR: Opportunity, Danger and Uncertainty Referential

Referent	Subcomponents	Instrument to Measure
MUISA:Mishel's Uncertainty in Illness Scale/ Appraisal Scale	MUIS: Mishel's Uncertainty in Illness Scale **Scores range from 34 to 170, with higher scores indicating greater uncertainty.**	Mishel's Uncertainty in Illness Scale (1981)
	A: Opportunity/Danger Ratio on Appraisal Scale. **Score on Opportunity Subscale over score on Danger Subscale.**	Appraisal Scale (Mishel and Sorenson, 1991)

$$ODUR = Y_1 Y_2$$

where Y_1 is the score on the Uncertainty Scale (MUIS) and Y_2 is the Opportunity/Danger Ratio (A). When the appraisal of opportunity exceeds that of danger, the overall appraisal is more positive. When the appraisal of danger exceeds that of opportunity, the overall appraisal is diminished.

Table 11.8 Referential for Coping
RCS: Referential of Coping Strategies

Referent	Subcomponent	Instrument to Measure
WOC Ways of Coping Scale	AFC: Affect-Control Coping Score. Number of behaviors that focus avoidance or distancing. *Sum of responses to items on the revised Ways of Coping Scale (WOC) that factor out as distancing and escape-avoidance.*	Ways of Coping Scale (Folkman and Lazarus, 1985)
	TC: Transformational Coping. Number of behaviors selected that focus on cognitive restructuring and trying new ways of being. *Sum of responses to items on the revised Ways of Coping Scale that factor out as positive reappraisal, confrontive coping, or growth-promoting.*	Ways of Coping Scale (Folkman and Lazarus, 1985)
	PSC: Problem-solving Coping. Number of behaviors selected that focus on positive action. *Sum of the responses to items on the revised Ways of Coping Scale that factor out as seeking social support, planful problem-solving, and accepting responsibility.*	Ways of Coping Scale (Folkman and Lazarus, 1985)

$$RCS = \frac{Y_4 Y_5}{Y_3}$$

where Y_3 is affect–control coping (AFC), Y_4 is transformational coping (TC) and Y_5 is problem–solving coping (PSC). The product of TC and PSC is diminished and AFC increases. Coping that contributes to experiential mastery is predominantly transformational and focused on solving problems.

Figure 11.9 Theory of Experiential Mastery

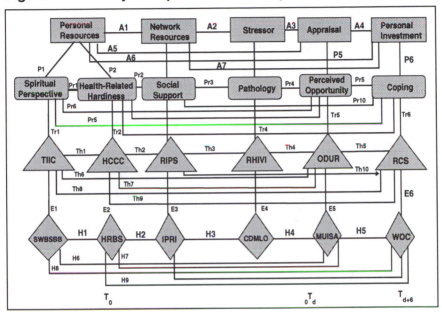

$$\text{Experiential Mastery} = 3 \frac{(\text{HCCC})\,(\text{RIPS})\,\text{THC}}{\text{RHIVI}} + \text{ODUR} + 5\,\text{RCS}$$

Intrinsic Theory

The relationships between the substantive terms are expressed as statements. Horizontal linkages are axioms, propositions, theorems and hypotheses. Axioms are statements linking constructs to constructs. A proposition links a concept to a concept, a theorem links a referential to a referential and a hypothesis links a referent to a referent. Vertical linkages are postulates, transformational statements and epistemic statements. A postulate links a construct with a concept, a transformational statement links a concept with a referential and an epistemic statement links a referential with a referent. The intrinsic part of the theory will be presented moving from the top of the schematic representation (abstract) to the bottom (empirical).

Axioms.

Axiom 1: Among persons confronted with life-threatening conditions, the greater the " personal resources at T_0", the greater the "network resources at T_0".

Axiom 2: Among persons confronted with life-threatening conditions, the greater the "network resources at T_0", the lesser the "stressor at $_0T_d$".

Axiom 3: Among persons confronted with life-threatening conditions, the greater the "stressor at $_0T_d$", the lesser the "appraisal at $_0T_d$" (Mishel, 1981).

Axiom 4: Among persons confronted with life-threatening conditions, the greater the "appraisal at $_0T_d$", the greater the "personal investment at T_{d+6}" (Maehr & Braskamp, 1986).

Axiom 5: Among persons confronted with life-threatening conditions, the greater the "personal resources at T_0", the greater the "appraisal at $_0T_d$" (Folkman, Lazarus, Gruen, & DeLongis, 1986).

Axiom 6: Among persons confronted with life-threatening conditions, the greater the "personal resources at T_0", the greater the "personal investment at T_{d+6}" (Holohan & Moos, 1987).

Axiom 7: Among persons confronted with life-threatening conditions, the greater the "network resources at T_0", the greater the "personal investment at T_{d+6}" (Holohan & Moos, 1987).

Postulates.

Postulate 1: Among persons confronted with life-threatening conditions, the greater the
" personal resources at T_0", the greater the 'spiritual perspective at T_0.'

Postulate 2: Among persons confronted with life-threatening conditions, the greater the
" personal resources at T_0", the greater the 'health-related hardiness at T_0.'

Postulate 3: Among persons confronted with life-threatening conditions, the greater the "network resources at T_0", the greater the 'social support at T_0.'

Postulate 4: Among persons confronted with life-threatening conditions, the greater the "stressor at $_0T_d$", the greater the 'pathology at $_0T_d$.'

Postulate 5: Among persons confronted with life-threatening conditions, the greater the "appraisal at $_0T_d$", the greater the 'perceived opportunity at $_0T_d$.'

Postulate 6: Among persons confronted with life-threatening conditions, the greater the "personal investment at T_{d+6}", the greater the 'coping at T_{d+6}.'

Propositions.

Proposition 1: Among persons confronted with life-threatening conditions, the greater the 'spiritual perspective at T_0', the greater the 'health-related hardiness at T_0'(Carson & Green,1992).

Proposition 2: Among persons confronted with life-threatening conditions, the greater the 'health-related hardiness at T_0', the greater the 'social support at T_0'.

Proposition 3: Among persons confronted with life-threatening conditions, the greater the 'social support at T_0', the lesser the 'pathology at $_0T_d$'.

Proposition 4: Among persons confronted with life-threatening conditions, the greater the 'pathology at $_0T_d$', the lesser the 'perceived opportunity at $_0T_d$'.

Proposition 5: Among persons confronted with life-threatening conditions, the greater the 'perceived opportunity at $_0T_d$', the greater the 'coping at T_{d+6}'.

Proposition 6: Among persons confronted with life-threatening conditions, the greater the 'spiritual perspective at T_0', the greater the 'perceived opportunity at $_0T_d$'.

Proposition 7: Among persons confronted with life-threatening conditions, the greater the 'health-related hardiness at T_0', the greater the 'perceived opportunity at $_0T_d$'.

Proposition 8: Among persons confronted with life-threatening conditions, the greater the 'spiritual perspective at T_0', the greater the 'coping at T_{d+6}'(Dunkel-Schetter, Feinstein, Taylor, & Falke, 1992).

Proposition 9: Among persons confronted with life-threatening conditions, the greater the 'health-related hardiness at T_0', the greater the 'coping at T_{d+6}'.

Proposition 10: Among persons confronted with life-threatening conditions, the greater the 'social support at T_0', the greater the 'coping at T_{d+6}' (Chiriboga, Jenkins, & Bailey, 1983).

Transformational Statements.

Transformational Statement 1: Among persons confronted with life-threatening conditions, the greater the 'spiritual perspective at T_0', the greater the TIIC at T_0.

Transformational Statement 2: Among persons confronted with life-threatening conditions, the greater the 'health-related hardiness at T_0', the greater the HCCC at T_0.

Transformational Statement 3: Among persons confronted with life-threatening conditions, the greater the 'social support at T_0', the greater the RIPS at T_0.

Transformational Statement 4: Among persons confronted with life-threatening conditions, the greater the 'pathology at $_0T_d$', the greater the RHIVI at $_0T_d$.

Transformational Statement 5: Among persons confronted with life-threatening conditions, the greater the 'perceived opportunity at $_0T_d$', the greater the ODUR at $_0T_d$.

Transformational Statement 6: Among persons confronted with life-threatening conditions, the greater the 'coping at T_{d+6}', the greater the WOCR at T_{d+6}.

Theorems.

Theorem 1: Among persons confronted with life-threatening conditions, the greater the TIIC at T_0, the greater the HCCC at T_0.

Theorem 2: Among persons confronted with life-threatening conditions, the greater the HCCC at T_0, the greater the RIPS at T_0.

Theorem 3: Among persons confronted with life-threatening conditions, the greater the RIPS at T_0, the lesser the RHIVI at $_0T_d$.

Theorem 4: Among persons confronted with life-threatening conditions, the greater the RHIVI at $_0T_d$, the lesser the ODUR at $_0T_d$.

Theorem 5: Among persons confronted with life-threatening conditions, the greater the ODUR at $_0T_d$, the greater the WOCR at T_{d+6}.

Theorem 6: Among persons confronted with life-threatening conditions, the greater the TIIC at T_0, the greater the ODUR at $_0T_d$.

Theorem 7: Among persons confronted with life-threatening conditions, the greater the HCCC at T_0, the greater the ODUR at $_0T_d$.

Theorem 8: Among persons confronted with life-threatening conditions, the greater the TIIC at T_0, the greater the WOCR at T_{d+6}.

Theorem 9: Among persons confronted with life-threatening conditions, the greater the HCCC at T_0, the greater the WOCR at T_{d+6}.

Theorem 10: Among persons confronted with life-threatening conditions, the greater the RIPS at T_0, the greater the WOCR at T_{d+6}.

Epistemic Statements.
Epistemic Statement 1: Among persons confronted with life-threatening conditions, the greater the TIIC at T_0, the greater the value of SWBSRS at T_0.
Epistemic Statement 2: Among persons confronted with life-threatening conditions, the greater the HCCC at T_0, the greater the value of HRHS at T_0.
Epistemic Statement 3: Among persons confronted with life-threatening conditions, the greater the RIPS at T_0, the greater the value of IPRI at T_0.
Epistemic Statement 4: Among persons confronted with life-threatening conditions, the greater the RHIVI at $_0T_d$, the greater the value of CMDLO at $_0T_d$.
Epistemic Statement 5: Among persons confronted with life-threatening conditions, the greater the ODUR at $_0T_d$, the greater the value of MUISA at $_0T_d$.
Epistemic Statement 6: Among persons confronted with life-threatening conditions, the greater the RCS at T_{d+6}, the greater the value of WOC at T_{d+6}.

Hypotheses.
Hypothesis 1: Among persons confronted with life-threatening conditions, the greater the value of SWBSRS at T_0, the greater the value of HRHS at T_0.
Hypothesis 2: Among persons confronted with life-threatening conditions, the greater the value of HRHS at T_0, the greater the value of IPRI at T_0.
Hypothesis 3: Among persons confronted with life-threatening conditions, the greater the value of IPRI at T_0, the lesser the value of CMDLO at $_0T_d$.
Hypothesis 4: Among persons confronted with life-threatening conditions, the greater the value of CMDLO at $_0T_d$, the lesser the value of MUISA at $_0T_d$.
Hypothesis 5: Among persons confronted with life-threatening conditions, the greater the value of MUISA at $_0T_d$, the greater the value of WOC at T_{d+6}.
Hypothesis 6: Among persons confronted with life-threatening conditions, the greater the value of SWBSRS at T_0, the greater the value of MUISA at oT_d.
Hypothesis 7: Among persons confronted with life-threatening conditions, the greater the value of HRHS at T_0, the greater the value of MUISA at $_0T_d$.
Hypothesis 8: Among persons confronted with life-threatening conditions, the greater the SWBSRS at T_0, the greater the value of WOC at T_{d+6}.
Hypothesis 9: Among persons confronted with life-threatening conditions, the greater the value of HRHS at T_0, the greater the value of WOC at T_{d+6}.
Hypothesis 10: Among persons confronted with life-threatening conditions, the greater the value of IPRI at T_0, the greater the value of WOC at T_{d+6}.

Testing the Gibbs Theoretical Explanation
Gibbs (1972) states that theory can be concisely and precisely stated using intrinsic statements. When stated precisely, theory can be tested. The epistemic statements and hypotheses would be used for testing of the theory. Complex models with multiple empirical indicators are likely to be difficult to test accurately due to measurement error. Linear structural equation models with unmeasured variables can be used to test theoretical propositions from such complex models (Hayduk, 1989; Herting, 1985).

CONCLUSION
Five possible theoretical explanations have been discussed for the phenomenon of women doing well with HIV infection. Theorists and researchers must quickly and assertively address the needs of this population. Nurses can facilitate mastery, and thereby, promote survivorship and quality of life.

Milluscak-Cooper and Miller (1991) summarized it well with the following words:

But even if the disease cannot be slowed down, living life in a fulfilling fashion, feeling good about yourself, and leaving your body in a peaceful way are worthwhile goals for all of us. How you think and how you feel are extremely important. They determine how you live as well as how you die. (p. 9)

REFERENCES

Antonovsky, A. (1984). The sense of coherence as a determinant of health. In R. D. Matarazzo, S. Weiss, J.A. Herd, & N. Miller (Eds.), *Behavioral health : A handbook of health enhancement and disease prevention* (pp.114-129). NY: John Wiley & Sons.

Banks, R. (1980). Health and the spiritual dimension: Relationships and implications for professional preparation programs. *Journal of School Health, 50,* 195-201.

Belcher, A. E., Dettmore, D., & Holzemer, S. P. (1989). Spirituality and sense of well-being in persons with AIDS. *Holistic Nursing Practice, 3* (4), 16-25.

Blalock, H. M. (1969). *Theory construction: From verbal to mathematical formulation.* Englewood, NJ: Prentice-Hall.

Boyle, A., Grap, M. J., Younger, J., & Thornby, D. (1991). Personality hardiness, ways of coping, social support, and burnout in critical care nurses. *Journal of Advanced Nursing, 16,* 850-857.

Brown, M.A., & Powell-Cope, G. M. (1991). AIDS family caregiving: Transitions through uncertainty. *Nursing Research, 40*(6), 338-345.

Butz, A. M., Hutton, J., Joyner, M., Vogelhut, J., Greenberg-Friedman, D., Schfeibeis, D., & Anderson, J. (1993). HIV-Infected women and infants: Social and health factors imnpeding utilization of health care. *Journal of Nurse-Midwifery, 38*(2), 103-109.

Carson, V. B., & Green, H. (1992). Spiritual well-being: A predictor of hardiness in patients with acquired immunodeficiency syndrome. *Journal of Professional Nursing, 8*(4), 209-220.

Carson, V., Soeken, K. L., Shanty, J., & Terry, J. (1990). Hope and spiritual well-being: Essentials for living with AIDS. *Perspectives in Psychiatric Care, 26,* 28-34.

Chiriboga, D. A., Jenkins, G., & Bailey, J. (1983). Stress and coping among hospice nurses: Test of an analytic model. *Nursing Research, 32,* 294-299.

Conrad, N. L.(1985). Spiritual support for the dying. *Nursing Clinics of North America, 20*(2), 415-426.

Cowles, K. V., & Rodgers, B. L. (1991). When a loved one has AIDS. *Journal of Psychosocial Nursing, 21*(4), 7-13.

Derdiarian, A. K., & Schnobel, D. (1990). Comprehensive assessment of AIDS patients using the behavioral systems model for nursing practice instrument. *Journal of Advanced Nursing, 15,* 436-446.

Dickinson, C. (1975). The search for spiritual meaning. *American Journal of Nursing, 75*(10), 178901794.

Dubin, R. (1978). *Theory building.* NY: Free Press.

Dunkel-Schetter, C., Feinstein, L. G., Taylor, S. E., & Falke, R. L. (1992). Patterns of coping with cancer. *Health Psychology, 11*(2), 79-87.

Ellison, C. W., & Paloutzian, R. F. (1978, August 29). *Assessing quality of life: Spiritual well-being and loneliness.* Paper presentation at the annual meeting of the American Psychological Association, Division 36, Toronto, Canada.

Fleishman, J. A. (1984). Personality characteristics and coping patterns. *Journal of Health and Social Behavior, 25,* 229-244.

Folkman, S., & Lazarus, R. S. (1985). If it changes it must be a process: Study of emotion and coping during three stages of a college examination. *Journal of Personality and Social Psychology, 48,* 150-170.

Folkman, S., Lazarus, R. S., Dunkel-Schetter, C., DeLongis, A., & Gruen, R. J. (1986).

Dynamics of a stressful encounter: Cognitive appraisal, coping, and encounter outcomes. *Journal of Personality and Social Psychology, 50,* 992-1003.

Folkman, S., Lazarus, R. S., Gruen, R. J., & DeLongis, A. (1986). Appraisal, coping, health status, and psychological symptoms. *Journal of Personality and Social Psychology, 50,* 571-579.

Forbis, P. A. (1988, May/June). Meeting patients' spiritual needs. *Geriatric Nursing,* 158-159.

Frankl, V. E. (1978). *The unheard cry for meaning: Psychotherapy and humanism.* NY: Simon and Schuster.

Frick, T. (1992, March/April). Women with HIV/AIDS: Dead but not disabled. *PAACNotes,* 66-67.

Gaskin, S., & Brown, K. (1992). Psychosocial responses among individuals with human immunodeficiency virus infection. *Applied Nursing Research, 5,* 111-121.

Gavzer, B. (1993, January 31). What keeps me alive. *Parade,* pp. 4-7.

Gibbs, J. P. (1972) *Sociological theory construction.* Hinsdale, IL: The Dryden Press, Inc.

Gloersen, B., Kendall, J., Gray, P., McConnell, J., Turner, J., & Lewkowicz, J. W. (1993). The phenomena of doing well in people with AIDS. *Western Journal of Nursing Research, 15*(1), 44-58.

Gorman, C. (1992, August 3). Invincible AIDS. *Time, 140*(5), pp. 30-34.

Gray, J.J. (1993). *Conceptual map of experiential mastery.* Unpublished manuscript. Texas Woman's University, Denton, TX.

Haase, J. E., Britt, T., Coward, D. D., Leidy, N. K., & Penn, P. E. (1992). Simultaneous concept analysis of spiritual perspective, hope, acceptance, and self-transcendence. *Image: Journal of Nursing Scholarship, 24,* 141-148.

Hall, B. A. (1990). The struggle of the diagnosed terminally ill person to maintain hope. *Nursing Science Quarterly, 3*(4), 177-184.

Hayduk, L. A. (1989). *Structural equation modeling with LISREL.* Baltimore, MD: John Hopkins University Press.

Herting, J. R. (1985). Multiple indicator models using LISREL. In H. M. Blalock (Ed.), *Causal models in the social sciences* (2nd ed.) (pp.263-319.) NY: Aldine Publishing.

Holahan, C. J., & Moos, R. H. (1987). Personal and contextual determinants of coping strategies. *Journal of Personality and Social Psychology, 52,* 946-955.

Johnson-Saylor, M. T. (1991). Psychosocial predictors of healthy behaviors in women. *Journal of Advanced Nursing, 16,* 1164-1171.

Jones, D., Adinolfi, A., & Gallis, H. A. (1991). Overview of HIV infection. In Glaxo, Inc. (Eds.), *Care of the patient with HIV infection* (2nd ed., pp. 1-66). Durham, NC: Clean-data, Inc.

Kaas, J. D., Friedman, R., Leserman, J., Zuttermeister, P. C., & Benson, H. (1991). Health outcomes and a new index of spiritual experience. *Journal for the Scientific Study of Religion, 30*(2), 203-211.

Laurence, L. (1991, June). The AIDS outrage: Doctors still don't believe women get AIDS. *Self,* 98-101.

Maehr, M. L., & Braskamp, L. A. (1986). *The motivation factor: A theory of personal investment.* Lexington, MA: D. C. Heath and Company.

McMillan, A. (1992). The human immunodeficiency virus. In C.Anderson & P. Wilkie (Eds.), *Reflective helping in HIV and AIDS* (pp. 33-48). Milton Keynes, EN: Open University Press.

Mikluscak-Cooper, C., & Miller, E. E. (1991). *Living in hope.* Berkeley, CA: Celestial Arts.

Mishel, M. H. (1981). The measurement of uncertainty in illness. *Nursing Research, 30,* 258-263.

Mishel, M. H. (1988). Uncertainty in illness. *Image: Journal of Nursing Scholarship, 20,* 225-232.

Mishel, M. H. (1990). Reconceptualization of the uncertainty in illness theory. *Image: Journal of Nursing Scholarship, 22,* 256-262..

Muldoon, M. H., & King, N. (1991). A spirituality for the long haul: Response to chronic illness. *Journal of Religion and Health, 30*(2), 99-108.

Nam, C. B., & Powers, M. G. (1983). *The socioeconomic approach to status measurement.* Houston, TX: Cap and Gown Press.

National Institutes of Health (1992). Women's interagency HIV study. *NIH Guide for Grants and Contracts, 21*(41), 10-14.

Nokes, K. M., & Carver, K. (1991). The meaning of living with AIDS: A study using Parse's Theory of Man-Living-Health. *Nursing Science Quarterly, 4,* 175-179.

Nyamathi, A., & Flaskerud, J. (1992). A community-based inventory of current concerns of impoverished homeless and drug-addicted minority women. *Research in Nursing and Health, 15,* 121-129.

Ochs, C. (1983). *Women and spirituality.* Totowa, NJ: Rowman and Allanheld.

Omer, H. (1984). Frames and symptoms: Some implications for strategic therapy. *Journal of Strategic and Systemic Therapies, 3*(2), 5-16.

Paloutzian, R. F.(1991). Purpose in life and value changes after conversion. *Journal of Personality and Social Psychology, 41*(6), 1153-1160.

Pearlin, L. I., & Schooler, C. (1978). The structure of coping. *Journal of Health and Social Behavior, 19,* 2-21.

Penney, A. (1991, June). A medical outrage. *Self,* 97.

Pollock, S. E. (1989). The hardiness characteristic: A motivating factor in adaptation. *Advances in Nursing Science, 11,* 53-62.

Pollock, S. E., & Duffy, M.E. (1990). The Health-Related Hardiness Scale: Development and psychometric analysis. *Nursing Research, 39,* 218-222.

Reed, P. G. (1992). An emerging paradigm for investigation of spirituality in nursing. *Research in Nursing and Health Care, 15,* 349-357.

Roth, P. D. (1988). Spiritual well-being and marital adjustment. *Journal of Psychology and Theology, 16*(2), 153-158.

Schwirian, P. M. (1981). Toward an explanatory model of nursing performance. *Nursing Research, 30,* 247-253.

Smeltzer, S. C. (1992). Women and AIDS: Sociopolitical issues. *Nursing Outlook, 40*(4), 152-157.

Sodestrom, K. E., & Martinson, I. M. (1987). Patients' spiritual coping strategies: A study of nurse and patient perspectives. *Oncology Nurse Forum, 14*(2), 41-46.

Stinchcombe, A. L. (1968). *Constructing social theories.* NY: Harcourt, Brace, and World.

Tilden, V. P., Nelson, C. A., & May, B. A. (1990). The IPR Inventory: Development and psychometric considerations. *Nursing Research, 39,* 337-343.

Van Servellen, G., Nyamathi, A. & Mannion, W. (1989). Coping with a crisis: Evaluating psychological risks of patients with AIDS. *Journal of Psychosocial Nursing, 27*(12), 16-21.

Vastyn, E. A. (1986). Spiritual aspects of the care of cancer patients. *CA-A Cancer Journal of Clinicians, 36*(2), 110-114.

Watzlawick, P., Beavin, J. H., & Jackson, D. D.(1967). *Pragmatic in human communication.* NY: W. W. Norton and Company.

Younger, J. B. (1991). A theory of mastery. *Advances in Nursing Science, 14,* 76-89.

Younger, J. B. (1993). Development and testing of the Mastery of Stress Instrument. *Nursing Research, 42,* 68-73.

Zaltman, G., LeMasters, K., & Heffring, M. (1982). *Theory construction in marketing: Some thoughts on thinking.* NY: John Wiley and Sons.

Considering Time in Theory and Research

Patti Hamilton

T he types of phenomena of interest to most social scientists are dynamic
processes embedded within evolving contexts. However, theories created
to understand these phenomena often depict static relationships among elements. Missing are theoretical representations of ways in which the direction,
strength and shape of the relations change over time. Without understanding
of the ways in which time influences relationships, researchers lack insight
into the effect of time on the variables measured and practitioners are ill equipped
to translate research findings into interventions in "real world" situations.

Take, for example, the relationship between patient education and adherence to treatment regimen. One might theorize that there is a positive relationship between these two variables. However, it is likely that the effect of education on behavior is neither instantaneous nor stable with regard to time. In
addition, the effect of education may "wear off" after a period of time. The
time interval between education and the adoption of new behavior and the
stability of effect are important theoretical issues with significant implications
for research and for the design of educational interventions.

A schema for examining dynamic relations was developed by Brinberg and
McGrath (1985) and may be of use to social science researchers and theorists
in analyzing theoretical relations. It points out quite clearly how time can
affect relations. The schema outlines ten features of relations to be considered
when planning research. These features include: presence or absence of theoretical relations between the variables "ij" along with the temporal order, logical order, direction of function, form of function, determinism versus
stochasticity and temporal stability of the ij relationship. In addition, antecedents of i in the ij relationship are considered as well as alternative antecedents
of j and moderator variables of the ij relations.

Using Brinberg and McGrath's schema, a researcher would first consider
the relations among variables to be investigated and describe the features of
those relations as they are theorized to be. Next, the investigator would determine whether the proposed study will provide information about the relations
as they are conceptualized and whether the subjects to be chosen provide opportunity to sample all relevant features of the relations.

An example of the Brinberg and McGrath validity schema applied to community health nursing research follows (see Figure 12.1). The researcher is
interested in determining the relationship between economic resources and
birth outcome in adolescent pregnancy. Economic resources would be measured by an array of indicators including income, living conditions and access
to health care. Birth outcome would be measured by birthweight, apgar at five
minutes and physical exam.

First, based on a literature review and clinical experience, the researcher
hypothesizes that *there is a relationship* between these variables. Next the
researcher considers the temporal order of this relationship. Economic re-

sources during pregnancy *come before* the birth outcome. The resources of interest may be the income of the parents of the adolescent, the income of the pregnant adolescent or that of the baby's father if the adolescent is married or living outside her parent's home. Likewise, the economic resources are thought to *lead to* the birth outcome, influencing the type of prenatal care received as well as the adolescent's nutrition and knowledge of good health practices, thus having an indirect causal affect on outcome.

The direction of the relationship might be hypothesized to be *positive*. In other words, as resources increase the quality of the birth outcome improves. The form of the relationship may be thought to be *nonlinear*. Nonlinear, as used here, refers to the notion that under certain circumstances the amount of change in the dependent variable may be out of proportion with change in the independent variable. In other words, outcomes may not improve in direct proportion to resources across all levels. At some levels of resources, slight increases greatly improve birth outcome while at other levels greatly increasing resources will yield no further improvement in outcome.

Deterministic relations are those that can be predicted with confidence when one has enough information about them. Stochastic relations are "unpredictable" in that similar conditions may produce different outcomes. Nurses often work with stochastic processes. Two people with the same chronic health conditions, living in similar circumstances, often differ in their responses to the condition. Two communities of similar size and resources may respond to the needs of their citizens differently. In this example, the relationship between resources and outcome is theorized to be *stochastic* in nature and may differ even between similar individuals.

Temporal stability concerns whether the relationship between resources and outcome will (a) remain the same, (b) fluctuate slightly or (c) change in variable or stable patterns over time. Birth outcome is not determined at the moment of delivery but is influenced by conditions across the pregnancy and even before conception. Therefore, the relationship between resources and outcome may *vary across time,* being more strongly correlated at one point than at another. Over time each feature of the relation between resources and outcome may vary. There may not be a significant observable relation between resources and outcome when resources and outcome are measured only at time of delivery. The relationship may only be detectable when resources are measured within three months of conception and outcome is measured at time of delivery. Temporal order may have relevance only when speaking of the first pregnancy. For example, a young woman giving birth to her first child may be setting in motion a spiral of diminishing resources which affects each subsequent birth outcome in a non-recursive manner. Resources become especially strained when the birth outcome of a pregnancy is poor, requiring prolonged hospitalization and expensive hospital care. The next pregnancy will likely be affected by the lower level of resources and may be at greater risk than the first pregnancy for a poor outcome. Therefore, the theoretical propositions regarding resources and outcome may be poorly representative of actual experience unless the influence of time and evolving processes are considered.

The final characteristics of the ij relationship include the extra-effect relations between i and j. These effects are often the basis of rival hypotheses according to Cook and Campbell (1979) as well as the auxiliary conditions

Figure 12.1 Model of Relation Between Resources and Birth Outcome

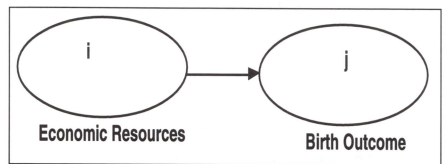

described by Blalock (1969). Certain antecedents of ij may alter the relationship. For example, life experiences, previous pregnancies and physical maturity of the young women can alter the ij relation by *preceding* it. The presence of needed services in a community will likely *moderate* the link between economic resources and birth outcome. The ij relation in communities in which services are readily available and accessible will differ from the ij relation in communities in which services are scarce resources. Finally, there are *antecedents* to birth outcome other than economic resources. Genetic conditions, substance abuse and overall health of the mother all contribute to birth outcome regardless of the ij relation.

These extra-effect relations are the features which a researcher hopes to control when conducting a study. One way to control for these relations is to use certain characteristics as control variables. Age of the adolescent could be controlled by holding it constant or by using it as a covariate in analysis. Moderator variables could be added to regression equations or used as grouping variables in ANOVA. Alternative antecedents to the ij relation might be added to path analysis diagrams and investigated through regression and residual analysis. Through careful planning, adequate data collection and appropriate analysis these threats to validity can be addressed in most studies. (See Chapter 15 for a more thorough discussion of the benefits of structural equation modeling for these types of analyses.)

TIME AS A CONFOUNDING VARIABLE

There is a more subtle and ubiquitous threat to understanding the "true" relation between variables that cannot be addressed by analysis techniques alone but is made explicit in Brinberg and McGrath's schema. This threat is the underlying effect of time on the nature of the relation of interest.

Features of Brinberg and McGrath's schema that are directly related to time are temporal order, logical order, direction and form of the relation, determinism versus stochasticism and temporal stability. In order to gain insight into these features a researcher will incorporate some strategy for sampling over time.

To investigate temporal and logical order between variables at least two strategies are used. First, and probably most common is the strategy in which subjects are sampled once on the variables of interest. The data are then analyzed using a correlation technique or path analysis in which proposed causal pathways are evaluated. The effects of time or sequence of events is inferred from the findings. The second strategy is less common and involves a longitudinal approach with measurement of variables on a number of occasions. In the example of the relationship between economic resources and birth outcome, a researcher might follow a cohort of young women with varying amounts of resources who are matched on other background characteristics. There might be multiple measures on the variable "resources" and only one observation of outcome at the time of birth. Of course, outcome could be measured after birth as well, yielding information about the predictive strength of birth weight, apgar, etc., for later well being of the infant.

Multiple measures of the independent variable(s), when based on sound theoretical planning, can enable the researcher to explore the form, direction, stochasticism/determinism and temporal stability of the relationship of interest. The researcher's conclusions about the form of the relation between resources and birth outcome are sensitive to the timing of analysis of that relation. For instance, if subjects' economic resources were measured weekly during pregnancy it is likely that there would be variation in the level of resources over the period. Eligibility for public assistance changes with pregnancy and living arrangements may be altered due to marriage, discord in the family or other circumstances. The level of economic resources during the period of interest will not remain constant. In addition, it is reasonable to theorize that there are 'critical periods' for maximum effect of resources on birth outcome. One of the periods may be the years immediately preceding conception while another critical point may be during the first trimester of pregnancy. Therefore, decisions must be made by the researcher about the timing of observations and the effect of that timing on conclusions drawn about form, direction, stochasticism/determinism and temporal stability of the relationship. The complexity of relationship between economic resources and birth outcome becomes much more evident when time is introduced into conceptualization and methodologies.

Research questions about the relationship between economic resources and birth outcome rest on underlying assumptions about the causal process that links economic resources to birth outcome. It is unlikely that a researcher conceptualizes the effect of economic resources on birth outcome to occur precisely at the time of birth. It is more likely that there is a hypothesized causal process which takes time to evolve. In addition, if the relation is non-linear one cannot measure at one level of resources and extrapolate a relation with outcome at other levels.

Sampling resources and comparing them to birth outcome at time of birth could lead to different conclusions for research and intervention depending on the 'true' underlying relationship between the variables. For example, the relation between resources and outcome may be one that rises slowly over the range of resources, reaching maximum correlation at high levels of resources. Or another case might be one in which the relation between resources and outcome is exponential in that small increases in resources have increasing correlation with improved outcome. Or yet another case may be that resources have a limited effect on outcome which is reached at relatively low levels of resources and adding more resources beyond that point yields no further increase in outcome. Of course there is another complicating factor in which the accumulation of effects across time may cloud the changing relationship. For example, the effects of early deprivation followed by increased resources may differ qualitatively from a situation in which resources were adequate at conception but then declined across the pregnancy. The effects of these two patterns may differ even when the total amount of resources across the pregnancy are equal in both cases.

The way to gain maximum insight into the form and direction of the relation between resources and outcome is to make multiple observations over a number of levels of the independent variable. As mentioned earlier, the young woman's access to economic resources varies across time. Therefore, the researcher would benefit greatly from theoretical direction regarding the form of the relation under scrutiny as well as the way the relation changes across time. Knowledge of the optimum times for observations rests on theoretical and clinical insight into the phenomena and the causal process.

Another feature of the relation is its deterministic or stochastic nature. A deterministic relation between economic resources and birth outcome would most resemble Figure 12.2a. In these types of processes the causal relation leads to outcomes that are predictable. Complex, fluctuating processes that cannot be predicted are said to be stochastic. They are likely to be dependent on factors outside the ij relation or on feedback among the variables making the output difficult to anticipate. These complex interactions make any but the most local and short term prediction of the outcome impossible. What is possible in stochastic processes is to determine an array of outcomes that can occur and the probability of each based on past experience. Without observations over time the researcher cannot begin to unravel the tangled relations they represent.

Temporal stability of the causal process cannot be assessed without multiple observations and the appropriate timing of those observations is necessary to gain knowledge regarding the temporal stability of a relation.

TIME-RELATED PROBLEMS WITH CURRENT CONCEPTUALIZATIONS, DESIGN AND METHODS
Conceptualizations

It is likely in the life sciences that the relation under study is non-recursive or circular. Few resources may lead to poor outcome but poor outcome might also result in high health care expenses and diminished resources for the next pregnancy. However, often the researcher is only concerned with the "snapshot" picture of the relation and will either overlook the feedback loop or change the model to represent the non-recursive nature of the relation. Until recently there were few approaches to addressing the problem of non-recursiveness in causal models. Blalock (1969) proposed a non-recursive block system in which blocks of relations could contain non-recursive links but the blocks themselves were recursive. The blocks were arranged hierarchically and assumptions were made about which variables were endogenous and which were exogenous. Each variable could not be related to all other variables as this would cause problems with model identification and make unique solutions of the simultaneous equations impossible. Blalock's system did provide for solutions of the equations describing the model but did so by adding exogenous variables to the model, not by considering time as a variable.

Our conceptualizations about relations are often limited by the constraints of the statistical methods we plan to use in analysis. For example, as a part of exploratory data analysis researchers examine the form and direction of a relationship. These forms have definite implications for subsequent analysis of the strength of the relations. When distributions are non-normal or bivariate relations are not linear the researcher transforms individual variables in order to meet the statistical assumptions of specific statistical analyses. This process of transformation is necessary for confidence in the statistical outcomes but may mask important features of the 'true' nature of the relations.

Assumptions about error in the process under investigation are also addressed in deciding which statistical tests are appropriate and what conclusions may be drawn from them. Error is assumed to be random and uncorrelated among variables. Error is also assumed to be separate from the relations of interests and its removal will not affect the conclusions drawn. These assumptions about error are necessary for interpretation of statistical findings; however, they may greatly over- simplify the complexity of the phenomena to be studied.

Designs and Methods

Common research strategies employed in nursing research currently include descriptive studies which are usually cross sectional, predictive studies using regression and/or path analysis and, for intervention studies, ANOVA (using gain scores or repeated measures), or ANCOVA and pre test scores used as covariates. The descriptive studies are most often one-time-only observations and the intervention studies use primarily single pre-test/single post test designs. Nursing research infrequently includes longitudinal studies or studies that measure the dependent variable on more than one occasion prior to the intervention and more than once following the intervention.

There are numerous threats to validity of the commonly used designs for measurement over time in nursing research. The paired t-test is perhaps the most problematic. The detection of change is limited with this design because it is assumed that any change would be linear and there is no means for discovering the process of change over the time period. ANCOVA is another often used analysis technique; however, meeting all the assumptions of this method is often impossible. The two most important assumptions of ANCOVA are:

1. homogeneity of within group regressions and
2. homogeneity of variances of the adjusted scores.

These assumptions are violated many times in intervention studies when the regression slopes are not constant across the intervention group and variances are higher in the treatment group, if the treatment causes change (Abraham & Neundorfer, 1990). With ANOVA-RM (repeated measures) it is assumed that each observation is paired with a specific treatment. If this is not the case, independence of error components in each observation cannot be assumed. Also, correlations among observations at different time points may not be uniform if treatments do not precede each observation, violating the assumption of equality of population correlation coefficients (Abraham & Neundorfer, 1990).

In addition to these threats in three of our most common methods of analyzing change in intervention studies there are threats to internal validity in the timing of our observations. Observations need to coincide with the optimal time for the causal process to occur. Limiting our research to single observation designs, even when pre-test post-test strategies are included results in serious limitations in our ability to gain knowledge of the complex relations between variables of interest. In order to gain information about the effect of time on relations, multiple samplings over time are called for. Kelly and McGrath (1988) suggest that the time interval between the variables be long enough to allow:

a. just enough time for causal processes to operate to their fullest;
b. but not so much time that some of it is empty of the operation of the causal process;
c. and not so much time that some other system forces have begun to operate so as to counter the causal forces under study; and
d. Finally, not so much time that the effects of the cause will have begun to wane (p. 47).

Knowledge of these time intervals will require systematic investigation and should precede predictive studies and intervention evaluations. Without accurate knowledge of the effect of time on the processes under investigation conclusions drawn from even the most rigorous studies are suspect.

Figure 12.2 Three Types of Relationships Between Variables

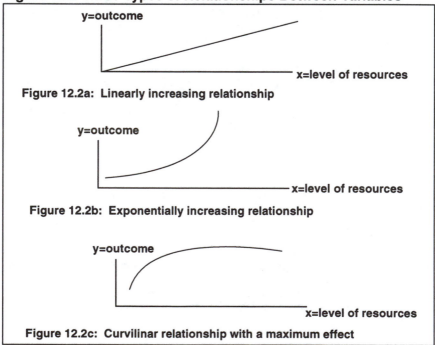

Figure 12.2a: Linearly increasing relationship

Figure 12.2b: Exponentially increasing relationship

Figure 12.2c: Curvilinar relationship with a maximum effect

AN ARGUMENT FOR THREE DIMENSIONAL THEORIES

I argue here for serious consideration of the effect of time on the relations of interest to nurse researchers. The models we use to represent dynamic relations among variables do so through simplifying assumptions which can distort or poorly depict 'reality'. The designs most often used in nursing research are inadequate to untangle the complex relations studied. Therefore, these designs limit generalizability of findings into 'real-world' contexts in which time is a significant factor. The need is great for relevant nursing research. One strategy for enhancing the relevance of our findings is to include time in our conceptualizations and methodologies.

WHAT WOULD THREE-DIMENSIONAL THEORY LOOK LIKE?

Below are examples of different forms of relations which may apply to the example of resources and birth outcome. They *do not* represent the influence of time of these relations over time but are static in nature.

Figure 12.2a illustrates a relation in which a unit change in resources in a positive direction is associated with a unit change in birth outcome in the same direction. This monotonic relationship continues over the range of resources. Figure 12.2b illustrates a positive relationship in which incremental small in-

Figure 12.3 Three Dimensional Relationship Between Two Variables

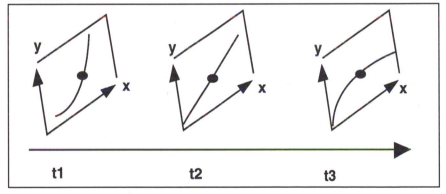

creases in resources have a small effect on outcome at first but then as resources continue to increase the effect on outcome becomes much greater and continues to increase without limit. Figure 12.2c depicts a positive relationship in which small increases in resources have slowly increasing positive influences on outcome until a limit or cap an effect is reached. At that point, adding more resources no longer has an increasing effect on outcome. This model is a bit more complex in that there is an upper limit to the process.

In each of the models above, time is ignored and only the bivariate relationship is depicted. But what if the relation is dependent on time? As an example, a model of resources and outcome is presented below with the addition of time as a third variable or third dimension. The figure illustrates that the shape of the relation can, and often does, change over time.

When time is introduced into a model as a third dimension, the complexity of the relation becomes more clear.

The shape and direction of the relation changes over time. Thus, time enters the model as a third dimension in a bivariate relation. The research implications of these changes include the necessity for sound theoretical rationale for the timing of observations. In addition, data transformation for linearity can mask the underlying complexity of the changing relation. The implications for interventions based on research of this phenomenon are extremely important. Targeting optimal times for interventions can be much more effective if the underlying process is understood. Increasing resources may have no effect, moderate effect or great effect depending on the timing of the intervention.

The first is the deterministic time–dependent covariates such as the day of the week, or clock time, calendar time or any function of time that is prespecified. The second classified group are the stochastic covariates that are generated by a stochastic mechanism external to the process that is studied. An example would be changes or fluctuations in student fees which may change the behavior of a person but which themselves are not influenced by the behavior. These types of covariates are called exogenous. The last type consist of stochastic covariates that are generated by a stochastic mechanism internal to the process being studied. These types of covariates are called endogenous. There are no specified conceptual problems with the first type of covariates. To overcome conceptual problems following the selection of a problem for conceptualization in the second and third types see Petersen (1995). Structural equation modeling may be considered as one method of data analysis, especially with large sample sizes.

SUMMARY

A full explication of the features of relations within a theory is necessary to guide the researcher in designing appropriate studies. However, the relations among variables cannot be fully understood without the addition of the effect of time on each. Because of the changing nature of the phenomena of interest to nurse researchers there is great need for theories which reflect the complexity encountered in the every day world. The application of research findings will take place in this every day world and will be only as relevant as the underlying theory. What is being argued for here is an expansion of current theory construction and application to include time as an influencing variable.

The inclusion of time in theory construction and application will necessitate implementing longitudinal designs. Time series and more advanced forms of dynamic analysis will need to be added to current ANOVA and regression techniques so common in nursing research. At the very least researchers would include the effect of time on research variables in disclosure of the assumptions and limitations of their studies.

REFERENCES

Abraham, I., & Neundorfer, M. (1990). *Advancing theory for nursing science through research.* Newbury Park, CA: Sage.

Allison, P.D. (1989). *Event history analysis.* Newbury Park, Sage Publications.

Allison, P.D. (1994). Using panel data to estimate the effects of events. *Sociological Methods & Research, 23*(2): 174-199.

Blalock, H. (1969). *Theory construction: From verbal to mathematical formulations.* Englewood Cliffs, NJ: Prentice-Hall.

Brinberg, D., & McGrath, J. (1985). *Validity and the research process.* Newbury Park, CA: Sage.

Browne, M.W., & Arminger, G. (1995). Specification estimation of mean and covariance structure models. In *Handbook for Statistical Modeling for the Social and Behavioral Sciences..* Editors G. Arminger, C.C. Clogg & M.E. Sobel. NY: Plenum Press.

Cook, D.T., & Campbell,D.T. (1979). *Quasi-experimentation: design and analysis issues for field settings.* Chicago: Rand McNally.

Cryer, J.D. (1986). *Time series analysis..* Boston: Duxbury.

Gibbs, J. (1972). *Sociological theory construction.* Hinsdale, IL: The Dryden Press, Inc.

Hsiao, C. (1995). Panel analysis for metric data. In *Handbook for Statistical Modeling for the Social and Behavioral Sciences..* Editors G. Arminger, C.C. Clogg & M.E. Sobel. NY: Plenum Press.

Kalbfleisch, J.D., & Prentice, R.L. (1980). *The statistical analysis of future time data.* NY: Wiley.

Kelly, J., & McGrath, J. (1988). *On time and method.* Newbury Park, CA: Sage.

McLaughlin, F.E., & Marascuilo, L.A. (1990). *Advanced nursing and health care research.* Philadelphia, PA: W.B. Saunders Co.

Pedhazur, E.J., & Schmelkin, L.P. (1991). *Measurement, design and analysis: An integrated approach.* Hillsdale, NJ: Lawrence Erlbaum Assoc.

Peterson, T. (1995). Analysis of event histories. In *Handbook for Statistical Modeling for the Social and Behavioral Sciences..* Editors G. Arminger, C.C. Clogg & M.E. Sobel. NY: Plenum Press.

Rao.C.R. (1958) Some Statistical Methods for Comparison of Growth Curves, *Biometrika, 14,* 1-17.

Stinchecombe,A.L. (1968). *Constructing Social Theories.* NY: Harcourt, Brace & World.

Tucker, L.R. (1958). Determinants of parameters of a functional relation by factor analysis. *Psychometrika.* 23, 19-23.

Part Three
Foundations and Methods of Theory Testing

Multivariate Analysis in Model Testing

Sally Northam and David Marshall

This chapter reviews multivariate analysis including what it is, what research questions it answers, what the statistical assumptions are for its use and what the computer output for a regression SPSS equation means. Multivariate analysis involves multiple independent variables as a "team" and examines their influence on a single dependent variable.

FUNDAMENTALS OF MULTIVARIATE ANALYSIS

A theorist determines the statistical technique used to analyze a model based on (a) the number of independent and dependent variables in the model; (b) the nature of the relationship among variables - continuous or discrete, linear or non-linear and (c) the determination of independent variable covariance (Tabachnick & Fidell, 1989; Pedhazur & Pedhazur, 1991). Multivariate analysis enables the scientist to examine relationships among variables simultaneously rather than examining two variables at a time (bivariate analysis). Multivariate analysis affords more realistic vantages on variable contributions within a model because the variance is less likely to be overstated when the independent variables are "teamed" to explain variance in the dependent variable rather than using simple correlations one by one. Multivariate analysis produces results which show the strength of relationship between a dependent variable and a cluster of independent variables, and the nature of the cluster itself. The ability to interpret a positive or negative correlation, or to interpret a factor analysis can be transferred to interpreting the cluster of independent variables revealed by multivariate analysis. The cluster score given by the multivariate analysis is a model of the dependent variable. A "good" model will correlate nicely with the dependent variable, or more generally, good models are well related with the actual phenomenon being studied. "Poor" models, ill-defined clusters of independent variables, will correlate weakly with the dependent variable.

Multivariate analysis is a technique of choice when a quantitative dependent variable is to be correlated with a set of independent variables containing quantitative variables or a mixture of quantitative and group indicator variables. An illustration of this with an example will follow later in the chapter.

Multiple regression is an appropriate statistical analytic procedure in research situations seeking to understand the impact of a number of independent variables on one dependent variable. Thus, it is appropriate for model testing when the model involves multiple independent variables and a single dependent variable. In modeling, the theorist proposes a schema of multiple causation involving a number of variables that impact the outcome variable. Regression analyses utilize correlations (termed betas in the regression testing) to look for significant relationships after which independent and dependent variables are plotted in the line of best fit. Prediction is then possible about the population based on the sample.

A simple correlation is a single number ranging from -1.0 to +1.0 that expresses the relationship between two variables. The absolute *size* of the correlation indicates the *strength* of the relationship between two variables, and the *sign* of the correlation reveals the way in which score values on the variables tend to go together or occur *simultaneously*. Regression utilizes correlations (betas) of independent variables to predict scores on a dependent variable. This prediction line is generated using the Least Squares Theory. The Least Squares Theory is a mathematical generation of a straight line equation determined so that the sum of the squared prediction errors for all observations is as small as possible. The general equation of a straight line is:

$$y = bx + a$$

where y = the criterion (dependent) variable
     b = the slope of the line = how many units of change in Y occur with every change in X
     x = the predictor (independent) variable
     a = the Y intercept of the line = where the regression line crosses the Y axis.

The determination of this regression formula utilizing Least Squares Theory is stated in terms of likelihood for prediction purposes. Utilizing the Principles of Maximum Likelihood, the scientist determines a probability value that findings similar to the sample set are likely in the population. Such generalization is frequently the goal of the researcher. Researchers want to study a sample and thereby know more about the population typified by the sample. Tantamount to sound generalization is utilization of an adequate sample.

Multiple regression, then, is a multivariate statistical technique used to examine the independent and cumulative effects of independent variables on one dependent variable. It answers research questions that deal with relationships among variables. The statistic is suited to model testing when the model is a simple one with clear directional theorems. (Multidirectional models with multiple dependent variables are better tested utilizing LISREL which expands insight into the variables and allows variables to be interdependent.) Multiple regression is not recommended as the only technique for model testing. The utilization of a number of statistical techniques in model testing augments insight into research questions much like looking at a landscape from different angles. Without the use of different statistical techniques, the researcher may miss important relationships, especially non-linear ones. Multiple regression examines for linear relationships among the independent variables and the dependent variable. If a line of best fit, based on the principle of least squares, is possible such that the majority of scores fall close to the line then the findings are significant and predictive of the population. Non-significant findings do not mean that the data is not valuable. Rather, nonsignificance means that there is no readily apparent linear relationship. There may be a non-linear relationship such as a curvilinear relationship. Scatterplots enable researchers to visually examine the spread of scores. If scores show homoscedasticity but are not linear other statistical techniques should be used to test the relationship. Unfortunately, many research studies utilize only linear testing and report nonsignificant relationships among variables when non-linear testing would have shown significant nonlinear relationships.

Multiple regression is an analysis of multiple variables and their contribution to one criterion (dependent) variable. Thus, it examines relationships among variables. In real life situations researchers know that rarely can a single independent variable be isolated as the sole influence on the dependent variable. Rather multiple factors generally influence a dependent variable. If a researcher does not study and express the contributions of the important independent variables on the dependent variables the research report is viewed skeptically and the variance contribution that a single variable makes on the outcome variable will likely be overstated leading to false impressions and misinformation. Thus multiple regression is a more powerful statistical test than simple correlations. Both correlations (such as Pearson's Product Moment Correlations) and multiple regression examine relationships of variables. Simple correlations allow a researcher to look at relationships between two variables at a time (bivariate analysis). Multiple regression allows a researcher to look at more than one independent variable at a time. In other words, is one variable correlated with several others working together as a "team" in typifying the ways in which people score on the dependent variable? Is there a discernible pattern in the ways people score on the dependent variable *and* simultaneously on the independent variables?

ASSUMPTIONS REGARDING THE USE OF MULTIPLE REGRESSION

Multiple regression is a *parametric statistic*. Parametric statistics presuppose that (a) the population is normally distributed, (b) variables are interval or ratio level, (c) a linear relationship exists and (d) variables have no multicollinearity. Representative samples drawn from a normally distributed population can be expected to have the majority of scores fall around the mean. Much of research utilizes the calculation of means and standard deviations. The mean is the mathematical average determined by dividing the sum of scores by the number of scores. The standard deviation mathematically averages the variability of scores away from the mean.

Sometimes samples are described as normally distributed, which means that half of the sample have scores higher than the mean and half of the scores fall below the mean. The majority of scores will fall within three standard deviations above and below the mean. Sixty eight percent of the population, and representative samples, have scores that fall one standard deviation above and below the mean. Another 13.6% have scores that lie in the area between one and two standard deviations from the mean and only a very small 2% will have scores greater than 3 standard deviations above and below the mean. Representative samples from normally distributed populations supply the researcher with statistics that the researcher can believe are 'true' of the population. This enables a researcher to gain insight into populations without trying to study each member of the population. Such insight fosters generalization.

Parametric statistics also stipulate that variables are measured on an *interval* or *ratio* level. Interval level variables are continuous variables incapable of having a zero value. Ratio level variables are continuous variables that may have a zero value. Both interval and ratio level variables have equal intervals between scores. Less emphasis is currently placed on the importance of this parametric rule, however, and dummy coding is frequently utilized to enable researchers to utilize multiple regression on lower ordinal (and sometimes, nominal) variables.

Regression analyses enable a researcher to *predict* population outcomes utilizing information generated from the sample. These analyses are based on a formula that plots sample data and examines for a linear relationship between independent and dependent variables. If a *linear* relationship exists the findings are significant and the multiple regression formula inserts a line in the sample data termed the line of best fit based on the Least Squares Theory. The majority of scores will fall close to the line. Those scores that fall far away from this line of best fit are termed outliers and they increase the residual. If our line of best fit is capable of being plotted such that most scores fall around the line we have been able to explain variance. (That means we have arrived at an equation that we feel we can utilize to predict scores in the population.) *Variance* is the change in the dependent variable that we can predict when we know the independent variable. In the case of multiple regression, a "team" of variables are utilized to explain change (variance) in the dependent variable. "For the most part, variance within a set of scores for a group of individuals occurs because different persons manifest different amounts of the attribute of interest" (Waltz, Strickland, & Lenz, 1991, p. 101).

For example, in situations involving hypercholesterolemia, researchers want to understand and predict the likelihood that the individual will develop heart disease. Researchers understand, however, that other variables must be taken into account such as age, sex and blood pressure. Regression is utilized to explain the variance in heart disease that is explained by these different variables. By summing variance (utilizing R^2) researchers strive to eventually explain as much about heart disease as possible. The part of heart disease that remains unexplained is termed the residual. The findings are significant if the p value obtained from the sample data elucidates a significant linear relationship and findings are not so random as to be unapplicable in generalizing to the population.

The sum of multiple simple correlations is not equal to the variance obtained utilizing multiple regression. Regression analyses can reveal shared variance among variables while minimizing the likelihood that explained variance will be overstated or inflated. If we added simple correlations we could conceivably exceed 100%. Regression analyses do not allow for this overstatement. Variance can be compared to a pie that is to be sliced into pieces. The total pie represents the dependent variable, for example, heart disease. Each variable studied will get a slice of the pie. That slice of pie represents a portion of the total pie and is expressed as a percent of the whole. If four independent variables (hypercholesterolemia, age, sex and blood pressure) are studied each would explain a portion of heart disease. There would remain a portion of heart disease that was unexplained (also referred to as error variance or residual). The researcher's goal is to explain as much about heart disease as possible. However, studying too many variables is like trying to slice a pie into too many slices. Each variable will explain little and is likely to be insignificant. The more variables studied the smaller the slice of the variance pie can be for each variable. A key role of the researcher is to thoughtfully plan the research study to include the most significant variables but not study too many variables and end up with nonsignificant findings that cannot be generalized to the population.

A fourth rule for utilizing multiple regression is that variables have no *multicollinearity* which means that the variables are interrelated. A key role for the researcher is to *select variables that overlap as little as possible.* Sex and age have no overlap and therefore have no multicollinearity. Hypercholesterolemia and blood pressure do have some overlap. That means the variables are interrelated. This is termed 'multicollinearity'. A researcher may decide that the conceptual framework supports that little overlap exists and the variables are too important to exclude one. If hypercholesterolemia explains a significant portion of the variance and is entered in the equation first it is likely that blood pressure will have less opportunity to explain variance because some of the variance was 'used up' in explaining hypercholesterolemia. If a significant portion of explained variance is found upon statistical analyses after blood pressure is entered, however, the researcher can state that the finding supports the unicollinearity of the variables and the lack of much shared variance. (The use of LISREL would be appropriate in situations where important variables had overlap and the conceptual framework of the research would not allow the elimination of the variable.)

Variance is influenced by the order of entry of variables into the computer equation. As in most statistical testing the initial variable entered in the equation has the greatest opportunity to 'use up' the variance and leaves less variance for remaining variables. Therefore, it is important that the researcher thoughtfully determine variable entry based on theory rather than allow the computer to control variable entry. Such computer control enhances the likelihood that sample dependent differences (that is, differences amplified in the sample that might not be typical of the population) will cause the computer to enter variables based on the sample and not based on theory that is felt grounded in the population attributes important to enable generalization. Further discussion of SPSS analysis using multiple regression will be presented shortly. This discussion of assumptions and variable entry order is included here to remind the reader that the value of the output is influenced by how well the assumptions are adhered to. It is not uncommon for some violation of the assumptions to occur, but thoughtful analysis of the schema of the research and the data must occur so that the researcher is insightful into the alternate explanations for findings other than the hypothesis being tested. That is, don't be too quick to believe that the significance or nonsignificance reported on the computer output answers the research question. Be sure to thoughtfully determine what assumptions may not have been met that could have impacted the results.

In summary, multivariate analysis (multiple regression) tests for relationships and reports that significant or nonsignificant results are found in the tested sample. This analysis leads a researcher to make research assumptions based upon the report of significance. The researcher must understand that the assumptions underlying the analysis are (a) the sample and population are normally distributed, (b) the variables are interval or ratio level, (c) the statistical technique only evaluates the presence of a linear relationship among the independent and dependent variables and (d) no multicollinearity of variables exists.

AN EXAMPLE OF MULTIVARIATE ANALYSIS AND EXAMINATION OF SPSS OUTPUT FOR REGRESSION

Multivariate analysis is a technique of choice when a quantitative dependent variable is to be correlated with a set of independent variables containing quantitative (interval or ratio level) variables or a mixture of quantitative and group indicator (nominal or ordinal level) variables. When group indicator variables are used, special coding is generally used to enable the researcher to examine and compare groups. Such coding is termed "dummy coding". Consider this example: systolic blood pressure is the dependent variable and sex, amount of weekly exercise and marital status are the set of independent variables. Sex, exercise and the indicator variables for marital status (dummy coded) were used as potential explanatory variables, with no guarantee that any of them would prove statistically or substantively significant. Marital group indicator variables were used because MARSTAT variable is multi-level nominal.

Table 13.1 Multiple correlation of systolic blood pressure with sex, exercise and marital status

VARIABLE	B	SE B	Beta	T	p
Exercise	-2.774	1.309	-.139	-2.119	.0353
Married	12.977	2.853	.304	4.547	.0001
Widowed	21.951	5.014	.296	4.378	.0001
Constant	130.133	3.962		32.847	.0001

R = .43, R^2 = .18, Adj-R^2 = .17, SE=19.37, F (3,217)=16.41, p<.0001

Examination of Table 13.1 shows a moderate correlation between systolic blood pressure and the combination of variables including exercise, being married and being widowed as reported on the SPSS printout. The multiple correlation coefficient is R=.43, which is nothing more than the Pearson correlation (r) between the dependent variable and the score on the cluster of independent variables. Notice that sex is not included as a significant part of the final correlation pattern, nor are the two remaining marital group indicator variables. Multiple regression can select a subset of all potential predictors, and leave some out which do not contribute to the increase in R.

Focusing on the figures under the label beta will conclude the interpretation of Table 13.1. Ignore the *size* of the Beta number. Only note the sign. A negative sign suggests that a high dependent variable score is paired with a low predictor score, and vice versa. A positive sign suggests that a high dependent variable score goes with a high score on the predictor variable. Marital status was "dummy coded". Dummy coding is a method of examining low level variables (nominal or ordinal) level variables by entering them in the computer data list by "assigning" them a number. An individual who is married receives a "1" for that variable. That same individual receives a "0" for the next variable of widowed. Thus "1" signifies membership in that group and "0" indicates membership in some other group. An individual who is widowed receives a "1" for widowed and a "0" for the married variable. This coding process enables the researcher to examine the influence of a variable such as marital status by looking at the subgroups of marital status. It produces a methodology for examining a variable that the researcher believes 'fits' into the model and is important in the conceptual framework, while overcoming the assumption that variables should be interval or ratio level in order to be statistically analyzed using multivariate analysis.

High systolic blood pressure accrues to people who do not exercise and are either married or widowed. Lower blood pressure accrues to all subjects who exercise and are in any other three categories of marital status (divorced, separated, never married), that is, are not either married or widowed. The strength of the relationship is revealed in R, while *nature of the cluster* is revealed in the *signs of the Beta figures*. Recall that a negative sign indicates a low score on one variable goes with a high score on the other. Positive signs indicate that high scores go together, and so do low scores on the two variables.

Low scores on exercise indicate no weekly exercise. High scores on indicator variables such as Married or Widowed register membership *in* those groups. The negative Beta for exercise, and positive Betas on being Married and being Widowed, are the basis for the assertion that being either Married *or* Widowed (one cannot be both) and not exercising go with high systolic blood pressure. What then goes with low systolic blood pressure?

The sizes of the Beta values (not the signs) indicate the relative importance of the included predictor variables. The Betas are standardized versions of the B values; the Beta mean is zero and its standard deviation is one. Unlike the B values, which are based on raw variable scores with varying means and standard deviations (generally, different 'ranges' on the variables), the Beta values can be compared in absolute size in determining which predictor contributes the most or the least to the value of R. The Beta values for Being Married and Being Widowed are each .30 (rounded to two places), suggesting that these categories of marital status are equally important in typifying systolic blood pressure, and over twice as impactful as the Exercise variable, having a Beta of .139 (ignoring its negative sign).

The presentation table contains essential elements which will all be defined later. However, it is apparent how simple the interpretation can be when focusing on *R*, the correlation between the dependent variable and the score on the cluster of independent variables, and on the signs of the *Beta* figures alone.

SPSS REGRESSION

The general program statements to perform multiple regression with SPSS utilizing the stepwise technique are given below:

Regression variables = names of dependent and independent variables

    / Criteria = Pin(.05) Pout (.051)
    / Dependent =
    / Stepwise =

The Variables = subcommand provides the names of the dependent and all the independent variables.

The Criteria = subcommand will include a variable in the correlation if its contribution is statistically significant at $p \leq .05$, and will remove an included variable if its significance level climbs above .05 during the stepwise correlation process.

The Dependent = subcommand is used to specify the name of the dependent variable.

The Stepwise = subcommand specifies the names of the independent variables. STEPWISE also provides a common approach to multivariate analysis when exploratory analysis is being done. The stepwise approach to multivariate analysis builds a result one variable at a time, or one step at a time; adding independent variables to the correlation one at a time if they increase the correlation in a statistically significant manner. STEPWISE regression does have the shortcoming of being influenced by sample dependent results, and is especially subject to error when small samples are utilized. Variable order entry is influenced by the strength of the relationship between the independent and dependent variables beginning with the independent variable that has the strongest relationship. It is appropriate for a researcher to utilize an alternate regression technique (FORWARD or HIERARCHICAL) whereby the order of variable entry is based on the theory regarding the population rather than sample dependent findings. This exploratory data analysis enhances insight into the data and forces the researcher to examine both sample results and the original theorized relationship among variables. To its credit, STEPWISE methodology with large samples elucidates what exists and allows the researcher less opportunity to manipulate the data. In model testing with large samples, STEPWISE facilitates insight into 'true' relationships among variables and enhances insight into the validity of the model.

CRITERIA = POUT (.051) removes a variable after a given step if it has become "non-significant" at that point.

Example

The SPSS REGRESSION procedure block below will provide multivariate analysis for the result under discussion. The mission is to determine if any or all of Subject sex, amount of weekly exercise taken, or marital status are significantly correlated with systolic blood pressure. The analysis uses systolic blood pressure as the dependent variable, with sex, exercise, and the indicator variables for marital status as independent variables.

REGRESSION VARIABLES = SYSBP, SEX, EXERCISE, MARRIED TO WIDOWED/
CRITERIA = PIN(.05) POUT(.051)/
DEPENDENT = SYSBP/
STEPWISE = SEX, EXERCISE, MARRIED TO WIDOWED/

Notice that all variables to be used as either dependent or independent variables are named in the VARIABLES = subcommand. Thereafter, analysis is specified by DEPENDENT = and STEPWISE = subcommands. The output from this SPSS program block will be presented. However, first simple guidelines for locating the material to be placed in a presentation table of results will be presented.

A stepwise multiple correlation analysis may include no steps, no predictor variables, if none of the candidate predictors is significantly correlated at $p \leq .05$ with the dependent variable. Stepwise may include only one step if but

Figure 13.1 MULTIPLE REGRESSION: Step One

Listwise Deletion of Missing Data

Equation Number 1 Dependent Variable. . SYSBP

Block Number 1. Method: Stepwise Criteria PIN .0500 Pout .0510

   SEX   EXERCISE   AMOUNT OF WEEKLY EXERCISE TAKEN

Multiple R	.27295	R and Beta are equal on Step 1,
R Square	.07450	though R is always positive, while
Adjusted R Square	.07027	a negative correlation can be
Standard Error	20.54211	expressed in Beta.

Analysis of Variance

	DF	Sum of Squares	Mean Square
Regression	1	7438.89293	7438.89293
Residual	219	92413.24282	421.97828

F = 17.62862   Signif F = .0000

Variables in the Equation

Variable	B	SE B	Beta	T	Sig T	
EXERCISE	-5.408662	1.288192	-.272945	-4.199	.0000	Exercise had the largest correla-
(Constant)	143.951529	3.199135		44.997	.0000	tion with BP

Variables not in the Equation

Variable	Beta	In Partial	Min Toler	T	Sig T	
SEX	-.021445	-.021662	.944296	-.320	.7493	
MARRIED	.1999970	.203804	.961332	3.074	.0024	Married
DIVORCED	-.046085	-.047894	.999588	-.708	.4797	should
SEPERATED	-.057384	-.059606	.998559	-.882	.3789	enter
WIDOWED	.186812	.188170	.939009	2.829	.0051	next step

Widowed would also be signif.

R is always positive, even though r, which is Beta for the variable entered at the first step, can be negative. Multivariate analysis produces "predicted" scores, that is, scores on the cluster of variables (even if the cluster temporarily contains only one variable at this step) which are as close in value to the dependent variable as possible. Thus, LOW predicted or cluster scores are seen to go with the LOW dependent variable scores, and HIGH cluster scores go with HIGH dependent variable scores; which is an operational definition of a positive relationship.

Figure 13.2 MULTIPLE REGRESSION: Step Two

```
Variable(s) Entered on Step Number
  2. . MARRIED

Multiple R              .33607
R Square                .11294
Adjusted R Square       .10480
Standard Error         20.15704

Analysis of Variance
                    DF          Sum of Squares      Mean Square
Regression           2            11277.37442       5638.68721
Residual           218            88574.76132        406.30624
```

F =	13.87792		Signif F = .0000	*Significance of R*		

<u>Variables in the Equation</u>

Variable	B	SE B	Beta	T	Sig T
EXERCISE	-4.629454	1.289216	-.233623	-3.591	.0004
MARRIED	8.532726	2.776098	.1999970	3.074	.0024
(Constant)	138.306671	3.636927		44.997	.0000

<u>Variables not in the Equation</u>

Variable	Beta In	Partial	Min Toler	T	Sig T
SEX	.008705	.008882	.895864	.131	.8960
DIVORCED	.010179	.010365	.884472	.153	.8788
SEPERATED	-.010576	-.010889	.905167	-.160	.8727
WIDOWED	.296268	.284884	.820200	4.378	.0000

Widowed should enter next step.

lation with the dependent variable. More than one step will be included, in fact, there will be k steps if there are as many as k significant correlates in the total set of independent variables. The last or final step is of greatest interest, as it contains results for all significant independent variables. Therefore, always begin by finding the last step. This step reports the R reflecting the "team" correlation of the independent variables with the dependent variable. Squared R is the variance in the dependent variable explained by the "team" of variables.

Do examine the intervening steps, however, so that insight is achieved into both the ordered entry and individual variable contributions at each step. The R square reflects the relative contribution of the variable entered at that step.

Following are copies of output from a STEPWISE regression run on SPSS. (Figures 13.1 - 13.3) All step output contains brief italicized annotations to assist understanding. Actual SPSS output contains no such annotations.

Compare the presentation table with the final step information on the printout (Figure 13.3). Notice that the Multiple R, R Square, Adjusted R Square, Standard Error, F = , DF, and Signif F = have been rounded to two places and inserted as a footnote to the body of the table containing results for "Variables in the Equation". This latter information has been rounded to three places in the presentation table; two places would be sufficient.

Notice that the SPSS output includes information about "Variables not in the Equation". None of these variables would be statistically significant at p < .05 if included at the next step, thus this is the final step. Look back at the intermediate results for steps 2 and 1, and at each step there were "Variables not in the Equation" which *would be* statistically significant if included at the next step, thus successive steps were performed. A variable added at a given

Figure 13.3 MULTIPLE REGRESSION: Step Three

```
Variable(s) Entered on Step Number
    3. . WIDOWED                        Widowed enters at this step.

Multiple R           .43004            Compare this R with that at step 2.
R Square             .18493
Adjusted R Square    .17367            Compare the increase in Adj R² from
Standard Error       19.36624          step to step

Analysis of Variance
                     DF         Sum of Squares        Mean Square
Regression           3          18465.99818           6155.33273
Residual             217         81386.13756          375.05133

F =      16.41197    Signif F  =  .0000    Significance of R
                     Variables  in the  Equation
Variable        B        SE B       Beta        T       Sig T
EXERCISE   -2.773726    1.309157   -.139975   -2.119    .0353
MARRIED    12.9769322    .853831   304122      4.547    .0000
WIDOWED    21.950580    5.013817   .296268     4.378    .0000
(Constant) 130.132636   3.961775              32.847    .0000
                     Variables  not in the  Equation
Variable    Beta In    Partial   Min Toler    T     Sig T
SEX         -.025032   -.026454   .808478    -.389   .6977
DIVORCED    .077402    .080090    .740790    1.181   .2390
SEPERATED   .045184    .047595    .766856     .700   .4845   No other
                                                             variables will
                                                             be signifcant at
                                                             p≤.01
End Block Number  1      PIN =   .050 Limits  Reached
```

This is the last step. See the message about .050 limits reached. The information of this step is to be tabled. The information under the header "Variables in the Equation" is the information to be placed in the presentation table. Above and to the left will be found **R** and other figures to be included as a footnote to the presentation table.

Table 13.2 Multiple correlation of systolic blood pressure with sex, exercise and marital status

VARIABLE	B	SE B	Beta	T	p
Exercise	-2.774	1.309	-.139	-2.119	.0353
Married	12.977	2.853	.304	4.547	.0001
Widowed	21.951	5.014	.296	4.378	.0001
Constant	130.133	3.962		32.847	.0001

R = .43, R² = .18, Adj-R² = .17, SE=19.37, F (3,217)=16.41, p<.0001 step is the one which will increase the correlation to the greatest degree using the STEPWISE regression model.

The following presentation table demonstrates the basic elements considered standard when constructing a presentation table for publication. Refer to both the presentation table and locations on the actual SPSS printout presented earlier to note the derivation of the numbers.

The terms utilized from the computer printout for presentation in a table are defined below:

R The Pearson correlation between systolic blood pressure and the score on the cluster of predictor variables.

R2 The square of R , revealing the proportionate reduction in error of predicting blood pressure, when the prediction is made from our cluster, rather than using the group mean blood pressure as our predictor.

Adj R^2 Shrinking the proportion of error reduction to a more realistic level, given our number of subjects and variables. Computed as Adj R 2 = $1 - (1-R^2)$ n - 1

SE Standard Error, or the average points of error in predicting blood pressure from our cluster.

B* The equation or weights for composing a raw score on the cluster of predictor variables. The equation for our data is displayed here in classical presentation form:

Predicted BP = 130.133-2.774 X EXERCISE + 12.977 X MARRIED = 21.951 X WIDOWED

The raw cluster score is formed for a Subject by multiplying their score on each independent variable by the weight for that variable, and then adding or subtracting the products according to sign, including the Constant. B gives us the weighted total of the independent variables, which sum is a model of the dependent variable.

Constant The predicted score on the dependent variable for any subject having scores of zero on all the independent variables, or for any Subject whose independent variable scores are unknown.

SE B Standard error of B, or an estimate of the population standard deviation of B. When large, may indicate that the predictor variables are too highly correlated; the condition of multicollinearity, which is consequential only when all predictors are assumed to be equally and uniquely important, and all are entered simultaneously. Otherwise, used in computing t for significance of B.

Beta The equation or weights for composing a standard-like score on the cluster of predictor variables. The Beta value for a predictor variable is multiplied by the standardized (z-score) value of that variable in producing a standardized cluster score. While the mean and variance of the predictor scores are respectively zero and one, the mean of the cluster score (the predicted value of the dependent variable) will be zero and its variance will be equal to R^2, not one, unless R = 1. Thus, the cluster score is "standard-like".

T* Statistical significance test value, modeling the B weight as if it were error of sampling when the true B is zero. Computed as T = B / SEB.

* Note: Capital letters of B and T correspond to capitals used in the SPSS printout.

Sig t The so-called level of statistical significance. When less than or equal to .05, we tend to believe that the B weight represents a "real" relationship, not an error of sampling around a true B of zero.

SAMPLE SIZE AND MULTIVARIATE ANALYSIS

Always use the largest samples possible, regardless of the research design or statistical analyses to be applied. Large samples yield statistics which are closer in value to true, though unknown, population values, a reflection of the Law of Large Numbers. Large samples contain more members of the population, and therefore have potential to harbor better approximations to the population values of quantities under study than do small samples.

Sample size for multivariate analysis in particular can be considered from several different perspectives. It is known that multivariate analysis results (the values of Beta and R) are more trustworthy when n = 200 or more. It is said that "the Betas bounce" or are unstable from sampling to sampling when n is smaller than 200, and especially so when n is trivially small. When true R is known (as it can be when a simulation is conducted or a population has been surveyed), small samples will yield values of R which fluctuate away from true R, greater than do samples of, say 200 or larger.

The number of subjects (n) must exceed the number of independent variables (**k**) in the analysis. As k approaches n, the value of R can become artificially large, reaching 1.0 when k = n. Plan to have no fewer than three subjects for every variable in the analysis, or n > k X. This number may not provide adequate statistical "power," however.

Another consideration does pertain to "power" (Cohen & Cohen, 1975) or the so-called probability of rejecting a false null hypothesis. The topics of Type II Error, accepting a false null hypothesis when R <> 0, and Type I Error, rejecting a true null hypothesis when R = 0[1] can be seen as controversial, because (a) lacking a population census the value of R is unknowable, and (b) p levels do not indicate probabilities that null hypotheses are either true or false. Assigning mathematical probabilities to these two Errors may not be as

Table 13.3 Sample size table for R, k and power

R	k	.70	Power .80	.90
.20	1	150	190	254
.20	2	187	234	306
.20	3	214	265	344
.20	4	237	291	374
.20	5	256	313	401
.20	10	332	400	503
.20	15	391	467	581

[1] Actually, the null hypothesis value of R^2 is equal to $(k-1)/(n-1)$, not zero, unless there is only one predictor variable, i.e., a simple Pearson r between variable.

Table 13.4 Sample size table for R, k and power

R	k	.70	Power .80	.90
.30	1	64	81	108
.30	2	80	100	130
.30	3	92	114	147
.30	4	102	125	160
.30	5	111	135	172
.30	10	146	175	218
.30	15	174	206	254

Table 13.5 Sample size table for R, k and power

R	k	.70	Power .80	.90
.40	1	34	43	57
.40	2	43	53	69
.40	3	50	61	78
.40	4	55	67	85
.40	5	60	73	92
.40	10	81	96	118
.40	15	98	114	139

important as using a large sample to provide as high a likelihood as possible of a sample which yields an R value close to that in the population. However, we present a table of required n's for achieving statistical power to detect R of varying sizes.

Each of the tables below present minimum required n to achieve adequate (.70) to excellent (.90) statistical power for varying numbers of variables (**k**). Select the table which provides the information for the minimum value of R to detect; that is, decide upon the smallest R that would be of practical interest to discover. The indicated sample size will provide statistical power to detect R of the minimum size or larger. For example, to detect R no smaller than .20, with power of .70, and 2 variables in the analysis, **n** must be no less than 187.

Table 13.6 Sample size table for R, k and power

R	k	.70	Power .80	.90
.50	1	20	25	33
.50	2	26	31	40
.50	3	30	36	46
.50	4	34	40	51
.50	5	37	44	55
.50	10	51	59	72
.50	15	62	72	86

Table 13.7 Sample size table for R, k and power

R	k	.70	Power .80	.90
.60	1	12	15	20
.60	2	16	20	25
.60	3	19	23	29
.60	4	22	26	32
.60	5	24	28	35
.60	10	34	39	47
.60	15	43	49	57

SUMMARY

This chapter has reviewed the utilization of multivariate analysis in model testing. The regression technique is appropriate in analyzing the cluster effects of a profile of independent variables on a single dependent variable. Research questions appropriately answered with this technique include: "How is a dependent variable related with two or more independent variables?" A "good" model will correlate nicely with the dependent variable and explain a significant portion of variance in the dependent (criterion) variable. A "poor" model is evidenced when clusters of independent variables correlate weakly,

Table 13.8 Sample size table for R, k and power

R	k	.70	Power .80	.90
.70	1	8	10	12
.70	2	11	13	16
.70	3	13	15	18
.70	4	15	17	21
.70	5	16	19	23
.70	10	24	27	32
.70	15	32	35	40

Table 13.9 Sample size table for R, k and power

R	k	.70	Power .80	.90
.80	1	5	6	7
.80	2	7	8	10
.80	3	8	10	11
.80	4	10	11	13
.80	5	11	13	15
.80	10	18	20	22
.80	15	24	26	29

and explain little variance in the dependent variable. Multiple regression is a linear technique. Researchers who believe that the model is sound, theoretically based, and yet are met with non-significant findings are encouraged to utilize non-linear methods of analysis as well as other exploratory data techniques. Inherent in understanding data are two principles: skepticism and openness (Hartwig & Dearing, 1989). "One should be skeptical of measures which summarize data since they can sometimes conceal or even misrepresent what may be the most informative aspects of the data, and one should be open to unanticipated patterns in the data since they can be the most revealing outcomes of the analysis." (p. 9)

"Effective researchers do not despair in the face of confounding and error; they guard against them and search them out. The means to do so reside in imaginative research design, measurement of potential confounders, informed analysis, and forceful inference." (Susser, 1994, p. 829)

REFERENCES

Cohen, J., & Cohen, P. (1975). *Applied multiple regression/correlation analysis for the behavioral sciences.* Hillsdale, NJ: Lawrence Erlbaum Associates.

Hamilton, L. C. (1992). *Regression with graphics: A second course in applied statistics.* Belmont, Ca: Duxbury Press.

Hartwig, F., & Dearing, B. E. (1989). *Exploratory data analysis.* Newbury Park, CA: Sage Publications.

Ott, R. L. (1988). *An introduction to statistical methods and data analysis.* Belmont, Ca: Duxbury Press.

Pedhauzer, E., & Pedhauzer, G. (1991). *Measurement, design, and analysis.* Hillsdale, NJ: Lawrence Erlbaum Associates, Publishers.

Sechrest, L., Perrin, E., & Bunker, J. (Eds.). (1990). *Research methodology: Strengthening causal interpretations of nonexperimental data.* U.S. Department of Health and Human Services: Public Health Service - Agency for Health Care Policy and Research.

Succer, M. (1994). The logic in ecological: I. The logic of analysis. *American Journal of Public Health, 84*(5), 825-829.

Tabachnick, B. G., & Fidell, L. S. (1989). *Using multivariate statistics.* Harper Collins Publisher.

Waltz, C.F., Strickland, O.L., & Lenz, F.R. (1991). *Measurement in nursing research.* Philadelphia, PA: F.A. Davis Company.

Multivariate Analysis of Categorical Data

Jan M. Nick and Margaret T. Beard

Powerful statistical methods for analysis of qualitative/categorical data have evolved over the past 15 years and have a foundation in theoretical statistics. These methods include the linear categoric regression model called log-linear, and the nonlinear or curvilinear categoric regression model which includes logit and probit models for theory and hypothesis testing (Agresti, 1989). Historically, outcome variables and explanatory variables were analyzed using a bivariate model for categorical data. Unfortunately, by computing regression analyses using dummy variables as regressors, several estimation problems arise when the dependent variable is categorical (Aldrich & Nelson, 1984; Holmes, Rogow, & Maynes, 1990). In fact, Holmes and others (1990) produced bivariate and multivariate analyses on the same data and discovered that the bivariate estimates of probabilities can be seriously in error as a result of the inability of bivariate probabilities to adjust for the effects of variables not included in the comparison. This error can be overcome by simultaneously analyzing the variables using the multivariate techniques described in this chapter. Now, with the advent of powerful and rapid computational technology, multivariate or simultaneous analyses can be computed for lower-order level data.

Terms used in these new techniques include odds ratios, marginal and conditional odds, general log-linear model, saturated or unsaturated models, effect parameters, logits and similar terms. Within the logit model, variations exist—namely a sequential nested logit and a joint logit model. Both the linear and nonlinear models provide correlation estimates and probabilities and are used to predict outcomes.

For many years, multinomial logit, probit and log-linear models have been used in disciplines interested in consumer "choice" responses which use categorical variables. Marketing, economics and education have used these methods to determine probabilities of different paths or choices a sample population chooses (Buckley, 1988; Kardes, Kalyanaram, Chandrashekaran, & Dornoff, 1993; Ribar, 1993; Siddhartham, 1991; Weiler, 1986, 1987). Nursing has recently begun to use these statistical analytic techniques (Vilhjalmsson, 1993).

The purpose of this chapter is to provide an introduction to multivariate analyses of linear and nonlinear categorical data, and the assumptions that must be met for valid results. In addition, how models are specified, and how they are tested will be covered. Finally, this chapter will provide information on common problems encountered in descriptive exploratory analysis, and provide a list of computer packages for estimation of multivariate models using categoric data. It is suggested that the reader refer to a textbook for details of analytic procedures as the purpose of this chapter is to merely introduce the availability of techniques for multivariate analysis of nominal and ordinal data.

Background

The origins of the log-linear model can be traced to the work of Pearson and Yule in the early twentieth century. Pearson proposed the chi(χ^2) square test that for the null hypotheses, the data were drawn from a multinominial with known probabilities (Sobel, 1995). Pearson further indicated a chi square test for the null hypotheses that two discrete random variables are independent. About the same time as Pearson's chi square, Yule proposed Yule's Q as a measure of the association between two dichotomous variables. Yule's Q is a function of the cross products (or odds) ratio which is the basic measure of association used in log-linear models. Pearson and Yule's work formed the bases for the tetrachoric correlation coefficient. Sobel(1995) view Pearson as the forefather of multivariate probit models and Yule as the forefather of the log-linear model.

In the first statistics course one learns of four types of measurement-nominal, ordinal, interval and ratio. This classification has been extended and refined, yet this basic classification is helpful for understanding. Types can be refined with reference to the kind of transformations under which they remain invariant, invariant meaning no change. Invariance refers to transformations that can be applied to numbers without changing the meaning of the interpretation of the empirical relations to which the numbers refer (Pedhazur & Schmelkin, 1991).

Nominal Level

The nominal level entails assigning numbers as labels to objects. That is, numbers are used as a substitute for names or other symbols that represent entities, objects or classes of objects. From a testing viewpoint, the identification of objects is important but of more relevance is the classification. Classifications are an integral part of theoretical formulation. When objects are classified into different categories, they are to be treated as different in kind, not in degree. Subjects are classified into a set of mutually exclusive and exhaustive categories which means each object (or subject) is assigned to only one category and that all objects (or subjects) are classified into the categories selected for use. If all objects or subjects do not fit into any of the existing categories, then new ones are added so that the requirement of exhaustiveness is met.

Nominal or categorical variables constitute a nominal level of measurement. A category is assigned a number with different numbers being assigned to different categories. The categorical numbers are identification symbols, therefore scale invariance is maintained under any substitution on one-to-one. This means that any number may be substituted for any other number as long as distinct numbers are used for distinct categories.

Ordinal Level

At the ordinal level, a predetermined rank or order among response classifications is made. Ordinal ranking indicates the categories are still mutually exclusive, but the categories increase (or decrease) in value. Monotonially, however the categories may not increase (or decrease) equally. For example, a patient, following a cerebrovascular accident, may be independent, or may need minimum assistance, moderate assistance, maximal assistance, or may be fully dependent. One can assign numbers 1-5 to these categories. Assigning numbers to entities, objects or persons so as to reflect their rank ordering on an attribute comprises an ordinal scale. The numbers assigned reflect the relation "greater than "or "more than.", therefore invariance will be maintained under any monotonic transformation of scale values.

Relationship to General Linear Models

Generally speaking, the linear and nonlinear categoric techniques have many similarities with ordinary regression. The log-linear model is similar to the general linear model used in multiple regression and analysis of variance. Therefore, it also must meet the same assumptions of the general linear model. The logistic models are nonlinear or distribution free, but are analogous to linear models for quantitative dependent variables. Both the log-linear and the logistic models examine the patterns of association among categorical variables in a multivariate contingency table, only using different methods for estimation. This will be covered later in the chapter. Regression procedures are used to predict numerical values on an interval or ratio scale for the dependent variable. However, with analysis using categoric variables, the logarithm of the *expected cell frequency* (not the expected criterion) is written as an additive function of the main effects and their interactions (Tracy, Sherry, Bauer, Robins, Todaro, & Briggs, 1984). When the dependent variable is dichotomous (or binary), an ordinary regression upon predictor variables can demonstrate how the probability of a response is affected. In another version of log-linear models, a dichotomous dependent variable can be treated as analogous to a regression with the independent variables affecting the odds on the dependent variable, that is, the ratio of favorable to unfavorable responses. Therefore, familiarity with regression techniques, analysis of variance and maximum likelihood estimation are necessary for testing and interpretation of the logistic and log-linear models.

The assumptions of regression are based on elegant algebra and geometry. Regression has status in most fields of research due to its geometrical, computational and interpretational (causal) properties. The geometric interpretations have been extended from linear parametric multivariate analysis to nonlinear nonparametric multivariate analysis. Using traditional multivariate analysis techniques, the researcher searches for linear relationships, works in linear planes or dimensions, and interprets with Euclidean geometry (i.e., hyperplanes, projections, and ellipsoids). Unfortunately, not everything behaves linearly. To deal with this problem, there are techniques available that search for nonlinear relationships between variables. In nonlinear techniques, classical techniques are made more general by optimal scaling and iteration, which is a basic property of nonlinear methods. There is a continued search for linear relationships such as linear regression and component analysis; however, transformations of the variables are built into these techniques.

LINEAR CATEGORICAL MODELS
Linear Models with Nominal Data

The general linear model is used to examine relationships among nominal categorical variables by analyzing expected cell frequencies whose function fits a linear trend. It involves fitting a log-linear function to the observed cell frequencies of a cross-classification table. The goal is to obtain the most parsimonious yet adequate description of the distribution of the data (Tracy et al., 1984). The log-linear model, derived from a normal distribution, is a recent development in contingency table analysis which applies new techniques to analyzing multidimensional tables. Prior to the advent of matrix operations and the development of sophisticated personal computers, the construction of multivariate models using purely categorical variables has been difficult to analyze.

If the data is not normally distributed or it's distribution is in question, higher-order interactions can be examined by collapsing continuous level data into categorical levels, and analyzing the data using a log-linear function. Normally distributed data tend to have the same variances (homogeneity of variance), but different means. Additionally the means are in a multi-dimensional space. Assumptions of log-linear modeling include normality of distribution and homoskedasticity, linear dependency, and nominal or ordinal data (Reiser and Schuessler, 1991). Log-linear multivariate analysis provides the odds of response x on the dependent variable. For ease and comfort of use, the astute researcher needs to become very familiar with odds ratios, marginal odds, and conditional odds if log-linear models are to be used.

These models can be viewed as analogous to analysis of simultaneous equations (Goodman, 1973 & 1978). Mare and Winship (1991) provide an overview of testing simultaneous equation models using the categorical log-linear approach. The general log-linear model is used to examine relationships among categorical variables by analyzing expected cell frequencies.

Log-linear models are used in various settings. With these models, one can analyze time series, examine simultaneously the effect of several categorical independent variables on a categorical dependent variable, and can also use causal modeling analogs (Mare & Winship, 1991). As with any model, parsimony is very important; however, with log-linear modeling, it is especially noteworthy.

Linear Models with Ordinal Data

While nominal log-linear models have been found in research literature for many years, recent attention has also been given to ordered log-linear model specification. Agresti (1989) reports that lack of differentiation between nominal and ordinal analytic techniques has served to obscure that subtleties between nominal and ordinal log-linear models and has caused this methodology to be poorly developed and poorly represented in the literature. In addition to odds ratios and marginal odds, ordinal log-linear models include row effects, column effects, row-column effects, uniform association and uniform interaction models. Ishii-Kuntz (1994) details a publication on the implementation and interpretation of ordered log-linear models. Unfortunately, when ordinal associations are found, a plethora of models are available to choose from. This may be disconcerting to the researcher. Therefore, Ishii-Kuntz (1994, p. 54) provides some guidelines for selecting which ordinal log-linear model fits best. Using the guidelines, a model should strive to be:

1. A parsimonious model containing the fewest parameters possible.
2. A model having a straightforward and reasonable interpretation.
3. A model with either all significant terms and no nonsignificant terms.
4. A high probability (p value) without over-specifying the model.
5. A well fitting nominal log-linear model initially; replaced later with some of the variables with ordered categories.
6. Guided first by theory and second by statistical outcomes.

If these guidelines are followed, a well fitting ordinal log-linear model should be the end result. This methodology is just beginning to advance contingency data analysis (Sobel, 1995), hazard rate analysis, paired data analysis (Yamaguchi, 1995), and item response theory and analysis (Agriesti, 1995).

Model Building
   Two merits of log-linear analytic procedures are flexibility in modeling and applicability to contingency table data The essential steps in log-linear modeling is to build a model for the expected frequencies in multidimensional cross-tabulation by introducing main effects and interaction effects. The objective in model specification is to describe the model by the set of "fitted marginals" used in estimating the expected frequencies under the model (Miller, 1991). Sometimes it is more convenient to work with the natural logarithms of the expected frequencies. Log-linear model specification and testing works well when multinomials are used because an assumption of this model is that the logarithms of the cell probabilities are a linear function of the logarithms of the marginal probabilities (Conover, 1980). Due to the iterative process involved with log-linear computations, computer packages are generally needed to determine the model.
   In statistical model building, the researcher explains the behavior of a variable "Y". In regression, the Y variable is usually the dependent variable. Suppose the theory suggests that k independent variables X_1, X_2, ...X_k influence the behavior of the dependent variable. Because the theory is imprecise as to the functional form of such relationships, a linear model can provide a useful approximation within the ranges of interest of the independent variables. In fact, when there is decreased variance among the responses, using either the log-linear or the nonlinear logistic models will provide similar answers. However, when there is a wide dispersion of responses, the logistic (logit) model is more accurate (Vilhjalmsson, 1993). This accuracy stems from the distribution free nature of the logistic model. Again, a word of caution—a sound theoretical base is more important in guiding the model than statistical results.
   Data that is typical of log-linear analytical method contingency tables are presented by Heuden and Moodaart (1995) and Elaison (1995). Some new log-linear models for the analysis of asymmetry in square contingency tables are suggested (Heuten & Moouaart, 1995). The logarithm of the expected frequency is divided into two parts, a symmetric part and a skew-symmetric part. The skew-symmetric part is decomposed, with graphical representations to assist in interpretation. A useful model has been developed to assess the influence of manifest variables on the row/column association while controlling for significant latent effects (Eliason, 1995). This model allows one to calculate distances between rows and columns and to partition the modeled association in the table into the percentage due to the manifest components

and the percentage due to the latent components. This model is applicable to a number of substantive problems in the health care area and in nursing. The strengths of the two-way-cross-classification is that it allows one to do the following: to partition the association in any two-way table into that portion due to unobserved factors and that portion due to observed factors, to assess the influence of the observed and latent dimensions on the odds of being in a specific row or column category, to measure the distances between rows and between columns as defined by the observed and latent dimensions, and to assess the relative contributions of each observed and unobserved dimension on the row/column association.

Sometimes subjects respond to a battery of questions (items) of a similar nature in a survey with each item having the same categorical scale. There are models that express logits for the response distributions in terms of subject and item effects. The models have interpretations referring to subject-specific comparisons of the items. One can estimate item parameters using estimates of main effect-parameters in corresponding quasi-symmetric log-linear models. Agresti (1995) demonstrates ordinal response models using adjacent-category logits and cumulative logits. For the two-item case, Agresti (1995) suggest models and corresponding parameter estimates for square ordinal contingency tables.

Testing Log-linear Models

Models can be evaluated by determining the proper "fit" to the data. This determination can be accomplished with either the Pearson chi-square statistic (χ^2) or the Likelihood-ratio chi-square statistic (χ^2) (Knoke & Burke, 1980). Several models can be evaluated during the testing phase to determine which model fits best by choosing the model with the lowest chi-square.

Log-linear models for contingency table analysis have major potential for adaptations and application in theory testing. For simultaneous model testing, extensions of the log-linear and logistic (logit) models can be accomplished. Recently, Mare and Winship (1991) tested several simultaneous equation models using log-linear and logistic approaches. Standard simultaneous equation models permit separation of structural relations of variables from their statistical associations, and isolation of distinct reciprocal effects. Mare and Winship (1991) were able to retain these qualities in their simultaneous log-linear and logistic models.

When the dependent variable is discrete or qualitative, the least squares method is not appropriate to use in analysis. If the dependent variable is binary, logit or probit are often used to estimate the relationship between the option selected and the characteristics of the alternatives in the data set (Weiler, 1987). When there are more than two alternatives in the choice set, the most widely used approach is the multinomial or conditional logit (MNL) (Weiler, 1987). However, the MNL has a very restrictive assumption called the IIA assumption. If the choices or categories have varying degrees of similarity or have between-set dependency, this assumption may prove problematic. In that instance the nested multinomial logit would be more appropriate to use. Model specification and testing can be accomplished with linear and nonlinear functions of categorical data, and better estimates of probabilities can be obtained by employing a multivariate approach based on the logistic (Holmes, Rogow, & Maynes, 1990) and/or log-linear models.

The proposed system for modeling (closely related to ordinary least-squares regression) is a d-systems analysis which was designed for causal modeling of small systems of categoric variables and can be viewed as the categorical counterpart to LISREL and EQS. The system produces linear flow graphs and corresponding equations (d-systems). In d-systems analysis, the effects of antecedent causes on dependent variables are expressed in terms of ranges in proportions (d for difference) rather than odds (see Knoke & Burke, 1980). This d-systems approach copes with the effect of interaction in a parallel fashion but has advantages over log-linear models in depicting causal transmittance through intervening variables. Tracy and others (1984) provide a simple and easily understandable sequential analysis and interpretation of a log-linear model using help-seeking as the dependent variable. Interested readers are encouraged to read this article for further detail into log-linear analysis.

NONLINEAR CATEGORICAL MODELS
Nonlinear Models with Nominal Data
Whenever the simple linear regression model does not appear to represent adequately the relationships between variables, or the distribution is nonparametric, the use of nonlinear regression is appropriate. In the usual multivariate analytic techniques, one searches for linear relationships between the variables, thus working in linear spaces and using interpretation from Euclidean (hyperplanes, projections, and ellipsoids). Newer computational statistics search for nonlinear relationships between multiple variables. In addition, if the model is a polynomial regression, a nonlinear model is commonly used. The statistical tool used to analyze nonlinear or nonparametrized categorical data is called the logistic function. The logistic function produces a coefficient which is commonly referred to as a logit. Logits are the log odds of the binary choice (Stynes & Peterson, 1984).

Logistic models require that the probability of responding dichotomously on each of the k items follows the path of a logistic curve as the continuous latent variable runs from its minimum to its maximum value (Reiser & Schuessler, 1991). The distribution for logit is derived from the random components which are independently and identically distributed according to the extreme value. This is called a Weibull distribution (Stynes and Peterson, 1984). The probit model is similar to the logit model except that probit transforms the regression into a normal Gaussian probability, and provides prediction using z scores according to a normal distribution. The normal distribution yields the probit model which is virtually indistinguishable from the logit model in the binary case and is statistically indistinguishable in the multinomial case (Stynes and Peterson, 1984). Therefore, logit and probit are generally referred to conjointly. Reiser and Schuessler (1991) present the logit/probit model conjointly in their comparison study of different multivariate models.

Logit and probit models are alternatives to the linear regression model for estimating a dichotomous variable and are two of the many nonlinear alternatives to the linear probability model. The logistic models (logit and probit) are the most developed, most common and most widely available alternatives to linear categorical regression models. Logit and probit analytic techniques are used extensively for modeling hierarchical choice responses. Marketing and economics literature is replete with research studies using logit and probit analyses (see Abe, 1991; Buckley, 1988; Kardes et al., 1993). Other disciplines such as the health sciences, sociology and psychology sparsely use these techniques. However, now these techniques can be found in the literature with little difficulty due to the advent of computerized data bases.

The logit and/or probit models examine the relationship between the dependent and independent variables by analyzing the probability (or expected odds) of a dependent variable as a function of the independent variable. The variables may be dichotomous or polytomous. Common examples of dichotomous dependent variables include success/failure, or pregnant/not pregnant. Examples of polytomous variables include choices between three or more paths such as not attempted, attempted and succeeded, or attempted and failed.

Logistic models are used to predict a continuous variable that stays in the range of 0-1 and have the underlying continuous variable with a probability of $Yi=p$. This makes the variable a function of its logit (Reiser & Schuessler, 1991). The logit is a coefficient estimate of it's fit within the proposed model, and is used to compare changes in proportions between different group. Logits can be used to measure differences or changes in a way that takes into account the different stages in the spread of information, attitudes or activities. In fact, this method of analysis can be used to measure the proportionality factor in the Stinchcombe model of theory construction.

There are generally two types of logit models found in the literature. These include the joint logit and a hierarchical nested logit. Siddharthan (1991) reports that it is customary in nested logit models to include choice-specific constants to capture the effects of unobserved variables, and to reduce measurement errors. The nested logit model is a sort of bridge between the restrictive uncorrelated utility function of the multinomial logit model and the general purpose multinomial probit model (Siddharthan, 1991). Most researchers use the hierarchical (nested) logit, but studies using the joint logit decision trees are also available in the literature (see Buckley, 1988; Kardes et al., 1993; Weiler, 1986). Probit and logit techniques were developed because the ordinary least squares regression estimates with a dichotomous variable are misleading when relationships are independent. Since a key assumption of ordinary least squares is that a constant variance of the error term across all observations is present, this assumption is violated when the function is nonparametrized as in probit and logit models.

Hierarchical models have a much different structure than linear compensatory models. Linear models use scores from weighted sums of attributes while hierarchical models use one of three models (Buckley, 1988). The hierarchical models include preference trees, the maximum likelihood and the nested multinomial logit analysis. All three models are similar in their function. The preference tree model is used with log-linear value functions. The maximum likelihood hierarchical model requires detailed information and uses rank order data with logistic function models. The nested logit model is also a logistic function model, but needs less data and can many times be obtained unobtrusively (Buckley, 1988). Hierarchical models are useful models for determining the structure or the process that is driving the behavior of the data.

Whenever the response or outcome studied is "choice" and variables surrounding that choice, the nested multinomial logit model is an appropriate formula to employ. The nested multinomial logit model has been used in other disciplines such as marketing research (Buckley, 1988), health care choices (Siddharthan, 1991), sociology (Reiser & Schuessler, 1991), education (Ribar, 1993) and nursing (Vilhjalmsson, 1993).

Siddharthan encourages the use of the nested multinomial logit model since it performs better to the independence of irrelevant alternatives (IIA) problems and is computationally less burdensome than the multinomial probit formulation. Large sample size is needed however to assure accuracy in the model estimation since nested logit formulations need to be fairly uniformly distributed across hierarchies in order to "nest" properly within each hierarchy (Siddharthan, 1991). Since nested logit uses an iterative process, empty nests could produce erroneous values at each level in the iterative process. However, since the nested logit model is computationally more difficult to estimate, Siddharthan (1991) recommends computing the joint logit first along with other statistical tests to determine if the assumption of independence of irrelevant alternatives (IIA) has been violated. (The rho_ can be used as a goodness-of-fit test in deciding whether a joint logit model or a nested model fits best). If this assumption has not been violated, then most likely, the joint logit estimation will suffice. However, if the IIA assumption has been violated, then recalculation using the hierarchical nested approach for obtaining logits should be employed.

Assumptions of the logistic models include independence of interaction, constant slope parameters (i.e., all variables have the same degree of association with the latent variables), are distribution free, and are categoric data (Reiser & Schuessler, 1991; Fleiss, 1981). The first assumption, one of independency and identical distribution implies that the relative probabilities between pairs of alternatives are independent of the number or the characteristics of the other alternatives. This property is called "independence of irrelevant alternatives" or IIA assumption (Weiler, 1986). The IIA assumptions are often violated in choices among alternatives, especially in cases where alternatives in the choice set can be viewed as having different degrees of similarity (Weiler, 1986). To see if the IIA assumption is violated or not, Hausman and McFadden (1984) recommend testing the coefficient vectors from the restricted and full choice sets. If the vectors are similar in value, then independence is supported and the IIA assumption has not been violated. When this is the case, the multinomial logit/probit models are appropriate. Hausman and McFadden (1984) provide the test statistic to estimate the equation.

Probit and logit parameters are estimated by maximum likelihood in contrast to ordinary regression least squares models including the log-linear models which are estimated by the least squares estimation method. With the least squares method, Gaussian-Markov assumptions are made. The conceptual difference between ordinary least squares (OLS) and maximum likelihood is that OLS is concerned with selecting parameter estimates that yield the smallest sum of squared errors in the fit between the model and data, while maximum likelihood estimation is concerned with selecting parameter estimates that imply the highest probability or likelihood of having obtained the observed sample "Y". Interpretation of the logit and probit models are similar to the linear regression model (Aldrich & Nelson, 1984, p.44). Instead of the usual F statistic and r^2 (square) that is used in linear regression, logit and probit use the chi square maximum likelihood ratio (G^2 square). In addition, a pseudo r-square statistic has been proposed for aiding in the interpretation of the logit and probit models. The likelihood ratio index is a pseudo r-squared which assesses how much more is explained by a model in which all subjects/respondents respond the same way (Buckley, 1988).

Reiser and Schuessler (1991) provide an excellent overview of the relationships between several categorical models including the logit/probit and the log-linear models. Examples using one and two parameter logit/probit, log-linear models are provided from actual data collected, and information on how to choose which model is appropriate is clearly demonstrated. In addition, Reiser and Schuessler introduce and compare several other models of mapping outcomes such as the latent variable conditional probability model (LATCON) and the conditional response probability model (RESCON).

Model Specification

When specifying a model, two steps are necessary. The first step consists of selecting the variables to be included in the model. The second step consists of specifying the functional relationship among the variables (Stynes and Peterson, 1984). Since the variables can theoretically remain the same in any of the models, it is the functional form that distinguishes between the log-linear, and logistic models. Progress in elegant statistical analytic techniques has led from descriptive statistics to predictive statistics. However, the predictive stage requires greater attention to the functional form and behavior of complex models, taking care not to violate assumptions (Stynes and Peterson, 1984). Statistical inference begins with the assumption that the model to be estimated and used to make inferences is correctly specified. It is presumed that substantive theory, not only gives rise to, but justifies the particular model.

In order to arrive at correct probabilities, the function (behavior) of the model must be identified correctly. It is the function that dictates the *type* of categorical model to use, whether it is a log-linear or logistic function. With prediction of outcomes, choosing the correct functional form is very important. The function depends on the pattern of percentage within the cells of the table as to which association the researcher should employ. Log-linear models are linear in their association. Logit and probit are considered nonlinear, but can be transformed to a linear function using the logit transformation. Agresti (1989) indicates how the logistic model can be transformed into a linear model using the logit transformation (with natural logarithm).

Once the correct function is specified, then the best model must be established. This is accomplished by comparing the maximum likelihood chi-square ($G\_$) estimations. Aldrich and Nelson (1984) state that the desired model is the one with the lowest chi-square. Intuitively, researchers are taught to look for largest chi-squares. However, in the case of model testing, the aim is not to look for the largest difference, but the similarity. The $G\_$ statistic can be used to determine the complexity of model needed, which explanatory variables are needed, the forms of their effects and whether interaction terms are needed (Agresti, 1989).

While log-linear models assume *constant* rates of change, the logistic models (i.e., logit and probit) permit *variable* rates of change. Logistic functions are restricted to 0, 1 interval and have a changing slope (not a constant slope). Log-linear models are most appropriate when variables are independent, having no interaction between them (IIA Assumption). If the function includes an interaction effect, then the logistic models (logit or probit) are more appropriate. Whereas log-linear associations can be either negative or positive, and assume a relatively straight line, logit and probit associations assume a sigmoidal curve in their functional forms and are considered asymptotic in the upper and lower limits (Vilhjalmsson, 1993). In general, as observed outcome proportions become extreme, the logit and probit models will yield models which are more parsimonious than log-linear models (Vilhjalmsson, 1993). The final goal of model analysis is to adequately describe the actual data distribution. Therefore, choosing the correct functional form is highly desirable.

The probability density function (pdf) is another useful tool to employ when deciding if the model is appropriately specified. The pdf describes the distribution of the association between variables (Abe, 1991). If the distribution is Gaussian (normal), Poisson, or gamma, then parametric regression techniques are appropriate. If the distribution is not normal or assumes a Weibull distribution, then nonparametric regression techniques are needed.

The advantages of using nonparametric regression are twofold. First, distributional assumptions such as normality and homoskedasticity are not involved which are generally associated with linear least squares techniques. Secondly, the model does not assume the parametric linear functional form (Abe, 1991). Any of the distributions can further assume an association between variables to include either monotonic, linear or nonlinear associations. The linear function assumes that a fixed increase (or decrease) in one variable will produce the same increase (or decrease) in the other variable (Vilhjalmsson, 1993). Nonlinear (sigmoid) specifications are defined as inherently interactive, and the rate of change in the probability of an outcome depends on the level of x but is not equal to it (Clearly & Kessler, 1982).

The decision about which function is most appropriate has been handled in one of two ways. The application of a general test for non-linearly has been recommended. (Vilhjalmsson, 1993). Other authors recommend computation of the log-linear, logit and probit coefficients of estimation to see which model fits best (Reiser and Schuessler, 1991; Agresti, 1989).

Hypotheses for the structure are stated, and then tested using the equations from the multinomial logit formulae. Possible hypotheses for testing the structure would look like this:

In a model for choice of x, either
a: the decision for x is nested within the decision of y
b: the decision for y is nested within the decision for x

Hypotheses for variables which influence the hierarchy can also be tested. Variables might include environmental and demographic variables. Coefficient estimates demonstrate the effects of the independent variables on the dependent variables whether using the joint logit model or the nested logit model. Buckley (1988) provides a good example of testing the structure and variables using the maximum likelihood ratio tests for exploratory analysis of model structure.

Model Testing

When testing to see which functional model is the best fit or the most appropriate, the most common method for model estimation is the maximum likelihood ratio chi-square statistic. Reiser and Schuessler (1991) demonstrated that when testing several functions (logit/probit, log-linear, and latent conditional probability models), best fit results can be ambiguous regarding the choice for the best model. In that case, parsimony (least number of variables kept in the model) would be preferable. Generally the logit and probit goodness-of-fit tests provide similar estimates and are considered the same. A strength of logistic function is the inclusion of interaction effects whereas the linear function does not include interaction effects. In nursing, interaction effects are especially important when working with the human response.

For model fitting strategies, Reiser and Schuessler (1991) suggest beginning with the logit/probit model as it is the most parsimonious. If it fits well, then the log-linear model with one latent variable, or a logit/probit model with two latent variables, LATCON and RESPCON will also fit well (LATCON and RESPCON are response consistency models). If logit/probit models fail to fit, then testing either the log-linear model or adding another variable to the logit model is suggested. Logit and probit models are useful for analyzing decisions of choice. Probit analysis is more ideally suited to analyze dichotomous dependent variables whereas logit models can be used for dichotomous or polytomous variables(Aldrich & Nelson, 1984). Generally speaking, however, probit analysis involves complex computations when more than two dichotomous outcomes are possible (Mare & Winship, 1991).

Probit and logit parameters are estimated by maximum likelihood in contrast to ordinary regression least squares models including the log-linear model which are estimated by the least squares estimation method. With the least squares method, Gaussian-Markov assumptions are made. The conceptual difference between ordinary least squares (OLS) and maximum likelihood is that OLS is concerned with selecting parameter estimates that yield the smallest sum of squared errors in the fit between the model and data, while maximum likelihood estimation is concerned with selecting parameter estimates that imply the highest probability or likelihood of having obtained the observed sample "Y". Instead of the usual F statistic and r^2 that is used in linear regression, logit and probit use the chi square maximum likelihood ratio (χ^2). In addition, a pseudo r^2 statistic has been proposed for aiding in the interpretation of the logit and probit models. The likelihood ratio index is a pseudo r-squared which assesses how much more is explained by the independent variables in an equation than is explained by a model in which all subjects/respondents respond the same way (Buckley, 1988). The uniqueness of the regression function of OLS and maximum likelihood is based on a single criterion and is linear in function while the nonparametric methods such as the ellipsoid method and the spherical kernal regression require the resolution of fit versus smoothness tradeoff in their regression equation (Abe, 1991). For analysis purposes, variables are frequently considered to be either continuous (i.e., weight, height, SAT scores) or categorical, where the categories are mutually exclusive. Examples include religious affiliation, sex, political party. A further refinement of categorical variables into categories that are ordered are possible.

A technique gaining in popularity is the minimum logit chi-square (Aldrich & Nelson, 1984; Grizzle et. al., l969; Kritzer, 1978). In minimum logit chi-square, the dependent variable to be explained is the probability of a particular response or outcome. In a model, main effects and interactions are specified through manipulation of a design matrix of effect-coded dummy variables.

Through this process the researcher is able to construct and estimate nonhierarchical models.

Hierarchical Linear Modeling

In hierarchical modeling, data may come from two and even three stage sampling designs. For example, in the national HIV study, clinics were selected from inner cities throughout the United States. From those clinics, sampling occurred over an eighteen month period. In the study, collateral background information on persons with HIV and the clinics were collected. The resulting data therefore contain variations and relationships among the variables that are contributed by both levels of sampling (i.e,, person level and clinic level). For the population as a whole, the distribution of the status of development of AIDS from being HIV positive is influenced by both person and clinic characteristics.

Disentangling sources of influence at the respondent level and institutional level of relationship were a problem prior to recent statistical and computational methods. There are programs available that provide efficient estimation of variation and relationships at two or more levels of these types of designs. Examples of programs include the HLM/2L and HLM/3L programs (Bryk & Raudenbush, 1992).

Descriptive and Exploratory Analysis

Frequently when categorical data are viewed by researchers, the data have been transformed from the raw form into frequency distributions of single variables and at times into cross-tabulations of two or more variables. In research that focuses on relationships among variables, the actual response in each category is ignored. Frequencies can be of great importance to policy-makers who need to know how many families are without health insurance, how many homeless are in need of food, shelter and health care, how many physicians will be needed in rural areas or how many children will need school availability.

Problems with Data Analysis Using Linear and Nonlinear Categorical Models

With any contingency or cross-tabulation table, the presence of empty cells presents a problem. When empty cells are present, the odds, odds ratios, and logits remain undefined when the denominator is zero. Therefore, research methodologists recommend arbitrarily adding anywhere from 0.2 to 0.5 to the empty cells in order to provide as small a denominator as possible (Evers & Namboodiri, 1977; Goodman, 1970).

Computer Programs Available

For nominal and ordinal log-linear, logit and probit analyses, many programs are available for the researcher to use in fitting the models discussed in this chapter to data.This presentation of software is merely an introduction and therefore is not meant to be comprehensive The programs include SAS, SPSSx, GLIM (see Agresti, 1989 for further discussion on those three programs), BMDP-4F (Brown, 1981), CDAS, ANOVAS and GAUSS. O'Brien and Wrigley (1980) review computer packages for the logit models, i.e., GLIM, BMDP and QUAIL. Application of log-multiplicative models to social relations such as social network are being used with GLIM. For an outline of the procedure see Anderson and Wasserman (1995). Clogg (1995) demonstrates how latent class models (LCM) arise naturally from theory and discusses the use of computer programs.. All of the programs discussed uses the principle of likelihood estimation and employ modern algorithms for maximization. There are many good programs available.

SAS

The SAS program has a procedure called CATMOD that can be used for log-linear model fitting using the Newton-Raphson algorithm (SAS). The program can be used with maximum likelihood estimation.by specifying that ML be used. The program can be used to output L square, fitted values, parameter estimates, and the covariance matrix of the parameter estimates. There are versions available for PC and mainframes. There is also a procedure available, GENMOD (SAS Institute, 1993) that can be used to fit generalized linear models. For detailed discussion of SAS the reader is referred to Hallahan (1995).

SPSS

PC and mainframe versions of LOGLINEAR and HILOGLINEAR are available in SPSS for fitting log-linear models (Norusis,1993, SPSS, 1994). Loglinear can be used to obtain ML estimates of log-linear models. With this program. One can obtain L square and df and user determined optional output, such as parameter estimates, fitted values, standard errors, and adjusted residuals. The HILOGLINEAR program is specifically for fitting hierarchical log-linear models with all variables treated as nominal. The program uses iterative promotional fitting (IPF) algorithm. A stepwise selection is available .The program only works for saturated models.To fit multinomial and Poisson log-linear models, the GENLOG program can be used. Presently, GENLOG runs under Windows with versions under other programs forthcoming.

Glim

Glim is a popular software package used for fitting generalized linear models (Frances, Green & Payne, 1993). With the program, one can obtain maximum likelihood estimates, input macros, and write small programs that are not available routinely in other programs. One can fit the models by using the Poisson error function and a model matrix.

BMDP

Mainframe and PC versions of two BMDP programs are available for use in fitting log-linear models. The 4F program is specifically designed for fitting log-linear models with all variables treated as nominal, and uses iterative proportional fitting (IPF) algorithm. This program can be used for an output of fitted values, Pearson residuals, parameter estimates, and standard errors, in addition to stepwise procedures. The 3R program is a nonlinear regression program that allows the user to input a likelihood function. This program can be useful in estimating log-linear models for ordinal variables, and for nonlinear models. See Sobel (1995) for useful hints before considering this program for nonlinear regression.

GAUSS

The GAUSS software package is a matrix programming language for the personal computer (Aptech Systems 1991a). The Markov, a GAUSS program written by J. Scott Long, is a program with a module for estimating log-linear models (Aptech Systems, 1991b). The module uses the Newton-Raphson algorithm. If all variables are treated as nominal, the program generates the appropriate model matrix. The user must supply the model matrix for the ordinal log-linear models For a detailed discussion of GAUSS and Markov see Long and Noss (1995). These authors describe GAUSS as an interactive calculator and a standard statistical package in which one specifies the data, variables and type of analysis and let the program do the computations.

CDAS

The Categorical Data Analisis System (CDAS) software is a personal computer program which allows one to estimate the models under discussion. The CDAS 3.50 (The Categorical DATA Analysis System, 1990) can be used for ordinal log-linear models, for log-nonlinear, standard errors for the estimates are obtained by jacknifing (Sobel, 1995). This program is distributed by Dr. Scott Eliason, Department of Sociology, University of Iowa, Iowa, City, Iowa 52242.

S-Plus

The S-Plus consist of programming language and an interactive environment under the UNIX operating system or Windows. In this program, generalized linear models can be fitted with the command "glm". For a comprehensive review of S-plus in data analysis the reader is referred to Schulman, Campbell and Kostello (1995). The authors highlight the modeling and graphic capabilities in addition to basic programming concepts; they also develop functions for bootstrapping and kernel density estimation.

SUMMARY

Multivariate analysis using categorical data has been unpopular historically for a number of reasons. The complexity of mathematical computations required in multivariate analyses, the use of categorical data for inference has traditionally been discouraged, have both contributed to a sparsity in the published literature. However, as this chapter indicates, categorical data, usually reported in frequencies and percentages, can be useful for further explanations when analyzed using a multivariate approach.

It was stressed that the functional relationship between variables in the model (linear or nonlinear) dictates whether log-linear, or the logistic model is used to describe, infer, or predict. Once the determination of independence of the variables (no interaction), and the distribution (Gaussian or Weibull) is described, guidelines are in place for choosing a log-linear or logistic model.

Due to the computations required for cross-tabulation of cells, problems are encountered when empty cells exist. These problems can be overcome by large sample sizes, and by adding an arbitrary number to empty cells. Authors have provided guidelines for doing this.

Many computer programs are available for analysis of log-linear and logistic models. Methods for estimating the log-linear models includes ordinary least squares (OLS), and for the logit and probit models, the maximum likelihood, chi-square or weighted least squares are used. In conclusion, for descriptive and exploratory analysis, frequency counts and the transforming of cross tabulations into frequencies in rows or column percentages or proportions, and analysis of contingency tables is a useful procedure that deserves greater attention in nursing.

REFERENCES
Abe, M. (1991). A moving ellipsoid method for nonparametric regression and its application to logit diagnostics with scanner data. *Journal of Marketing Research, 28,* 339-346.

Agresti, A. (1989). Tutorial on modeling ordered categorical response data. *Psychological Bulletin, 105*(2), 290-301.

Agresti, A. (1995). Logit models and related quasi-symmetric log-linear models for comparing responses to similar items in a survey. *Sociological Methods and Research, 24*(1), 68-95.

Anderson, C.J., & Wasserman, S. (1995) Log-multiplicative models for valued social relations. *Sociological Methods and Research, 24*(1), 96-127.

Aldrich, J., & Nelson, F. (1984). *Linear probability, logit, and probit models.* Beverly Hills: SAGE Publications

Aptech Systems. (1991a). *GAUSS: Programming manual.* Kent, WA: Aptech Systems.

Aptech Systems. (1991b). *Markov: A statistical environment for GAUSS.* Kent, WA: Aptevh Systems.

Buckley, P. G. (1988). Nested multinomial logit analysis of scanner data for a hierarchical choice model. *Journal of Business Research, 17,* 133-154.

Brown, N. B. (1981). BMDP-4F: Two way and multiway frequency tables—Measures of association and the loglinear model. In W. J. Dixon (Ed.), *BMDP statistical software.* Berkeley: University of California Press.

Bryk, A. S., & Raudenbush, S. W. (1992). *Hierarchical linear models.* Newbury Park, CA: Sage Publications.

Bryk, A. S., & Raudenbush, S. W. (1992). *HLM 2/3, Hierarchical linear modeling with the HLM/2L and HLM/3L programs.* Chicago: SSI.

Clearly, P. D., & Kessler, R. C. (1982). The estimation and interpretation of modifier effects. *Journal of Health Social Behavior, 23,* 159-169.

Clogg, C. C. (1995) Latent class models. In G. Arminger, C.C. Clogg, & M.S. Sobel (Eds.), *Handbook of statistical modeling for the social and behavioral sciences.* NY: Plenum Press.

Conover, W. J. (1980). *Practical nonparametric statistics* (2nd ed.). NY: John Wiley & Sons.

Eliason, S. R. (1995) Modeling manifest and latent dimensions of association in two-way cross-classifications. *Sociological Methods & Research, 24*(1), 30-67.

Evers, M., & Namboodiri, N. K. (1977). A monte carlo assessment of the stability of log-linear estimates in small samples. *Proceedings of the American Statistical Association, Social Statistics Section.* Washington, DC: American Statistical Association.

Fleiss, J. L. (1981). *Statistical methods for rates and proportions* (2nd ed.). NY: John Wiley & Sons.

Francis, B. Green, M., & Payne, C. (1993). *The Glim System, Release 4 manual* , Oxford: Clarendon Press.

Goodman, L. A. (1970). The multivariate analysis of qualitative data: Interaction among multiple classifications. *Journal of the American Statistical Association, 65,* 226-256.

Goodman, L. A. (1973). Causal analysis of data from panel studies and other kinds of surveys. *American Journal of Sociology, 75,* 1135-91.

Goodman, L. A. (1978). *Analyzing qualitative/categorical data.* Cambridge: Abt Books.

Grizzel, J. E., Starmer, C. F., & Koch, G. G. (1969). Analysis of categorical data by linear models. *Biometrics, 25,* 489-504

Hallahan, C. (1995) Data analysis using SAS. *Sociological Methods & Research, 23*(3), 373-391..

Hausman, J., & McFadden, D. (1984). Specification tests for the multinomial logit model. *Econometrics, 52,* 1219-1240.

Heuden,P.G.M & Moouaart, A. (1995). Some new bilinear models for the analysis of asymmetry in a square contingency table. *Sociological Methods & Research, 24*(1), 7-29.

Holmes, R. A., Rogow, R., & Maynes, S. S. (1990). A multivariate logit analysis of the outcomes of arbitration decisions in British Columbia. *Evaluation Review, 14*(3), 247-263.

Ishii-Kuntz, M. (1994). *Ordinal log-linear models.* Newbury Park: SAGE Publications.

Kardes, F. R., Kalyanaram, G., Chandrashekaran, M., & Dornoff, R. J. (1993). Brand retrieval, consideration set composition, consumer choice, and the pioneering advantage. *Journal of Consumer Research, 20*(6), 62-75.

Knoke, D., & Burke, P. (1980). *Log-linear models.* Beverly Hills: SAGE Publications.

Kritzer, H. M. (1978). An introduction to multivariate contingency table analysis. *American Journal of Political Science, 22*(1), 187-226.

Long, J.S., & Noss, B. (1995) Data analysis using GAUSS and Markov. *Sociological Methods and Research, 23*(3), 308-328.

Mare, R. D., & Winship, 0. (1991). Loglinear models for response and other simultaneous effects. *Sociological Methodology, 21,* 199-234.

Norusis, M. J. (1988). *SPSSX advanced statistics guide, 2nd ed.* NY: McGraw-Hill.

Norusis, M. J. (1993). *SPSS for windows advanced statistics, release 6.0.* Englewood Cliffs, NJ: Prentice-Hall.

Pedhazur, E.J., & Schmelkin (1991). *Measurement, design, and analysis: An integrated approach.* Hillsdale, NJ: Lawerence Erlbaum Associates.

O'Brien, L. G., & Wrigley, N. (1980). Computer programs for the analysis of categorical data. *Area, 12,* 263-268.

Reiser, M., & Schuessler, K. F. (1991). A hierarchy for some latent structure models. *Sociological Methods and Research, 19,* 419-465.

Ribar, D. 0. (1993). A multinomial logit analysis of teenage fertility and high school completion. *Economics of Education Review, 12*(2), 153-164.

SAS Institute, Inc. (1993). *SAS technical report P-243, SAS/STAT software. The GEBMOD procedure, release 6.09.* Cary, NC: SAS Institute, Inc.

SAS. (1987). *SAS/STAT Guide for personal computers, version 6.* Cary, NC: SAS Institute, Inc

Schulman, D.A., Campbell, A.D., & Kostello. (1995). Data Analysis Using S-Plus. *Sociological Methods & Research,* (3).

Siddharthan, K. (1991). Evaluation of behavioral demand models of consumer choice in health care. *Evaluation Review, 5*(4), 455-470

Sobel, M. E. (1995) The Analysis of Contingency Tables. In G. Arminger & M.E. Sobel (Eds.), *Handbook of statistical modeling for the social and behavioral sciences.* NY: Plenum Press.

SPSS, Inc. (1994). *SPSS 6.1 for windows update.* Englewood Cliffs, NJ: Prentice-Hall.

Stynes, D., & Peterson, G. (1984). A review of logit models with implications for modeling recreation choices. *Journal of Leisure Research, 4,* 295-310.

Tracy, T. J., Sherry, P., Bauer, G. P., Robins, T. H., Todaro, L., & Briggs, S. (1984). Help seeking as a function of student characteristics and program description: A logit-loglinear analysis. *Journal of Counseling Psychology, 31*(l), 54-62.

Vilhjalmsson, R. (1993). Life stress, social support and clinical depression: A reanalysis of the literature. *Social Sciences Medicine, 37*(3), 331-342.

Weiler, W. 0. (1986). A sequential logit model of the access effects of higher education institutions. *Economics of Education Review, 5*(1), 49-55.

Weiler, W. 0. (1987). An application of the nested multinomial logit model to enrollment choice behavior. *Research in Higher Education, 27*(3), 273-282.

Yamaguchi, K. (1995) Introduction to the special issue on log-linear and log-multiplicative models. *Sociological Methods & Research, 24*(1), 3-6.

Structural Equation Modeling

Donna A. Bachand and Margaret T. Beard

The arrival of new types of multivariate techniques offers potential for re-shaping research of nursing phenomena. Structural equation modeling (SEM), an advanced multivariate statistical technique, is more theory-driven and confirmatory in nature than traditional path analysis or factor analysis techniques. The SEM approach has been described as an extension of multiple regression and factor analysis, yet is more powerful than either of these techniques alone (Bynner & Romney, 1985). Because SEM requires a priori specification of modeled relationships and permits detailed assessment of measurement error, the method is well suited for inferential purposes, even with nonexperimental designs. This chapter offers an overview of the historical, theoretical and statistical foundations of SEM and describes potential applications to the process of theory development.

HISTORICAL BACKGROUND

The historical evolution of structural equation models is difficult to trace, as statistical models have unfolded with many contributors in diverse fields of study. Three components have been identified as contributing to the present state of the science: (a) path analytic techniques; (b) the conceptual synthesis of latent variable and measurement models and (c) general estimation procedures (Bollen, 1989).

Sewall Wright (1921), considered the founder or inventor of path analysis, proposed a set of rules for writing equations that relate the correlations of variables to parameters depicted in a path diagram. The path diagram provides a pictorial representation of a simultaneous equation system illustrating relations between all variables in the system. Equations describing the system are equivalent to covariance structure equations. Wright advocated solving these equations for the unknown parameters and substituting sample correlations for their population counterparts to obtain estimates of modeled parameters. As a special application of multiple regression, path analysis addresses questions concerning the direction and strength of causal influences hypothesized by the model.

The earliest factor analytic models were proposed by Charles Spearman (1904), who theorized that diverse mental abilities can be explained by a single underlying factor. He devised a method for estimating correlations between latent factors and observed variables based on the assumption that different tests of mental ability correlate only because of their common relationship with this general factor. These confirmatory factor models were equivalent to contemporary measurement models which examine the strength of hypothesized effects of latent constructs on observed variables.

The pioneering work of Wright and Spearman influenced generations of scientists, but the methods were mathematically daunting until the development of general estimation procedures. Computational procedures for factor analysis and maximum likelihood estimation were not available until the late

1960s and early 1970s, and their use was limited to scientists with strong mathematics and computer science backgrounds. The advent and successive releases of "user friendly" software programs, such as LISREL (Jöreskog & Sörbom, 1993) and EQS (Bentler, 1993), have contributed dramatically to the state of the art in structural equation modeling.

THEORETICAL FOUNDATIONS OF STRUCTURAL EQUATION MODELING

Causal Modeling

Causal modeling is a heuristic tool for producing empirical estimates of hypothesized relationships among constructs. Thinking causally about a process and constructing a path diagram to illustrate it enables the analyst to generate explicit hypotheses about how various elements of the process influence or relate to each other. With causal modeling, the researcher can sort out the best-fitting model from among several competing models of relationships among variables with different orderings.

An important caveat in causal modeling relates to the relevance of both theoretical and methodological concerns. While causal modeling is largely a statistical enterprise, the models one chooses to test should be based on sound theoretical reasoning. Theory postulates how latent constructs are ordered and interrelated in a model. Constructs may be exogenous or endogenous, depending on how they are believed to operate empirically. Constructs may be correlated or exert direct or indirect causal effects. Relationships may be unidirectional or reciprocal. In order to maximize confidence in the statistical output of any test, the model must be well specified and substantively meaningful.

Causal Inference

Philosophers and scientists frequently disagree regarding the nature and value of causation in theory construction. On the one hand, causal models provide powerful tools for prediction; on the other, researchers cannot directly observe causation but merely infer it from statistical correlation (Blalock, 1971).

Cook and Campbell (1979) cite three logical criteria for inferring cause: covariation between the presumed cause and effect, temporal precedence of the cause and elimination of rival explanations of the cause-effect relationship. These criteria are easily met in laboratory research settings via experimental design. Nursing research, however, is typically conducted in field settings characterized by lack of experimental control. Hinshaw (1984) argues that causal inference is nevertheless feasible if nurse investigators employ causal modeling strategies to test theoretical models. Using this approach, each condition of causality can be satisfied through theoretical assumptions rather than design procedures, as in experimental strategies.

The condition of covariation, for example, can be met by identifying all relevant concepts or variables and specifying how they interrelate and how they influence the dependent variable. Staging the concepts in terms of their impact on each other as well as the dependent variable strategically satisfies the time ordering condition. The final condition, elimination of rival explanations, can be dealt with by closing the model, that is, by assuming all relevant concepts are included in the model and all extraneous ones are excluded (Hinshaw, 1984).

Structural equation analysis does not establish causation; no statistical procedure can. However, the structural equation modeling approach does offer what Bullock, Harlow, and Mulaik (1994) refer to as "compelling potential." They write:

In our view, structural modeling does offer the potential to reach tentative causal statements. By continuously testing structural equation models, researchers may discover whether the causal hypotheses and functional equations on which their models are based are useful for explaining variables that are related to one another. (p.262)

A model provides a formal representation of a theory, which is an approximation of reality (Bollen, 1989). Thus, model building and model modification involve a process of successive approximations. Because of the approximate nature of models and the inability to directly observe causality, causal inferences are always tentative, though one may place varying degrees of confidence in the relations. A model can never be proved valid. A good fit between model and data does not guarantee a "true" model, but may offer a plausible approximation of reality.

STATISTICAL FOUNDATIONS OF STRUCTURAL EQUATION MODELING
Distribution, Mean, and Variance

The cornerstones of structural equation modeling are the location (mean) and spread (variance) of a distribution. A distribution describes the spread of a set of values collected from a well-defined universe of possible values. The "normal" distribution, also referred to as the normal curve, bell-shaped curve, or Gaussian distribution has a characteristic shape indicative of the probability of observing expected values in a large population. The normal distribution has a mean of zero and standard deviation of one. That is, values are centered around zero and the majority of values (95%) are spread out between two standard deviations above and below the mean.

The mean of a distribution represents an average value and as such, provides a "best guess" for predicting the value of any case randomly selected from the distribution. Variance is calculated as the average of squared deviations from the mean, or the standard deviation squared. Squaring the deviations prevents positive and negative deviations from canceling each other out. Variance therefore produces a measure of the spread of cases around the mean. Variance is small if values or cases cluster near the mean; variance is large if values or cases deviate far from the mean.

Covariance is a measure of the relationship or dependence between two variables. Covariance implies that values of one variable change depending on the values of another variable. If values of two variables are plotted for each case in the distribution, their covariance characterizes the way the points cluster. Covariance is similar to correlation; in fact, correlations are standardized to have unit variance.

Covariance in SEM

SEM procedures emphasize covariances rather than individual cases (Bollen, 1989). The means, variances and covariances of observed variables comprise the data set. The means, variances and covariances of latent constructs, structural links among constructs, and structural links between constructs and their indicators are unknowns that will be estimated.

The goal of statistical analysis is to minimize differences between observed sample covariances and covariances predicted by a model. The basic hypothesis is that the covariance matrix of observed variables is a function of the set of parameters or links between variables. If a model is correct and the parameters are known, the population covariance matrix can be exactly reproduced. The technique involves comparing a matrix containing variances and covariances implied by a model (Σ) with a matrix of variances and covariances observed in a sample (S). If the fit is adequate, the model "fits" the data; in the ideal situation the difference between Σ and S is insignificant.

Maximum Likelihood Estimation

Maximum likelihood estimation is the most commonly used statistical procedure for computing parameter estimates from covariances. Estimation essentially involves fitting the model-implied covariance matrix with the sample covariance matrix. In other words, the unknown parameters of the model are iteratively estimated in such a way that the implied matrix Σ comes as close as possible to the sample matrix S. Under the assumptions of normal theory, estimation yields coefficients for structural parameters (paths) along with a standard error which serves as a measure of precision for each estimate. These coefficients are interpreted as either factor loadings or path coefficients, depending on which parameters they describe.

Goodness-of-Fit

Maximum likelihood provides estimates based on optimal fit between model and data. With a good data set it is quite possible to estimate a wide variety of models, whether or not those models make theoretical or empirical sense. If maximum likelihood estimates reflect poor fit, the model should be reformulated or rejected outright. However, appropriate estimates might be achieved by multiple competing models. For this reason, model adequacy cannot be evaluated on the basis of parameter estimates alone.

The chi square (χ^2) test is generally used as a measure of overall model fit. A small statistically nonsignificant chi square indicates a small discrepancy between sample data and modeled covariances, whereas a large significant finding justifies rejecting the model. Deciding how large chi square should be poses a difficult issue, because the test is sensitive to sample size and to kurtotic distributions. The power of the test may not be sufficient to detect differences between Σ and S in samples smaller than 50 to 100 observations (Hayduk, 1988). On the other hand, the likelihood of rejecting a "good" model increases in very large samples. Nonnormal distributions can also distort chi square. Highly peaked or excessively flat distributions can lead to erroneous rejection of models that might fit normally distributed data well (Bollen, 1989).

Several adjuncts to chi square have been reported in the literature. Most fit indices are derived from chi square; newer measures attempt to account for sample size or for degrees of freedom in the model. Examples of these are introduced in a later section of the chapter.

Fundamental Equations and Matrices

All SEM operations are based on three equations and eight matrices. Equations resemble regression equations except that they are typically written in Greek notation. The first equation describes relationships among structural model components:

$$\eta = \beta\eta + \Gamma\xi + \zeta$$

where η is a vector of endogenous constructs, β is a matrix of structural coefficients among the endogenous constructs, Γ is the matrix of structural coefficients among exogenous constructs, ξ is the vector of exogenous constructs, and ζ is an error or disturbance term. Thus, the basic structural equation expresses the endogenous constructs as a linear combination of all other constructs in the model plus error.

Two other equations express relationships between latent variables and their indicators. One equation is written for endogenous and one for exogenous variables. These are:

$$y = \Lambda_y \eta + \varepsilon$$
$$x = \Lambda_x \xi + \delta$$

where y and x are the observed endogenous and exogenous indicators, Λ_y and Λ_x are matrices of structural coefficients between latent constructs and their indicators, and ε and δ are vectors containing measurement errors for y and x, respectively. These two equations convey the fundamental SEM assumption that measured variables are produced by their underlying latent constructs.

These basic equations contain four matrices of structural coefficients that can be estimated if statistical assumptions are met. Since the error terms are assumed to represent random error, their means should equal zero, and they should be independent or mutually uncorrelated. Additionally, the error terms are assumed to be uncorrelated with the latent constructs they measure.

Four variance/covariance matrices are required to complete the model. Diagonal elements of these matrices are variances; and the off-diagonal elements are covariances. For example, the phi (ϕ) matrix contains the variances of exogenous constructs on the main diagonal, and the covariances among pairs of exogenous constructs on the off-diagonal. The diagonal elements of psi (Ψ) are error variances in ζ, or the amount of variance in η that remains unexplained by the variables in the equation. The off-diagonal elements are the covariances among the ζ's. Similarly, the elements of theta delta ($\Theta\delta$) and theta epsilon ($\Theta\varepsilon$) contain variances and covariances of the measurement errors in x and y.

The preceding information is, by necessity, abstract. A detailed mathematical foundation for SEM is presented in Loehlin (1987), Hayduk (1988), and Bollen (1989) as well as the statistical manuals for EQS (Bentler, 1993) and LISREL (Jöreskog & Sörbom, 1993).

THE STRUCTURAL EQUATION MODELING PROCESS
Model Building Strategies

Jöreskog (1993) distinguishes between three model building strategies. In the strictly confirmatory situation, the researcher constructs a single conceptual model, collects data to test it and either accepts or rejects the model based on results of the test. This approach is rarely undertaken because most scientists are unwilling to reject their models outright without further investigation. In the alternate models approach, the researcher constructs several competing models, obtains data from a single sample and selects the best-fitting model. This data-driven approach is relatively uncommon in the health sciences because few researchers specify alternate models a priori.

The most common strategy in practice is the model generating situation in which the researcher specifies and tests a tentative model with a data set, then continues to refine and retest the model until acceptable fit is achieved. The process may be data-driven or theory-driven, but the ultimate goal is to generate a model that not only fits the data but is also theoretically interpretable. The model generating approach is analogous to the five steps of SEM identified by Bollen (1989): model specification, identification, estimation, testing fit and respecification.

Steps in SEM Applications

Model Specification. The first and perhaps most critical step involves designing a path diagram depicting relevant causal processes among concepts. These theoretical relationships form a structural model that can be translated into a system of equations for statistical testing. Although specification of the structural model is largely theoretical, methodological issues cannot be overlooked. Statistical tests are based on the general linear model; if relationships are nonlinear the test may be invalid.

Table 15.1 summarizes terminology commonly employed in specifying structural equation models. In labeling path diagrams, observed variables are enclosed in squares and labeled as x or y, depending upon whether they are modeled as endogenous or exogenous. Latent variables or constructs are enclosed in circles and assigned the Greek letter ξ or η in LISREL analyses or F (for factor) in EQS language. Including disturbance or error terms in the diagram is useful for applying the rules of identification which are discussed in a subsequent section.

Each line or link in a path diagram represents an equation. A system of equations can be written to describe the entire model by following two rules. For each variable with a one-way arrow pointing to it, there will be one equation in which this variable is on the left-hand side. The right-hand side of each equation, then, is the sum of the terms equal to the number of one-way arrows pointing to that variable. Each term is the product of the path coefficient and the variable from which the path originates, plus the associated error term.

Identification. Identification is a statistical rather than theoretical issue. Most researchers try to specify models that have substantive meaning; such models may become extremely complicated with large numbers of constructs interrelated in very complex patterns. SEM does estimate very complex models, but only if they are identified. In the most general sense, identification implies that there is sufficient information to solve the equations. In other words, the number of covariances between measured variables must be greater than the number of causal parameters to be estimated (Long, 1983).

A model may be just identified, under-identified, or over-identified. Just-identified means that there is a one-to-one correspondence between the number of covariances and the number of parameters to be estimated. Although a unique set of parameter estimates can be determined from a just identified model, the results are scientifically uninteresting because there are no degrees of freedom and the model cannot be rejected (Byrne, 1994). An under-identified model cannot be tested because there is insufficient information to uniquely solve all of the equations implied by the model; attempts to estimate models that are not identified, therefore, result in arbitrary estimates and meaningless interpretation of the parameters. An over-identified model has more covariances than parameters and can be tested.

Table 15.1. Structural Equation Modeling Terminology

Variable Type	Greek Name	Error Term	Causal Parameter	Model Type	Associated Matrices
X independent indicator manifest observed measured exogenous	none	(delta)	λx (lambda x) the path from ξ-X or from the latent variable to its indicator	measurement models, CFA models, or path models of observed variables	Δx - structural coefficients among exogenous indicators θ - measurement error covariances for X variables
Y dependent indicator manifest observed measured endogenous	none	(epsilon)	y (lambda y) the path from -Y or from the latent variable to its indicator	measurement models, CFA models, or path models of observed variables	Λ - structural coefficients among endogenous indicators measurement error covariances for Y variables
latent unmeasured independent exogenous or intervening factors	ξ (ksi)		Γ (gamma) the causal path from - ξ – λ or an exogenous to an endogenous variable	structural models of latent variables	- structural coefficients for latent exogenous variables (phi) - the covariances among exogenous latent variables
latent unmeasured endogenous dependent factors	η (eta)	(zeta)	(beta) β the causal path between endogenous latent variables	structural models of latent variables	- structural coefficients for latent endogenous variables (psi) - the covariances among structural disturbance terms or 's

The identification problem can be resolved prior to testing by fixing or constraining model parameters to meet certain rules of matrix algebra. The first of these is the order condition (Long, 1983). The order condition is a necessary but not sufficient condition which implies that if an equation in a system of equations is identified, it must follow that the number of variables excluded from the equation is greater than or equal to the number of equations in the system minus one. To meet the condition, the researcher first writes an equation for each structural parameter in the model and subsequently decides, based on theoretical concerns, which parameters to fix or constrain so that the number of variables excluded from the system equals the number of equations in the system.

A second condition is referred to as the rank condition (Long, 1983). The rank condition is both necessary and sufficient for identification. In order to satisfy the rank condition, the researcher must write the matrices for structural coefficients between exogenous (β) and endogenous (Γ) constructs. A new matrix β# is formed by excluding the row for the equation being considered and deleting all columns with nonzero elements in the excluded row. Similar operations are performed for the new matrix Γ#; an equation is identified if, and only if, the rank of the matrix produced by joining β# and Γ# equals the number of equations in the system minus one.

The t-rule is a necessary but not sufficient condition which is very easy to implement (Byrne, 1994). To apply the t-rule, first count the number of data points in the model; these are the variances and covariances of the observed variables, p. With p variables there are $p(p+1)/2$ data points. Then calculate the number of free parameters to be estimated. Every line in the path diagram that is not fixed or constrained is considered an unknown parameter to be estimated. The number of data points must exceed the number of parameters, and the difference between the two provide the degrees of freedom.

Hayduk (1988) describes simpler procedures for preventing and testing under-identification. The first involves re-estimating the model coefficients several times, beginning with different sets of start values. If maximum likelihood estimates repeatedly converge on the same set of final estimates, the model is identified. An alternate method is useful when the identification status of a particular equation is in question. The researcher estimates the model twice: once with the relevant coefficient free and again with the coefficient fixed at some value believed or known to be different from the estimated value. If this exercise results in a substantial decrement to the overall model fit, the coefficient's value was uniquely determined.

A related difficulty commonly encountered in SEM occurs when the population matrix Σ is not positive definite. Positive indefiniteness, like identification, is a mathematical problem. If all elements on the diagonal of a matrix (the variances) are not positive nonzero numbers, the matrix cannot be inverted and the model cannot be estimated. Potential causes of indefiniteness include collinearities in the data set, pairwise deletion of missing data in small samples, outliers or nonnormal distributions in the data, analyses of nominal or ordinal data based on Pearson correlations and under-identification (Wothke, 1993).

Wothke (1993) offers useful guidelines for diagnosing and correcting situations that give rise to positive indefiniteness. As previously noted, the problem of identification must be resolved prior to estimating the model. With respect to diagnosis, the researcher can screen the data for outliers and collinearities, plot variable distributions to examine normality, and consider listwise deletion of missing observations. Furthermore, the researcher should take into account the level of measurement for each variable. Maximum likelihood procedures are based on Pearson correlations that assume interval or ratio measurement; if variables are strictly ordinal or nominal, polyserial or biserial correlations should be used and the model estimated by the weighted least squares procedure.

Finally, the LISREL program offers a special feature called the ridge option for removing negative values along the matrix diagonal. Adding a ridge simply entails multiplying the diagonal elements by a constant greater than one. Adding a ridge transforms the data to allow computation, but does not provide diagnostic insight into the original indefiniteness issue.

Estimation. Estimation is the procedure for testing the model. Several methods of estimation are available in LISREL and EQS, but the classic and most widely used is maximum likelihood (ML). Maximum likelihood is a fitting function that minimizes the difference between the observed sample covariance matrix Σ and the implied population covariance matrix . In less statistical terms, ML systematically searches different possible population values and selects those parameter estimates which are most likely to be correct, given the sample observations.

Estimation procedures yield several types of information about the model including overall fit statistics, individual parameter estimates, and error variances and covariances. An important first step in SEM is to test the measurement model. The measurement model includes only those relationships between latent constructs and their empirical indicators. The resulting estimates are analogous to factor loadings, and their associated error variances are useful in assessing the reliability of empirical indicators. The parameter estimates should be consistent with the theory; confirming the hypothesized factor structure is the primary goal of this step. Serious misfit between the measurement model and the data may mean that the chosen indicators are not valid and reliable. In this case the model must be respecified prior to proceeding with the structural model test, because reliability of measurement is always a prerequisite to inference.

The structural model test incorporates relationships among the latent constructs. Structural parameter estimates can be interpreted as path coefficients which signify the strength and direction of hypothesized relationships. Standard errors and T-values assist in evaluating whether the estimates are statistically significant. Unreasonable or nonsignificant estimates may be produced by a poor model but may also reflect sampling error, missing data, or test assumption violations. Design issues are important in SEM, as in all research methods. If structural parameter estimates cannot be interpreted substantively the researcher should consider both theoretical and methodological sources of bias and consider respecifying the model.

Testing Fit. A primary objective of SEM is to test the fit between a theoretical model and a set of empirical data. The most commonly reported measure of fit is the chi square (χ^2) goodness of fit statistic. Although chi square is a statistical test, it is more appropriate to consider the result a measure of fit rather than a pure test of fit. Chi square measures the difference between the sample covariance matrix and the fitted covariance matrix. Therefore, in contrast with the typical inferential test, a small *nonsignificant* chi square is desirable. In SEM significance implies that the model does not adequately describe the sample.

Chi square is calculated as N-1 times the minimum value of the fit function, where N is the sample size (Jöreskog, 1993). Because of its inherent sensitivity to sample size, chi square should not be considered the sole indicator of fit. Furthermore, it is usually possible to improve chi square by adding parameters to the model whether or not there are theoretical reasons to do so. For these reasons multiple fit indices should be evaluated before rejecting a model.

Additional measures of fit include the goodness-of-fit index (GFI) and adjusted goodness-of-fit index (AGFI). The GFI is robust against departures from normality and is independent of sample size. The GFI has an unknown statistical distribution; as there is no standard of comparison, the index should be interpreted with caution (Jöreskog & Sörbom, 1982). The AGFI is adjusted for the degrees of freedom in the model and is used to compare one structural model with another. The range of GFI and AGFI is 0 to 1.0; the closer the indices are to 1.0, the better the fit between the data and the model.

The root mean square residual (RMR) provides another measure of fit. The RMR is used to compare the residuals in different models proposed to explain the same data. A small RMR indicates minimal error in the model.

The root mean square error of approximation (RMSEA) estimates the degree of lack of fit based on discrepancies between the population matrix and the fitted matrix. The formula for computing the RMSEA takes degrees of freedom into account, so this value does not necessarily improve as parameters are added to the model. Values range from 0 to 1, with smaller results indicating smaller error of approximation and therefore better fit.

Respecification. The analyst has two options for dealing with a poor-fitting model: Reject the model altogether or respecify and retest it. Unfortunately there is no formula for respecifying a model, but there are strategies for diagnosing and improving sources of misfit.

First, examine the matrix of residuals. Residuals are the elements in the sample covariance matrix S that are poorly reproduced by the fitted matrix Σ. Large residuals may occur in a wide variety of situations ranging from non-normal bivariate distributions to nonlinear relationships, but are generally indicative of specification errors. Residuals provide clues concerning misspecified paths, but can also be misleading. Paths should not necessarily be altered on the basis of these parameters alone; incorrect respecifications can improve overall model fit and at the same time impact correlations between remaining paths in the model.

Structural equation modeling packages offer alternate methods for respecifying problematic paths. LISREL, for example, calculates a modification index (MI) for each fixed parameter in the model. The MI estimates the predicted decrement in chi square that can be achieved by freeing a parameter and re-estimating the model. EQS offers a similar test called the Lagrange multiplier (LM) test along with a parameter change statistic that gives the value which would be obtained when a fixed parameter is freed in a subsequent analysis. Implementing changes based on either the MI or LM results should be an iterative process; that is, parameters should be freed one at a time and the new solution examined before proceeding with additional changes. The latest version of EQS provides a unique test for evaluating sets of parameters multivariately. The Wald test can be used to determine whether sets of parameters could be simultaneously set to zero without sacrificing model fit. In essence, the Wald test locates redundant paths.

Despite such statistical advances, the analyst must exercise caution in respecifying parameters. Paths should only be altered in light of the theory being tested. Adding or deleting parameters in the interest of fit can result in a model of nonsense.

CONCLUSION

Despite its many advantages, SEM poses difficulties for novice users. Although widely used in econometrics and the political and social sciences since the late 1960's, the method is relatively new to many researchers. Much of the literature describing SEM requires considerable mathematical sophistication. Fortunately, contemporary software designers are motivated to produce marketable statistics programs that do not mandate knowledge of programming language. Today's scientists are therefore free to concentrate on the methodology of theory construction. Structural equation analysis provides a powerful test of the researcher's theory. As nurse researchers become more sophisticated in theory development, advanced data analytic techniques gain importance as critical research tools.

REFERENCES

Aaronson, L. S., Frey, M. A., & Boyd, C. J. (1988). Structural equation models and nursing research: Part II. *Nursing Research, 37*(5), 315-318.

Asher, H. B. (1983). *Causal modeling (2nd ed.)*. Beverly Hills, CA: Sage Publications.

Bentler, P. M. (1993). *EQS structural equations program manual*. Los Angeles, CA: BMDP Statistical Software.

Berry, W. D. (1984). *Nonrecursive causal models*. Beverly Hills, CA: Sage Publications.

Blalock, H. M. (1971). *Causal models in the social sciences*. Chicago, IL: Aldine-Atherton.

Bollen, K. A. (1989). *Structural equations with latent variables*. NY: John Wiley.

Bollen, K. A., & Long, J. S. (1993). *Testing structural equation models*. Newbury Park, CA: Sage Publications.

Bollen, K. A., & Stine, R. A. (1993). Bootstrapping goodness-of-fit measures in structural equation models. In K.A. Bollen and J.S. Long (Eds.). *Testing structural equation models*. Newbury Park, CA: Sage Publications.

Boomsma, A. (1985). Nonconvergence, improper solutions, and starting values in LISREL maximum likelihood estimation. *Psychometrika, 50*(2), 229-242.

Boyd, C. J., Frey, M. A., & Aaronson, L. S. (1988). Structural equation models and nursing research: Part I. *Nursing Research, 37*(4), 249-252.

Browne, M. W. (1982). Covariance structures. In D.M. Hawkins (Ed.). *Topics in applied multivariate analysis*. Cambridge: Cambridge University Press.

Bullock, H. E., Harlow, L. L., & Mulaik, S. A. (1994). Causation issues in structural equation modeling research. *Structural Equation Modeling, 1*(3), 253-267.

Bynner, J. M., & Romney, D. M. (1985). LISREL for beginners. *Canadian Psychology, 26*(1), 43-49.

Byrne, B. M. (1994). *Structural equation modeling with EQS and EQS/Windows*. Thousand Oaks, CA: Sage Publications.

Cook, T. D., & Campbell, D. T. (1979). *Quasi-Experimentation design and analysis issues for field settings*. Boston, MA: Houghton Mifflin.

Hayduk, L. A. (1988). *Structural equation modeling with LISREL*. Baltimore, MD: The Johns Hopkins University Press.

Hinshaw, A. S. (1984) Theoretical model testing: Full utilization of data. *Western Journal of Nursing Research, 6* (1), 5-9.

Jöreskog, K. G. (1993). Testing structural equation models. In K.A. Bollen and J.S. Long (Eds.). *Testing structural equation models*. Newbury Park, CA: Sage Publications.

Jöreskog, K. G., & Sörbom, D. (1982). Recent developments in structural equations modeling. *Journal of Marketing Research, 19*,404-416.

Jöreskog, K. G., & Sörbom, D. (1989). *LISREL 7: A guide to the program and applications*. Chicago, IL: SPSS, Inc.

Jöreskog, K. G., & Sörbom, D. (1993). *LISREL 8: Structural equation modeling with the SIMPLIS command language*. Hillsdale, NJ: Lawrence Erlbaum Associates.

Loehlin, J. C. (1987). *Latent variable models: An introduction to factor, path, and structural analysis*. Hillsdale, NJ: Lawrence Erlbaum Associates.

Long, J. S. (1983). *Covariance structure models: An introduction to LISREL*. Newbury Park, CA: Sage Publications.

Pedhazur, E. J. (1982). *Multiple regression in behavioral research (2nd ed.)*. NY: Holt, Rinehart, and Winston.

Pruzek, R. M., & Lepak, G. M. (1992). Weighted structural regression: A broad class of adaptive methods. *Multivariate Behavioral Research, 27*(1), 95-129.

Saris, W. E., & Satorra, A. (1993). Power evaluations in structural equation models. In K.A. Bollen and J.S. Long (Eds.). *Testing structural equation models*. Newbury Park, CA: Sage Publications.

Spearman, C. (1904). General intelligence objectively determined and measured. *American Journal of Psychology, 15*, 201-293.

Wothke, W. (1993). Nonpositive definite matrices in structural equation modeling. In K.A. Bollen and J.S. Long (Eds.). *Testing structural equation models*. Newbury Park, CA: Sage Publications.

Wright, S. (1921). Correlation and causation. *Journal of Agricultural Research, 20,* 557-585.

LISREL 8 Analysis

Donna A. Bachand

N urses investigate complex relationships among complex phenomena. Traditional methods of examining cause-effect relationships are often inefficient for such models. Meeting the assumptions of path analysis, for example, poses a number of conceptual and methodological constraints that limit the complexity of models which can be tested empirically. Structural equation analysis, however, offers a powerful statistical tool as it encompasses factor analysis, path analysis and analysis of variance or covariance in a single theory-testing framework.

Although many software packages are available for both mainframe and personal computers, this chapter focuses on the LISREL 8 (Scientific Software International) program developed by Jöreskog and Sörbom (1993). The program is available in DOS, extended DOS and Windows versions. The regular DOS version can be installed and run on an IBM-compatible 286 without a math coprocessor. Extended-DOS or Windows versions require the following system features:

- 386sx, 386 or 486 CPU
- PC-DOS or MS-DOS (version 3.0 or later) and Windows 3.1
- MDA, CGA, EGA, VGA or MCGA compatible video card
- Hard disk and one diskette drive
- Minimum of 2 MB RAM
- Math co-processor

DEFINITIONS AND ASSUMPTIONS

LISREL is an acronym for linear structural equation analysis. Other terms such as structural equation modeling (SEM), covariance structure modeling and latent variable modeling are used interchangeably in the literature. LISREL is one of many statistical modeling tools that employ matrix algebra to estimate covariances among a system of equations. The term 'structural' implies causality. In postulating a structural relation between two variables, the researcher asserts an invariant cause-effect relationship rather than a simple association.

As the name implies, the method is founded on the general linear model and therefore holds the same assumptions (see Table 16.1). A considerable body of research documents LISREL's robustness to violations of normal distribution as long as sample sizes are sufficiently large (Jöreskog & Sörbom, 1993). Special features of SEM allow the researcher to either relax assumptions or account for them. The assumption of perfect measurement can be relaxed, for example, by obtaining multiple measures for each latent construct.

Careful data screening and appropriate transformation procedures can reduce problems associated with minor departures from linearity. LISREL also offers numerous choices among estimation techniques. Although maximum likelihood estimates are robust with continuous variables, alternate methods

Figure 16.1 Theoretical Model of Quality of Life

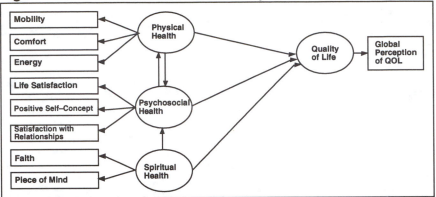

¹This model is derived from a larger model currently under study by the author.

such as weighted least squares are more appropriate with ordinal data because they do not assume normal distribution of covariances. Estimation methods are discussed later in this chapter.

RESEARCH QUESTIONS AND HYPOTHESES

The primary objective of structural equation modeling is to test theory, or perhaps more appropriately stated, to test the fit between a conceptual model and a set of observations. SEM procedures emphasize covariances rather than cases (Bollen, 1989). Traditional statistical methods minimize functions of observed and predicted individual cases. SEM, on the other hand, minimizes the difference between covariances observed in the sample data and covariances predicted by the model. The null hypothesis may be written as a general equation:

$$\Sigma = \Sigma(\Theta)$$

where Σ is the population covariance matrix of observed variables, Θ is a vector containing model parameters and $\Sigma(\Theta)$ is the covariance matrix implied by the model. In other words, the hypothesis asserts that the covariance matrix of observed variables is a function of a set of parameters. If the model were correctly specified and the parameter values known, the population covariance matrix could be exactly reproduced and the null hypothesis subjected to a statistical test of significance. The appropriate statistic is the χ^2 goodness of fit test. Jöreskog (1993) actually refers to the χ^2 statistic as a badness of fit test because a significant difference from zero implies a poor fit between model and data. Fit assessment is discussed in greater detail in a subsequent section of this chapter.

In addition to overall fit, LISREL estimates the strength and statistical significance of the parameters (paths) specified by the model. Since the measurement model is essentially a common factor model, parameter estimates can be interpreted as factor loadings. The larger the parameter estimate, the stronger the relationship between an empirical indicator and its associated latent construct. Error terms yield information about measurement error or reliability of

Table 16.1 LISREL Assumptions

1.	Normal or near–normal distribution of scores on x's and y's and the error terms δ and ε.
2.	Linearity of bivariate relationships.
3.	ζ is uncorrelated with V or error in structural equations is not related to values of the latent exogenous variables.
4.	ε is uncorrelated with η, or error in measuring y is not related to the latent endogenous variables.
5.	δ is uncorrelated ς, or error in measuring x is not related to the latent exogenous variables.
6.	ς, ε, and δ are mutually uncorrelated.

empirical indicators. Generally speaking, the larger the error the more unreliable the measure. Multitrait-multimethod analysis must be carried out to diagnose the source of error variance. Structural parameter estimates are interpreted as effect coefficients. These values provide information about the strength and direction of proposed paths or structural relationships among the latent variables. T-statistics and P-values reported for each coefficient indicate statistical significance from zero.

DATA SCREENING AND MANAGEMENT

Statistical tests are only valid if the inherent assumptions are met. Careful data screening is therefore an essential prerequisite to model testing. Screening can be accomplished with SPSSX (Scientific Software International) or any other statistical package. However, the PRELIS program computes a wide variety of moment matrices not available elsewhere. The current version (PRELIS 2) will read any ASCII file, list all values found in the raw data, report the number and relative frequency of each data value and display a bar chart to graphically depict the distribution of values.

Data Manipulation

Variables and Scale Types. An important first step in data screening is to determine the type and scale of each variable. Many variables of interest to nurse researchers are ordinal. Although it is common practice to treat ordinal variables as continuous, this practice is not feasible in maximum likelihood estimation. Ordinal variables do not have origins or specific units of measurement, so their means, variances and covariances have no theoretical meaning. Correlations (specifically, Pearson product moment correlations) consistently underestimate relationships between ordinal variables (Jöreskog & Sörbom, 1993).

PRELIS 2 distinguishes between continuous, ordinal, censored and fixed variables. Censored variables have a high concentration of cases at the upper or lower tail of the distribution. For example, 'weeks of gestation' appears skewed because of a ceiling effect around 42 weeks — any resulting correlation calculated with this variable will be biased. Treating this variable as censored reduces skewness and produces better estimates. Censoring "spreads out" a distribution by replacing maximum or minimum values with their corresponding normal scores. After censoring, variables are treated as continuous.

By default, the program classifies all variables with fewer than 16 categories as ordinal and all others as continuous. The researcher must specify censored or fixed variables.

Missing Values. Missing values can create enormous problems in LISREL.
Matrix algebra operations require that values on the diagonal of the matrix be
positive. If the diagonal elements are zero or negative the matrix is nonpositive
definite and LISREL will not run. When covariances are computed by pairwise
deletion of missing data, the resulting matrix may be nonpositive definite, particularly when the sample is small (Wothke, 1993).

Listwise deletion is practical if there are only a few missing cases and the
deletion process does not jeopardize an already small sample size. PRELIS 2
offers a method for imputing missing values or substituting real values for the
missing values. The imputation procedure scans the data set for patterns and
replaces a missing value for a case with a value from another case that has a
similar response pattern over a set of matching variables. The researcher must
specify the matching variables as well as the variable to be imputed. PRELIS
scans all cases for which there are no missing values on both the matching
variables and the variable to be imputed, calculates a value and performs the
substitution. If no such cases exist, imputation is not possible (Jöreskog &
Sörbom, 1993b). The imputation approach yields less biased structural parameter estimates than pairwise deletion, listwise deletion or mean substitution procedures (Brown, 1994).

Recoding Observations and Creating New Variables. The recode command is useful in many familiar situations. The researcher may wish to di-
chotomize a variable, collapse several categories of a variable or reorder negatively worded items on a survey. Recoding is primarily intended for ordinal
variables, but may also be used with continuous variables.

A new variable can be created as some function of an existing variable. For
example, variables can be weighted by adding or multiplying a constant. The
new variable command is particularly useful in calculating scale scores or factor scores as a linear combination of existing variables. The new variable is
subsequently treated as any other variable with regard to missing values, recode
statements and transformations. Unlike the earlier version, PRELIS 2 performs all operations in the order specified in the input file. The researcher can
either recode variables and then select a subset of cases on the recoded values
or select cases first and recode variables only for those cases.

Testing the Assumptions. PRELIS displays a bar chart for both univariate
and bivariate distributions of ordinal variables, gives a histogram for continuous variables and calculates statistical tests of normality. For ordinal variables, absolute and relative frequencies are given in univariate and bivariate
contingency tables. The mean, standard deviation, skewness and kurtosis are
reported for each continuous variable and for any censored ordinal variables.
PRELIS also performs tests of multivariate skewness and kurtosis for all continuous variables jointly. Tests of homogeneity are available for ordinal variables to determine whether marginal distributions are significantly different.
Homogeneity tests must be requested in the input file; all other tests are computed by default unless turned off. The investigator may opt not to print bi-

variate contingency tables or multivariate statistics tables as these become lengthy with large models.

Data Transformations. Power and logarithmic transformations are available to improve non-normal distributions of continuous variables. The procedures will also transform ordinal or censored variables, but the output will not be meaningful. Writing a power or log command implies that all variables listed on the command line be transformed using the same procedure. The investigator may choose the default procedures or use any transformation in the general power or log families of equations.

Choosing a Matrix to Analyze
Selecting the appropriate matrix to analyze always depends on the type of data available. A covariance matrix is optimal when all variables are continuous. In this situation, any estimation technique will yield consistent results. If one or more variables in the data set is ordinal, a correlation or asymptotic covariance matrix should be analyzed in order to obtain non-biased estimates.

The user can specify which matrix to analyze on the output line. However, PRELIS computes the appropriate matrix depending on the type of variables contained in the data. Pearson product moment correlations will be computed for ordinal or continuous variables; this is the KM option. The PM option calls for computation of polychoric or polyserial correlations between ordinal or ordinal and continuous variables, respectively. The CM option computes the covariance matrix. All computed matrices assume an underlying normal distribution. If data screening indicates violations of this assumption, the asymptotic covariance matrix should be requested.

THE PRELIS RUN
Control Lines
Control lines tell PRELIS how to operate. Each line begins with a specific name, the first two letters of which are recognized by the program. Title or comment lines are optional, but must not begin with characters that could be read as control lines. For example, DA signifies the data line. When the program encounters DA, it expects to encounter a list of data parameters to read, not a comment line. If PRELIS cannot find the data parameters, the program stops.

For each problem run, a minimum set of control lines must be entered in order. Required lines include title, data (DA), raw data (RA) and output (OU). These lines tell PRELIS what kind of data to look for, where to locate the raw data and how to save or print the output. All other lines are optional: variable labels, scale types, treatment of missing data, transformation or recoding procedures, case selections and statistical procedures. Table 16.2 lists the required and optional control lines.

Figure 16.2 depicts a theoretical model of quality of life.[1] To test the model, data were collected from 174 adults diagnosed with cancer. Subjects responded to a series of questions about their physical, psychosocial and spiritual status and evaluated their global perception of quality of life.

Each empirical indicator for the exogenous constructs actually consists of a pair of items—one to evaluate satisfaction and one to measure the importance of that particular aspect of life. The two items are measured on six-point Likert

Table 16.2 Required and Optional Control Lines for PRELIS

Required	Optional	General Comments
	Title	• may include as many lines as desires • may be 10127 characters long
DA (data line)		• NI specifies the number of variables • NO specifies the number of cases • MI may be used to denote missing values • TR=LI or PA may be used to request listwise or pairwise deletion of missing data. LI is the default.
	LA (labels)	• may be entered in free or FORTRAN format • may be read from an external file • if not named, variables are numbered VAR1, VAR2, etc.
RA (raw data)		• must be read from an external file • may be read in free or FORTAN format • will be read as a matrix with one case per row and one variable per column
	Scale types	• OR declares variable(s) as ordinal • CO declares variable(s) as continuous • CA censors variables above, or at the upper end of the distribution • CB censors below or at the low end • CE censors above and below
	PO or LO (power or log transformations)	• used to transform specified variables prior to computing correlations • intended for transforming CO variables
	RE (recode)	• NE creates a new variable as some function of an existing variable • use to collapse categories or recode negatively worded survey items
	SC (select cases)	• use to select subsets of cases for analysis (e.g., all females or all cases with specific scores)
	RG (regression)	• must include the keyword ON to regress specified y variables onto specified x variables
OU (output)		• MA denotes the type of matrix to compute • S specifies which parameters to save and where to save them • P specifies which parameters to print

scales and then multiplied to obtain scores for each indicator. This is accomplished by creating a new variable for each pair of satisfaction-importance items; the new variables will be used in subsequent LISREL analyses. Control lines for the data screening run are given below.

```
PRELIS DATA SCREENING FOR THE QOL STUDY
DA NI=17 NO=174 MI=-9 TR=LI
LA
SCOMFORT SENERGY SMOBILE SRELATE SLIFESAT SSELFCON
SPEACE SFAITH
ICOMFORT IENERGY IMOBILE IRELATE ILIFESAT ISELFCON IPEACE
IFAITH QOL
RA FI=QL.RAW
CO QOL
NE COMFORT=SCOMFORT*ICOMFORT
NE ENERGY= SENERGY*IENERGY
NE MOBILITY=SMOBILITY*IMOBILITY
NE RELATION=SRELATE*IRELATE
NE LIFESAT=SLIFESAT*ILIFESAT
NE SELFCON=SSELFCON*ISELFCON
NE PEACE=SPEACE*IPEACE
NE FAITH=SFAITH*IFAITH
OU MA=PM SM=QLEX.PM XB
```

The control lines inform PRELIS there are 17 variables for 174 cases. Missing values are coded as -9, and listwise deletion is requested. The LA command assigns labels for the 17 variables. The RA line indicates the raw scores for each variable are stored in an external file called QL.RAW. Since no fortran format is specified for either labels or data, the program will read both in free format in the order encountered.

The CO line defines QOL as a continuous variable; all others are ordinal by default. The next eight lines compute new variables with the NE command. These variables will be used later in LISREL analyses. Finally, the output line specifies that a product-moment matrix should be calculated and saved in a file called QLEX.PM for later use in LISREL. The XB command instructs the program not to print the bivariate contingency tables. These tables provide information about how subjects score on pairs of variables. In this example, the resulting output exceeded 6000 lines of print, so the function was "turned off." Output of the problem run is abbreviated in Table 16.3.

Reading the Output

PRELIS output always begins by repeating the control lines followed by a count of missing values for each variable. After listwise deletion, the total effective sample size for this example is 164; 10 cases have missing data. Bar charts for the ordinal variables clearly indicate skewed distributions for the eight new variables. This finding is not unexpected, as most subjects in the sample rated these eight aspects of life as highly important on a scale of 1 to 6. Quality of life ratings are also slightly skewed in this sample. The histogram provides a graphic representation of the numerical statistics summarized in

Table 16.3 LISREL Output Example

```
The following lines were read from file D:\LISREL8W\EXAMPLE.PR2:

PRELIS2 EXAMPLE RUN
DA NI=17 NO=174 MI=-9 TR=LI
LA
SCOMFORT SENERGY SMOBILE SRELATE SLIFESAT SSELFCON SPEACE SFAITH
ICOMFORT IENERGY IMOBILE IRELATE ILIFESAT ISELFCON IPEACE IFAITH QOL
RA FI=QL.RAW
CO QOL
NE COMFORT=SCOMFORT=ICOMFORT
NE ENERGY=SENERGY=IENERGY
NE MOBILITY=SMOBILE=IMOBILE
NE RELATION=SRELATE=IRELATE
NE LIFESAT=SLIFESAT=ILIFESAT
NE SELFCON=SSELFCON=ISELFCON
NE PEACE=SPEACE=IPEACE
NE FAITH=SFAITH=IFAITH
OU MA=PM SM=QLEX.PM XB


NUMBER OF MISSING VALUES PER VARIABLE
  SCOMFORT    SENERGY    SMOBILE    SRELATE    SLIFESAT   SSELFCON    SPEACE     SFAITH
      0           0          0          0          2          2          0          0
  ICOMFORT    IENERGY    IMOBILE    IRELATE    ILIFESAT   ISELFCON    IPEACE     IFAITH
      4           0          0          2          0          0          0          0
      QOL     COMFORT     ENERGY   MOBILITY    RELATION    LIFESAT    SELFCON     PEACE
      0           4          0          0          7          2          0          0
    FAITH
      0


DISTRIBUTION OF MISSING VALUES
TOTAL SAMPLE SIZE =   174

NUMBER OF MISSING VALUES    0    1    2    3    4
            NUMBER OF CASES 164  0    5    2    3
LISTWISE DELETION
TOTAL EFFECTIVE SAMPLE SIZE =   164


UNIVARIATE DISTRIBUTIONS FOR ORDINAL VARIABLES

  COMFORT FREQUENCY PERCENTAGE BAR CHART
      5         4        2.4    ||||
      6         6        3.7    ||||||
      9         2        1.2    ||
     10        12        7.3    ||||||||||||
     15         4        2.4    ||||
     18         6        3.7    ||||||
     20        14        8.5    ||||||||||||||
     24        16        9.8    ||||||||||||||||
     25        20       12.2    ||||||||||||||||||||
     30        44       26.8    |||||||||||||||||||||||||||||||||||||||||||||
     36        36       22.0    |||||||||||||||||||||||||||||||||||||

  ENERGY FREQUENCY PERCENTAGE BAR CHART
      4         2        1.2    ||
      5         2        1.2    ||
      6         7        4.3    |||||||
     10         2        1.2    ||
     12         3        1.8    |||
     15         5        3.0    |||||
     18         8        4.9    ||||||||
     20        21       12.8    |||||||||||||||||||||
     24        50       30.5    ||||||||||||||||||||||||||||||||||||||||||||||||||
     25        14        8.5    ||||||||||||||
     30        44       26.8    ||||||||||||||||||||||||||||||||||||||||||||
     36         6        3.7    ||||||

  MOBILITY FREQUENCY PERCENTAGE BAR CHART
      5         4        2.4    |||
      6         4        2.4    |||
     10         2        1.2    ||
     12         3        1.8    |||
     15         4        2.4    |||
     16         1        0.6    |
     18         5        3.0    ||||
     20         5        3.0    ||||
     24        25       15.2    |||||||||||||||||||||||||
     25        11        6.7    |||||||||||
```

Table 16.3 LISREL Output Example (cont.)

```
RELATION FREQUENCY PERCENTAGE BAR CHART
    4        2         1.2     |
    6        4         2.4     ||
   12        2         1.2     |
   15        3         1.8     ||
   18        9         5.5     |||||
   20       11         6.7     ||||||
   24       19        11.6     |||||||||||
   25       10         6.1     ||||||
   30       23        14.0     |||||||||||||
   36       81        49.4     |||||||||||||||||||||||||||||||||||||||||||||||||

LIFESAT FREQUENCY PERCENTAGE BAR CHART
   10        4         2.4     ||||
   12        6         3.7     ||||||
   15        7         4.3     |||||||
   16        2         1.2     ||
   18       20        12.2     ||||||||||||||||||||
   20        5         3.0     |||||
   24       15         9.1     |||||||||||||||
   25       12         7.3     ||||||||||||
   30       50        30.5     ||||||||||||||||||||||||||||||||||||||||||||||||||
   36       43        26.2     |||||||||||||||||||||||||||||||||||||||||

SELFCON FREQUENCY PERCENTAGE BAR CHART
    3        2         1.2     |
    5        2         1.2     |
   10        8         4.9     |||||
   15        4         2.4     |||
   16        2         1.2     |
   18        2         1.2     |
   20        3         1.8     ||
   24        5         3.0     |||
   25       14         8.5     |||||||||
   30       47        28.7     |||||||||||||||||||||||||||||
   36       75        45.7     |||||||||||||||||||||||||||||||||||||||||||||||

PEACE FREQUENCY PERCENTAGE BAR CHART
   10        2         1.2     |
   15        6         3.7     ||||
   16        1         0.6     |
   18        2         1.2     |
   20        9         5.5     ||||||
   24       11         6.7     |||||||
   25       20        12.2     |||||||||||||
   30       73        44.5     ||||||||||||||||||||||||||||||||||||||||||||||
   36       40        24.4     |||||||||||||||||||||||||||

FAITH FREQUENCY PERCENTAGE BAR CHART
   15        4         2.4     |||
   18        2         1.2     |
   20       12         7.3     |||||||||
   24       10         6.1     |||||||
   25       17        10.4     ||||||||||||
   30       63        38.4     |||||||||||||||||||||||||||||||||||||||||
   36       56        34.1     ||||||||||||||||||||||||||||||||||||||
```

```
UNIVARIATE SUMMARY STATISTICS FOR CONTINUOUS VARIABLES
VARIABLE    MEAN   ST. DEV.  SKEWNESS  KURTOSIS  MINIMUM FREQ.  MAXIMUM FREQ.

   QOL    72.207   17.866    -0.956     0.503     20.000    2   98.000    2
```

```
TEST OF UNIVARIATE NORMALITY FOR CONTINUOUS VARIABLES
                 SKEWNESS           KURTOSIS      SKEWNESS AND KURTOSIS
            Z-SCORE P-VALUE    Z-SCORE P-VALUE    CHI-SQUARE P-VALUE
     QOL    -2.897   0.002      1.389   0.082        10.322   0.006
```

```
TEST OF MULTIVARIATE NORMALITY FOR CONTINUOUS VARIABLES
                 SKEWNESS           KURTOSIS      SKEWNESS AND KURTOSIS
            Z-SCORE P-VALUE    Z-SCORE P-VALUE    CHI-SQUARE P-VALUE
             3.794   0.000      1.254   0.105        15.965   0.000
```

```
HISTOGRAMS FOR CONTINUOUS VARIABLES

          QOL
FREQUENCY PERCENTAGE LOWER CLASS LIMIT
    4        2.4        20.000       ||||
    4        2.4        27.800       ||||
    8        4.9        35.600       ||||||||
```

Table 16.3 LISREL Output Example (cont.)

```
   28       17.1      66.800     ||||||||||||||||||||||||||||||
   36       22.0      74.600     |||||||||||||||||||||||||||||||||||||||
   30       18.3      82.400     |||||||||||||||||||||||||||||||||||
   18       11.0      90.200     ||||||||||||||||||||||
```

```
                        CORRELATIONS AND TEST STATISTICS
              (PE=PEARSON PRODUCT MOMENT, PC=POLYCHORIC, PS=POLYSERIAL)
                                         TEST OF MODEL        TEST OF CLOSE FIT
                          CORRELATION  CHI-SQU.  D.F. P-VALUE   RMSEA  P-VALUE


   COMFORT VS.      QOL   0.805 (PS)   73.063     19   0.000    0.132   0.000
   ENERGY VS.       QOL   0.741 (PS)   66.885     21   0.000    0.115   0.000
   ENERGY VS.   COMFORT   0.731 (PC)  178.089    109   0.000    0.062   0.113
   MOBILITY VS.     QOL   0.396 (PS)  140.030     19   0.000    0.177   0.000
   MOBILITY VS. COMFORT   0.628 (PC)  177.667    109   0.000    0.062   0.117
   MOBILITY VS.  ENERGY   0.721 (PC)  170.067    120   0.002    0.050   0.468
   RELATION VS.     QOL   0.528 (PS)   41.278     17   0.001    0.093   0.027
   RELATION VS. COMFORT   0.553 (PC)  155.924     89   0.000    0.068   0.053
   RELATION VS.  ENERGY   0.584 (PC)  152.142     98   0.000    0.058   0.224
   RELATION VS. MOBILITY  0.466 (PC)  141.923     98   0.002    0.052   0.405
   LIFESAT VS.      QOL   0.553 (PS)   66.171     17   0.000    0.133   0.000
   LIFESAT VS.  COMFORT   0.456 (PC)  234.892     89   0.000    0.100   0.000
   LIFESAT VS.   ENERGY   0.402 (PC)  165.828     98   0.000    0.065   0.077
   LIFESAT VS. MOBILITY   0.408 (PC)  152.881     98   0.000    0.058   0.213
   LIFESAT VS. RELATION   0.236 (PC)  152.332     80   0.000    0.074   0.016
   SELFCON VS.      QOL   0.578 (PS)   62.754     19   0.000    0.118   0.000
W_A_R_N_I_N_G: The iterations did not converge
               The correlation may not be correct. ERROR CODE 205.
   SELFCON VS.  COMFORT   0.476 (PC)  161.912     99   0.000    0.062   0.122
   SELFCON VS.   ENERGY   0.379 (PC)  128.845    109   0.094    0.033   0.899
   SELFCON VS. MOBILITY   0.375 (PC)  137.775    109   0.033    0.040   0.784
   SELFCON VS. RELATION   0.412 (PC)  169.477     89   0.000    0.074   0.012
   SELFCON VS.  LIFESAT   0.540 (PC)  144.261     89   0.000    0.062   0.149
   PEACE VS.        QOL   0.341 (PS)   18.642     13   0.135    0.046   0.503
   PEACE VS.    COMFORT   0.388 (PC)  159.385     79   0.000    0.079   0.005
   PEACE VS.     ENERGY   0.447 (PC)  138.535     87   0.000    0.060   0.183
   PEACE VS.   MOBILITY   0.425 (PC)  147.434     87   0.000    0.065   0.087
   PEACE VS.   RELATION   0.344 (PC)  107.618     71   0.003    0.056   0.306
   PEACE VS.    LIFESAT   0.521 (PC)  103.004     71   0.008    0.052   0.409
   PEACE VS.    SELFCON   0.650 (PC)  132.333     79   0.000    0.064   0.112
   FAITH VS.        QOL   0.507 (PS)   18.258     11   0.076    0.063   0.295
   FAITH VS.    COMFORT   0.408 (PC)  128.739     59   0.000    0.085   0.003
   FAITH VS.     ENERGY   0.373 (PC)   93.246     65   0.012    0.051   0.438
   FAITH VS.   MOBILITY   0.461 (PC)  119.737     65   0.000    0.072   0.042
   FAITH VS.   RELATION   0.158 (PC)   83.114     53   0.005    0.059   0.261
   FAITH VS.    LIFESAT   0.587 (PC)  118.989     53   0.000    0.097   0.003
   FAITH VS.    SELFCON   0.454 (PC)  122.767     59   0.000    0.081   0.008
   FAITH VS.      PEACE   0.838 (PC)   85.016     47   0.001    0.070   0.083
            PERCENTAGE OF TESTS EXCEEDING 0.5% SIGNIFICANCE LEVEL : 24.7%
            PERCENTAGE OF TESTS EXCEEDING 1.0% SIGNIFICANCE LEVEL : 49.2%
            PERCENTAGE OF TESTS EXCEEDING 5.0% SIGNIFICANCE LEVEL : 49.2%


PRELIS2 EXAMPLE RUN:


         CORRELATION MATRIX
            QOL     COMFORT    ENERGY   MOBILITY   RELATION   LIFESAT   SELFCON   PEACE

    QOL    1.000
 COMFORT   0.085    1.000
  ENERGY   0.741    0.731     1.000
 MOBILITY  0.396    0.628     0.721    1.000
 RELATION  0.528    0.553     0.584    0.466     1.000
  LIFESAT  0.553    0.456     0.402    0.408     0.236     1.000
  SELFCON  0.578    0.476     0.379    0.375     0.412     0.540     1.000
    PEACE  0.341    0.388     0.447    0.425     0.344     0.521     0.650    1.000
    FAITH  0.507    0.408     0.373    0.461     0.158     0.587     0.454    0.838


          THE PROBLEM USED  99312 BYTES (= 1.4% OF AVAILABLE WORKSPACE)
END OF PROBLEM
```

table form. These findings might be improved by imputing missing values and censoring the ordinal variables.

The table of correlations and test statistics yields correlations and significance levels for each pair of variables. PC and PS refer to the type of correlation; in this example polychoric (PC) and polyserial (PS) correlations were computed. Among all possible pairs, 24.7% were significant at the 0.5% level. The correlations are also displayed in matrix form.

TRANSLATING PATH DIAGRAMS TO EQUATIONS
Specifying Relationships

An initial task in SEM involves specifying a path diagram. The path diagram is actually a graphical representation of a system of simultaneous equations—a picture of the hypothetical relationships postulated by the theory to be tested. Every line in the diagram is associated with an equation. A major advantage of path diagrams is that many researchers can identify modeled relations more easily than their associated equations.

By convention, observed variables are enclosed in squares and labeled x (exogenous) or y (endogenous). Latent constructs are enclosed in circles or elipses and labeled with the Greek letters ξ (exogenous) or η (endogenous). Disturbance or error terms are also included in the diagram but are not enclosed: δ represents error in measuring the x variable, ε is the measurement error for y and ζ denotes error in an equation.

Arrows signify relations. A straight single-headed arrow represents an assumed causal relationship in the direction of the point. In other words, the variable at the base of the arrow is the "cause" variable, and the one at the arrow's tip is the "effect" variable. Two straight single-headed arrows depict reciprocal causation or a feedback loop. A curved two-headed arrow implies simple correlation. The absence of a link or arrow is theoretically meaningful;

Figure 16.2 Path Diagram for a Latent Variable Model

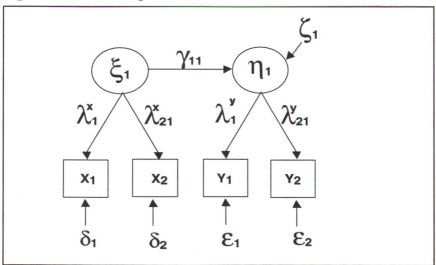

in this situation, the researcher specifies that no association exists. Figure 16.2 illustrates a path diagram for a latent variable model.

Each arrow is associated with a coefficient. In structural equation models, coefficients are usually labeled with Greek letters and a two-number subscript. The first number in the subscript denotes the variable *to* which the arrow points and the second is the variable *from* which the arrow originates. In the above model, for example:

The path from ξ_1 to x_1 is $\lambda_{11}^{(x)}$ or simply $\lambda_1^{(x)}$
The path from ξ_1 to x_2 is $\lambda_{21}^{(x)}$
The path from η_1 to y_1 is $\lambda_{11}^{(y)}$ or simply $\lambda_1^{(y)}$
The path from η_1 to y_2 is $\lambda_{21}^{(y)}$
The path from ξ_1 to η_1 is γ_{11}

Using these conventions, the researcher can write all the necessary model equations by following two simple rules. For each variable with a one-way arrow pointing to it, there must be one equation in which this variable is on the left side. The right-hand side of each equation is the sum of the terms equal to the number of one-way arrows pointing to that variable; each term is the product of the coefficient associated with the arrow and the variable from which the arrow originates. Thus, for the simple model in Figure 16.1:

$$x_1 = \lambda_1^{(x)}\xi_1 + \delta_1$$
$$x_2 = \lambda_{21}\xi_1 + \delta_2$$
$$y_1 = \lambda_1^{(y)}\eta_1 + \varepsilon_1$$
$$y_2 = \lambda_{21}\eta_1 + \varepsilon_2$$
$$\eta_1 = \gamma_{11}\xi_1 + \zeta_1$$

The SIMPLIS command language of LISREL8 permits the user to specify equations without using mathematical notation. For each dependent variable, one equation can be written by listing the variables upon which it depends. Relationships are simply specified as:

left-hand variable = right-hand variables OR
TO variable = FROM variables

In path terminology, the same relationship is written 'FROM variable - > TO variables' to signify a path or one-way arrow from the FROM variable to each of the TO variables listed.

TESTING THE MEASUREMENT MODEL
Modeling Latent Constructs

Many concepts of interest to nurses are actually constructs, or highly abstract non-observable phenomena. Constructs such as quality of life, motivation, social support and hardiness are not directly measurable. Because constructs are not directly observable, theory cannot be tested directly. It is therefore essential to translate the theory into a statistical model that is testable.

This task involves much more than drawing a path diagram and calculating regression coefficients. The researcher must not only know the theory well, but must also make methodological decisions aimed at maximizing information gain while minimizing bias. An initial task in modeling is to define the latent constructs in terms of their relevant dimensions and to select empirical indicators to measure them. Both theoretical and measurement considerations come into play in the selection process, but the result is a measurement model which can be subjected to statistical reliability and validity tests.

It is imperative to test the measurement model prior to estimating the structural model. If the measurement model fails to hold—that is, if the indicators chosen to measure a construct do not actually measure that construct—then subsequent tests of the theoretical model are meaningless. Jöreskog (1993) recommends testing the measurement model in stages, first by carrying out the procedure for each construct separately, then for paired constructs, and finally for all constructs simultaneously. This is rarely accomplished in practice, however, since many empirical indicators may load onto or correlate with more than one latent variable.

Specifying Factor Structures

The measurement model is essentially a factor model (Long, 1983) which describes relationships between latent and observed variables. In other words, this model links each latent construct with a set of empirical indicators hypothesized to represent the construct. Again, using Figure 16.2 as an example, the measurement portion of the model proposes a factor structure consisting of two indicators for ξ and two for η. These are x_1 and x_2 and y_1 and y_2, respectively. Measurement models may be tested for the exogenous and endogenous factors separately and for the two variables simultaneously. Note that the only relationship depicted in Figure 16.2 not included in the measurement model is γ_{11}, the structural (causal) path between ξ and η.

Scaling the Latent Variables

Imagine that a latent construct is measured by two indices—a self-report measure and an objective rating scale. In most practical situations, values obtained with these measures are not comparable unless both are continuous ratio-level variables having the same origin and unit of measurement. Furthermore, the latent variable itself is implied rather than directly measured, so it has no scale whatsoever. In order to interpret the program output, the researcher must set a scale for each latent variable.

Scaling may be accomplished two ways in LISREL 8 (Jöreskog & Sörbom, 1993). The investigator may identify one of the empirical indicators as a reference variable or "best" indicator for the construct and assign a non-zero coefficient to that indicator. This coefficient (usually 1) defines the unit of measurement for the latent construct. If no reference variable is identified, the program will standardize the latent construct so that its unit of measurement equals the population standard deviation.

Estimating Reliability and Validity

Reliability refers to consistency of measurement (Nunnally, 1978) or the part of a measure that is free of purely random error. In SEM, reliability is the squared correlation of a measure and its latent construct (Bollen, 1989). In SEM theory, the ξ variables exert direct systematic effects on the x variables — any other source is variance in x is attributable to error. Thus, the stronger the systematic variance, the higher the reliability of a measure. Of course, the x variables can be correlated among themselves. In this situation, the squared multiple correlation coefficient (R^2) for x provides the best estimate of reliability.

Validity refers to whether an indicator measures what it is supposed to measure (Nunnally, 1978). Content validity requires a qualitative judgement and cannot be assessed statistically. The researcher must define relevant domains of each construct and select empirical indicators for these domains based on the theory. Criterion validity is typically estimated by the correlation between a measure and some established criterion variable (Nunnally, 1978). In SEM, the two variables of interest are either x or y indicators. Traditional correlation "coefficients" are not necessarily informative in SEM because the values of indicators are generated by the latent constructs. Again considering the model in Figure 16.1, the correlation between x_1 and x_2 is affected by both λ_{11} and λ_{21}. These paths are further influenced by their associated error terms.

Construct validity is concerned with whether an indicator correlates with other indicators from a theoretically specified domain (Nunnally, 1978). Imagine two latent constructs ξ_1 and ξ_2. If the theory hypothesizes a positive correlation between these two constructs, then their empirical indicators should also correlate positively. However, the correlation between empirical indicators in latent variable models is attenuated by correlations between the latent variables (the λs) and by error. If the two ξ variables do not correlate as predicted (because of sampling error or any other source of error), neither will the indicators. This situation does not necessarily imply that the measures lack validity. In SEM, bivariate correlations are less meaningful than their underlying structural linkages (Bollen, 1989).

Bollen (1989) offers an alternative definition of validity in structural equation modeling. He defines validity as the magnitude of the direct structural relation between a measure and its latent construct. For example, the researcher hypothesizes that x_1 is a valid measure of ξ_1 and tests this hypothesis by examining the direct causal link between them. Lambda (λ) coefficients, squared multiple correlations and unique error variances provide information about the fit between empirical indicators and their latent constructs.

ESTIMATING THE STRUCTURAL MODEL
General Assessment of Model Fit

Chi square (χ^2) provides a general indicator of how well the model fits the sample data. A small χ^2 value indicates a good fit or a small discrepancy between sample covariances and covariances predicted by the model. Most authors advise caution in using χ^2 as the sole criterion of model efficacy (Bollen, 1989; Jöreskog, 1993; Gerbing & Anderson, 1993). It is always possible to generate one or even several models to fit a given data set, whether or not the model holds substantive meaning. Jöreskog and Sörbom therefore recommend examining the total LISREL solution including parameter estimates with their standard errors, χ^2 and other measures of overall fit, residuals matrices and modification indices.

Evaluating Parameter Estimates and Standard Errors

LISREL 8 prints parameter estimates, standard errors of estimates, T-values and squared multiple correlations for each relationship specified by the model.

The parameter estimates should have the correct sign and reasonable magnitudes. Unreasonable parameter estimates may mean that the model is incorrectly specified or may reflect sampling error, missing data or biases introduced by analyzing the wrong matrix with an inappropriate estimation method. The T-value reported for each estimate indicates how different that estimate is from zero. T-values greater than 2 generally imply statistical significance. The squared multiple correlation or R^2 measures the strength of relationships — the larger the R^2, the stronger the relationship. If the parameter estimates are judged as substantively interpretable, then overall fit can be assessed. If not, the researcher should attempt to diagnose possible theoretical or methodological reasons for the estimates and consider respecifying the model.

Evaluating Overall Fit

LISREL 8 output yields multiple indicators of model fit derived from several families of fit statistics. All of these statistics are functions of χ^2. There is no widely agreed upon standard for comparing the utility of these test statistics. The only consensus is that multiple indices selected from different families should be reported (Bollen, 1989).

At a minimum, χ^2 should be examined with its associated degrees of freedom. Chi square can be improved by adding or freeing parameters, whether or not these parameters are substantively important. Examining the χ^2 to degrees of freedom ratio yields limited information about model fit in light of parsimony. Again, there is no accepted standard of comparison, but ratios of 2:1 or 3:1 are commonly reported. More sophisticated indices of parsimony-based fit have recently been reported in the literature (Williams & Holahan, 1994) and are included in the output of LISREL 8.

Jöreskog and Sörbom (1989) suggest evaluating the goodness of fit index (GFI) and adjusted goodness of fit index (AGFI) as additional indicators of model fit. The GFI and AGFI were developed to offset problems associated with sensitivity to sample size. Although the indices have received criticism, they are still reported in the LISREL output. Indices should range between 0 and 1, with higher numbers indicating greater fit.

The root mean square error of approximation (RMSEA) is strongly recommended in recent literature (Browne & Cudeck, 1993). This test estimates the degree of lack of fit based on discrepancies between the population covariance matrix and a fitted covariance matrix. Since the estimate accounts for degrees of freedom in the model, it does not necessarily improve as parameters are added to the model. The RMSEA can range from 0 to 1, with smaller values indicating less error of approximation and therefore better fit. Values of 0.08 or less are deemed reasonable and those over 0.1 justify rejecting the model.

Evaluating Residuals and Modification Indices
Residuals

Unacceptable fit statistics warrant a more detailed analysis of potential sources of misfit. A logical starting point is the residuals matrices. LISREL prints fitted and standardized residual matrices. By default, these are given in summary form as the largest, smallest and median values along with a stem leaf plot. Fitted residuals are produced by subtracting fitted from observed moment matrices. These values should be small compared to the elements in the observed moment matrix but are difficult to interpret.

The standardized residuals are usually more interpretable. These values are computed by dividing the fitted residuals by their standard errors. LISREL computes residuals for every pair of observed variables. A large positive residual means the model underestimates or does not account for the variance between two variables. Adding parameters to account for this variance will usually improve model fit. A large negative residual implies overestimation of variance; deleting this path should improve fit.

Residuals greater than 2.58 are usually considered significant, so the program lists these variables. If desired, the user can request the entire residuals matrix and Q-plot rather than summary statistics. Ideally, residuals in a Q-plot fall on a 45 degree line if the model fits well. Patterns outside the 45 degree line may occur with nonlinearity, non-normality or specification errors in the model. Outliers generally indicate specification errors.

Modification Indices

LISREL calculates a modification index (MI) for every fixed parameter in the model. The MI estimates the predicted decrease in χ^2 obtained if a single constraint is relaxed and the entire model re-estimated. The largest MI indicates which parameter to free in order to improve the model. Parameters should be freed one at a time and only when there is a substantive reason to do so. Parameters should not be relaxed just to achieve better model fit if those paths cannot be interpreted in light of the theory.

THE LISREL RUN
Setting Up the Run

Choosing an Appropriate Estimation Method. LISREL 8 fits the model covariance matrix S by one of seven estimation procedures. Maximum likelihood (ML) is the default method unless the program encounters an asymptotic covariance matrix or the user specifies an alternate method. If an asymptotic covariance matrix is provided, weighted least squares (WLS) is the default method. Other available procedures include unweighted least squares ULS), generalized least squares (GLS), two-stage least squares (TSLS) and diagonally weighted least squares (DWLS).

Writing the Command File. The command file is a program that controls LISREL execution. As previously stated, LISREL 8 will accept either SIMPLIS or LISREL 7 input files, but the two languages cannot be mixed. The remainder of this section addresses SIMPLIS syntax.

Required commands. SIMPLIS command files contain "header" lines followed by user input. For example, the header 'Title' may precede the title of the program. Title lines are optional in LISREL. If encountered, the program will read title lines until it encounters a line beginning with the keywords 'observed variables' or 'labels.' Any line beginning with an exclamation point (!) will be treated as a comment or title line. The first required header is labeled 'observed variables' or 'labels.' Although the terms are synonymous, the former is useful in distinguishing models that also contain latent variables.

Variables must then be listed in the order encountered in the data file. If the data are stored on a floppy disk, the command should give the filename. All variables contained in the data file do not have to be included in a particular study. The user can list the variables of interest and LISREL will read only those given on the command line.

The next line must tell LISREL which data to analyze. This command may instruct the program to read raw data or the appropriate matrix from an external file or the data/matrix may be written directly into the program. The most logical approach is to compute and save the appropriate covariance matrix with PRELIS and simply tell LISREL where to find it. This approach is especially feasible with large data sets.

Sample size must be given on the next line. If no sample size is stated, the program will stop.

The only additional required lines describe the modeled relationships or paths as described in an earlier section. The header line 'relationships,' 'relations,' or 'equations' is optional, but each relationship in the model must be clearly specified on a separate line.

Optional commands. If the model contains latent variables, these are listed in the same manner as the observed variables described earlier but under the header 'unobserved variables' or 'latent variables.' Observed and unobserved variables cannot have the same names. To set a scale for any latent variable, one of its indicators can be defined as a reference variable by assigning it a fixed non-zero value. Other parameters in the model can be fixed at some known value or constrained to be equal.

Options can be selected to customize the program either by writing command lines or by abbreviating the commands on the 'options' line. For example, the command 'Print Residuals' instructs the program to print residuals in matrix form along with a fitted covariance or correlations matrix and a Q-plot of standardized residuals. The default output contains a summary of residuals and standardized residuals.

Figure 16.3 The Measurement Model

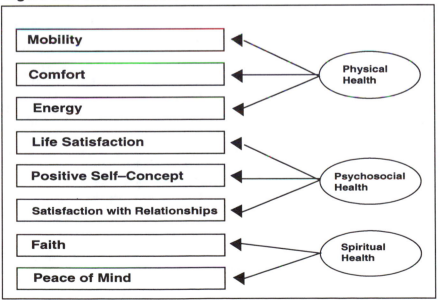

SIMPLIS Example
The Measurement Model. The measurement portion of the quality of life model is illustrated in Figure 16.3. In this example, only the exogenous portion of the model will be tested. Structural relationships among the latent constructs are not included in the measurement model. The following command lines will be read by LISREL8:

LISREL8 Example Run: The Measurement Model
Observed Variables
Comfort Energy Mobility Relations Lifesat Selfcon Peace Faith
Correlation Matrix from file QLEX.PM
Sample size 174
Latent Variables
PHEALTH PSHEALTH SHEALTH
Relationships
PHEALTH=Comfort-Mobility
PSHEALTH=Relations-Selfcon
SHEALTH=Peace Faith
!Setting the scale for latent variables
Comfort=1*PHEALTH
Energy Mobility=PHEALTH
Relations=1*PSHEALTH
Lifesat Selfcon=PSHEALTH
Faith=1*SHEALTH
Peace=SHEALTH
Let the errors of PHEALTH-SHEALTH correlate
Print Residuals
Admissibility check=off
End of Problem

These command lines define the observed and latent variables and specify measurement relationships among them. Latent variables are scaled by defining a reference variable for each. Error variances among the latent variables are allowed to correlate; otherwise, the model is not identified. The admissibility check in LISREL stops computations after 20 iterations unless turned off, as in this example. Output from this example is abbreviated in Table 16.4.

After reading the command lines, the output gives the correlation matrix computed earlier with PRELIS. The solution converged after 12 iterations. Maximum likelihood estimates, error variances, T-values and significance levels (in parentheses) are reported for each empirical indicator. Note that paths from reference variables are not estimated, although their associated error and the squared multiple correlation coefficients are. Although the paths from empirical indicators to latent constructs are nonsignificant, the R^2 values indicate modest reliability for most indicators.

[2] This statement actually provides a test that these constructs are reciprocally related. The model can be estimated first without the equality constraint and again with the constraint. The resulting difference in chi square between the two models (with one degree of freedom) should be negligible if the paths are indeed equal.

Table 16.4 Output from the Problem Run

```
Table 4.  Output from the Problem Run


LISREL8 Example Run: The Measurement Model
Observed Variables
Comfort Energy Mobility Relations Lifesat Selfcon Peace Faith
Correlation Matrix from file QLEX.PM
Sample Size 174
Latent Variables
PHEALTH PSHEALTH SHEALTH
Relationships
PHEALTH=Comfort-Mobility
PSHEALTH=Relations-Selfcon
SHEALTH=Peace Faith
!Setting the scale for latent variables
Comfort=1*PHEALTH
Energy Mobility=PHEALTH
Relations=1*PSHEALTH
Lifesat Selfcon=PSHEALTH
Faith=1*SHEALTH
Peace=SHEALTH
Let the errors of PHEALTH-SHEALTH correlate
Print Residuals
Admissibility check=off
End of Problem

Sample Size =   174

LISREL8 Example Run: The Measurement Model

        CORRELATION MATRIX TO BE ANALYZED

             Comfort    Energy   Mobility    Lifesat    Selfcon      Peace
            --------  --------  --------   --------   --------   --------
  Comfort     1.00
   Energy     0.68      1.00
 Mobility     0.65      0.77      1.00
  Lifesat     0.44      0.46      0.41      1.00
  Selfcon     0.52      0.38      0.32      0.53      1.00
    Peace     0.42      0.49      0.43      0.50      0.61      1.00
    Faith     0.43      0.49      0.51      0.61      0.51      0.81
 Relation     0.40      0.46      0.38      0.24      0.44      0.45

        CORRELATION MATRIX TO BE ANALYZED

               Faith   Relation
            --------  --------
    Faith     1.00
 Relation     0.19      1.00


LISREL8 Example Run: The Measurement Model
Number of Iterations = 12

LISREL ESTIMATES (MAXIMUM LIKELIHOOD)

 Comfort = 1.00*PHEALTH, Errorvar.= 0.41  , R² = 0.59
                               (0.053)
                                7.62

  Energy = 1.16*PHEALTH, Errorvar.= 0.20  , R² = 0.80
          (0.097)                (0.044)
           11.93                  4.69

Mobility = 1.11*PHEALTH, Errorvar.= 0.27  , R² = 0.73
          (0.096)                (0.045)
           11.61                  5.88

 Lifesat = 0.69*PSHEALTH, Errorvar.= 0.47  , R² = 0.50
          (0.074)                 (0.071)
           9.29                    6.68

 Selfcon = 0.69*PSHEALTH, Errorvar.= 0.46  , R² = 0.51
          (0.074)                 (0.070)
           9.36                    6.58

   Peace = 0.93*SHEALTH, Errorvar.= 0.25  , R² = 0.75
```

Table 16.4 Output from the Problem Run (cont.)

```
        Faith = 1.00*SHEALTH, Errorvar.= 0.12  , R² = 0.88
                                     (0.046)
                                       2.67


PSHEALTH = 0.21*Relation, Errorvar.= 0.96, R² = 0.042
            (0.070)
             2.92

Error Covariance for PSHEALTH and PHEALTH = 0.46
                                          (0.074)
                                            6.24
Error Covariance for SHEALTH and PHEALTH = 0.44
                                          (0.075)
                                            5.83
Error Covariance for SHEALTH and PSHEALTH = 0.77
                                           (0.076)
                                            10.17



                    GOODNESS OF FIT STATISTICS

         CHI-SQUARE WITH 17 DEGREES OF FREEDOM = 161.43 (P = 0.0)
            ESTIMATED NON-CENTRALITY PARAMETER (NCP) = 144.43

                 MINIMUM FIT FUNCTION VALUE = 0.93
           POPULATION DISCREPANCY FUNCTION VALUE (F0) = 0.83
          ROOT MEAN SQUARE ERROR OF APPROXIMATION (RMSEA) = 0.22
        P-VALUE FOR TEST OF CLOSE FIT (RMSEA < 0.05) = 0.00000036

              EXPECTED CROSS-VALIDATION INDEX (ECVI) = 1.15
                   ECVI FOR SATURATED MODEL = 0.42
                   ECVI FOR INDEPENDENCE MODEL = 5.09

   CHI-SQUARE FOR INDEPENDENCE MODEL WITH 28 DEGREES OF FREEDOM = 863.93
                       INDEPENDENCE AIC = 879.93
                          MODEL AIC = 199.43
                         SATURATED AIC = 72.00
                       INDEPENDENCE CAIC = 913.21
                          MODEL CAIC = 278.45
                        SATURATED CAIC = 221.73

               ROOT MEAN SQUARE RESIDUAL (RMR) = 0.16
                       STANDARDIZED RMR = 0.16
                   GOODNESS OF FIT INDEX (GFI) = 0.83
            ADJUSTED GOODNESS OF FIT INDEX (AGFI) = 0.64
            PARSIMONY GOODNESS OF FIT INDEX (PGFI) = 0.39

                    NORMED FIT INDEX (NFI) = 0.81
                  NON-NORMED FIT INDEX (NNFI) = 0.72
               PARSIMONY NORMED FIT INDEX (PNFI) = 0.49
                 COMPARATIVE FIT INDEX (CFI) = 0.83
                 INCREMENTAL FIT INDEX (IFI) = 0.83
                  RELATIVE FIT INDEX (RFI) = 0.69

                       CRITICAL N (CN) = 36.81


    STANDARDIZED RESIDUALS
```

	Comfort	Energy	Mobility	Lifesat	Selfcon	Peace
Comfort	0.00					
Energy	-0.54	0.00				
Mobility	-0.56	1.29	0.00			
Lifesat	2.80	2.76	1.63	1.45		
Selfcon	4.57	0.17	-0.97	4.67	1.51	
Peace	0.38	0.85	-0.85	0.21	4.96	0.00
Faith	-0.33	-0.83	0.92	4.62	-1.37	0.00
Relation	5.26	6.00	5.06	1.76	5.33	5.97

```
    STANDARDIZED RESIDUALS
```

	Faith	Relation
Faith	0.00	
Relation	2.53	- -

Table 16.4 Output from the Problem Run (cont.)

```
  MEDIAN STANDARDIZED RESIDUAL =      0.89
  LARGEST STANDARDIZED RESIDUAL =     6.00

STEMLEAF PLOT
 - 1|40
 - 0|986530000000
   0|22499
   1|34568
   2|588
   3|
   4|667
   5|0133
   6|00
LARGEST POSITIVE STANDARDIZED RESIDUALS
RESIDUAL FOR  Lifesat AND  Comfort   2.80
RESIDUAL FOR  Lifesat AND   Energy   2.76
RESIDUAL FOR  Selfcon AND  Comfort   4.57
RESIDUAL FOR  Selfcon AND  Lifesat   4.67
RESIDUAL FOR    Peace AND  Selfcon   4.96
RESIDUAL FOR    Faith AND  Lifesat   4.62
RESIDUAL FOR Relation AND  Comfort   5.26
RESIDUAL FOR Relation AND   Energy   6.00
RESIDUAL FOR Relation AND Mobility   5.06
RESIDUAL FOR Relation AND  Selfcon   5.33
RESIDUAL FOR Relation AND    Peace   5.97


          THE MODIFICATION INDICES SUGGEST TO ADD THE
  PATH TO  FROM       DECREASE IN CHI-SQUARE    NEW ESTIMATE
Peace      PSHEALTH            28.0                 1.01
Faith      PSHEALTH            20.7                -0.86
PHEALTH    PSHEALTH            23.3                 1.22
PHEALTH    Relation            23.3                 0.25


THE MODIFICATION INDICES SUGGEST TO ADD AN ERROR COVARIANCE
  BETWEEN    AND      DECREASE IN CHI-SQUARE    NEW ESTIMATE
Selfcon   Comfort            22.5                 0.19
Peace     Lifesat            19.2                -0.17
Peace     Selfcon            17.0                 0.16
Faith     Mobility            9.7                 0.08
Faith     Lifesat            17.8                 0.17
Faith     Selfcon            15.8                -0.16
Relation  Peace              36.3                 0.26
Relation  Faith              26.0                -0.22


          THE PROBLEM USED   10344 BYTES (=  0.1% OF AVAILABLE WORKSPACE)

                      TIME USED:     9.2 SECONDS
```

Table 16.5 LISREL The Structural Model Output

```
The following lines were read from file SMODEL.LI8:

LISREL8 Example Run: The Structural Model
Observed Variables
Comfort Energy Mobility Relations Lifesat Selfcon Peace Faith QOL
Correlation Matrix from file QLEX.PM
Sample Size 174
Latent Variables
QUALITY PHEALTH PSHEALTH SHEALTH
Relationships
QOL=QUALITY
Comfort-Mobility=PHEALTH
Relations-Selfcon=PSHEALTH
Peace-Faith=SHEALTH
Comfort=1*PHEALTH
Energy Mobility=PHEALTH
Relations=1*PSHEALTH
Lifesat Selfcon=PSHEALTH
Faith=1*SHEALTH
Peace=SHEALTH
SHEALTH=PSHEALTH PHEALTH
QUALITY=PHEALTH PSHEALTH SHEALTH
Set path from PHEALTH to PSHEALTH equal to path from PSHEALTH to PHEALTH
Let the error of PHEALTH-SHEALTH correlate
Set the error variance of QOL to 0
Print Residuals
Admissibility check-off
End of Problem

Sample Size =    174

LISREL8 Example Run: The Structural Model

          CORRELATION MATRIX TO BE ANALYZED

              Peace     Faith      QOL     Comfort    Energy    Mobility
            --------  --------  --------  --------  --------  --------
    Peace      1.00
    Faith      0.81      1.00
      QOL      0.41      0.29      1.00
  Comfort      0.42      0.43      0.39      1.00
   Energy      0.49      0.49      0.25      0.68      1.00
 Mobility      0.43      0.51      0.11      0.65      0.77      1.00
  Lifesat      0.50      0.61      0.25      0.44      0.46      0.41
  Selfcon      0.61      0.51      0.25      0.52      0.38      0.32

          CORRELATION MATRIX TO BE ANALYZED

              Lifesat   Selfcon
            --------  --------
  Lifesat      1.00
  Selfcon      0.53      1.00


LISREL8 Example Run: The Structural Model
Number of Iterations = 27

LISREL ESTIMATES (MAXIMUM LIKELIHOOD)

    Peace = 1.01*SHEALTH, Errorvar.= 0.18   , R² = 0.82
          (0.068)                  (0.043)
           14.79                     4.12

    Faith = 1.00*SHEALTH, Errorvar.= 0.20   , R² = 0.80
                                     (0.043)
                                      4.55

      QOL = 1.00*QUALITY,, R² = 1.00
          (0.055)
           18.30


  Comfort = 1.00*PHEALTH, Errorvar.= 0.40   , R² = 0.60
                                     (0.053)
                                      7.55

   Energy = 1.15*PHEALTH, Errorvar.= 0.20   , R² = 0.80
          (0.095)                   (0.043)
```

Table 16.5 LISREL The Structural Model Output (cont.)

```
            (0.094)                        (0.046)
            11.66                          6.15

Lifesat = 0.74*PSHEALTH, Errorvar.= 0.46  , R² = 0.54
          (0.074)                        (0.071)
          10.00                          6.47


Selfcon = 0.72*PSHEALTH, Errorvar.= 0.48  , R² = 0.52
          (0.074)                        (0.071)
          9.83                           6.69


QUALITY = 0.38*SHEALTH + 0.064*PHEALTH + 0.025*PSHEALTH, Errorvar.= 0.85,
          (0.23)          (0.15)          (0.25)
          1.62            0.43            0.10

          R² = 0.15

SHEALTH = 0.092*PHEALTH + 0.71*PSHEALTH, Errorvar.= 0.22  , R² = 0.72
          (0.14)          (0.12)                        (0.065)
          0.67            6.14                          3.45


          COVARIANCE MATRIX OF LATENT VARIABLES

                QUALITY    SHEALTH    PHEALTH    PSHEALTH
                --------   --------   --------   --------
QUALITY          1.00
SHEALTH          0.35       0.80
PHEALTH          0.21       0.42       0.60
PSHEALTH         0.34       0.76       0.52       1.00


                  GOODNESS OF FIT STATISTICS

       CHI-SQUARE WITH 15 DEGREES OF FREEDOM = 104.97 (P = 0.00)
            ESTIMATED NON-CENTRALITY PARAMETER (NCP) = 89.97

                MINIMUM FIT FUNCTION VALUE = 0.61
        POPULATION DISCREPANCY FUNCTION VALUE (F0) = 0.52
        ROOT MEAN SQUARE ERROR OF APPROXIMATION (RMSEA) = 0.19
    P-VALUE FOR TEST OF CLOSE FIT (RMSEA < 0.05) = 0.00000035

            EXPECTED CROSS-VALIDATION INDEX (ECVI) = 0.85
                 ECVI FOR SATURATED MODEL = 0.42
                 ECVI FOR INDEPENDENCE MODEL = 4.88

CHI-SQUARE FOR INDEPENDENCE MODEL WITH 28 DEGREES OF FREEDOM = 827.55
                  INDEPENDENCE AIC = 843.55
                      MODEL AIC = 146.97
                    SATURATED AIC = 72.00
                 INDEPENDENCE CAIC = 876.82
                     MODEL CAIC = 234.31
                   SATURATED CAIC = 221.73

          ROOT MEAN SQUARE RESIDUAL (RMR) = 0.055
                 STANDARDIZED RMR = 0.055
          GOODNESS OF FIT INDEX (GFI) = 0.88
       ADJUSTED GOODNESS OF FIT INDEX (AGFI) = 0.71
       PARSIMONY GOODNESS OF FIT INDEX (PGFI) = 0.37

              NORMED FIT INDEX (NFI) = 0.87
            NON-NORMED FIT INDEX (NNFI) = 0.79
         PARSIMONY NORMED FIT INDEX (PNFI) = 0.47
            COMPARATIVE FIT INDEX (CFI) = 0.89
            INCREMENTAL FIT INDEX (IFI) = 0.89
             RELATIVE FIT INDEX (RFI) = 0.76

                  CRITICAL N (CN) = 51.40


     STANDARDIZED RESIDUALS

              Peace      Faith      QOL      Comfort     Energy    Mobility
              --------   --------   --------  --------   --------  --------
Peace          0.00
Faith          0.00       0.00
QOL            2.80      -2.80       0.00
Comfort       -0.22       0.09       4.40      0.00
```

Table 16.5 LISREL The Structural Model Output (cont.)

```
Selfcon       3.40       -2.23       -0.04       3.52      -1.83      -2.5[
              STANDARDIZED RESIDUALS

                  Lifesat   Selfcon
                  --------  --------
Lifesat            0.00
Selfcon            0.00      0.00

SUMMARY STATISTICS FOR STANDARDIZED RESIDUALS
SMALLEST STANDARDIZED RESIDUAL =   -4.33
  MEDIAN STANDARDIZED RESIDUAL =    0.00
 LARGEST STANDARDIZED RESIDUAL =    4.40

STEMLEAF PLOT
 - 4|30
 - 3|
 - 2|852
 - 1|865
 - 0|5200000000000000
   0|1128
   1|56
   2|38
   3|245
   4|4
LARGEST NEGATIVE STANDARDIZED RESIDUALS
RESIDUAL FOR       QOL AND       Faith  -2.80
RESIDUAL FOR Mobility AND         QOL  -3.98
RESIDUAL FOR  Lifesat AND       Peace  -4.33
LARGEST POSITIVE STANDARDIZED RESIDUALS
RESIDUAL FOR       QOL AND       Peace   2.80
RESIDUAL FOR  Comfort AND         QOL   4.40
RESIDUAL FOR  Lifesat AND       Faith   3.21
RESIDUAL FOR  Selfcon AND       Peace   3.40
RESIDUAL FOR  Selfcon AND     Comfort   3.52

THE MODIFICATION INDICES SUGGEST TO ADD AN ERROR COVARIANCE
  BETWEEN      AND     DECREASE IN CHI-SQUARE     NEW ESTIMATE
QOL        Peace            7.9                      0.13
QOL        Faith            7.9                     -0.13
Comfort    QOL             19.4                      0.22
Mobility   Faith           12.5                      0.09
Mobility   QOL             16.0                     -0.18
Lifesat    Peace           21.7                     -0.18
Lifesat    Faith           17.2                      0.16
Selfcon    Peace           17.3                      0.16
Selfcon    Faith           13.2                     -0.14
Selfcon    Comfort         20.7                      0.18


         THE PROBLEM USED    10688 BYTES (= 0.2% OF AVAILABLE WORKSPACE)

                    TIME USED:    11.9 SECONDS
```

Chi square for the measurement model is significant at 161.43 with 17 degrees of freedom, indicating poor overall fit of the model. The RMSEA is 0.22, which reflects unacceptable error of approximation. Modification indices suggest four paths and several error covariances can be modified to improve overall fit. One of these is a structural path that should be freed in the structural model test. The other three path MI's indicate that peace and faith may load onto psychosocial health as well as spiritual health, and that personal relationships load onto physical as well as psychosocial health. These paths are substantively interpretable and should be freed in subsequent tests to achieve substantial decrements in χ^2.

Standardized residuals are large for several bivariate pairs of indicators. These values suggest the model underestimates the variance between the associated pairs. One problematic variable is relation (satisfaction and importance of interpersonal relationships). Adding parameters or allowing relation to correlate with comfort, energy, mobility, and self concept should reduce error variance and improve the model.

Figure 16.4 The Structural Portion of the Model

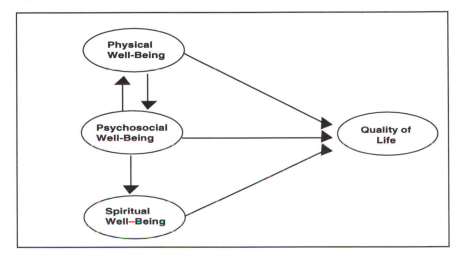

Testing the Structural Model. After respecifying the measurement model, the structural model can be tested. Figure 16.4 depicts the structural portion of the quality of life model. Note that although the structural test does estimate all free parameters including error variances and measurement paths, the relationships of interest are those among the latent variables themselves.

When all indicators and structural paths are included, the model is not identified and cannot be estimated. Identification can be achieved by constraining paths to decrease the number of free parameters to be estimated. In the following example, the reciprocal relation between physical and psychosocial health is constrained as equal.[2] Additionally, the error variance of QOL is set to zero because the single indicator is hypothesized to perfectly measure QUALITY, or quality of life.

The command lines and output appear in Table 16.5. Structural paths between exogenous variables and quality of life are smaller than expected, but the paths among the exogenous variables are strongly positive and statistically significant. Overall fit is nonsignificant, and the χ^2 to degrees of freedom ratio

is high. The RMSEA and RMR are acceptable; however, overall fit is poor .
Modification indices again suggest allowing the error covariance among the
indicators to correlate freely. By freeing these parameters one at a time, the
overall χ^2 can be substantially improved.

REFERENCES
Bollen, K. A. (1989). *Structural equations with latent variables*. NY: John Wiley.

Brown, R. L. (1994). Efficacy of the indirect approach for estimating structural equation models with missing data: A comparison of five methods. *Structural Equation Modeling, 1*(4), 287-316.

Browne, M.W., & Cudeck, R. (1993). Alternative ways of assessing model fit. In K.A. Bollen, and J.S. Long, (Eds.). *Testing Structural Equation Models*. Newbury Park, CA: Sage Publications.

Gerbing, D. W., & Anderson, J. C. (1993). Monte Carlo evaluations of goodness-of-fit indices for structural equation models. In K.A. Bollen and J.S. Long (Eds.). *Testing structural equation models*. Newbury Park, CA: Sage Publications.

Jöreskog, K. G. (1993). Testing structural equation models. In K.A. Bollen and J.S. Long (Eds.). *Testing structural equation models*. Newbury Park, CA: Sage Publications.

Jöreskog, K. G., & Sörbom, D. (1989). *LISREL 7: A guide to the program and applications*. Chicago, IL: SPSS, Inc.

Jöreskog, K. G., & Sörbom, D. (1993) *LISREL 8: Structural equation modeling with the SIMPLIS command language*. Hillsdale, NJ: Lawrence Erlbaum Associates.

Long, J. S. (1983). *Covariance structure models: An introduction to LISREL*. Newbury Park, CA: Sage Publications.

Nunnally, J. C. (1978). *Psychometric theory (2nd Ed.)*. NY: McGraw-Hill Book Company.

Wothke, W. (1993). Nonpositive definite matrices in structural equation modeling. In K.A. Bollen and J.S. Long (Eds.). *Testing structural equation models*. Newbury Park, CA: Sage Publications.

EQS 4.02 Windows Analysis

Margaret T. Beard, Donna A. Bachand and Verdell Marsh

S tructural equations modeling (SEM) programs were devised to make advanced analytic methods available to statisticians. However, data analysts without advanced mathematics, matrix algebra and Greek knowledge have been hesitant to use the method. EQS, a registered trademark of BMDP Statistical Software, Inc., is a computer program developed by Peter Bentler of UCLA to meet both theoretical and statistical needs of the scientific community. At the theoretical level, EQS offers multivariate techniques based on methods more general than those which stem from multinormal distribution theory. Methodologically, EQS provides a general and powerful approach to statistical modeling that does not require knowledge of Greek notation or matrix algebra.

The program is available for a wide variety of computer systems such as IBM mainframes running OS/MVS, high performance UNIX workstations, IBM 386 and 486 PC's running MS-DOS and Macintosh computers. The most recent version, 4.02, is written for Microsoft Windows. The Windows version is improved and expanded with a graphical user interface. The new interface allows the analyst to input raw data, impute missing values, visually inspect and plot data and carry out sophisticated data exploration and transformation procedures. Most importantly, the user can construct the necessary set of specifications and equations to run the program without extensive use of syntax.

This chapter introduces diverse structural equation models made possible with EQS setups. The goal is to provide the reader with fundamental information about how EQS can be used to screen data and analyze a variety of models, including factor analyses, multitrait-multimethod analysis and the analysis of covariance and mean structures.

BACKGROUND INFORMATION

Linear structural equation modeling is a useful technique for specifying, estimating and testing hypothesized relationships in a path diagram or system of substantively meaningful variables. Although the basic ideas of structural modeling are very simple, technical mathematical and statistical language can foreshadow the basic principles applied. One of the first published SEM packages was the LISREL program developed by Karl Jöreskog and Dag Sörbom. The early releases of LISREL required specifying eight matrices for measurement and structural models in Greek notation. A prepublication release of EQS opened the possibility of modeling structural equation systems in simple language (Brecht, Tanaka, & Bentler, 1986). The first public release of EQS enabled even novice modelers to run jobs successfully (Bentler, 1985). Each successive release of the program has introduced new methods for model improvement, new statistical tests and fit indices and more general models while becoming more user-friendly.

The latest release has an "easy-build" option that constructs a model automatically. Thus, more time can be spent analyzing data and refining models than on writing program code. The easy-build feature prompts the user for visual specifications that are used to create the command language; the program generates equations and variance-covariance matrices based on user input. All one needs to know to obtain an automatic model is the conceptual approach used by EQS and the meaning of statistics and program specifications. Of course, users should know the basic ideas of modeling as presented in the program manual to ensure that the options selected really implement the model as intended. The model and data specifications are derived from options selected in a series of well defined dialog boxes rather than specific EQS syntax. The researcher can always write a program file if desired, but an advantage of using the easy-build feature is that it is not necessary to keep referring to the manual for correct syntax.

DATA SCREENING AND EXPLORATION
Entering Raw Data
Raw data can be entered in spreadsheet format, where each row represents one case with one column for each variable. The drop down data menu first asks the user to state the number of cases and variables, and then automatically creates the correct number of rows and columns. The menu also requests user specification of missing data values; the system default is 9999. After coding, the raw data can be saved in an external file labeled with the extension '.ess' for future use. In fact, raw data must be stored in an external file, because only correlation or covariance matrices can be read directly from the program input file. EQS will read any ASCII file or a variety of spreadsheet files, but saving in '.ess' files is highly recommended because they contain system-specific language to assist the program in locating variables.

Variables are labeled in EQS notation as V1, V2, V3, and so on. Assigning variable names is as simple as clicking on the data information menu, double-clicking on a V in the variable list, and typing a label for that variable. Naming variables is optional, but helpful in interpreting output and creating charts or plots.

Once created, data files can be rearranged in various ways. For example, the researcher may initially choose to save demographic data in one file and later join this file with another data set. The 'join' command will place the two files side-by-side to form a single file. When joining data files it is important to ensure that the data are entered sequentially in each file so that each row corresponds to the same subject or case. Data files can also be merged, or placed end-to-end. The 'merge' command is useful for combining data sets that were originally entered as separate groups. The 'save as' command permits the user to save joined or merged files in their entirety or to select and save subsets of variables.

Similarly, the user can input data into a large matrix and later partition the data into subsets of variables. This step can save considerable computer time and memory when working with only a few variables from a large survey.

Data Screening
The EQS 4.02 program offers a full range of procedures for exploratory data analysis that were formerly available only through separate packages such as

SPSS, SAS or BMDP. Continuous and categorical data can be visually inspected via several plot functions such as histograms, box plots, pie charts and bar charts. Scatterplots and regression lines can be displayed for bivariate relations. Plots can be customized to produce publication-quality figures with a laser printer.

A new feature of EQS Windows permits inspection of missing data and detection of outliers simply by clicking an icon. On a color screen the entire data matrix appears dark, while outliers are colored green and missing data points, yellow. Special dialog boxes provide more specific information about these data. For example, outliers are defined by default as values occurring 3 standard deviations from the mean; this value can be changed in the missing data specifications box. The missing data processing box gives an option to mark outliers to the data editor or to impute missing values. Outliers can be temporarily removed from the data by clicking and dragging them with a mouse to an area on the screen that resembles a black hole. After removal, the regression equation, R^2, and confidence intervals are automatically recomputed. The user can repeat this operation with all the outliers and interactively re-evaluate the regression statistics to determine how the outliers affect the sample. To recover the points, simply double-click on the black hole icon. If a decision is made to exclude these data points from future analyses, they can be marked to the data editor.

Data Transformation

Data screening may suggest a need to transform variables. The data transformation menu contains several standard operations such as log or log-normal transformation, square and cubic root transformation, and sine-cosine transformation, among others. Alternatively, the user can create an equation with the calculator pad to manipulate variables. This utility is helpful not only for transforming non-normal data, but also for creating new variables as sums or products of existing variables. Consider the common situation in which several questionnaire items are summed to obtain a subscale score. This task is accomplished by clicking relevant variables from the variable list along with the + sign on the calculator pad. As always, new or transformed variables should be labeled and saved with the 'save as' command.

Descriptive Analyses

The analysis menu offers basic tools for computing descriptive statistics, t-tests, cross-tabulations, one and two-way ANOVA's, correlations and covariance matrices, linear regressions and exploratory factor analyses. Each of these features is comparable to tests provided by standard statistical packages; only the factor analysis option will be discussed here. This option is designed for exploratory factor analytic (EFA) situations in which relationships between observed and latent variables are either unknown or previously untested. In this situation, rather than propose and confirm a specified factor structure, the analyst examines correlations or "loadings" to determine how a set of indicators relates to a number of potential factors. The goal of EFA is to discover a minimal number of factors underlying the measured indicators (Byrne, 1994). In EQS, the analyst can conduct EFA to examine factor structures in the data and retain those findings for later use in specifying a measurement model.

THE BENTLER-WEEKS MODEL

The EQS program implements the Bentler-Weeks model for representing a system of variables. In SEM, the main parameters of concern include the path coefficients, variances and covariances implied by a model. These parameters must be estimated from sample observations; estimation can only be accomplished by mathematically transposing the data into the model parameters. The mathematical system of representation varies with a particular SEM program. The program in EQS is derived from the Bentler-Weeks model, which characterizes all variables as either independent or dependent. In EQS independence or dependence is not necessarily related to a variable's position in a path diagram; the Bentler-Weeks concept of independence is much broader in scope. An independent variable has no unidirectional arrow pointing toward it in a path diagram. Within this system, any variable that is not dependent is independent, including residual variables. Independent variables may also include observed variables or factor scores depending upon how the model is specified; they are considered independent because they are never regressed onto other variables in the system. Residuals are independent because they influence the observed variables, even though the residual-to-observed variable paths are not estimated. The variances and covariances of independent variables represent parameters to be estimated by the program.

A dependent variable is any variable with an arrow pointing toward it. Dependent variables can be expressed in an equation as some function of other variables. In other words, dependent variables are explained by other variables in the model. In the Bentler-Weeks system, the variances of dependent variables and covariances among dependent variables are not considered parameters of the model; rather, they are explained by the parameters of the model.

THE EQS PROGRAM

A wide variety of models can be tested with EQS. This section provides an overview of EQS notation and programming language and illustrates potential uses of the program. Readers should consult the EQS program manual and user's guide for a detailed description of the mathematical foundation of techniques employed by the program.

Regression Analyses

Linear regression is useful in predicting the scores on a dependent variable from one or more independent variables. The regression procedure estimates weights for each independent variable to yield a predicted score for each case that is as close as possible to the actual dependent variable score using a least square criterion (Bentler & Wu, 1993). Regression coefficients and residuals can be obtained with EQS by specifying a model of measured variables and requesting ordinary least squares estimates.

Confirmatory Factor Analyses

Confirmatory factor analysis (CFA) can be viewed as a submodel of the more general structural equation model approach (Pedhazur & Schmelkin, 1992). CFA tests the measurement model of hypothesized relationships between latent factors and their indicators. The primary objective of CFA concerns testing the theorist's hypothesis about how a domain of variables are structured. In other words, the researcher specifies a priori how many factors are operating in a system and which variables relate to each factor. In EQS, CFA techniques can be employed in both single group and multiple group analyses to test the factorial validity of a measuring instrument; examine validity within a multitrait-multimethod framework; or to test invariance of factor structures, latent mean structures or causal structures.

Multitrait-Multimethod Analyses

Multitrait-multimethod matrix analysis provides a means of assessing convergent, construct, and discriminant validity. Fiske and Campbell (1959) developed this validation process by examining a matrix of intercorrelations among tests of at least two traits measured by at least two methods each. Measures of the same trait should covary more strongly with each other than with measures of different traits using different measures. Validity values of the same trait and the same method should be higher than correlations among different traits by the same method.

Within the CFA framework the multitrait-multimethod matrix is explained in terms of underlying constructs rather than observed variables. Convergent and discriminant validity are assessed in light of parameter estimates, and it is possible to test hypotheses concerning these types of validity. The method also provides separate estimates of variance due to traits, methods, and error in addition to estimated correlations for both trait and method factors (Byrne and Goffin, 1993).

Multiple Group Analyses

Most SEM users are familiar with traditional applications in which data are collected from a single sample to test a theoretical model. Failing to reject a model with one test provides limited support for the theory in question. Multiple group analyses and cross-validation studies are vital to the process of theory development. The primary task of multiple group studies is to ascertain whether the model holds across different samples. Byrne (1994) poses five questions that may be addressed in multiple group analyses. These are:

1. Is the measurement model group invariant? In other words, do the items on an instrument operate the same across different populations such as different genders or age groups?
2. Is the structural model group invariant? That is, are relationships among the latent variables the same in different groups?
3. Are certain paths in the causal structure invariant across groups? In this situation, individual paths are tested rather than the structural model as a whole.
4. Do the latent means of particular factors differ across populations?
5. Does the factor structure of an instrument replicate across independent samples of the same population?

EQS Notation

EQS treats all variables as either observed or latent. Observed variables are labeled V; these include the measured variables given in the data set. All measured variables are labeled sequentially as V1, V2, V3, and so forth unless the user designates specific variable names. It is important to note here that variables are read from the data file in numerical order rather than by variable name. During the process of respecifying models, variables can be deleted or rearranged by the analyst, but the program will continue to read the data sequentially. If, for example, V2 is eliminated from the model, the analyst must ensure that the program language reflects the exclusion. Otherwise, the results will be erroneous or at least uninterpretable.

All remaining variables are unmeasured. These include the latent variables, error terms, and disturbances. Latent variables are factors, designated as F in EQS language. The capital letter E denotes error in measuring V, while D represents error or disturbance in prediction. One E is associated with each V and one D corresponds to each F in the model.

Model Specification

Four basic steps are recommended for specifying models in EQS. These are:

1. Draw a path diagram to represent the model. In keeping with standard SEM conventions, factors (F's) are enclosed in circles and their indicators (V's) appear in boxes. Error (E) and disturbance (D) terms need not be enclosed, but should be included in the diagram to facilitate writing the equations and identifying the model.
2. Write equations for the model. As previously discussed, there will be one equation for each dependent variable in the model. Any variable with an arrow aimed toward it must have an associated equation.
3. Indicate the parameters to be estimated with an asterisk (*). List all nonfixed coefficients from the equations as well as all independent variable variances and covariances. Recall that the paths from error terms to measured variables are not estimated, but fixed to 1.0; however, the E's should be marked with an asterisk because their variance will be estimated. Depending on the model in question, path coefficients, factor variances, factor covariances, and error variances are potential parameters to estimate.
4. Identify the model. To apply the t-rule for identification, first count the number of data points implied by the model. With a model of p variables, there will be p(p+1)/2 data points. Next count the number of parameters to be estimated; these are the number of asterisks in the diagram. Finally, subtract the number of parameters from the number of data points to obtain the degrees of freedom. The goal of identification is to achieve an overidentified model with more data points than parameters and positive degrees of freedom.

Program Statements

All statistical packages require the user to write an input file of commands or keywords that follow a set of syntax rules. These files should be saved with the extension '.eqs.' These are considered the "working files" of the program, and their output will automatically be labeled with the extension '.out.'

EQS reads primary and secondary keywords organized in a paragraph structure. Within each paragraph the primary keyword appears on the first line; this line essentially identifies the paragraph which follows. For example, the keyword /EQUATIONS signals that modeled equations will appear on the next few lines. Secondary keywords are subcommands or individual statements within each paragraph. Primary keywords must always be preceded with a slash (/), and no other information can be placed on this line. Secondary keywords can be placed on the same line, but must be separated by a semicolon. Comment lines or descriptive statements preceded by an exclamation mark (!) will be printed in the input file, but are ignored in executing the program. Paragraphs describing model specifications, equations, and variances are required; all others are optional.

Required and Optional Keywords and Paragraphs

The first paragraph keyword /TITLE is optional. After the title line, the user may type as many words or lines as necessary to describe the study. Although not required to run an EQS analysis, title lines are particularly helpful when multiple analyses are conducted to improve or re-estimate the model.

The first required command is /SPECIFICATIONS, which may be abbreviated /SPE. This paragraph defines the data and the method of analysis. Required data definition subcommands include CASES and VARIABLES, or CAS and VAR. The user must specify the total number of cases in the sample, regardless of whether all cases will be used in the analysis. VARIABLES refers to the total number of variables in the data set, not the number to be included in the current run.

The METHOD or ME subcommand may also be included in the /SPE paragraph to request an estimation method. Maximum likelihood (ML) is the default method, but a wide variety of alternative methods are also available, including estimates based on elliptical and arbitrary distributions. This command is optional; if none is given, ML will be computed. ROBUST statistics can be requested for any method except arbitrary GLS. These statistics correct for non-normality in large samples and also computes a Bentler-Satorra chi square statistic. The command for obtaining robust statistics is ME=ML, ROBUST.

The MATRIX (MA) keyword refers to the type of data matrix to be analyzed. A covariance matrix is assumed by default. If the covariance matrix will be entered into the input file, a paragraph heading /MATRIX is required prior to entering the actual matrix. If raw data are to be read from an external file, the user must instruct EQS where to find the matrix as well as how to read it on the DATA (DA) line. In the Windows environment, this means the user should give the drive, path, and filename enclosed in single quotes. Data are read in free format unless the user specifies a Fortran format.

The next major paragraph names modeled variables. The /LABELS command is optional. If no labels are given, the program numbers variables and factors sequentially, as previously noted.

The second required paragraph begins with the keyword /EQUATIONS or / EQU. The equations specify the model, and should be written and verified with care. From the path diagram, one equation is written for each dependent variable. The dependent variable always appears on the left side of the equation with all direct explanatory variables, including error variables, on the right side. The user must insert asterisks for each parameter to be estimated. EQS assumes that non-asterisked parameters are fixed, and these parameters will not be estimated. Of course, parameters can be constrained to 0, 1.0, or some other user-defined value in this paragraph.

Information about independent variable variances must be included in the / VARIANCES or /VAR paragraph. Each variance to be estimated should be marked with an asterisk. Variances can be fixed to 1.0 or some predetermined start value. In accordance with the Bentler-Weeks model, dependent variable variances are never specified.

The /COVARIANCES or /COV paragraph is optional unless the model contains covariances. Free covariances are designated by typing a pair of variables separated by a comma followed by an asterisk. The statement F1, F2 = * instructs EQS to estimate the covariance between factors one and two. Each variable in a covariance statement should also have its variance specified in the preceding /VAR paragraph. Covariances can only be estimated for independent variables.

EQS Program Example

The following example illustrates the use of EQS in testing a model of quality of life. The basic model hypothesizes that quality of life is directly influenced by three important life dimensions: physical health, psychosocial health, and spiritual health. These dimensions are labeled in the input file as factors one, two and three (F1, F2, F3). Quality of life is the dependent variable of the path model, labeled as factor four (F4) in the program. The input file for the measurement model appears in Table 17.1.

Table 17.1 Measurement Model Input File

```
/TITLE
QOL Measurement Model
/SPECIFICATIONS
 DATA='C:\EQSWIN\QLRAW.ESS'; VARIABLES= 9; CASES=  70;
 METHODS=ML;
 MATRIX=RAW;
/LABELS
V1=mobility; V2=comfort; V3=energy; V4=lifesat; V5=selfcon;
V6=relation; V7=faith; V8=peace; V9=QOL;
/EQUATIONS
V1 = + *F1  + E1;
V2 = + *F1  + E2;
V3 = + *F1  + E3;
V4 = + *F2  + E4;
V5 = + *F2  + E5;
V6 = + *F2  + E6;
V7 = + *F3  + E7;
V8 = + *F3  + E8;
V9 = + *F4  + E9;
/VARIANCES
F1 = 1;
F2 = 1;
F3 = 1;
F4 = 1;
E1 = *;
E2 = *;
E3 = *;
E4 = *;
E5 = *;
E6 = *;
E7 = *;
E8 = *;
E9 = 1;
/COVARIANCES
/LMTEST
 PROCESS=SIMULTANEOUS;
/END
```

The input file specifies that raw data are read for 9 variables on 70 cases from a file named QLRAW.ESS. Maximum likelihood estimation is requested on line 5. Lines 8 and 9 list the variable names in the order encountered in the data file. The next nine lines contain the equations which specify the model: V1, V2 and V3 measure F1; V4, V5 and V6 measure F2; V7 and V8 measure F3; and F4 is measured by a single indicator V9.

Lines 21 through 33 depict modeled variances. Note that variances of the four factors are fixed at 1.0 and will not be estimated. These elements are fixed in order to set a scale for each factor. As the sole indicator of F4, the error variance of V9 is also fixed. The Lagrange multiplier test (LMTEST) is invoked on line 35. This test will provide parameter change statistics to identify how the model can be improved by relaxing these constraints.

Program output is abbreviated in Table 17.2. The first section of the printout summarizes sample statistics including the mean, skewness, and kurtosis for each variable as well as a measure of multivariate kurtosis. This output permits assessment of whether variable distributions meet the test assumptions, but is only given when raw data are read in. Before using a correlation or covariance matrix for input, the data should be screened in greater detail via the descriptive statistics and plot functions described elsewhere in this chapter.

Univariate statistics for this example indicate acceptable skewness and kurtosis for most variables; only relation is kurtotic. Mardia's coefficient is the multivariate statistic for kurtosis. The normalized estimate of 8.34 suggests a multivariate nonnormal distribution. Case numbers 26, 32, 43, 55, and 68 provide the largest contribution to multivariate kurtosis. These cases represent probable outliers; such cases can be marked and either removed from the sample or analyzed separately in future runs. The decision to delete cases cannot necessarily be based on their contribution to kurtosis alone because there is no standard "cutoff" value for comparison. Case values listed on the printout should be compared to the normalized estimate. In this example, the estimates for all five cases deviate greatly from the normalized (mean) estimate, and are therefore probably outliers.

The next section of output gives the covariance matrix computed from raw data or from correlations and standard deviations given in the input file. This matrix will be used to calculate parameter estimates and goodness of fit indices. A summary of the Bentler-Weeks structural representation follows. This information is helpful in ensuring that the model in the input file is specified as the user intended.

Residuals and standardized residuals matrices are given next, followed by a summary of the bivariate pairs contributing the largest residuals. Generally speaking, the residuals should be small and evenly distributed among the variables if the model represents the data well. Standardized residuals are usually more interpretable because the values can be compared to one another. These values can be used to diagnose problems in the model; large standardized residuals occur when variables are not adequately explained by the model. The twenty largest standardized residuals are listed in table format. In our example output, the covariances between V7 and V5, V9 and V5, V9 and V7, V7 and V4 and V8 and V5 appear as the five largest residuals. Variables 5, 7, 8, and 9 appear most frequently in the "top twenty" estimates; these variables are clearly not explained by the model. In respecifying the model, possible correlates or antecedents of these variables should be modified.

Table 17.2 Measurement Model Output

```
DATA IS READ FROM C:\EQSWIN\QLRAW.ESS
THERE ARE 9 VARIABLES AND 70 CASES

SAMPLE STATISTICS
                              UNIVARIATE STATISTICS

VARIABLE       MOBILITY  COMFORT  ENERGY   LIFESAT  SELFCON

MEAN             4.8261   4.1594   4.8571    5.1250   4.5429

SKEWNESS (G1)   -1.1458  -0.6636  -1.1542   -1.7780  -0.8590

KURTOSIS (G2)    0.2858  -0.5395   0.4422    2.4242  -0.3977


VARIABLE        RELATION  FAITH    PEACE     QOL

MEAN             5.2609   4.8429   4.9286    65.3000

SKEWNESS (G1)   -1.9963  -1.1246  -0.9641    -0.7847

KURTOSIS (G2)    3.9165   0.6983   0.7677    -0.4264


                         MULTIVARIATE KURTOSIS

MARDIA'S COEFFICIENT (G2,P) =        28.0581
NORMALIZED ESTIMATE =                 8.3415
```

CASE NUMBERS WITH LARGEST CONTRIBUTION TO NORMALIZED MULTIVARIATE KURTOSIS:

```
CASE NUMBER    26       32        43        55    68

ESTIMATE    287.8878  102.1303  117.8037  101.9211  136.0864
COVARIANCE  MATRIX TO BE ANALYZED: 9 VARIABLES BASED ON 70 CASES.
```

	MOBILITY V1	COMFORT V2	ENERGY V3	LIFESAT V4	SELFCON V5
MOBILITY V1	2.028				
COMFORT V2	1.185	2.337			
ENERGY V3	1.030	1.400	1.892		
LIFESAT V4	0.447	0.406	0.293	1.812	
SELFCON V5	0.757	0.888	0.818	0.938	2.107
RELATION V6	0.239	0.337	0.309	0.697	0.933
FAITH V7	0.607	0.636	.847	1.005	1.405
PEACE V8	0.507	0.579	0.468	0.661	0.822
QOL V9	18.660	22.388	19.725	13.543	25.212

	RELATION V6	FAITH V7	PEACE V8	QOL V9
RELATION V6	1.236			
FAITH V7	0.683	1.468		
PEACE V8	0.352	0.742	0.966	
QOL V9	11.900	20.859	10.384	661.749

Table 17.2 Measurement Model Output (con't)

BENTLER-WEEKS STRUCTURAL REPRESENTATION:

NUMBER OF DEPENDENT VARIABLES = 9
DEPENDENT V'S :   1   2   3   4   5   6   7   8   9

NUMBER OF INDEPENDENT VARIABLES = 13
INDEPENDENT F'S :   1   2   3   4
INDEPENDENT E'S :   1   2   3   4   5   6   7   8   9

RESIDUAL COVARIANCE MATRIX (S-SIGMA) :

	MOBILITY V1	COMFORT V2	ENERGY V3	LIFESAT V4	SELFCON V5
MOBILITY V1	0.000				
COMFORT V2	0.000	0.000			
ENERGY V3	0.000	0.000	0.000		
LIFESAT V4	0.447	0.406	0.293	0.000	
SELFCON V5	0.757	0.888	0.818	0.000	0.000
RELATION V6	0.239	0.337	0.309	0.000	0.000
FAITH V7	0.607	0.636	0.847	1.005	1.405
PEACE V8	0.507	0.579	0.468	0.661	0.822
QOL V9	18.660	22.388	19.725	13.543	25.212

	RELATION V6	FAITH V7	PEACE V8	QOL V9
RELATION V6	0.000			
FAITH V7	0.683	0.000		
PEACE V8	0.352	0.000	0.000	
QOL V9	11.900	20.859	10.384	0.000

AVERAGE ABSOLUTE COVARIANCE RESIDUALS   =   3.4609
AVERAGE OFF-DIAGONAL ABSOLUTE COVARIANCE RESIDUALS   = 4.3261

STANDARDIZED RESIDUAL MATRIX:

	MOBILITY V1	COMFORT V2	ENERGY V3	LIFESAT V4	SELFCON V5
MOBILITY V1	0.000				
COMFORT V2	0.000	0.000			
ENERGY V3	0.000	0.000	0.000		
LIFESAT V4	0.233	0.197	0.159	0.000	
SELFCON V5	0.366	0.400	0.410	0.000	0.000
RELATION V6	0.151	0.198	0.202	0.000	0.000
FAITH V7	0.352	0.344	0.508	0.617	0.799
PEACE V8	0.362	0.385	0.346	0.500	0.576
QOL V9	0.509	0.569	0.557	0.391	0.675

	RELATION V6	FAITH V7	PEACE V8	QOL V9
RELATION V6	0.000			
FAITH V7	0.507	0.000		
PEACE V8	0.322	0.000	0.000	
QOL V9	0.416	0.669	0.411	0.000

LARGEST STANDARDIZED RESIDUALS:

V7,V5	V9,V5	V9,V7	V7,V4	V8,V5
0.799	0.675	0.669	0.617	0.576

V9,V2	V9,V3	V9,V1	V7,V3	V7,V6
0.569	0.557	0.509	0.508	0.507

V8,V4	V9,V6	V9,V8	V5,V3	V5,V2
0.500	0.416	0.411	0.410	0.400

V9,V4	V8,V2	V5,V1	V8,V1	V7,V1
0.391	0.385	0.366	0.362	0.352

Table 17.2 Measurement Model Output (con't)

GOODNESS OF FIT SUMMARY

INDEPENDENCE MODEL CHI-SQUARE = 353.655 ON 36 DEGREES OF FREEDOM

INDEPENDENCE AIC = 281.65479   INDEPENDENCE CAIC = 164.70896
MODEL AIC = 143.09994   MODEL CAIC =   52.14207

CHI-SQUARE =   199.100 BASED ON   28 DEGREES OF FREEDOM
PROBABILITY VALUE FOR THE CHI-SQUARE STATISTIC IS LESS THAN 0.001

BENTLER-BONETT NORMED   FIT INDEX= 0.437
BENTLER-BONETT NONNORMED FIT INDEX= 0.307
COMPARATIVE FIT INDEX = 0.461

MEASUREMENT EQUATIONS WITH STANDARD ERRORS AND TEST STATISTICS

MOBILITY=V1   =   .934*F1   +   1.000 E1
                      .168
                     5.573

COMFORT =V2 =   1.269*F1   +   1.000 E2
                      .177
                     7.156

ENERGY =V3   =   1.103*F1   +   1.000 E3
                      .160
                     6.897

LIFESAT =V4   =   .838*F2   +   1.000 E4
                      .169
                     4.969

SELFCON =V5 =   1.120*F2   +   1.000 E5
                      .185
                     6.042

RELATION=V6   =   .832*F2   +   1.000 E6
                      .142
                     5.879

FAITH =V7   =   1.000*F3   +   1.000 E7
                      .125
                     8.004

PEACE =V8   =   .742*F3   +   1.000 E8
                      .117
                     6.343

QOL =V9   =   25.705*F4   +   1.000 E9
                     2.191
                    11.730

STANDARDIZED SOLUTION:

MOBILITY=V1   =   .656*F1   +   .755 E1
COMFORT =V2 =   .830*F1   +   .558 E2
ENERGY =V3   =   802*F1   +   .597 E3
LIFESAT =V4   =   .622*F2   +   .783 E4
SELFCON =V5 =   .772*F2   +   .636 E5
RELATION=V6   =   .749*F2   +   .663 E6
FAITH =V7   =   .825*F3   +   .565 E7
PEACE =V8   =   .755*F3   +   .655 E8
QOL =V9   =   .999*F4   +   .039 E9

Table 17.2 Measurement Model Output (con't)

LAGRANGE MULTIPLIER TEST (FOR ADDING PARAMETERS)

ORDERED UNIVARIATE TEST STATISTICS:

NO	CODE PARA	CHI-SQUARE	PROB	PARA	CHANGE
1	2 3	F3,F2	40.531	0.000	0.990
2	2 12	V9,F1	28.249	0.000	18.102
3	2 3	F4,F1	28.249	0.000	0.704
4	2 12	V9,F3	26.886	0.000	18.228
5	2 3	F4,F3	26.886	0.000	0.709
6	2 12	V9,F2	26.727	0.000	18.225

MULTIVARIATE LAGRANGE MULTIPLIER TEST BY SIMULTANEOUS PROCESS IN STAGE 1

CUMULATIVE MULTIVARIATE STATISTICS   UNIVARIATE INCREMENT

STEP	PARAMETER	CHI-SQUARE	D.F.	PROB.	CHI-SQUARE	PROB.
1	F3,F2	40.531	1	0.000	40.531	0.000
2	V9,F1	68.780	2	0.000	28.249	0.000
3	V9,F3	95.666	3	0.000	26.886	0.000
4	V9,F2	122.394	4	0.000	26.727	0.000
5	F3,F1	139.535	5	0.000	17.141	0.000
6	V5,F1	149.751	6	0.000	10.217	0.001

The goodness of fit summary first gives a χ^2 for the independence model. This statistic is a likelihood ratio test for the null model in which all variables are independent or uncorrelated. The alternate model, if correctly specified, should differ significantly from the null model. In this example, the large χ^2 (353.655, 36 df) suggests that it does.

Akaike's information criterion (AIC) is printed first for the independence model and then the hypothesized model. This criterion is useful in evaluating the best model fit among multiple alternative models. The AIC accounts for the number of parameters estimated in the model, thereby providing a parsimony-based fit index. The goal is to select a model with an AIC closest to zero, as it will have the best χ^2 value for the most parsimonious set of parameters.

The next chi square value (199.100 with 28 df) is reported for the hypothesized QOL model. This value is statistically significant ($p < 0.001$), so the model should be rejected as currently specified. The comparative fit index (CFI) accounts for sample size and has been shown to reflect fit relatively well, even in small samples. The CFI ranges from 0 to 1, and values greater than .9 indicate acceptable fit. The CFI finding of .461 for the QOL example demonstrates serious misfit.

The next section of output yields measurement equations. These are the parameter estimates, which are first presented as unstandardized. In the unstandardized solution each variable has an estimate, standardized error, and significance test statistic. The test statistic indicates whether an estimate is different from zero; values that exceed 1.96 are significant at the 0.05 alpha level. All estimates for the hypothesized model are significant and, with the exception of QOL, the errors are small.

The standardized solution rescales variables so that the variance is equal to 1.0. All variables, including the error terms are rescaled so that all coefficients are comparable. The standardized residual variance in an equation can be calculated as the square of the error variable's coefficient. Subtracting this value from 1 yields the squared multiple correlation (R^2) for the equation. The equation for mobility, for example, appears in the standardized solution as V1 = .656*F1 + .755E1. $R^2 = 1 - .755^2 = .43$. Thus 43% of variance in V1 is explained by F1.

The LM test results appear in two tables. The first table gives univariate test statistics for those fixed parameters that will substantially decrease χ^2 if freed in subsequent runs. Alongside the χ^2, parameter change values reveal estimates the parameters would take on if they were freely estimated rather than fixed. The multivariate table compares cumulative multivariate statistics with their associated univariate increments. Bentler (1993) recommends using the multivariate test whenever possible because it provides information about relaxing multiple constraints simultaneously. In the present example, the multivariate solution suggests freeing parameters between factors F3 and F2, F3 and F1, and F2 and F1. Of course, these paths will be estimated in the full structural model. Findings also suggest that V5 should be allowed to correlate with F1 and F4, and V7 also "loads" onto F4. Only the path from V5 to F1 is substantively interpretable. Recall that F4 represents quality of life, the endogenous factor of the model. F4 is measured by a single indicator, V9, which measures subjective perceptions of QOL. Allowing V9 to correlate with factors other than F4, or estimating paths from exogenous variables to an endogenous factor does not make theoretical sense as the model is currently conceptualized. However, statistical findings warrant reconsidering the original conceptualization.

Input and output for the structural model analysis appears in Table 17.3. The model is tested for illustrative purposes only; the measurement model should be substantially improved before the full structural model can be estimated and interpreted with any degree of confidence.

In this model V5 was permitted to correlate with F1 and F2 and the factor covariances were added. Overall, results are similar to those reported previously for the measurement model. The χ^2 is smaller (52.160 with 21 df) but still significant. The Satorra-Bentler scaled chi square (S-χ^2) is reported in this analysis because robust statistics were requested in the input file. The S-χ^2 corrects for nonnormality in the data; in this example, the resulting value of 31.41 is marginally significant at the .067 level, indicating a better fit than the non-robust value. The LM test results recommend adding only one additional path from F3 to F1. Most standardized residuals range from -0.1 to 0.3 but again, several bivariate pairs pose serious specification issues.

The solution provides evidence that the hypothesized model does not fit the data well. The sample size (N=70) is very small and most data are not normally distributed. Although maximum likelihood estimates are robust to violations of multivariate normality in large samples, other types of estimators should be explored in this small sample consisting primarily of categorical data. At a minimum, variables should be transformed to approximate a normal distribution and outliers evaluated separately. If these procedures fail to improve fit estimates, the model can be reformulated as recommended.

Table 17.3 The Structural Equation Model

```
/TITLE
QOL Improved structural model
/TITLE
QOL Structural Model #2
/SPECIFICATIONS
 DATA='C:\EQSWIN\QLRAW.ESS'; VARIABLES= 9; CASES=  70;
 METHODS=ML,ROBUST;
 MATRIX=RAW;
/LABELS
V1=mobility; V2=comfort; V3=energy; V4=lifesat; V5=selfcon;
V6=relation; V7=faith; V8=peace; V9=QOL;
/EQUATIONS
V1 = + *F1  + E1;
V2 = + *F1  + E2;
V3 = + *F1  + E3;
V4 = + *F2  + E4;
V5 = + *F1  + *F2  + E5;
V6 = + *F2  + E6;
V7 = + *F3  + E7;
V8 = + *F3  + E8;
V9 = + *F4  + E9;
/VARIANCES
F1 = 1;
F2 = 1;
F3 = 1;
F4 = 1;
E1 = *;
E2 = *;
E3 = *;
E4 = *;
E5 = *;
E6 = *;
E7 = *;
E8 = *;
E9 = *;
/COVARIANCES
F2 , F1 = *;
F3 , F2 = *;
F4 , F1 = *;
F4 , F2 = *;
F4 , F3 = *;
/LMTEST
 PROCESS=SIMULTANEOUS;
/END

DATA IS READ FROM C:\EQSWIN\QLRAW.ESS
THERE ARE  9 VARIABLES AND   70 CASES

 TITLE:  QOL Structural Model

 SAMPLE STATISTICS

              UNIVARIATE STATISTICS
```

VARIABLE	MOBILITY	COMFORT	ENERGY	LIFESAT	SELFCON
MEAN	4.8261	4.1594	4.8571	5.1250	4.5429
SKEWNESS	-1.1458	-0.6636	-1.1542	-1.7780	-0.8590
KURTOSIS	0.2858	-0.5395	0.4422	2.4242	-0.3977

Table 17.3 The Structural Equation Model (con't)

VARIABLE	RELATION	FAITH	PEACE	QOL
MEAN	5.2609	4.8429	4.9286	65.3000
SKEWNESS	-1.9963	-1.1246	-0.9641	-0.7847
KURTOSIS	3.9165	0.6983	0.7677	-0.4264

MULTIVARIATE KURTOSIS

MARDIA'S COEFFICIENT =   28.0581
NORMALIZED ESTIMATE =   8.3415

CASE NUMBERS WITH LARGEST CONTRIBUTION TO NORMALIZED MULTIVARIATE KURTOSIS:

CASE NUMBER	26	32	43	55	68
ESTIMATE	287.8878	102.1303	117.8037	101.9211	136.0864

COVARIANCE MATRIX TO BE ANALYZED: 9 VARIABLES BASED ON   70 CASES.

	MOBILITY V1	COMFORT V2	ENERGY V3	LIFESAT V4	SELFCON V5
MOBILITY V1	2.028				
COMFORT V2	1.185	2.337			
ENERGY V3	1.030	1.400	1.892		
LIFESAT V4	0.447	0.406	0.293	1.812	
SELFCON V5	0.757	0.888	0.818	0.938	2.107
RELATION V6	0.239	0.337	0.309	0.697	0.933
FAITH V7	0.607	0.636	0.847	1.005	1.405
PEACE V8	0.507	0.579	0.468	0.661	0.822
QOL V9	18.660	22.388	19.725	13.543	25.212

	RELATION V6	FAITH V7	PEACE V8	QOL V9
RELATION V6	1.236			
FAITH V7	0.683	1.468		
PEACE V8	0.352	0.742	0.966	
QOL V9	11.900	20.859	10.384	661.749

DETERMINANT OF INPUT MATRIX IS   0.23591E+03

RESIDUAL COVARIANCE MATRIX (S-SIGMA) :

	MOBILITY V1	COMFORT V2	ENERGY V3	LIFESAT V4	SELFCON V5
MOBILITY V1	0.000				
COMFORT V2	-0.027	0.000			
ENERGY V3	0.007	0.018	0.000		
LIFESAT V4	0.561	0.559	0.423	-0.088	
SELFCON V5	0.606	0.683	0.645	-0.141	0.153
RELATION V6	0.326	0.455	0.409	0.035	0.103
FAITH V7	0.607	0.636	0.847	-0.016	0.080
PEACE V8	0.507	0.579	0.468	0.083	0.072
QOL V9	7.406	7.183	6.890	2.318	6.901

Table 17.3 The Structural Equation Model (con't)

	RELATION V6	FAITH V7	PEACE V8	QOL V9
RELATION V6	-0.052			
FAITH V7	-0.102	0.000		
PEACE V8	-0.092	0.000	0.000	
QOL V9	3.271	6.444	2.224	123.556

AVERAGE ABSOLUTE COVARIANCE RESIDUALS = 3.9017
AVERAGE OFF-DIAGONAL ABSOLUTE COVARIANCE RESIDUALS = 1.4368

STANDARDIZED RESIDUAL MATRIX:

	MOBILITY V1	COMFORT V2	ENERGY V3	LIFESAT V4	SELFCON V5
MOBILITY V1	0.000				
COMFORT V2	-0.012	0.000			
ENERGY V3	0.004	0.009	0.000		
LIFESAT V4	0.292	0.272	0.228	-0.049	
SELFCON V5	0.293	0.308	0.323	-0.072	0.073
RELATION V6	0.206	0.268	0.267	0.023	0.064
FAITH V7	0.352	0.344	0.508	-0.010	0.046
PEACE V8	0.362	0.385	0.346	0.063	0.050
QOL V9	0.202	0.183	0.195	0.067	0.185

	RELATION V6	FAITH V7	PEACE V8	QOL V9
RELATION V6	-0.042			
FAITH V7	-0.076	0.000		
PEACE V8	-0.084	0.000	0.000	
QOL V9	0.114	0.207	0.088	0.187

AVERAGE ABSOLUTE STANDARDIZED RESIDUALS = 0.1524
AVERAGE OFF-DIAGONAL ABSOLUTE STANDARDIZED RESIDUALS = 0.1808

LARGEST STANDARDIZED RESIDUALS:

V7,V3	V8,V2	V8,V1	V7,V1	V8,V3
0.508	0.385	0.362	0.352	0.346

V7,V2	V5,V3	V5,V2	V5,V1	V4,V1
0.344	0.323	0.308	0.293	0.292

V4,V2	V6,V2	V6,V3	V4,V3	V9,V7
0.272	0.268	0.267	0.228	0.207

V6,V1	V9,V1	V9,V3	V9,V9	V9,V5
0.206	0.202	0.195	0.187	0.185

GOODNESS OF FIT SUMMARY

INDEPENDENCE MODEL CHI-SQUARE = 353.655 ON 36 DEGREES OF FREEDOM

INDEPENDENCE AIC = 281.65479   INDEPENDENCE CAIC = 164.70896
MODEL AIC = 10.16034   MODEL CAIC = -58.05806

Table 17.3 The Structural Equation Model (con't)

```
CHI-SQUARE =    52.160 BASED ON   21 DEGREES OF FREEDOM
PROBABILITY VALUE FOR THE CHI-SQUARE STATISTIC IS LESS THAN 0.001

SATORRA-BENTLER SCALED CHI-SQUARE =   31.4153
PROBABILITY VALUE FOR THE CHI-SQUARE STATISTIC IS    0.06702

BENTLER-BONETT NORMED   FIT INDEX=    0.853
BENTLER-BONETT NONNORMED FIT INDEX=    0.832
COMPARATIVE FIT INDEX =    0.902

MEASUREMENT EQUATIONS WITH STANDARD ERRORS AND TEST STATISTICS
(ROBUST STATISTICS IN PARENTHESES)

MOBILITY=V1   =    .947*F1    +    1.000 E1
                   .164
                   5.760
              (    .185)
              (   5.111)
   COMFORT =V2 =   1.279*F1   +    1.000 E2
                   .166
                   7.704
              (    .174)
              (   7.367)

ENERGY  =V3   =   1.080*F1   +    1.000 E3
                   .152
                   7.097
              (    .185)
              (   5.838)
   LIFESAT =V4  =    .928*F2   +    1.000 E4
                   .152
                   6.120
              (    .194)
              (   4.788)

SELFCON =V5   =    .316*F1   +    1.204*F2   +    1.000 E5
                   .163            .141
                   1.939           8.514
              (    .189)      (    .132)
              (   1.671)      (   9.102)
   RELATION=V6 =    .714*F2   +    1.000 E6
                   .127
                   5.604
              (    .169)
              (   4.210)

FAITH  =V7   =   1.145*F3   +    1.000 E7
                   .120
                   9.515
              (    .135)
              (   8.510)
   PEACE  =V8   =    .648*F3   +    1.000 E8
                   .109
                   5.961
              (    .130)
              (   4.975)
```

Table 17.3 The Structural Equation Model (con't)

```
QOL =V9      =   12.589*F4     +      1.000 E9
                     2.373
                     5.304
                 (   2.098)
                 (   6.001)
```

STANDARDIZED SOLUTION:

```
MOBILITY=V1   =      .665*F1   +    .747 E1
COMFORT =V2   =      .837*F1   +    .547 E2
ENERGY  =V3   =      .785*F1   +    .619 E3
LIFESAT =V4   =      .673*F2   +    .739 E4
SELFCON =V5   =      .226*F1   +    .861*F2   +      .507 E5
RELATION=V6   =      .629*F2   +    .778 E6
FAITH   =V7   =      .945*F3   +    .326 E7
PEACE   =V8   =      .660*F3   +    .752 E8
QOL     =V9   =      .543*F4   +    .840 E9
```

LAGRANGE MULTIPLIER TEST (FOR ADDING PARAMETERS)

ORDERED UNIVARIATE TEST STATISTICS:

NO	CODE	PARAMETER	CHI-SQUARE	PROBABILITY	PARAMETER CHANGE
1	2 3	F3,F1	15.794	0.000	0.554
2	2 12	V7,F1	5.204	0.023	0.285
3	2 12	V3,F3	5.134	0.023	0.285
4	2 12	V8,F4	4.999	0.025	0.190
5	2 12	V3,F2	3.844	0.050	0.251
6	2 12	V3,F4	3.388	0.066	0.190
7	2 12	V8,F2	3.348	0.067	1.396
8	2 12	V7,F2	3.141	0.076	1.695
9	2 12	V4,F3	1.814	0.178	1.403
10	2 12	V6,F3	1.534	0.215	1.034

	CUMULATIVE MULTIVARIATE STATISTICS			UNIVARIATE INCREMENT		
STEP	PARAMETER	CHI-SQUARE	D.F.	PROB	CHI-SQUARE	PROB
1	F3,F1	15.794	1	0.000	15.794	0.000

SUMMARY

EQS windows is a program which allows even the novice user to perform advanced statistical analyses. This has been an introduction; for details the reader is referred to the Program Manual and the User's Guide. EQS 5 is expected in a few months. However, the version presented is the most recent available. This program can be run without extensive use of syntax as has been illustrated. How to screen, explore, and transform data has been indicated. Using EQS to compute descriptive statistics was also presented. A special feature of the program is the Bentler-Weeks model. Among models that can be tested with the EQS program are regression, confirmatory factor analyses, and multitrait-multimethod analyses. A program run of EQS was illustrated with "Quality of Life in Cancer Patients " data. The authors are desirous that readers of this chapter gain knowledge and an appreciation of the EQS program.

REFERENCES

Bentler, P. M. (1976). Multistructural statistical model applied to factor analysis. *Multivariate Behavioral Research, 11,* 3-25.

Bentler, P. M., & Weeks, D. G. (1980). Linear structural equations with latent variables. *Psychometrika, 45,* 298-308.

Bentler, P. M. (1986). *LaGrange Multiplier and Wald Tests for EQS and EQS/PC.* LA: BMDP Statistical Software.

Bentler, P. M., & Wu, E. J. C. (1993). *EQS/Windows user's guide: Version 4.* LA: BMDP Statistical Software.

Bentler, P. M. (1993). *EQS structural equations program manual.* LA: BMDP Statistical Software.

Berkson, J. (1980). Minimum chi square, not maximum likelihood. *The Annals of Statistics, 8,* 457-487.

Bollen, K. (1989). *Structural equations with latent variables.* NY: John Wiley.

Brecht, M. L., Bentler, P. M., & Tanaka, J. S. (1986). A case study in evaluating statistical computer programs: Comparison of three programs for specifying and testing structural equation models. *Journal of Educational Technology Systems, 14,* 217-227.

Byrne, B. M., & Goffin, R. D. (1993). Modeling MTMM data from additive and multiplicative covariance structures: An audit of construct validity concordance. *Multivariate Behavioral Research, 28*(1), 67-96.

Byrne, B. M. (1994). *Structural equation modeling with EQS and EQS/Windows.* Thousand Oaks, CA: Sage.

Cole, D. A. (1987). Utility of confirmatory factor analysis in test validation research. *Journal of Consulting and Clinical Psychology, 55*(4), 584-594.

Fiske, D. W., & Campbell, D. T. (1959). Convergent and discriminant validation by the multitrait-multimethod matrix. *Psychological Bulletin, 56,* 81-104.

Shaping Social Policy Through Empirical Influences

Betty N. Adams

T his chapter introduces social policy within a framework for illustrating the nature of interaction between entities (both person and object). Policy is acknowledged as being influenced by values and as the instrument which provides order in the allocation of scarce resources. Policy is influenced by the values of those in position to set policies and also by those outside the policy making arena. Policy is also motivated by the element of power as a driving force for influencing process and outcomes of decision making.

Social policy is addressed broadly, reflecting on organized approaches directed toward an established end. Derivations of social policies and policy making, such as health and public policy, are illustrated to depict the connection between policy making and politics (formally and informally). The inspiration of various beliefs and values, both from the individual to policy makers, is conveyed to describe the smoke screen which conceals and tarnishes often the affects of politics in defining social policy. Issues relating to social policy and research are raised to depict the lack of reliance on empirical evidence in directing policy making. In view of the fact that social policy exists because of the scarcity in resources, it behooves policy makers to target decision making for action or in-action where the greatest effect can be achieved.

WHAT IS SOCIAL POLICY?

Policy defines the values of a social system and directs the manner in which worth and benefits are actualized to accomplish a pre-conceived goal. Policy is authoritative and decisive, planned and directed in delineating the allocation of scarce resources. Regardless of the setting, i.e., social, political, organizational or the work place, policy institution is analogous. Also, because policy issues are driven by values, the framework for operation executes in a cyclical fashion creating initially an agenda justified by perceived goals.

Accordingly, social policy (Mason, Talbott, & Leavitt, 1993) is merely a construct of public policy designed to promote and guard the public's health, safety and welfare. The economic status in connection with populace demographics and political forces influence the development of social policy. However, in spite of the linkage, research has shown that there is a diffusion in the economic prominence and value when in connection with public or welfare-state programs (Wilensky, Luebbert, Hahn, & Jamieson, 1985).

Social policy is designed to protect the public's welfare. The public's ideas and interests are embedded to effect policy making in response to social concerns and needs. This is accomplished through an exchange of ideas, beliefs and values orientation between individuals, groups and policy makers. Often, social policy arises out of a problem or situation that is believed to be a threat to the community or nation as a whole. These occurrences are usually incidences in which policies already in existence do not have the scope or resources to adequately address the social conditions.

A likely example of the aforementioned was the response of the Communicable Disease Center (CDC) instantaneously developing regulations to limit the spread of the Human Immune Deficiency Virus (HIV). This action was kindled in response to public fear and reaction to the case involving Kimberly Bergalis and four other individuals claiming to lack the capacity for evaluating the risk of HIV infection from practitioner to client. Bergalis and the others had received dental treatments from a dentist in Florida believed to be infected with HIV (Bradley, 1993; Glantz, Mariner, & Annas, 1992).

Coerced to respond, the Communicable Disease Center proposed a risk prevention or restrictive policy without clarifying the distinction between regulating things or procedures from that of regulating people. The criticism was that the policy did not support the communicability of HIV and instead compromised the rights of health care practitioners (Glantz, et al., 1992).

In the strategy for dealing with HIV, the magnitude of society's influence on policy making has been unyielding throughout state and local municipalities. Consequently, policies to protect social welfare have been created across disciplines and occupations to protect the public in the spread of HIV. Those in health related professions, service occupations and numerous others have had to change the way they deliver services to the public (Louisiana Revised Statutes [LARS], 1992; *Connecticut Medicine,* 1992; Brown, Phillips, Brown, Knowlan, Castle, & Moyer, 1994). These noted changes have been made through the creation of policies designed to enhance or limit an individual or group's scope of practice. The Louisiana Senate proposed legislation in 1992, Bill Number 790, authorizing the disclosure of HIV test results to state health care boards for licensees regulated by said boards. The Bill was suspended following several attempts and later referred to committee. Had the Bill passed, those health care providers testing positive for HIV would have been subjected to disciplinary charges had they failed to notify the board which regulated their practice. Also, the opportunity to practice a health related profession and deliver services to the public may have been prohibited (Louisiana Revised Statutes [LARS], 1992).

Since social policy is fostered through the political socialization of people with beliefs and values shared through generations, individuals in an aggregate form become the dominant force in declaring what is purposive and rational. As issues evolve, this socialization is challenged by personal interests of individuals to phenomena and also individual control over resources of interests to others (Brown, 1991). Thus, a bridge or linkage always exists between individuals or groups and policy makers. Often, the perceived intimidation brought on by social issues and pertinent policies usually have connection with a threat to economic security and public welfare.

Such has been the social response to HIV. Beside affecting the livelihood of health care practitioners and recipients of health services, there is the belief that HIV will increase at an unyielding proportion by 2004, having the greatest social threat to women and children (Weiss & Louria, 1994). The prediction is an endemic, worldwide problem. In spite of the passage of the Americans With Disabilities Act at the federal level, and numerous other state legislation, it is questionable whether coping between individuals and policy makers on this social issue will endure.

FRAMEWORK FOR POLITICAL INFLUENCE: POLICY MAKING FOR SOCIAL CHANGE

Policy making implies having the authority to direct some kind of behavior for action or inaction. A policy, which is derived through policy making, commands or permits elected and appointed governmental officials, representatives of organizations or interest groups and individuals to behave in a certain way. The policy takes on variations in description depending upon the entity it is designed to address. Also, there are numerous variations in policy making impacting all aspects of society in relation to the community, nation and the world.

Private policy originates through organizations or exclusive institutions in society. In this grouping of policy, the goal is to maintain or bring about some kind of reverberation that shows solidarity and control by a defined body. There is a collective stance and trust that the structure for behavior as defined by private policy will sustain the continuance and stability of the organization. Petersen (1988) refers to this structure for policy making as organizational model. Similarly, Mason and others (1993) use the idiom for the same structure as institutional model.

The most familiar pattern for policy making is public policy, which affects how people behave in response to governmental goals which are defined and directed through legislation, regulation and court decisions. In this structure, people or the citizenry have input in the goals for policy making. Most commonly, this is accomplished through a demonstration of the right to vote which selects and permits elected members of the constituency to serve in represen-

Figure 18.1 Influences on Policy Making

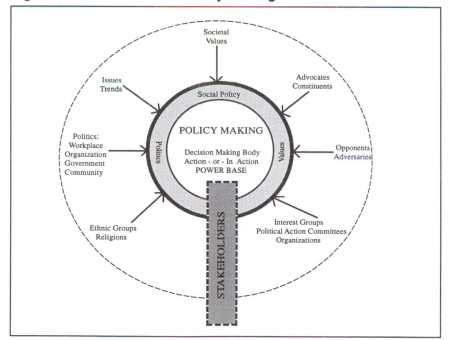

tation of the public in meeting perceived goals. In actuality, the elected officials respond to the public good by engaging in policy making to bring about structure in how the good of the public can best be accomplished for the betterment of society. Oftentimes, the goals sought by the policy makers are not endorsed by the constituency, thereby causing discontent and unrest in the action or inaction taken by the electorate.

Governmental policy making emulates a rational model (Petersen, 1988; Starling, 1988). It is rational because it directs goals and outcomes that are not totally in control by the policy maker. There is a respect for goals and expected outcomes that have to be reached within a prescribed allocation of resources. Starling (1988) advocates six principles that encircle a rational approach to policy making. These are concentration, clarity, changeability, challenge, coordination and consistency.

It is often not appreciated that the policy maker does not possess a total repertoire of internal assets necessary for addressing and setting policies rationally for a constituency or the whole of society. The question of clarity in the goals set in an electorate's platform may not be concentrated congruent with the resources the policy maker has available to meet goals. So the question arises in a rational approach, how flexible or changeable can a policy be defined to show consistency in what may have generated as a campaign promise and later is influenced by changing conditions in society. Consequently, the challenge to the electorate is the assurance of similarity and realism in respect to the intended goals by relying on sound facts and reasoning through coordinated efforts of other resources. Thus, in the rational approach to policy making, there must be reliance on the exchange of information generated through collaboration with others and most specifically through empirical evidence.

Social policy originates in a public domain. In consideration of illustrations by Mason and others (1993), social policy evolves in a group and systems model. Competing groups have vested interests in social issues and entities influenced through lobbying and negotiations with policy makers for input in goal setting and feedback on outcomes. Social issues evolve in representation to decisions on health, education, jobs, and overall social welfare. These situations proliferate tensions and contradictions between the public and private sectors in the manner in which resources should be allocated to meet social concern.

Petersen (1988) relates to the above design by suggesting bargaining models as the structure for influencing social policy. These bargaining models are the ideological and pluralist. In the former example, individuals and those who are not elected officials are distant in the interpretation of social issues and concerns. A likely illustration would be in deciding on the best approach for governmental policy on birth control. The question remains miles apart. Is pro-life the answer? Is pro-choice the answer? These become opposing ideologies because the goals and objectives are so broad and undefined.

Petersen (1988) asserts that in the pluralist bargaining model, there is the desire to compromise between policy makers and the people. Therefore, input is sought from the outside for guiding decision making. Consequently, policy makers may be persuaded in bargaining to set policies based more on intuition rather than inclusive of empirical evidence. The impact of the above may or may not reflect the intended goals as beneficial to the social good.

In consideration of the four models for influencing policy making (rational, pluralist, ideological and organization) as suggested by Petersen (1988), the subsequent sections of this chapter illustrate the similarities and differences in these models when applied to policy making in government, organizations and the public arena. Also, there are forthcoming discussions of the above in respect to common settings where policy making and politics operate, such as the work place, community (at large), government and in organizations, associations, leagues, etc. The latter has been characterized most vividly by Mason and others (1993).

RATIONAL MODEL FOR DECISION MAKING AND COLLECTIVE BARGAINING

Graham Room (1979) illustrates a two dimensional paragon for social policy, referred to as the rational model. One dimension represents formal rationality which is achieved through the actions of public officials in developing policy. The second dimension is substantive rationality representing the choice of the public to pursue change in social policy goals.

The rational model permeated the nineteenth century when people were in search of political understanding and unanimity. The rational citizen was one who strived for what was good and just in dominance over the political environment. Confidence was in those who were elected by the public to carry out the common good. Therefore, it was one's obligation to participate in ideas and actions out of a sense of civic responsibility and ultimate accountability for the exercise of power within a socially acceptable value system (Wirt & Kirst, 1982).

Peterson (1988) explains the rational model as a correspondence between goals and outcomes that are external to policy makers. Rational process is used to plan future actions for decision making in generating policy for any organized body and setting. The question to be addressed is in the structure selected for rational decision making in policy planning, such as empirically based (descriptive theory) or value-based (normative theory) process. Empirical findings depict how things are in society. The value-based accentuates how things ought to be in answering to a social concern (Mayer, 1985). In both, decision making is the purpose. Concerns of the populace include the rational relationship of policy planning in respect to the means justifying the ends, or developing plans to meet a goal-oriented decision in promoting social welfare in response to social concerns. The politician is concerned about the populace's response or interpretation (voter or constituent) to decisions made and actions taken in implementing policy. Mayer (1988) states that:

> Planning and politics are inextricably related. Every public decision involves choices among important values which can only be made through a political process. Also, any political leader who wishes to stay in power must show progress in solving vexing social problems, which requires rationality about substantive issues. (p. 2)

Alternatives in policy making are pathways that are open and often pursued by either external forces and policy makers. Rational decision making identifies limits in the range of alternatives to policy issues, even though it may not determine which alternative to select within a given range. For example, social policy has been responsive to the unquenchable desire of the public for a better health care system through the enactment of the Social Security Act in

1935. During the last several decades, public policy created the Medicaid
Program to meet the needs of the uninsured and underinsured (Mason, et al.,
1993). Contention for the above is rationalized because of the aging and job-
less population, improved technology designed to render more expedient diagnoses and treatments, and most importantly, the power of advocates, manu-
facturers, and policy makers in directing the public's stake in health care
(Wilensky, et al., 1985). An example would be when health care escalated in
the 1990s with less consumers able to pay, nurses offered an alternative community nursing approach to meet the needs of people more economically. The
model for this program was suggested later under the Omnibus Budget Reconciliation Act of 1988. Finally, after much lobbying, in 1991 a community
demonstration project by nurses as providers was permitted (Mason, et al.,
1993).

Alternatives to policy issues are conveyed usually to demonstrate the importance or gravity of resolving an agenda through policy making. Values
consistently lead the transaction in policy making and also in the implementation and evaluation of policy. The pattern continues to evolve as the results of
policy evaluations become new agenda that are contemplated through the definition of values. Mason and others (1993) acclaim this configuration exists
for policy generation in organizations, communities, the work place and government.

The intent of substantive rationality is the articulation of alternatives in social policy brought on by selective retrospective evaluation of policy effectiveness. This latter dimension of substantive rationality fabricates social policy
development operating in an empirical milieu, formally or informally arranged.
As Room affirms (1979), deficiencies in policy successes may occur because
the original analysis of the social problem or issue that stimulated a policy
development may not be consistent and relevant in respect to societal changes
since the original policy was adopted. Also, in substantive rationality, the
public's expectations of the policy are not congruent with the measures for
demonstrating effectiveness.

PLURALIST MODEL: A BARGAINING APPROACH

The pluralist model (Petersen, 1988), as a participatory model for political
socialization (Mayer, 1985) asserts that as there are more than one, or more
than two kinds of ultimate realities and as issues change in society, participating groups and the alliances among them will change. A pluralist state in
society is one in which members of diverse ethnic, racial, religious or social
groups maintain an autonomous participation in the development of their traditional culture or special interests within the confines of a common civilization. The objective of the pluralist is to bring in harmony the public and the
collectives' plans for policy and alternatives to policy.

Room upholds (1979) that to appreciate the development of social policy, it
is necessary to examine the implications for social stratification and political
order. The criticism of formal rationality is the creation of social policies to
benefit the interests of capitalism. The populace, therefore, cannot participate
in rational policy making and thus are enslaved to the greed and insatiability of
individuals and organized groups who are in position to best articulate and
influence policy makers. Nevertheless, in a democratic society, reliance is on
the active participation of the populace in social policy development. Therefore, the implementation and ultimate impact of social policy is affected by

exclusion or inclusion of the public throughout policy development. The best posture is pursuing substantive rational policy development with collective participation.

According to Peterson (1988), the pluralists are politically active groups that concentrate their energy on those issues that have the greatest immediate impact on their desires and values. Those inside the political system who serve as policy makers seek to satisfy the interests of groups in order to maximize the vote and remain elected. The political system responds to the interests of groups in relation to the significance and character of the group. Those groups that are relatively small, homogeneous and concentrate on a specific area of public policy, tend to receive the greatest satisfaction from the political system. Consequently, the intent of the participatory model is to increase opportunity for all parties to take part so when policies are planned, there will be a better fit and consensus in the actions or alternatives taken (Mayer, 1985).

To be assured of pluralist views, the participatory model of planning may be patterned in citizen participation through opinion surveys, public forums or input to advisory committees. Also, participation may be demonstrated through selection of nonpartisan groups authorized to engage in alternative planning for collective interest. The aforementioned represents a framework for citizen participation in policy making which became a pluralist perspective in the 1960s with the acknowledgment that certain groups had been removed from the formal process of political decision making. This recognition was actualized through the civil rights movement and the war on poverty (Mayer, 1985).

In speculating on the implications of the pluralist model, there is the realization of a socially agreed exception of assuring that diversity in groups, the public and collectives, is acknowledged and respected. Thus, this belief is accomplished through involvement and participation of pluralists in the context of an open process that guarantees reconciliation in policy planning. The outcome is the security of a more integrated system for decision making on issues.

The pluralist model is synonymous in structure to the allegiant model illustrated by Wirt and Kirst (1982). This model arose as a perceived threat of the immigrant urban migration of the early nineteenth century. Many felt that this urban migration would dilute American values in our socially acceptable way of responding to social issues and concerns. In other words, "the immigrant was to be swayed from dirty parties, patronage, and ethnic group conflict to accept nonpartisanship, the merit system, and a harmony of community interests" (Wirt & Kirst, 1982). The strategy was compromise.

The compromise approach by the dominant pluralist group is a sympathetic response to the interests of all groups focusing on a common variance of issues. The pluralist is "realistic about the need for cooperation among a wide range of interests in order to keep a complex system a viable functioning entity, the compromiser will search for ways of satisfying, at least minimally, the various competing interests with a claim to be heard" (Peterson, 1988, p. 41). As in the past, imperialism and allegiance to a better society by working together and adopting a communal set of values void of conflict is the pluralist's socialization for effective policy planning. Consequently, dominant pluralist groups and policy makers recognize that the participation between and among groups on issues is a transient bargaining relationship. Even though a group remains intact, its relationship with other groups and policy makers may be represented as an opponent on one issue, neutral on another and simply a confederate on another.

IDEOLOGICAL MODEL: A BARGAINING MODEL

Peterson (1988) describes the ideological model also as a bargaining model for policy making in which there are two distinct ideas characterized by an issue. Unlike the pluralist, components of the two sides are miles apart and do not seek compromise for decision making in policy formation. The ideologies articulate the interests of broad inclusive social roles, i.e., race, class, religion, ethnicity, values and beliefs. Thus, commitment is to broad objectives on issues which spun conflict over principles rather than competition among specific concerns.

The ideologists' mainstay is in how economic and social policies impact their social roles and welfare, which according to Peterson (1988) can be characterized as a two dimensional political thought or policy position: internal consistency, cohesion and comprehensiveness. Ideologies intersect across these dimensions as a representation of interdependencies among social, economic and political institutions. For instance, a shift in economic structure automatically warrants the inclusion of social and political institutions, since interference and disruption reciprocate involvement or disequilibrium in response to social issues.

The ideologists are consistent in values orientation and reaction to social issues. Ideologists establish coalitions as strategies for policy making and these coalitions become dominant when building support for similar issues viewed important for inclusive social groups. The description in the consistency in the concept of ideology, which operates as a political belief system, is less appropriate when concerns are questions on the posterity of individuals or groups representing exclusive social roles. Regardless of how venomous a social issue may be, distinct groups such as garbage collectors, certified public accountants, homeless people and so forth, all would have interests in a particular or exclusive concern representative of their ideology.

The ideological model as a bargaining structure for influencing policy making can be summarized through various observations (Peterson, 1988). First of all, ideological bargaining on policies always involve groups and individuals who continue to be committed to broad social objectives which guarantee consistency in protecting their economic and social welfare interests. Consistency in commitment is the goal verses compromising on issues such as the pluralist would do.

Secondly, the ideological model portrays consistency in the reaction to social issues over time. The ideologue participates in similar broad situations congruent to his invariable perspective on policy questions, especially those involving race and class in correlation to social and economic well being. The tendency to share interests and views with liberals or exclusive groups is not the intent of ideologists.

In consideration of the social formulation of a group, such as a political party, there is in the structure ideologies that reflect comprehensiveness, coherency and consistency. Even though maximizing the vote is the ultimate interest of political parties, the voters' reactions to social concerns are observed within the ideological perspective of the party. There is consistency in the manner selected for response to the voter by the ideological bargaining group as there is consistency with the coalitions that are aligned by the group. This illustration is clear if one focuses on what ideologies, for example, the Democrats and Republicans represent and the groups they are known to coalesce. In other word, Democrats are perceived to have established coalitions with organized labor; whereas Republicans are perceived to be aligned with the values orientation of affluent businesses whose belief is the welfare protection of those who are empowered to generate a high standard of living. Thus, the above illustrates the third highlight in characterizing the ideological model as a bargaining type.

Lastly, ideologies are ingrained in comprehensiveness and coherency. The values orientation is like an old cliche, "It's better to fight than quit." Therefore, the priority is not necessarily in winning, as it is in being consistent on the stance taken in protecting the groups' interests for social and economic stability.

ORGANIZATIONAL MODEL

Organizational model implies solidarity. The members set the interests and are committed unitarily to operate by using standard operating procedures. In this structure, change is slow in the manner in which business or policies are defined. The consistency is the appreciation and respect for interdependency among all components of the organization. Even though there may be internal bargaining, unity is always the ultimate intention.

Organizations are viewed as autonomous and self-guiding in an enclosed system. Since goals and objectives are defined and actions are taken in an undifferentiated and isolated pattern, standard operating procedures serve as routines for the organization relating to the special interests of the structure. Also, because change in goals and objectives is slow, there is always reluctance and hesitancy in moving from an agreed set of values and interests which have been adopted and internally understood by the members and constituents of the organization. Petersen (1988) presents organizational model as representing a natural-system approach, entwined in movement via its routines, interests and the shared values of its members. Consequently, in view of the above explanation, organizations are limited in scope or policies in resolving unanticipated crises or disruptions. If the solution is not in the standard operating procedures, then there is not an appropriate repertoire or relative alternative. Also, because the interests of the organization are limited and confined, its members may encounter inconvenience or turbulence when in need of special assistance.

However, in consideration of this natural-system approach to organizations, there is more consistency in shared values among members than conflict. "Members typically adhere to certain norms that distinguish them from other groups in society..." (Petersen, 1988, p. 114). The above is more profound, especially when the members represent a profession. They share values and also trust in the unified structure as an interdependent mechanism for shaping decision making and direction. As Petersen (1988) asserts, what is most important for organizational members in not so much the power that can be gained internally as it is maintaining the natural-systems approach which assures its members protection and autonomy for common interests, values and routines. For a graphic presentation of the rational, pluralist, ideological and organizational models for policy making, see Figure 18.2.

Figure 18.2 Policy Making for Social Change

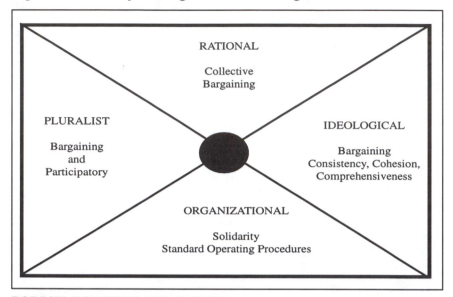

POLICY, POLITICS AND VALUES

Often, we presume politics to be decorous only to politicians. We blunder in our understanding that all play the role of influencing or making policies, formally and informally, in our existence in any social group. This could be family or community association, as well as conventionally in our professional organizations, the work place, and if we aspire to engage, through the public vote in government at the local, state and federal levels. "Politics is a neutral term. It means influencing ... the allocation of scarce resources..." (Mason, et al, 1993, p. 6) by persuading others to change their values and ideas by adopting the values and decisions of another. In brief, policy operates within politics and a value system to bring change in the allocation of resources for social advancement.

Those most often in position to influence others are the elected or selected policy makers who usually are politicians. Policy makers epitomize a seat of power because they are in position to engage in action or inaction in allocating something of value which others depend on or desire. Power is having control over others and events by being in position to deliver certain goods on one's own terms. Consequently, a policy maker, whether functioning in a rational, pluralist, ideological or organizational structure has the leeway to exert control and jurisdiction outside of external conditions and intimidations.

Policy makers and those bodies and entities outside a policy making domain are all influenced by values. Resources, privileges, positions, etc. sought are dictated by values and perceived worth. Values are expressed through individuals and groups' judgements about something being good or bad. Thus, according to McNally (1994), " a value is both a judgment and an emotional response..." (p. 111). For example, Americans for the most part, associate democracy as a value associated with freedom and equality, even though evidence does not always show this in action (McNally, 1994).

The members operating in a rational, pluralist, ideological or organizational models (previously illustrated as structure for political influence) share a common system of values (Petersen, 1988). These values are incorporated in the beliefs which guide the action of choices and decision making (see Figure 18.1). Consequently, it is human nature that policy makers and those outside the policy making domain are influenced by the values they hold within.

When policy makers and groups are faced with a social issue, the strategy for action or inaction is guided by the values orientation related to the issue. Those individuals and entities on the outside may decide to invade the policy makers in a manner that is congruent with the values orientation of the body. On the other hand, the decision may be to endorse the policy makers' stance with or without noticeable support of the body. The latter closely illustrates the pluralists because their most operative value is to be in accord with what is most civil. As previously addressed, in an ideological structure, there are wide variations in values which usually precipitate conflict and dissention when entities are competing for the same limited resources especially in the forms of money, time, opportunity, information, education, etc. (Mason, et al., 1993). Sometimes the values conflicts evolve into stressors that are transferred through out a political system by policy makers, individuals and group influences (Refer to Figure 18.2 for an illustration depicting influences on policy making).

POLICY AS PROACTIVE TO EFFECT SOCIAL POLICY AND WELFARE: WIC AS AN EXAMPLE

Generally, social policy is initiated through the sphere of governmental influence, underpinning some public issue or strategy. Because of the nature of policy making, what is often intended as policy usually never results as such. Therefore, it is sometimes very difficult to measure the impact of social policy. Instead, political analysts tend to dwell on the measurement of program descriptions in addition to the cost of implementation as the criteria for meeting the expectations of the policy.

Starling (1988) suggests six criteria for appraising the effectiveness of a policy. The criteria for assessment are referred to as side effects, efficiency, strategy, compliance, justice and intervention effect. These criteria are applicable as programs are developed to meet a policy, as well as for ongoing programs and after implementation of programs.

The effectiveness of a social policy on nutrition can serve as an example when applying Starling's (1988) six criteria. The *Special Supplemental Food Program for Women, Infants, and Children,* better known as WIC, was created by Public Law 92-433 and enacted on September 26, 1972 to meet a national nutrition need (United States Department of Agriculture [USDA], 1980). WIC was justified in support of the "substantial numbers of pregnant, postpartum, and breast feeding women, infants and young children from families of inadequate income" (USDA, 1972). It was the position of policy makers that families with inadequate incomes were in high risk of having inadequate nutrition and health care. Thus, the initial intent of WIC was to serve as an adjunct to good health care practices during periods when women, infants and children's growth and development are most vulnerable.

In the last 20 years, (United State Department of Agriculture [USDA], 1988), WIC has been augmented to include prevention of drug abuse and overall improvement in the health status of families by blending cultural diversity and customary health care practices. WIC, as a program to address a social policy on nutrition, has been delivered to the public via local public health and welfare agencies as well as private nonprofit health care agencies. Strategies to address the nutrition needs of families have been distributed by means of individual and group community sessions. The goal has been to provide nutrition education to achieve a positive change in dietary habits by considering the family's socioeconomic status and personal preferences.

Agencies that offer the WIC program must provide for families at risk, referrals to services for substance abuse counseling and treatment. Also, families are to be monitored in their success of accessing services and the progress made to guarantee an improvement in health status.

The question is whether WIC, designed to meet a social policy, has demonstrated and achieved an improved health care status for women, infants and children of families at risk. Over the 24 years that WIC has been operating, has there been a significant lowering in the maternal-infant-child morbidity and mortality rates because of better nutrition understanding and practice? An empirical response to the above questions is anticipated as a logical representation of the public: taxpayers, voters, health organizations, politicians, etc. Therefore, policy makers are responsible for reporting to the public facts about the successes and failures of the WIC program in meeting a nutrition policy.

Reporting is essential if the policy is to remain in effect through its previously designed program(s), such as WIC, or through some other social program. Hence, the framework offered by Starling (1988), culminating with an evaluation component, is a rational order to undertake in generating a creditable report to the public.

To answer scientifically, one would begin by defining the *side-effects* or externalities of the WIC program. Much of the same phenomenon as what educators exclaim as the hidden curriculum, which are those events or occurrences that become components of the program that were never intended but nonetheless create side effects which alter the intended expectation of the policy. These are the unintended consequences.

Hearings before the Select Committee on Nutrition and Human Needs of the United States Senate, Ninety-fourth Congress (1976), addressed expressed concerns that the Department of Agriculture was not appropriating adequate funding to support WIC. Instead, the USDA created regulations which engendered more bureaucracy and perceived hardships on mothers and children needing nutritional assistance. There was conflict in the importance of WIC by Congress which had doubled expenditures for WIC in 1973 and extended the program for 3 more years. Also, there was the question of the depth of implementation of WIC by the USDA because actions had been taken by the Department to halt the implementation of WIC prior to the initial three years' deadline for the program.

As opponents and proponents of social programs wane, the argument had been misadministration of WIC by the USDA. In actuality, it had been decided by the Department not to expend WIC in areas with existing commodity supplemental food programs (CSFD). The CSFD also was under the jurisdiction and regulation of the USDA. Congressional supporters argued that it was better to guarantee that high-risk mothers and babies were fed well at the stages of prenatal and postnatal, than it was to attempt to impact a baby that grows up to be a slow learner, mentally retarded, and malnourished (USDA, 1972).

The WIC program is operated via local agencies (public welfare and private non-profit) through Medicaid. The first local project was approved for funding on August 29, 1973 in Kentucky as a pilot program. Since 1980, WIC has operated throughout the United States and territories, Puerto Rico and the Virgin Islands (USDA, 1980). The regulatory statutes of WIC are global which create an opportunity for flexibility in operation through the numerous facets in which the program is operated. Usually, these go unnoticed because who is going to argue that mothers and babies should be deprived of adequate nutrition and preventive care. Thus, the unintended consequences or side-effects become more important and have to be dealt with as if they were initially the intended policy.

The WIC program has endured side-effects reflected in three principles which have surfaced in social policy and characterized by Charles Murray (1984, pp. 211-218):

1. Any program, however generously designed, will necessarily leave many more worthy claimants uncovered and thus exert pressure for expansion.
2. Any program will also necessarily provide benefits to unworthy or unintended free riders.
3. Most programs hurt more people than they help.

Side-effects or unintended consequences occur in programs to effect social policy often because of a lack of clarity and understanding of specifically what segment in society the related programs are to serve. Also, there may be discrepancy in who is eligible to sub-contract these services for the government. The Department of Agriculture was concerned about duplicating programs to meet a nutrition policy, such as the conflict between the CSFP and WIC. However, WIC was defined specifically for prenatal and postnatal women and children (infancy to under five years of age) at nutritional risk needing more than the food available through CSFP. Therefore, to abort continued criticism of ineffectiveness of WIC, the Department of Agriculture sought external consultation for assistance in developing more guidelines for defining what constituted broad nutritional risks (USDA, 1980).

Efficiency is the second criterion for determining if a policy is proactive (Starling, 1988). The question are: What will be the direct cost to taxpayers? Have the goals been reached? Do they exceed the intent? How much extravagance has occurred in implementation and where has expenditure been most demonstrated? Are mothers and babies experiencing a better and healthier start after having participated in the WIC program?

Starling (1988) argues that the governmental sphere has not supported policy making through the incorporation of research findings. Empirical evidence is most lacking in programs operated by government. Thus, too often policy makers are void of information generated through research needed to aid them in decision making to best support the welfare of the public.

The next appraisal criterion according to Starling (1988) is to determine if a policy is *proactive* in depicting what it was suppose to accomplish and whether the changes or amelioration subsequent to implementation are explainable in respect to implicit theories. Officials of the Department of Agriculture reported to the Select Committee on Nutrition and Human Needs of the United States Senate (1976) on the progress of WIC in meeting the nutrition policy. The authorized appropriation was $250 million (expended over six to seven months) to cover a caseload of nearly 1.5 million women, infants, and children by 1976. The strategy of the Department of Agriculture had been to decelerate the growth of participants to less than a million, thereby serving 830,000 in WIC by 1976. The reason given was to establish a more orderly movement of participants with funding extended over a longer period of time without disruption during the transition quarter that was not covered in the appropriation. This proactive strategy by the USDA was open to scrutiny and criticism by the Select Committee (United States Congress, Senate, 1976).

The Department of Agriculture rationalized its stance by illustrating that affirmative action priority had been given to communities already participating in the supplemental food and food certificate programs. The rationale was to support the special population WIC served and ease the administrative costs, provide extended medical determinations and also add nutrition education. The Department of Agriculture attested that the above represented a foundational support of one social program promoting another without duplication and instead demonstrating civic accountability and moral responsibility. Simply, those at risks, especially women, infants and children deserved adequate nutrition, therefore, it was prudent that services be spread out at a rate that would not compromise efficiency. Also, the Department of Agriculture testified that to fully meet the needs of the special population, it was prudent to broaden the definition of nutrition risk to include anemia, inadequate growth and inadequate diet for women with high risk pregnancies. Also, to guarantee program efficiency, parameters were being developed to assess when a woman or child was no longer a nutritional risk.

Compliance is the fourth criterion (Starling, 1988). Did the program truly accomplish what it set out to do? Is the WIC program reaching the low socioeconomic and poor mothers and babies? Is the maternal-child policy through the WIC program morally right and correct? Is justice being served through the WIC program?

The values in society change. Social programs held in high esteem in one era may be perceived otherwise as time goes on. This same pattern of change is reflected in the manner in which social policies are derived. In reflecting again on WIC as a program to meet a nutrition policy, the USDA presented its biennial report on the status of compliance (USDA, 1980) . The report covered a brief overview of how the money had been spent and the 1.2 million people who had been served since 1973, roughly 20 per cent of all persons eligible. The majority of the report outlined fundamental areas that needed to be inclusive in future funding comprised of more diversity in sub-cultures of the low socioeconomic groups, and especially breast feedings mothers and infants and children. Recommendations were made that WIC increase the number of participants to at least 50 per cent of the nation's eligible population. This would be met by combining the efforts of WIC with other related social policy activities, such as the Indian Health Service (IHS). Also, the suggestion was that nutrition education be more diversified for Hispanics, Asian refugees, migrants, Native Americans and other specialized populations. This design would mean a more cooperative effort between the USDA and USPH/IHS with the aim targeted at those populations that were not being met through WIC in its present design.

Starling (1988) illustrates the final criterion, which is the *intervention effect* of the policy. The challenge is comparing the outcomes of a program after implementation with what would have happened if the program were not executed. In other words, having policy or no policy, certain phenomena do occur (Mohr, 1992). Therefore, the sure way of explaining the intervention effect is through research. The techniques should employ control groups to clearly justify whether the intervention was the reason for the demonstrated outcomes or some external, unintended force. The methodology to evaluate the intervention effect should focus a times-series format. Trends before and during the intervention should be correlated to describe the magnitude of the social condition. The evaluation should ask the questions: Were social conditions ameliorated during and with the intervention? Were the conditions significantly improved or did things relatively remain the same? Were there perhaps other relationships that dominated the time period in which the intervention was in effect?

The aforementioned questions illustrate the term impact analysis of a program carried out via human activities to affect the state of some objects or phenomena. Again, like the hidden curriculum, the evaluator appraising the effectiveness of a social policy must concertize the outcomes generated clearly as expected and also acknowledge the intended consequences of the intervention.

Using WIC as an example of a social program to meet a nutrition policy, the USDA engaged in evaluation of each expected outcome of the program. Reflecting on the nutrition education tailored for various cultural groups, the survey results revealed that three-fourths of the programs reporting employed a nutritionist who may not have been responsible exclusively for WIC. There was much diversity in the methods applied in rendering nutrition education. Some sites used one-to-one sessions and others used group sessions. In some cases the person providing the nutrition education may have been a nutritional aid or a WIC technician. The setting for the nutrition classes did not render always comfortable space and opportunity to meet with individuals who may have missed a previous session (USDA, 1990).

In respect to the above WIC survey findings, Mohr's (1992) suggestion would be that the program theory applied for WIC's nutrition education component should be tested in terms of the intervention. The latter serves as substantive rationality which impacts the relevance of the program theory and purpose. Second, the next step is the quantification of program effectiveness through research designs that offer comparisons between those subjects included in the intervention and the control group. In the case of WIC, a smaller population of eligible individuals/groups was served than the policy intended. The program may have been effective with those participating in WIC. However, it becomes important to know how much of the larger population not reached actually remains in critical need of nutrition education.

SOCIAL POLICY AND RESEARCH ISSUES

In any situation a policy always has social ramifications and impact, strongly driven by the values of the originator and the society in which it was designed to benefit. Oftentimes, with or without birth in a research base, a policy may be contradictory for constituents or the social dilemma it was designed to serve. Therefore, it is wise for policy makers to seek input through empirical findings prior to or during the implementation of policies.

Policy research can lead to a fundamental analysis of social problems and provide pragmatic and action-oriented recommendations for consideration by policy makers in alleviating the quandary of social concerns. Majchrzak (1984) suggests that to maximize the greatest gain from policy research; it is advisable first to know the audience and stakeholders dependent on the study results. This includes those who will be users of the policy as well as those who may be affected because of the policy. The above is important because the intent of social policy is to allocate scarce resources for fundamental change where it can make the greatest contribution.

"Policy research explicitly incorporates values" (Majchrzak, 1984, p. 20). The recommendations from the policy research will be questioned to the extent a social problem has been clarified, thus making the research multidimensional in nature. Values dominate all the elements that arise if the policy is or is not implemented or changed in the manner in which it is offered. Therefore, the impact and role of values, even from the researcher's perspective must be identified and focused for successful policy research.

Policy research effects policy making via issues generation in aversive interventions. There are pros and cons on whether social policy should exist to support or not support inimical treatments options as remedy or control of health related problems for various facets of society. Gerhardt, Holmes, Alessandri, and Goodman (1991) challenge the efficacy of aversive intervention to reduce problematic behavior in the developmental disabled. Parmenter (1991) discusses the shift in the Australian health care system to de-emphasize the institutionalization of the intellectually handicapped as influenced by the emerging practices in America and other western nations (Fisher, Dorwart, Schlesinger, Epstein, & Davidson, 1992). In the latter, the policy has been a move from governmental support of large segregated hospitals to small cooperative integrated community based living. The consequence has been new intervention without substantial manpower support and a refusal to adopt changing values of empowering the mentally disabled and families in the process. Consequently, in both examples, aversive interventions in respect to social policies have raise empirical questions.

The 1990 policy on HIV proliferated legal and ethical attention to other social issues, such as informed consent, significant risk, confidentiality, and the right to work. It is through research that solutions will evolve to provide for policy makers direction in the relevance of education, enforcement of safety measures, and the regulation of high risks to prevent the spread of HIV (Bradley, (1993). When the above is actualized, human and economic expenditure will be protected because policy makers will have the resources to effect rational and socially accepted change in respect to HIV.

It has been 30 years since a national policy on health has been passed, which was during the Lyndon Johnson's era. This policy was Medicare and Medicaid which was to expand the accessibility of health care to special populations. Also, this legislation changed the organization in which health care services were dispersed for the indigent and elderly (Goldfield, 1993; Friedman, 1990). In spite of the resources that have been placed in Medicare and Medicaid, the criticism is the lack of program data suitable for policy analysis and research to adequately evaluate the effectiveness of health interventions.

The frequent condemnation of Medicaid is that it does not deliver to the poor what it planned to do; supposedly access to quality health care (Davidson, 1993; *Hospitals*, 1990). Also, despite the expansive identification of Medicaid services to children, the smallest portion of allocations from Medicaid are appropriated to children (Cartland, McManus, & Flint, 1993). The latter has been attributed to a void in consideration of the political magnitude of varying ideologies on Medicare and Medicaid compounded with the lack of adequate research for rational decision making.

The outcry continues among ordinary individuals and policy makers about the resources spent on health services in the United States, in spite of the country's high infant mortality rate among industrialized nations. Certainly, in consideration of the value of investing in the welfare of children combined with enhancing the nation's stance as an economic base, policy makers support more federal action to improve child and maternal health services by expanding Medicaid eligibility in the 1980s and 1990s. These policy changes have been instituted without sufficient research for direction. The alternative approach has been to merely change the definition of child health to preventing childhood illnesses and infant mortality (Sardell, 1990; Wagner, 1990).

The choice should be to promote social policy development through continued research designed to re-form aversive treatment to potential treatment options in inimical situations. Thus, the role of policy making is essential for progress in fundamental societal undertakings. It is through empirical ventures that parity will occur for the importance of social policy in shaping and supporting the social existence.

SUMMARY

Social policy exists to gain the greatest asset in the distribution of necessary resources to maintain humanity. Because there are limitations in resources, there is the need to create and assert an instrument for distributing what it essential. This can be assured only through scientific means in which substantial rationale directs the actions to be taken in maintaining social welfare. In consideration of the question of essentiality, the perception of values becomes a dominant force to be reckoned with by policy makers and the entities which influence policy making from the outermost. In either position, there is the belief that certain interests and authorities lie with one object verses another. Again, the premise should be to support empirical evidence for more truth in effecting social policy.

REFERENCES

Bradley, S.L. (1993). Human immunodeficiency virus infection in the healthcare worker. *Journal of Association of Nurses AIDs Care, 4*(1), 37-47.

Brown, D.J. (1991). Foundation of social theory. Essay review. *Educational Administration Quarterly, 27*(4), 563-566.

Brown, L.S., Phillips, R.Y., Brown, C.L., Knowlan, D., Castle, L., & Moyer, J. (1994). HIV/AIDs policies and sports: The National Football League. *Medicine Science Sports Exercises, 26*(4), 403-407.

Cartland, J.D., McManus, M.A., & Flint, S.S., 1993. A decade of Medicaid in perspective: What have been the effects on children? *Pediatrics, 91*(2), 287-95.

Davidson, S.M., 1993. Medicaid: Taking stock. *Journal of Health Politics, Policy, and Law, 18*(1), 43-74.

Fisher, W.H., Dorwart, R.A., Schlesinger, M., Epstein, S., & Davidson, H., 1992. The role of general hospitals in the privatization of inpatient treatment for serious mental illness. *Hospital Community Psychiatry, 43*(11), 1114-1119.

Friedman, E., 1990. Medicare and Medicaid at 25. *Hospitals, 64*(15), 38,42, 46, passim.

Gerhardt, P., Holmes, D.L., Alessandri, M., & Goodman, M. (1991). Social policy on the use of aversive interventions: Empirical, ethical, and legal considerations. *Journal of Autism and Developmental Disorders, 21,* 265-280.

Glantz, L.H., Mariner, W.K., & Annas, G.J. (1992). Risky business: Setting public health policy for HIV infected health care professionals. *Milbank Quarterly, 70*(1), 43-49Gold-field, N. (1993). Medicare and Medicaid: The first successful effort to increase access to health care. *Physician Executive, 19*(4), 6-11.

HIV/HBV infected health care workers. *Connecticut Medicine, 56*(4), 213-216.

Louisiana Revised Statutes. (1992). Senate bill number 790.

Confidentiality of HIV test result; disclosure (LARS 40:1300.14(B)(15). Baton Rouge, LA: State Library of Louisiana, User Services Branch.

Majchrzak, A. (1984). *Methods for policy research.* Newbury Park, NJ: Sage Publications, Inc.

Mason, D.J., Talbott, S.W., & Leavitt, J.K. (1993). *Policy and politics for nurses. 2nd ed.* Philadelphia, PA: W.B. Saunders Co.

Mayer, R.R. (1985). *Policy and program planning: A developmental perspective.* Englewood Cliffs, NJ: Prentice-Hall, Inc.

Mohr, L.B. (1992). *Impact analysis for program evaluation.* Newbury Park, CA: Sage Publications, Inc.

Murray, C. (1984). *Losing ground American social policy, 1950-1980.* NY: Basic Books, Inc.

National Advisory Council on Maternal, *Infant, and Fetal Nutrition: 1980 Biennial Report (1980).* United States Department of Agriculture.

Parmenter, T.R. (1991). Has social policy left research behind? *Australia and New Zealand Journal of Developmental Disabilities, 17,* 1-8.

Petersen, P.E. (1988). *School politics Chicago style.* Chicago, IL: The University of Chicago Press.

Recommendations: HIV/HBV infected health care workers. *Connecticut Medicine, 56*(4), 213-216.

Room, G. (1979). *The sociology of welfare.* NY: St. Martin's Press.

Sardell, A. (1990). Child health policy in the United States: The paradox of consensus. *Journal of Health, Politics, Policy, and Law, 15*(2), 271-304.

Starling, G. (1988). *Strategies for policy making.* Chicago, IL: The Dorsey Press.

United States Congress. Senate Select Committee on Nutrition and Human Needs. (1976). *WIC and commodity supplemental food programs: Hearing before the select committee on nutrition and human needs of the United States Senate, Ninty-fourth Congress* (DHHS Publication No. OCLC 2282704). Washington, DC: U.S. Government Printing Office.

United States Department of Agriculture. (1980). *National advisory council on maternal, infant, and fetal nutrition: 1980 biennial report.* Washington, DC: U.S. Department of Agriculture, Food, Nutrition Services.

United States Food and Nutrition Service. (1988). *A study of WIC participant and program characteristics* (DHHS Publication No. A 98.17). Washington, DC: U.S. Government Printing Office.

Wagner, L. (1990). Medicaid expansions dodge budget knife; funds will aid hospitals, children, elderly. *Modern Healthcare, 20*(45), 26-27.

Weiss, S.H., & Louria, D.B. (1994). Quo vadis: Perinatal AIDs issues—2004. *Clinical Perinatology, 21*(1), 179-98.

Wilensky, H.L., Luebbert, G.M., Hahn, S.R., & Jamieson, A.M. (1985). *Comparative social policy.* Berkeley, CA: University of California.

Wirt, F.M., & Kirst, M. W. (1982). *Schools in conflict.* Berkeley, CA: McCutrhan Publishing Corporation.

Future Trends in Theory Construction and Testing

Margaret T. Beard and Betty N. Adams

T he purpose of this chapter is to reflect on the past and give recognition to future trends in theory construction and testing. In this endeavor, views of scientific knowledge development, future trends, nursing practice of the 21st century, biological theories, laws in biology, intervention outcomes and the relevance to policy making, computer modeling, models, and simulations will be presented.

SCIENTIFIC KNOWLEDGE DEVELOPMENT

One ultimate aim of theory construction and the testing of theory is knowledge development. Two competing theories of scientific knowledge development are the theory of evolution and the theory of revolution. These theories are efforts to describe and explain the life cycle of scientific ideas developed through discovery, confirmation, alteration or modification and ultimately discarded as progress in scientific history.

The evolutionary view of scientific knowledge development was influenced by Darwin's formulation of evolution. Tolumin (1967, 1972) applied Darwin's principles in conceptualizing scientific development as proceeding through progressive stages with the premise being that knowledge development is a cumulative, uninterrupted process upon which successive ideas, facts or theories build, adding to a reservoir of knowledge. In support of this view, one could hold for alternate theories as justification for sound scientific practice and progress in scientific growth. This view could be regarded as a piecemeal approach in which facts are added one at a time. Scientists can, thus, draw from this depository to solve problems.

The revolutionary view of scientific knowledge development is based on the concept of Kuhn's paradigm (1970). This is the view that science proceeds in a zigzag fashion with periods of radical alterations of scientific ideas. This new perspective is referred to as a paradigm that amounts to a revolution. While there are critics of both views, evolutionary and revolutionary theories can be useful in providing an explanation of phenomena, thereby increasing understanding and knowledge.

The competing theories of evolution and revolution have implications for further development of nursing knowledge and the pitfalls and future progression of knowledge in nursing. Abdellah and Levine (1994) have presented an assessment of nursing research for theory building, the past, present and future by demonstrating how methods have evolved; why certain methods are used and the limitations and strengths of methodologies. Thus, methodologies in nursing research have evolved from descriptive to analytic variety and sophistication.

Abdellah and Levine (1994) cite the effort placed on the analytical side of the research process in theory development in nursing, and the insufficient attention to the quality of the data generated. The methodologies evolving as having the greatest relevance for the future in theory building in nursing are qualitative and quantitative methods, especially coalesced with clinical trials, outcome measures, and secondary data analyses (Abdellah & Levine, 1994). Qualitative methods are theory generating and quantitative methods are related more to testing theory.

FUTURE TRENDS
Informatics
In spite of the circumscribed knowledge generated through theory building in nursing, some inroads have been made, most noticeably in the transformation of advanced nursing practice. This development has been strengthened through the identification of outcome measures and the advent of informatics. Outcomes are pre-determined and constitute change in some phenomena. Informatics is the study, collection and management of information using computer storage and retrieval.

Nursing informatics is the integration of nursing, computer and information science for the purpose of identifying, collecting, processing and managing data to support the expansion of nursing knowledge. Thus, research priorities for nursing informatics should include symbolic representation of nursing phenomena and evaluative research on the effects of systems in the processes and outcomes of nursing care (American Nurses Association [ANA], 1994). The other priority should be nursing's use of data and information in delivering patient care and the affects of different levels of expertise and factors, such as situations generated through organizational policy in the work place (Skiba, 1993).

Social Concerns
The Agency for Health Care Policy and Research (AHCPR) was established in 1988 with a focus on the development of clinical practice guidelines, outcome measures and effectiveness research (Short & Hennessy, 1994). Nursing will have an important role and impact in shaping the nation's health agenda and restructuring the health care system. Future nursing research will be highly pertinent to policy formulation as findings impact health care, nursing practice and social issues, especially economic conditions. Nurses already are involved in the care of the homeless, victims of AIDs and drug abusers. All of the aforementioned are examples of vital social concerns reflective in the national goals for policy making.

The Joint Commission for Accreditation of Hospital Organizations (JCAHO) has shifted focus from standards compliance to clinical outcomes measurement. The concentration is on records and outcome indicators through the utilization of computers. In other words, computerized patient records will influence future health care in terms of data entry, retrieval and utilization.

The National Institute of Nursing Research (NINR) has priority statements for research to form the national research agenda for the year 2000 with a focus for each year. The areas of emphasis projected are as follows: (a) 1995, community based nursing models; (b) 1996, effectiveness of nursing interventions in HIV/AIDs; (c) 1997, cognitive impairment; (d) 1998, living with chronic illness and (e) 1999, bio-behavioral factors related to immunocompetence (National Center for Nursing Research, 1992).

Recent and Future Trends

Over the years, there have been debates about the relevance of causal modeling for explaining phenomena in theory development and testing. However, with the advancement of computer technology, there is increased acceptance and use of causal modeling in structural equation modeling. The application of the above has enhanced the development of methods for dealing with not only interval and ratio level data, but also nominal and ordinal data, or a combination of these. More thorough information can be attained and applied when analyzing categorical data by delineating more diversity in the levels of categories. For example, in examining the communicable disease, Auto-Immune Deficiency Syndrome (AIDS), the researcher can examine the treatment mode, home care provider, drug therapy and other related factors by applying hierarchial categorical analysis. The importance of this statistical evolution is the availability of analyzing large data sets thereby lessening the chance of type one or type two error and explaining errors in variables and models.

Error can be hypothesized and measured with structural equation modeling. Whereas in the past with multiple regression analysis, the assumption had to be made that there was no measurement error. In time series analysis, occurrences in events can be displayed in three dimensions in which there is the advantage of examining the magnitude of the event occurring over time. Thus,..."the nature of statistics itself has changed, moving from classical notions of hypothesis testing toward graphical, exploratory modeling that exploits the flexibility of interactive computing and high-resolution display" (Fox & Stein, 1995, p. 267).

Structural Equation Modeling

Structural equation modeling is a useful technique to evaluate intervention outcomes (Bagozzi & Heatherton, 1994). When evaluating intervention programs designed to influence outcomes, frequently investigators are faced with confounding background variables to be controlled, in addition to intervening and mediating variables. Since the former is assumed to have a causal effect on outcomes, the impact of intervening variables should be estimated instead of controlled.

Short and Hennessy (1994) found that the mean difference accurately estimates the total effect of the treatment on the outcomes, but does not allow for decomposition of treatment effects attributable to intervening variables. In multiple regression, the treatment effect is defined as a unique component that does not consider relations among intervening variables. In contrast, structural equation modeling not only provides an accurate estimate of the total treatment effect, but also allows for decomposition of effects in those directly related to the treatment and those operating through theoretically specified intervening causal variables.

Short and Hennessy (1994) demonstrate the similarities and differences between mean difference analysis in using t-test, single-equation multiple regression and structural equation modeling. The argument for using the structural equation modeling approach is to estimate effects for interventions in which changes occur as a result of theoretically specified intervening variables.

New research methods resulting from advanced technologies provide new challenges for scientists, especially biomedical scientists. Special attention to ethical, legal and social policy issues related to the use of these newer technologies will have to be rendered. The future trend will be to give knowledge an expanded meaning to include verbal information, numerical data, images and imagery. There will be methodological analytical variety and sophistication to cope with increasing environmental complexity, turbulence and paradox. The increasing departure from linear thinking and movement toward nonlinear characteristics is represented by the new sciences of Chaos Theory, quantum mechanics and Field Theory.

Computer Simulation

Computer modeling technology has an important role in structuring and understanding the complexity of biological systems. However, because of the tendency for physiological complications, it is difficult to precisely predict behavior during experimental investigations, as biological systems do not always behave as expected. Simulations on biological systems may be carried out with digital or analog computers. Hybrid computers, which are a combination of analog and digital computers, are used often to simulate biological system behaviors.

Simulation and Modeling

Simulation and modeling are important investigative techniques in any research activity because they provide a methodology for the design, development, experimentation, analysis and evaluation of an experiment. Simulation of a particular situation provides a common base of techniques in studying a diversity of projects. Biological explanations may be tested by simulation or by modeling.

Models

Models have been grouped in various ways. Hardy (1974) lists types of models as analog, icons and symbols. An analog model directs attention to resemblances between theoretical entities and familiar subject matter. An example would be the use of a mechanical device to explain the activity of the heart, such as the electrocardiographic device. Iconic models are used as a direct representation of the desired subject, such as a hemodialysis machine to represent the processes of the kidney. Thus, a symbolic model represents phenomena figuratively, such as using concepts to illustrate a problem of interest.

Models can be built from the perspective to solving a problem. The problem is first analyzed into components of the various hierarchical levels of interest. At each level, analogous and homologous behavior is sought across the entire taxonomic domain of biology and within mathematical and computer simulations.

The Committee on Models for Biological Research was convened by the National Research Council to determine the relevance or limitation of biomedical research models (Morotwitz, 1989). However, developments in computer science and informatics have led to data bases that may be rapidly accessed and manipulated to extract generalizations and relations (together known as knowledge structures). From the large data base, the committee came up with "the notion of a matrix of biological knowledge..."(Morotwitz, 1989, p. 177).

Cox and Miller (1990) define the role of models as substantive, empirical and indirect. Substantive models are those that connect directly with subject considerations. The aim of substantive models is to explain what is observed in terms of processes (mechanisms) by quantities that are not directly observed, and to obtain some theoretical notions as to how the system under study works. Empirical models represent dependencies in idealized form thought likely to be present. Indirect models are used to suggest methods of analyses which can be accessed by success in specific application, a direct practical approach. Indirect models are used also to study the properties of particular techniques of analyses.

Science is the systematic organization of knowledge about the universe based on explanatory hypotheses which are testable. Science advances by gradually developing more comprehensive theories by formulating conjectures of greater generality through the description of observations. These observations initially may appear to be unrelated to a certain event. This phenomenon can be illustrated by considering the Mendelian principles of inheritance in which observations appear to be unrelated at first, such as the proportions of characteristics transmitted from parents to offspring. The preservation of inheritance is continued through generations as discontinuity in traits, combining with alternative traits with features sometime present in the parents but not being present in progenies.

In the future, more emphasis will be placed on the biological basis of phenomena for describing, understanding, and predicting events. A 10 year plan to enhance biological underpinnings of nursing research and training is a part of the research agenda of the National Institute of Nursing Research (Cowan, Heinrich, Lucas, Sigmon, & Hinshaw, 1993).

In view of the above, biologists and physical scientists have become interested in modeling biological phenomena (Morotwitz, 1989). This response has generated interest because of the realization that data standing alone do not represent knowledge. Therefore, the attempt has been to quantitatively describe and explain phenomena via observations. This has been accomplished by treating a biological system as a physical state in which there is an interaction between energy and matter. The end thereby being a highly organized, complex, physical state. Nevertheless, a question to be considered is whether the present techniques of physical science are sufficient to explain biological phenomena. Also, will new techniques in modeling biological phenomena emerge and be more powerful.

Biological phenomena are better understood by applying laws of biology other than Mendel's Law. These are laws of conservation, thermodynamics, gas, and the universal law of natural selection, which translates as the better ones replace the less than good ones. Some related theories to these laws in biology are those of antibody formation, stochastic processes, clonic selection, acquired immunity and Selye's Theory on Stress.

The theory of stochastic processes has been useful in understanding biological phenomena at various levels of complexity, from the molecular to the ecological levels. Thus, modeling of biological systems via stochastic processes allows the incorporation of the effects of other events and factors (Bartholomew,

1973). In summary, theories in the developmental phase gradually allow the scientist to observe regularities and patterns which eventually lead to laws. The result being the relevance of laws as aiding in the determination of the predictability of occurrences in phenomena.

Theory structure and biology have implications for knowledge development in all disciplines. In taking physics as an example, it is proper to begin with observations and proceed to constructs. The level of abstraction leads to mass, space, and related motions because theory deals with forces, force fields, and radiation. A continuance in a reductionist methodology leads to atoms, electrons, probability distribution function, and more abstract functions.

Constructs of physics are constrained by methodological overviews such as causality, connectivity and extensibility. There is movement from constructs to observational domains where predictions of phenomena are subjected to testing and the possibility of falsification.

Nursing as an applied science has a collection of illustrative emerging possibilities for developing theory that focuses on specific rather than general nursing phenomena. The composition or makeup is linked closely to nursing practice and reflects the values and knowledge of the profession, serving as a basis for the challenge and development of substantive knowledge. Chinn (1994) has compiled a selection of commentaries of mid-range theory representative of the above. The mid-range theory provides a specific conceptual focus based on the foundational concepts and values of nursing. These include concepts and values, such as health and wholeness, social and cultural context, growth and development, caring relationship, diversity, and complexity. The phenomena of theoretical focus are crisis, stress, protection, social support, lifestyle change, and self-transcendence.

The papers represented in the book, *Developing Substance: Mid-Range Theorizing,* (Chinn, 1994), illustrate a wide-range of methods and stages in the process of theory building. Some papers are critiques of existing theories viewed from a nursing perspective. There is an example of theory generating research using a grounded theory methodology in the identity of self as infertile. There is an illustration of theory derivation in developing a theory of smoking relapse and a theory of deductive formulation using developmental theories to cultivate a nursing theory of self-transcendence. The models presented in the above are social support, stress-coping, health belief, health and vitality, and health care professionals facilitating self-care and maternal role sufficiency.

THE FUTURE OF NURSING
Nursing for the Twenty-First Century

Nursing as a scientific discipline evolved rapidly and has been influenced by the principles of logical positivism. The basic thinking about nursing has changed and continued into the twentieth century, supported by prevailing late nineteenth century economic, social and political norms. Nursing, first as a training, moved from a hospital based setting and then to higher education in the university. Today, nursing's caricature is no longer perceived as the handmaiden to the physician; instead nursing is a recognized scientific discipline in its own right.

The evolution of nursing theories indicates that structures of the past are not adequate for the future. The authors of this book suggest that in the twenty-first century, the nursing paradigm will be influenced by emerging environmental changes. Some factors contributing to changes will be the continuing increase in health care costs, health care reform, the growth and contribution of the National Institute of Nursing Research, new technological advancements and the empowerment of people to engage in self care and preservation. The thesis of this book asserts that for nursing to cope with increasing environmental complexity, turbulence and paradox, there will be a departure from linear thinking and a movement toward nonlinear characteristics accomplished through the new sciences of Chaos Theory, Field Theory and quantum mechanics. Also, nursing's organizational structure of the twenty-first century will dictate development along the principles of these new sciences.

EMERGING ENVIRONMENTAL TRENDS
Economic growth and abundant natural resources will no longer be the norm. Since the 1973 Arabian oil embargo, the economies of the United States and major industrialized nations have experienced a decline (Marcus, 1993). Some developing countries have experienced average growth rates of more than 5 per cent, most noteworthy of these are Taiwan, Brazil and Yugoslavia. Nevertheless, all industrial nations are facing an era in which exponential growth is beginning to absorb resources at faster rates than that of new technologies (Heilbroner, 1989). Thus, the decline in growth stems from the scarcity of natural resources.

Another emerging trend is an increasing demand for organizations and businesses to shift from an economic focus to a social welfare focus (Gopalan, Ramakrishnan, & Nicholson, 1992). There has been an increase in corporate contributions to social programs in reaction to social pressures demonstrating a productivity rating of 1.78 per cent after tax income in 1960 to 3.48 per cent in 1989 (Carroll, 1993). This demand on businesses to support social programs come at a time when businesses are experiencing limited growth in resources. Recent legislation such as the American With Disabilities Act and proposed legislations to support health care and welfare reforms and a policy on parental leave all suggest that businesses must share the responsibilities in providing such programs.

Cavanagh (1990) describes fourteen emerging values adopted by business as representative in coping with the quandary and perplexity to social pressure for welfare reform in the workplace. These values present business as a servant of society with its central role to be that of the individual. There is the acceptance of the roots of religion as having a bearing on the creed of business by recognizing the importance and concern for others with a vision of hope and prosperity. The intent should be the empowerment of people-institution-nation as interdependent by acknowledging support for liberation and self-denial (Davis & Botkin, 1994). These business values appeal for local control, efficiency, and flexibility in innovations with more participation of consumers and citizens in long-range perspectives, especially in management decisions for utilization of scare resources.

NURSING'S RESPONSE TO EMERGING ENVIRONMENTAL TRENDS
The future of nursing will be influenced by new technologies, political and socio-economic factors, health care reform, and the new sciences and philosophies of science. Nurses will not adhere to the traditional determinism, but

instead will move away and observe the complex patterns of relationships in the workplace, organizations, and policy making settings.

Quantum physics is based on the uncertainty principle (Hawking, 1988). For many years philosophers and scientists believed that humans live in a universe which is orderly and completely predictable. As science progressed in the study of particles and waves, the dual characteristics observed in electromagnetic waves led to the conceptualization of uncertainty in nature. The linear relationship of deterministic Newtonian science has been shaken. Theorists have been able to include a world view of the uncertainty of nature. Nurses are concerned also about the uncertainty principle in their encounters with clients

Chaos Theory (Glick, 1987) will assist in understanding these complex relationships. According to Stinchecombe (1968), theory ought to assist one in inventing explanations to phenomena. The conceptualization that systems are in chaos when it becomes impossible to know what state they will be in next is an acceptable explanation for the diversity in which nursing will exist. Therefore, from Chaos Theory has come the realization that chaotic systems, observed over time, will eventually demonstrate an inherent orderliness (Wheatley, 1992b).

Computer simulations of chaotic nonlinear systems observed over time create pictures which are called strange attractors (Glick, 1987). These computer pictures are often described as beautiful images created as the computer goes through thousands and sometimes millions of iterations of nonlinear equations. The patterns produced take on definite shapes within specific limitations (Glick, 1987). Therefore, from Chaos Theory comes the realization that throughout the universe, order exists within disorder and disorder in order (Wheatley, 1992b).

Nurses can glean valuable insights from Chaos Theory. Gathering additional information will not improve predictability. Over a period of time, the strange attractor (order) will reveal itself. Reductionist thinking is destroyed as with Quantum Theory, which implies that the nurse should not rely solely on specific events in futuristic thinking but should look for patterns in complex relationships.

Field Theory evolved to explain forces acting to influence change (Lewin, 1951). Thus, Fanizationalield Theory developed to explain forces exerted on each other by two bodies of mass separated by a distance. Principles of Field Theory explain this as action-at-a-distance (Resnick & Halliday, 1966).

Fields are invisible forces affecting bodies over space, such as electromagnetic and magnetic forces (Hawking, 1988). School children observe the patterns of iron filings as they are placed near a magnet. The patterns that result from magnetic fields demonstrate the action of invisible forces influencing change.

Thus, from Field Theory nurses can gleam two valuable implications as the twenty-first century approaches. First, the acknowledgement that events or entities which appear to be separated and isolated may actually be related. Secondly, the definable relationships among entities can be determined by relying on the fundamental importance of empirical evidence. This then is representative of the process in developing scientific theory (Hardy, 1985).

Nurses should look for forces of relatedness among events recognizing that there are invisible forces that have an influence on nursing. Nursing's vision, values, and culture are examples of unseen forces impacting the profession (Wheatley, 1992a). Implications of quantum physics, Chaos Theory, and Field Theory as contributing to the scientific development and growth of nursing knowledge are suggestive that nurse researchers give particular notice to patterns of complex relationships.

SUMMARY OF IMPLICATIONS FOR NURSING

Central to the scientific development of nursing knowledge and practice is the realization that the physical world is naturally full of uncertainty, chaos, and patterns of complex relationships. If the physical world functions under such conditions, then the question to be asked is whether it is nursing's role to control dynamic and complex environments, or instead accept and adapt to them.

Nursing has in the past been successful in adapting to new environmental realities. As nurse administrators, nurse managers, deans, and case managers approach new challenges, perhaps an analysis of organizational culture may prove helpful (Schein, 1985). Organizational culture is the pattern of basic assumptions that a given group has invented, discovered or developed in learning to cope with problems of external adaptation and internal integration. Thus, organizational culture worked well enough to be considered valid and therefore should be taught to new members as the correct way to perceive, think, and feel in relation to those problems.

The idea inherent in this definition is that the organization and its environment has an interacting set of complex relationships that can be managed by a pattern of basic assumptions and values. There is no inherent reference to linear relationships as espoused in Newtonian physics. What is clear and implied are the existence of nonlinear patterns of relationships of new scientific management. Thus, this is nursing's challenge for transcending in the new environmental awakenings of the twenty-first century.

REFERENCES

Abdella, F. G., & Levine, E. (1994). *Preparing nursing research for the 21st century.* NJ: Springer Publishing Company, Inc.

Bagozzi, R. F., & Heatherton, T. F. (1994). A general approach to representing multifaceted personality constructs: Application to state self-esteem. *Structural Equation Modeling, 1,* 35-67.

Bartholomew, D. J. (1973). *Stochastic models for social processes* (2nd ed.). NY: John Wiley & Sons.

Carroll, A. B. (1993). *Business and society. Ethics and stakeholders management* (2nd ed.). Cincinnati, OH: South Western Publishing.

Cavanagh, G. F. (1990). *American business values* (3rd ed.). Englewood Cliffs, NJ: Prentice-Hall.

Chinn, P. (1994). *Developing substance: Midrange-theorizing.* MD: Aspen Publishing.

Cowan, M. J., Heinrich, J., Lucas, M., Sigmon, H., & Hinshaw, A. S. (1993). Integration of biological and nursing sciences: A 10 year plan to enhance research and training. *Research in Nursing and Health, 16,* 3-9.

Cox, D. R., & Miller, H. D. (1965). *The theory of stochastic processes.* NY: John Wiley & Sons.

Davis, S., & Botkin, J. (1994). *The monster under the bed: How business in mastering the opportunity of knowledge for profit.* NY: Simon & Schuster.

Fox, J., & Stine, R. (Eds.). (1995). Introduction to the special issues on computing environments. *Sociological Methods and Research, 23,* 267-281.

Glick, J. (1987). *Chaos. Making a new science.* NY: Penquin Books.

Gopalan, S., Ramakreshnan, K. R., & Nicholson, R. W. (1992). *Shift in the value orientation of the United States. Some social and economic implications for developing countries. Proceedings at the University Consortium for Social Development.* Washington, DC:

Hardy, M. E. (1974). Theories: Components, development, evaluation. *Nursing Research, 23,* 100-106.

Hardy, M. E. (1985). *Strategy for theory development by nursing. Proceedings of the Second Annual Nursing Science Colloquium.* Boston University, MA:

Hawking, S. W. (1988). *A brief history of time.* NY: Banton Books.

Heilbroner, R. V. (1989). *The making of economic society* (8th ed.). Englewood Cliff, NJ: Prentice-Hall.

Kuhn, T. S. (1970). *The structure of scientific revolutions* (2nd ed.). Chicago, IL: University of Chicago Press.

Lewin, K. (1951). *Field theory in social science.* NY: Harper and Brothers.

Marcus, A. A. (1993). *Business and society: Ethics, government, and the world economy.* Boston, MA: Irwen Publishers.

Morotwitz, H. J. (1989). Models, theory, and the matrix of biological knowledge. *BioScience, 39,* 177-179.

Author. (1992). *Update: National Center for Nursing Research.* Bethesda, MD: National Center for Nursing Research.

Resnick, R., & Halliday, D. (1966). *Physics.* New York: John Wiley & Sons.

Schein, E. H. (1985). Coming to a new awareness of organizational culture. *Sloan Management Review, Winter, 3-15.*

Short, L. M., & Hennessy, M. (1994). Using structural equation to estimate effects of behavioral interventions. *Structural Equation Modeling, 1,* 68-80.

Skiba, D.J. (1993). *Priorities for research in nursing informatics. Connections:* A publication for the NLN's Council for Nursing Informatics. NY: National League for Nursing.

Stinchecombe, A. L. (1968). *Constructing social theories.* NY: Harcourt, Brace & World.

Author. (1994). *The scope of practice for nursing informatics.* Washington, DC: American Nurses Association.

Tolumin, S. (1967). The evolutionary development of natural science. *American Scientists*

Tolumin, S. (1972). *Human understanding: The collective use and evolution of concepts.* Princeton, NJ: Princeton University Press.

United States Department of Health and Human Services. (1991). *Healthy people 2000: National health promotion goals and disease prevention objectives* (DHHS Publication No. 91-50212). Washington, DC: U.S. Printing Office.

Wheatley, M. J. (1992a). *Leadership and the new science.* San Francisco, CA: Barrett-Kaehler.

Wheatley, M. J. (1992b). Searching for order in an orderly world: A poetic for post-machine-age managers. *Journal of Management Inquiry, 1,* 337-342.

Part Four
Appendix

Appendix

Included in this appendix are the structural equations and matrices which correspond to the structural equation model depicted in Figure 7.7.

Measurement Model

Lambda x - The measurement of the x variables

$$
\begin{vmatrix} X_1 \\ X_2 \\ X_3 \\ X_4 \\ X_5 \\ X_6 \\ X_7 \\ X_8 \end{vmatrix}
=
\begin{vmatrix} 1 & 0 & 0 & 0 \\ \lambda_{21} & 0 & 0 & 0 \\ 0 & 1 & 0 & 0 \\ 0 & \lambda_{42} & 0 & 0 \\ 0 & 0 & 1 & 0 \\ 0 & 0 & \lambda_{63} & 0 \\ 0 & 0 & 0 & 1 \\ 0 & 0 & 0 & \lambda_{84} \end{vmatrix}
$$

Lambda y - The measurement of the y variables

$$
\begin{vmatrix} Y_1 \\ Y_2 \\ Y_3 \\ Y_4 \\ Y_5 \\ Y_6 \end{vmatrix}
=
\begin{vmatrix} 1 & 0 \\ \lambda_{21} & 0 \\ \lambda_{31} & 0 \\ \lambda_{41} & 0 \\ 0 & 1 \\ 0 & \lambda_{62} \end{vmatrix}
$$

Theta delta - The measurement error of the x variables.

$$
\theta_\delta =
\begin{vmatrix}
\theta_{11} \\
\theta_{21} & \theta_{23} \\
\theta_{31} & \theta_{32} & \theta_{33} \\
\theta_{41} & \theta_{42} & \theta_{43} & \theta_{44} \\
\theta_{51} & \theta_{52} & \theta_{53} & \theta_{54} & \theta_{55} \\
\theta_{61} & \theta_{62} & \theta_{63} & \theta_{64} & \theta_{65} & \theta_{66} \\
\theta_{71} & \theta_{72} & \theta_{73} & \theta_{74} & \theta_{75} & \theta_{76} & \theta_{77} \\
\theta_{81} & \theta_{82} & \theta_{83} & \theta_{84} & \theta_{85} & \theta_{86} & \theta_{87} & \theta_{88}
\end{vmatrix}
$$

Theta epsilon - The measurement error of the y variables.

$$
\theta_\varepsilon =
\begin{vmatrix}
\theta_{11} \\
\theta_{21} & \theta_{23} \\
\theta_{31} & \theta_{32} & \theta_{33} \\
\theta_{41} & \theta_{42} & \theta_{43} & \theta_{44} \\
\theta_{51} & \theta_{52} & \theta_{53} & \theta_{54} & \theta_{55} \\
\theta_{61} & \theta_{62} & \theta_{63} & \theta_{64} & \theta_{65} & \theta_{66}
\end{vmatrix}
$$

Structural Model

Beta Matrix - The effects of the latent endogenous variables on each other

$$
\beta =
\begin{vmatrix}
0 & \beta_{12} \\
\beta_{21} & 0
\end{vmatrix}
$$

Gamma Matrix - The effects of the latent exogenous latent endogenous variables

$$
Y =
\begin{vmatrix}
Y_{11} & Y_{12} & Y_{13} & Y_{14} \\
Y_{21} & Y_{22} & Y_{23} & Y_{24}
\end{vmatrix}
$$

Phi Matrix - The variance, covariance matrix of latent exogenous variables

$$\beta \quad = \quad \begin{vmatrix} \phi_{11} \\ \phi_{21} & \phi_{22} \\ \phi_{31} & \phi_{32} & \phi_{33} \\ \phi_{41} & \phi_{42} & \phi_{43} & \phi_{44} \end{vmatrix}$$

Psi Matrix - The variance, covariance matrix of residuals

$$\psi \quad = \quad \begin{vmatrix} \psi_{11} \\ \psi_{21} & \psi_{22} \end{vmatrix}$$

Equations and Corresponding Matrices for the Model

Equations for X-Variables:

$$X1 = \xi_1 + \delta_1$$
$$X2 = \lambda_{21} + \xi_1 + \delta_2$$
$$X3 = \xi_2 + \delta_3$$
$$X4 = \lambda_{42} + \xi_2 + \delta_4$$
$$X5 = \xi_3 + \delta_5$$
$$X6 = \lambda_{63} + \xi_3 + \delta_6$$
$$X7 = \xi_4 + \delta_7$$
$$X8 = \lambda_{84} + \xi_4 + \delta_8$$

$$\begin{vmatrix} X1 \\ X2 \\ X3 \\ X4 \\ X5 \\ X6 \\ X7 \\ X8 \end{vmatrix} = \begin{vmatrix} 1 & 0 & 0 & 0 \\ \lambda_{21} & 0 & 0 & 0 \\ 0 & 1 & 0 & 0 \\ 0 & \lambda_{42} & 0 & 0 \\ 0 & 0 & 1 & 0 \\ 0 & 0 & \lambda_{63} & 0 \\ 0 & 0 & 0 & 1 \\ 1 & 0 & 0 & \lambda_{84} \end{vmatrix} \begin{vmatrix} \xi_1 \\ \xi_2 \\ \xi_3 \\ \xi_4 \end{vmatrix} + \begin{vmatrix} \delta_1 \\ \delta_2 \\ \delta_3 \\ \delta_4 \\ \delta_5 \\ \delta_6 \\ \delta_7 \\ \delta_8 \end{vmatrix}$$

Equations for Y-Variables:

$$Y1 = \eta_1 + \varepsilon_1$$
$$Y2 = \lambda_{21} + \eta_1 + \varepsilon_2$$
$$Y3 = \lambda_{31} + \eta_1 + \varepsilon_2$$
$$Y4 = \lambda_{41} + \eta_1 + \varepsilon_4$$
$$Y5 = \eta_2 + \varepsilon_5$$
$$Y6 = \lambda_{62} + \eta_2 + \varepsilon_6$$

$$
\begin{vmatrix} Y1 \\ Y2 \\ Y3 \\ Y4 \\ Y5 \\ Y6 \end{vmatrix}
=
\begin{vmatrix} 1 & 0 \\ \lambda_{21} & 0 \\ \lambda_{31} & 1 \\ \lambda_{41} & 0 \\ 0 & 1 \\ 0 & \lambda_{62} \end{vmatrix}
\begin{vmatrix} \eta_1 \\ \eta_2 \end{vmatrix}
+
\begin{vmatrix} \varepsilon_1 \\ \varepsilon_2 \\ \varepsilon_3 \\ \varepsilon_4 \\ \varepsilon_5 \\ \varepsilon_6 \end{vmatrix}
$$

Structural Equations:

$$\eta_1 = \beta_{12}\eta_2 + Y_{11}\xi_1 + Y_{12}\xi_2 + Y_{13}\xi_3 + Y_{14}\xi_4 + \zeta_1$$
$$\eta_2 = \beta_{21}\eta_1 + Y_{21}\xi_1 + Y_{22}\xi_2 + Y_{23}\xi_3 + Y_{24}\xi_4 + \zeta_2$$

$$
\begin{vmatrix} \eta_1 \\ \eta_2 \end{vmatrix}
=
\begin{vmatrix} 0 & \beta_{12} \\ \beta_{21} & 0 \end{vmatrix}
\begin{vmatrix} \eta_1 \\ \eta_2 \end{vmatrix}
+
\begin{vmatrix} Y_{11} & Y_{12} & Y_{13} & Y_{14} \\ Y_{22} & Y_{22} & Y_{23} & Y_{24} \end{vmatrix}
\begin{vmatrix} \xi_1 \\ \xi_2 \\ \xi_3 \\ \xi_4 \end{vmatrix}
+
\begin{vmatrix} \zeta_1 \\ \zeta_2 \end{vmatrix}
$$

Hypotheses

Hypotheses can be generated from the associations of the latent exogenous variables and the latent endogenous variables. Hypotheses generated from the LISREL model are:

Among asymptomatic, HIV positive adults:
1. The greater the personal resources, the more the immume system be comes stable or improves.
$$> \xi_{1,} > \eta_{1}$$

2. The greater the personal resources, the greater the viral inactivity
$$> \xi_{1,} > \eta_{2}$$

3. The greater the physical health, the more the immune system becomes stable or improves.
$$> \xi_{2,} > \eta_{1}$$

4. The greater the physical health, the greater the viral inactivity.
$$> \xi_{2,} > \eta_{2}$$

5. The greater the psychological health, the more the immune system stabilizes or improves.
$$> \xi_{3,} > \eta_{1}$$

6. The greater the psychological health, the greater the viral inactivity.
$$> \xi_{3,} > \eta_{3}$$

7. The greater the spiritural growth, the more the immune system stabilizes or improves.
$$> \xi_{4,} > \eta_{1}$$

8. The greater the spiritual health, the greater the viral inactivity.
$$> \xi_{4,} > \eta_{2}$$

Part Five
Index

—A—

—B—

—C—

—H—

—P—

—V—

—W—

—Y—

LC 95-060045

ISBN: 0-923950-12-5